THE REVOLT OF THE JUDGES

THE REVOLT OF
THE JUDGES

The Parlement of Paris and the Fronde
1643-1652

BY A. LLOYD MOOTE

PRINCETON UNIVERSITY PRESS
PRINCETON, NEW JERSEY

L.C. CARD: 78-155003

ISBN: 0-691-05191-7

This book has been composed in Linotype Granjon
Printed in the United States of America
by Princeton University Press

To

John B. Wolf

PREFACE

THERE ARE several books which examine the history of the Parlement of Paris and many more that trace the course of the Fronde, but there is, as yet, no comprehensive study of the role played in that mid-seventeenth-century upheaval by the famous high court of law. This book is designed to fill that gap. The scope of this study is much broader than I envisaged at the beginning of my research on the topic. One of the prime reasons for the magnitude of the subject is that what I call the "revolt of the judges" is full of paradoxes, the greatest being the fact that a body of royal officials dedicated to the enforcement of law and the principle of royal absolutism could rebel against the king's administration. To come to any understanding of that paradox, the causes and nature of that parlementary Fronde have to be placed in their broad historical setting, and at the same time within the specific context of institutional structure, governmental practices, and social conditions of the early seventeenth century. This framework is the subject of the first part of the book. Two additional sections have been required to analyze the complexities of the Fronde itself, a cluster of attacks by virtually every social group, geographic area, and political institution of France on the administration of Louis XIV's youthful years. Though it is perhaps unavoidable that the study of revolutions be undertaken chronologically, given the inherent characteristic of constant, rapid change, there is a weakness in a narrowly narrative approach: the tendency to lose sight of the significance of the interdependence of all the elements of the upheaval. In the case of the Fronde, this problem has been found in the accounts of one historian after another, with the result that the important role of the Parlement of Paris has been obscured. Scholars have succumbed to the convenience of dividing the complex cluster of revolts into neat chronological compartments—the early parlementary phase and the later princely-noble one—thus confusing and distorting more than they explain. From my initial examination of sources, it became clear that the role played by the Parlement of Paris from the beginning of the movement for state reform, in 1643-1648, to the collapse of the military revolts by the great nobles, in 1652, was the factor that explained most satisfactorily all phases of the Fronde. The parlementary judges were deeply committed to the cause of reform, and yet they were involved in the royal-noble quarrels. In addition, they were inextricably connected with protest movements by wealthy and poor Parisians, peasants in the surrounding area, various social groups in the outlying provinces, and the activities of many other corporations of judicial and financial officials throughout the realm. Hence, while recognizing that the parlementarians' role was the central theme of the Fronde, I was faced with the task of analyzing the involved social, economic, and political considerations and relating them to the revolt of the judges. After attempting to force the subject into a largely topical mold, which was as unsatisfactory as a chronological account, I compromised by combining analysis and narrative within fairly distinct periods of the Fronde. Thus, as in traditional accounts, I have treated in chronological sections of the book first the parlementary Fronde, and then the noble Fronde. But within each period, the Parlement's response to changing conditions is related to the activities of other judicial and financial corporations, to the contemporaneous agitations of noble factions and peasant communities, to Parisian politics as well as provincial affairs.

As this study took shape, it had to contend with the arguments of past and present historians over the nature of the Fronde. Therefore, references have been made to interpretations of other scholars, although an effort has been made to keep historiographical issues under control. They are important, but the subject under survey is the history of the Fronde, not the history of its history. The latter should illuminate the former, not vie with it for the attention of the reader. At this point, it may be helpful to mention the three broad areas of historical contention: the dispute between nineteenth-century liberal and monarchist historians over the legality of the rebel movement (in which liberals portrayed the Fronde as a legitimate movement against tyranny on behalf of individual rights and limitations on the state, while monarchists described it as an illegal attempt to strip the monarchy of its legitimate powers protecting the state and its inhabitants); the more recent discussion between Marxists and non-Marxists over the political relations of the various socio-economic groups involved in the Fronde; and the lively current debate on the so-called "general crisis of the seventeenth century" which links the Fronde with political turmoil elsewhere in the 1640's and 1650's. All three controversies raise important questions about the causes, nature, and results of the Fronde, questions that are an essential part of this book.

Ernst Kossman and Boris Porschnev have analyzed in detail the historiography of the Fronde, and hence the issue of its legality. From my own reading of the rather substantial secondary literature, it became apparent that the question was indeed very important, but badly posed because it was taken out of the context of seventeenth-century political and institutional conditions. Monarchist historians have all too hastily branded the noble and parlementary opposition as a destructive assault on the legally constituted royal government, having no aim beyond the vague notion of restoring selfish medieval privileges of some subjects. The reader of such proroyal accounts, if he does agree with their view of the Fronde as illegal, narrowly conceived, and destructive of state order and unity, will neverthe-less want to know how such an allegedly pathetic uprising could have lasted as long as it did. Liberal apologists of the Fronde's legiti-macy, on the other hand, have made the movement look stronger than it was by describing it as a constructive, constitutional move-ment firmly rooted in medieval beliefs in individual liberty and at the same time anticipating the French Revolution's modern ideals of liberty, equality, and fraternity. After reading these liberal accounts, the reader will still want to know why such a supposedly strong constitutional movement failed to realize its ideals. In short, instead of trying to resolve the question-begging argument between mon-archist and liberal scholars over the Fronde's legality, we must examine the fact that in combining legal precedent with pragmatic activity in a seventeenth-century setting, the Fronde bequeathed a very ambiguous legacy. No exclusive examination of the medieval Parlement of Paris, let alone medieval French history, will com-pletely explain that legacy. This does not mean that there are no connections between the two periods. Indeed there are parallels. The sister court known as the Chambre des Comptes of Paris played a role in the Parisian opposition to Charles V in the fourteenth cen-tury. In 1415, the same court, along with the Parlement and the Grand Conseil, joined in pressing for state reforms, as it did during the parlementary Fronde. A century later, the Parlement of Paris became the virtual center of French government after François I's defeat and capture by Spanish forces in Italy. And that high court went on to make common cause with the great nobles against alleged misgovernment by François' ministers. As late as 1588-1589, the parlementarians invested agents of the rebel noble League with quasi-royal powers, somewhat as their descendants did for Condé in the last months of the Fronde. During the next decade, the sovereign courts in Paris, led by the Parlement, even tried to organize joint sessions aimed at forcing financial reforms on Henri IV, surely an anticipation of the Chambre Saint Louis at the outset of the parlementary Fronde in 1648. Yet, despite these ties and the court's veneration of the past, the judges of the 1640's and 1650's were dealing with a different political, economic, and social situation, and they knew it. Their interests were broader, their place in that upheaval was much more central, and their impact on events was far more profound.

The lessons to be learned from historians concerned with social relationships are more valuable than those of scholars concentrating narrowly on politics and the question of legality. Boris Porschnev's careful examination of so-called "popular" uprisings by the rural and urban poor on the eve of the Fronde has forced political historians to consider that mid-century upheaval "from the bottom up," to use a phrase now in vogue, rather than only from the perspective of the political and social elite, the judges and nobles. Roland Mousnier, on the other hand, has added another dimension to the Fronde by his emphasis on the connection between peasants and town workers at the bottom of the social scale and the parlementary judges and great nobles at the top. Yet, though the stress of both men on the social ramifications of the Fronde has helped show why the upheaval was so widespread, neither scholar has succeeded any better than old-style liberal and monarchist historians in explaining its length and intensity. Porschnev argues that the Fronde failed because temporary unity against the monarchy by the peasant-artisan element and the parlementary-noble class broke down over underlying class hatred between these two groups. However, this view clearly ignores the intensity of the separate, but mutually influencing revolts of virtually all social elements. Equally misleading is Mousnier's assertion that the Fronde, although far more dangerous than Porschnev suggests, was eventually overcome by skillful dividing of the opposition by an astute monarchy. This analysis fails to explore the factor of the limited resources of both sides that helped turn the Fronde into a long and ultimately chaotic conflict. Nevertheless, the provocative studies of both Porschnev and Mousnier were of value in that they led me to consider the parlementary Fronde in a much broader social context than I would otherwise have done. And they strengthened my conviction of the centrality of the role played by the Parlement of Paris, itself, in containing both the anarchical and authoritarian potential within the Fronde.

Although historical considerations of the so-called seventeenth-century crisis are still in a preliminary stage, and have not yet provided a satisfactory definition of the term, let alone given a clear picture of the place of mid-century France in the broader European situation, we can at least extract some general symptoms of European crisis from the relevant literature. Countries throughout early seventeenth-century Europe were plagued by economic uncertainty, costly and devastating interstate wars, efforts by central administrations to impose law, order, and desperately needed taxes on rebellious subjects, and finally, by the appearance of corrupt ministers, courtiers, or financiers whose virtual embezzlement robbed the royal treasury and private subjects. However, the collision of the imperious state and rebellious subjects varied in intensity from country to country. France's Fronde was a more broadly based cluster of revolts than England's better known and more successful Great Rebellion, and it also had some parallels in abortive Catalonian and Neapolitan revolts against Spain. There were signs, for a while, that Denmark might experience rebellion, and Sweden came still closer to a political upheaval, while Russia and Poland were racked by seething unrest. Even the normally placid Dutch republic witnessed a bitter struggle for leadership which was resolved only when the would-be absolutist William II died suddenly, permitting the rival "regent" class to assume control of Dutch politics. But the diverse nature of these regional upheavals makes it hazardous to suggest any major issue as the same basic reason for tension and polarization within each state, even if Sir George Clark has hinted by his description of the mid-century experience as a great "watershed" that some great issue was at stake.

Fortunately, preliminary studies of the general European situation provide enough clues for a specialist on one state to put that country's mid-century experience somewhat in the broader contemporary context. I am particularly indebted to Hugh Trevor-Roper for the broad picture, and to Ernst Kossman, John Elliott, and Michael Roberts for their suggestive treatment of not only the European crisis theme but of the particular situation, respectively, in the French and Dutch, Spanish, and Swedish states. Clearly, the general problems which the French state faced at mid-century were not unique to France: its adverse economic conditions, the weight of foreign wars, and corrupt financiers. It also had the clash of wartime centralization with an alienated political-social elite of nobles, officials, and merchants, similar to that in Olivares' Spain and Charles I's England. The sullen hostility by French peasants and artisans to royal taxation which flared into defiant riots was the same as that occurring as far away as the Russia of Tsar Alexei. Yet there were peculiar aspects of the French crisis which defy all attempts to explain its course and denouement purely in terms of broad European forces. My objective has been to explain the role of the Parlement of Paris during the Fronde and, in so doing, to attempt to render the peculiar nature of the French mid-century experience intelligible. For the enigma of the Fronde and the baffling, ambivalent role of the parlementary judges are two sides of the same coin. General European conditions explain much of the background, and the outcome of the Fronde, in turn, should shed light on the nature of European states in the succeeding age of Louis XIV. However, the unique composition of that peculiarly French institution, the Parlement of Paris, sheds more light on the French version of the crisis than does any other factor, either within France or in Europe as a whole.

It would be relatively easy to place all the foregoing components of the Fronde in a rigid institutional framework, conjuring up an image of an inevitable clash between a monarchy set on governmental centralization and a court of law rallying the diverse opposition. Such impersonal forces, institutions pressed by war on the one hand and ingrained legalism on the other, did clash in the 1640's. Nevertheless, human beings make history, and it was very human administrators and judges who helped to make the Fronde what it was. At crucial moments between 1648 and 1652, as well as before and after those terminal dates of the Fronde, the human element spelled the difference between what might have been and what actually occurred. Errors in judgment, astute tactical moves by the queen mother, chief minister Mazarin, and judges like Mathieu Molé, Omer Talon, and Pierre Broussel, frequently became the deciding factors. It was the blending of institutional responses and individual reactions, along with closely connected military, social, and ideological forces, which together shaped the course of the enigmatic cluster of rebellions. In seeking to give proper weight to the role of individuals, there is of course the danger of reading moral judgments into the past, a danger which is magnified by concentrating on one institution. But the evaluations of the roles of persons in this book are, as far as possible, historically based, and are designed to bring more sharply into focus the issues involved and the alternatives which were open to the protagonists.

I am indebted to many persons and institutions. Those who are acquainted with seventeenth-century France and Europe will recognize how much my interpretation has been built on the foundations laid by other historians, even where it differs sharply with their views. This is particularly true of the work of Ernst Kossman, a great historian of the Fronde, and of Roland Mousnier, whose productivity and insight have been demonstrated in a host of studies on the seventeenth century. To John Wolf, who introduced me to seventeenth-century France, guided my doctoral work on the subject, and has given me constant encouragement as scholar, critic, and friend, I am especially grateful. Orest Ranum has contributed immeasurably through discussions ranging over many topics. I owe a particular debt to him and Herbert Rowen, both of whom read the entire typescript. My former colleagues, Ivo Lambi, Richard Grassby, and Edmund Beame, read earlier versions and provided important suggestions and criticisms. Needless to say, I bear sole responsibility for the debatable elements that remain. Institutional assistance has also been gracious and indispensable. A grant from the American Philosophical Society made it possible for me to work in the Cabinet des Manuscrits and Département des Imprimés of the Bibliothèque Nationale and, briefly, at the Bibliothèque Mazarine. At an earlier stage, the University of Minnesota generously provided me with an excellent substitute for archival research: microfilms of several bulky manuscripts held by archival libraries in Paris. Some additional information was uncovered after the book was written, while I was working in archival collections on another project financed by a National Endowment for the Humanities grant. The material has been incorporated, mainly in footnotes. Librarians at a number of institutions have been helpful: at the universities of Minnesota and Toronto, Queen's University, the Widener and Houghton libraries at Harvard University, the Bibliothèque Nationale, Bibliothèque Mazarine, and Bibliothèque de l'Institut, as well as the Archives des Affaires Etrangères. I wish also to express my appreciation to Mrs. Jane Lenel for her thoughtful and thorough work at the copyediting stage of this study, and to thank Princeton University Press for selecting her to work with me. My greatest debt is to my wife, Barbara, who has contributed by her encouragement, patience, and typing.

Los Angeles   A. LLOYD MOOTE
November 21, 1970

CONTENTS

PART I

PRELUDE TO THE FRONDE

1610-1648

CHAPTER ONE

FRENCH GOVERNMENT AND
SOCIETY IN 1610

IN THEORY, the governmental structure that Louis XIII inherited in 1610 was deceptively simple.[1] The king (or regent, if he were under thirteen) exercised sovereign authority in executive, legislative, judicial, and military affairs. He was assisted by a small number of loyal, efficient, and very able persons who constituted what can be called the royal "administration."[2] Originally a single council, the administration had become divided into four councils: a *conseil d'état* or *conseil des affaires*, for general policy; a *conseil d'état et des finances*, for financial policies; a *conseil des finances*, in charge of the actual acquisition and allocation of revenues; and a *conseil des parties*, an organ of executive justice. The personnel of the councils included councilors of state, who participated in discussions on policies, and *maîtres des requêtes*, who provided the councils with pertinent information. These councils worked closely with a select num-

---

[1] The standard legal and institutional histories contain much of the information in this chapter. See especially F. Olivier-Martin, *Histoire du droit français des origines à la Révolution*, Paris, 1951; R. Doucet, *Les Institutions de la France au XVIe siècle*, 2 vols., Paris, 1948. However, the actual practices of the French government at the beginning of the seventeenth century did not always fit the somewhat rigid, mechanical pattern described by legal scholars. I have had to draw my interpretation of those practices as much from a wide reading of contemporary sources as from the facts as established by historians.

[2] By adopting the modern term "administration," there is a danger of misleading the reader, for the word implies that the inner circles of seventeenth-century royal government had a far more clear-cut position within the governmental structure than was actually the case. Indeed, the lack of a seventeenth-century descriptive noun attests to the absence of an administration in the modern sense. However, alternative phrases being still less satisfactory, this term must be used to describe the machinery and personnel in charge of royal policy-making. "Government" refers to every agent and agency of the state, including the very judicial and financial officials who were in conflict with the central administration during the Fronde. "Ministry" is not used because it might allude too narrowly to the chief minister. "Council of state" denotes the formal, leading council which was often bypassed by the ruler and ministerial aides. The once accepted use of "Crown" is totally misleading except in very specific instances; all officials, and particularly the Parlement of Paris which was the central element in the opposition of the Fronde, claimed to be part of the Crown since they represented the king in dealing with his subjects.

ber of great state functionaries, who were either ministers or in the process of assuming a ministerial role. The minister of finance (*surintendant des finances*) was assisted by a *contrôleur général* and a few *intendants des finances*. The titular head of justice was the chancellor, who appended the royal seals to legal documents drafted in the councils. The other major persons of the administration were the four secretaries of state, who signed state letters and were just beginning to emerge as embryonic ministers for war, foreign affairs, the royal household, and other internal affairs. Beneath this conciliar-ministerial administration were thousands of officials entrusted with the implementation of the king's conciliar decisions, the enforcement of his laws, collection of taxes, and the maintenance of order.

In practice, this pyramid of king, conciliar personnel, and judicial, financial, and police officials was far from a perfect instrument of royal authority. Over the centuries, it had helped the monarchy break down the virtually independent status of *les grands* (the highest ranking nobles and the royal princes), as well as some basic privileges of the clergy, municipal authorities, and provincial assemblies of estates. Royal authority became absolute in the sense that the king was considered to be "absolved" or freed from any formal controls by subjects or their moribund Estates General. Ministers, councilors, and officials believed in the principle of the divine right of kings which made the king accountable to God alone for his actions, and all swore to uphold the king's will.[3] There remained serious governmental weaknesses which were to hamper the "absolute" monarchy's efforts to meet the gigantic problems of war, economic depression, and endemic rebellion, facing all states in the first half of the seventeenth century.

Although some of the difficulties can be traced to inefficiency at the conciliar-ministerial level, on the whole the royal administration was to prove as obedient and effective in the future as it had in the past. Councilors, maîtres des requêtes, and ministers actively participated in the decisions of the king, and, therefore, had little reason to feel alienated; moreover, most of them were *commissaires* (a term which derives from the fact that they held temporary commissions), serving at the pleasure of the regent or king. The authority of the few who held permanent offices could be circumvented if necessary.

---

[3] On contemporary divine-right beliefs, see R. Mousnier, "Comment les français du XVIIe siècle voyaient la constitution," *XVIIe Siècle*, nos. 25-26 (1955), 9-36.

The secretaries of state, who bought their positions, could simply be stripped of important duties. The chancellor, who held office for life, could be deprived of the royal seals, and his functions transferred to a specially appointed keeper of the seals (*garde des sceaux*). The maîtres des requêtes, who purchased their offices and had the right to bequeath them at will, could be kept from the council chambers or ignored by the king when he chose members of special commissions. Personal rivalries of ministers, jurisdictional disputes between councils, or sheer confusion over the functions of different types of conciliar agents could be smoothed over by an inner council composed of the king, his most trusted adviser or favorite minister, and a few additional friends, ministers, and councilors who had the monarch's confidence.

A more basic weakness emerged in the form of permanent officials (*officiers*) entrusted with the execution of decisions by the king and his commissaires. These state servants blanketed the country with a complex network of governmental corporations. To simplify the picture, France in 1610 can be described as divided into broad geographic regions, each with its own set of corporations for civil and criminal justice, taxation and financial litigation, and examination of officials' accounts.[4] Within each broad category, a quasi-hierarchical arrangement existed. For civil and criminal affairs, each broad district had a parlement, which was theoretically sovereign, though subject to royal review. Beneath that tribunal were several regionally based, intermediate courts (*présidiaux*), and beneath them many types of petty courts, most notably those headed by *baillis* in northern France and *sénéchaux* in the south. The same geographic area had a "sovereign" court for tax suits—*cour des aides*—and a host of subordinate officials headed by the *élus*, entrusted with the initial imposition of taxes. For accounting, there was a "sovereign" *chambre des comptes*, and beneath it several bureaus of *trésoriers de France*, which supervised royal domains, roads, and the work of the *élus*. Thus central France, composed of the oldest provinces in the realm, had a parlement, chambre des comptes, and cour des aides, seated in Paris, and a host of *présidiaux, baillis, sénéchaux, trésoriers,*

---

[4] However, boundaries were not always drawn with any precision for judicial districts, and there were often minor variations in the area (*ressort*) under the common jurisdiction of criminal and financial tribunals. See E. Esmonin, "Donnés statistiques sur le règne de Louis XIII," *Etudes sur la France des XVIIe et XVIIIe siècles,* Paris, 1964, p. 243.

and *élus* in various towns. Each of the more recently acquired provinces on the periphery of the realm had its own complement of these tribunals and bureaus: in Normandy, Brittany, Guienne, Provence, Languedoc, Burgundy, Dauphiné, and by the late 1630's also in Metz-Toul-Verdun and Navarre. In addition, the entire realm was under the jurisdiction of the *Grand Conseil,* a "sovereign" court which adjudicated ecclesiastical disputes affecting the state from its base in Paris. Finally, there existed in every province a few military-administrative officials who were not, strictly speaking, officiers. These were the provincial governors, their *lieutenants généraux,* and the governors of fortresses. Members of the high nobility, or princely families, holding temporary commissions rather than permanent offices, they acted as executors of the royal will just as did the judicial and financial officials. Originally, they had been the chief military officers in an area; by the beginning of the seventeenth century, they were used chiefly to add weight to the king's decisions by personally authorizing their implementation. A governor might cooperate with the financial and judicial officials of his province in maintaining law and order, or he might antagonize them by trying to make them his underlings, or entice them into joining a rebellion by nobles against the Crown.[5]

These officers constituted an important group of subjects who were part of the government and yet lacked the consultative role which bound the ministers, councilors, and maîtres so closely to the monarchy. In the early seventeenth century they numbered some forty thousand persons, or one official for every four hundred subjects.[6] Closely attached to them was the still greater number of

[5] We need a thorough examination of sixteenth- and seventeenth-century governors to supplant the vague descriptions in legal histories, and to test the diametrically opposed interpretations by G. Zeller, "L'Administration monarchique avant les intendants: Parlements et gouverneurs," *Revue Historique* cxcvii (1947), 180-215; and R. Mousnier, "Notes sur les rapports entre les gouverneurs de province et les intendants dans la première moitié du XVIIe siècle," ibid. ccxxviii (1962), 339-350. One can still read with profit the perceptive comments on the subject in G. d'Avenel, *Richelieu et la monarchie absolue,* 4 vols., Paris, 1895, iv, 108-129.

[6] This figure is generally accepted. By 1664, according to Jean-Baptiste Colbert, there were 30,000 financial officials and 70,000 judicial offices. A list made in 1665 by the *bureaux des finances* limited the total figure to 45,780, with an evaluation of 419,630,000 *livres.* J. P. Charmeil, *Les Trésoriers de France à l'époque de la Fronde,* Paris, 1964, pp. 16-18, 456-479, has the most precise information for a single category of officials.

marshals, pages, clerks, and legal assistants (*avocats, procureurs, notaires*) who crowded the law courts and financial bureaus. Each of these officials was deeply committed to his profession, holding a permanent office, in contrast to the temporary commissaires in the royal administration, and protected against arbitrary removal by a law of 1467. As a deeply entrenched bloc of career servants, the officiers posed a threat from within the government which was potentially far more serious than a rebellion by outside social groups. If they were antagonized by the monarch or chose to support revolts by his subjects, they could make the task of ruling France virtually impossible. By merely failing to carry out their functions, or by exercising their powers independently of the royal will, they could make a mockery of absolute monarchy.

The existence of these officers made the early seventeenth-century French state unique in an age noted for its variety of governmental forms. Central and eastern European states were dominated by the aristocracy. Whether they acted as lords on their estates or as royal servants at the central or local levels of government, these nobles tended to think and act as members of a social group. The change from private to public posture was largely a change of title. The situation in the Dutch republic was not very different, despite the fact that non-noble elements constituted the governing elite. Town officials, members of the provincial assemblies and States General, and well-to-do commoners (such as bondholders, landowners, and a few merchants) were often one and the same, combining public and private affairs in the interest of their loose social grouping. The Spanish empire was closer to the French state in the development of a career service. Yet the phenomenon was largely confined to Castile; in the other Iberian provinces, the Italian possessions, and the Spanish Netherlands, few royal officials stood between monarch and subject. England was notorious for its rudimentary governmental structure. Its elementary machinery for collecting taxes and its system of law enforcement at the local level by a few unpaid representatives of the landed classes are proof that England was one of the most undergoverned states in Europe. Different from all these were the French officers, a broad governing "class," acting as state servants rather than as members of a social group, and serving as intermediaries between king and subjects.

7

2

THE EMERGENCE of the officers had given the theoretically unitary monarchy a governmental dualism: the king had his administrative commissaires to help him establish policies, and his permanent officers to implement them. In theory, this implied separation of powers was innocuous enough. But in actuality, it provided such unanticipated latitude for the judicial and financial officials that it thwarted the efforts of successive kings to enforce royal sovereignty over the so-called sovereign courts and lesser corporations in judicial, legislative, and administrative matters. For underlying the seeming separation of powers was a chaotic overlapping of powers. This confusion was fostered in large part by the lack of a coherent and common set of laws for the realm; and, one might add, the absence of unified laws even within each governmental region. Only constant directives from the king and his councils could have prevented the individual courts and bureaus from making their own decisions about the applicability of laws. In effect, the officers became legislators and administrators, initiating as well as implementing policies.[7]

This overlapping of functions was reinforced by a "police" authority inherent in every corporation of officers. Police authority was the obligation to issue regulatory *arrêts* (in some cases, *ordonnances*) in the collective name of law, order, and justice, and all officials issued such orders on behalf of what was called "good administration." Some of these quasi-executive decrees applied to a single, unprecedented case in dispute, many were binding for similar cases in the future, and all went beyond past laws, being applicable to situations never anticipated by royal legislation, or simply closing gaps in the existing body of law.[8] Moreover, the officers, especially in the parlements, kept an excellent record of these *arrêts*. Indeed, as late as the 1650's, the future minister of Louis XIV, Jean-Baptiste Colbert, lamented that for some matters the Parlement of Paris had a better archival system than the royal administration. Therefore, the officiers had an obvious advantage over the monarch. Before the king

[7] Zeller, "Parlements et gouverneurs," pp. 184-185, 187; G. Pagès, "Essai sur l'évolution des institutions administratives en France du XVIe siècle à la fin du XVIIe," *Revue d'Histoire Moderne* VII (1932), 8-57. The phrase "confusion of powers" was used by d'Avenel (*Richelieu* IV, 130-132), in a brilliant, but often overlooked discussion.

[8] P. A. Chéruel, *Dictionnaire historique des institutions, moeurs et coutumes de la France*, 2 vols., Paris, 1910, II, 1053.

8

in his councils might even be aware of an issue that had come to a tribunal's attention, the judges would already have glanced at their archives, found a precedent for an appropriate response, and issued a decree which might very well conflict with royal interests.[9]

Though in the strict sense, the officiers never legislated, the famous judicial review of the law courts and some of the financial corporations gave them an important role in legislation. Just as police authority made them administrators, their uncontested right to register all new laws made them legislators. The monarch had to submit legislation for registration in the appropriate bureau or court so that the officials who enforced the laws could know their contents, and publish this information for subjects. This provided the registering body with an opportunity to modify or reject new laws.

In part, this use of registration to block the king's will was an illegal procedure; the officials simply usurped the king's role as legislator by "verifying" a projected law: deciding whether it was in the interest of the king, conformed to existing laws, or would be obeyed by subjects. If the answer to any of these questions was negative, the officiers could remonstrate to the king through written or oral objections. Whenever the officials considered remonstrances to be too mild a form of criticism, they simply refused to register the legislation or appended their own amendments, thus, in effect, altering the new law. Illegal as this procedure was, it did have some justification in current governmental procedures; otherwise, it would have been suppressed by the monarchy.[10] The officiers argued persuasively that their police powers included the right to object to legislation that might cause rebellion, or at the very least a weakening of respect for the king. Judicial review also stemmed from the officials' duty to hear appeals by subjects against new laws affecting the latter. And it followed faithfully the practice at the chancellery, where the

[9] J.-B. Colbert, *Lettres, instructions, et mémoires*, ed. P. Clément, 7 vols., Paris, 1861-1882, I, 252; VI, 5, 20-21.

[10] P. R. Doolin, *The Fronde*, Cambridge, 1935, pp. 11, 68, seems to be using modern notions of legislation when he interprets judicial review as a legislative matter. Nevertheless, his somewhat formalized categorization of the distribution of functions between monarchy and the sovereign courts comes closer to an understanding of early modern practices than the completely unhistorical criticisms of judicial review to be found in the works of legal historians, e.g., E. D. Glasson, *Le Parlement de Paris, son rôle politique depuis le règne de Charles VII jusqu'à la Révolution*, 2 vols., Paris, 1901. The excellent study by J. H. Shennan, *The Parlement of Paris*, Ithaca, 1968, especially pp. 159-160, does place judicial review in the proper context.

chancellor reviewed all royal acts affecting justice before deciding whether he would seal and dispatch them.[11] To be sure, French kings had always objected that judicial review could not be construed to include outright rejection or crippling amendments, but they had never questioned the right to verify and remonstrate. Having conceded this, monarchs found it very difficult to prevent verification from leading logically to a veto. Judicial review became such a regular practice that even remonstrances were serious affronts to royal authority. Until the king answered the objections and either convinced or compromised with his officers, the new law remained unregistered, unenforced, and unacceptable to subjects.[12]

It was also virtually impossible to control the judicial functions, per se, of criminal, civil, and financial tribunals. Monarchs claimed royal monopoly over cases of high treason against the king's sovereignty (*lèse-majesté*), and permitted judgment by tribunals of crimes affecting only subjects. But in practice, it was difficult to make a clear distinction between ordinary and state crimes. And though there was also a broad "reserved authority" of the king, which gave him the right as the embodiment of justice in the state to take back from any court at any time the judicial functions the monarchy had bestowed on it, it was impossible for the king to interfere constantly with litigation in the courts. By default, and often with royal approval, the courts took charge of great state trials as well as petty suits.

It cannot be emphasized too strongly that the above-mentioned powers of the officers were not only deeply embedded in traditional governmental practices, but proceeded logically from the very nature of French government. Had the officials' power lacked such a solid base, monarchs would have dealt much more easily with courts and bureaus. Historians who have argued categorically that the officers were acting illegally through their use of judicial review, or that they were usurping the king's executive and legislative roles, have misunderstood the governmental problems facing the monarchy in 1610, and consequently rendered the Fronde unintelligible. The

[11] Olivier-Martin, *Histoire du droit français*, pp. 452, 542.

[12] Ibid., pp. 573-604; E. Maugis, *Histoire du Parlement de Paris de l'avènement des rois Valois à la mort d'Henri IV*, 3 vols., Paris, 1913-1916, 1, 674-703; A. de Boislisle, ed., *Chambre des Comptes de Paris*, Rogent le Rotrou, 1873, intro.; Zeller, "Parlements et gouverneurs," pp. 155-156.

danger to the king from his officers actually stemmed more from the legality than the illegality of their actions.[13] Nor is it appropriate to argue, as generations of scholars have, that the officers should have left the task of mediating between king and subjects to the much more representative Estates General, an assembly composed of clergy, nobles, and commoners. The truth is that the French Estates General was not an institution, but only an irregularly summoned body that had no real power and was on the point of extinction in 1610. Considering its impotence during the religious wars, which brought forth a flood of pamphlets urging the sovereign courts to fill the vacuum,[14] nothing could have been more natural than for the officers to use their powers to become mediators between king and subjects. Indeed, the French parlements were in one major respect far more potent political institutions than their English namesake, the Stuart Parliaments. Generations of historians have erroneously inferred that the parlementary judges were doomed to political impotence because they lacked Parliament's legislative and representative traits,[15] while the truth is that French parlements combined many of the powers of Parliament and the chief English courts, King's Bench and Common Pleas. The only correct conclusion is that the corporations of French officials were more powerful, and better suited to the French situation than any legislative, representative assembly could have been, whether it was an Estates General, a Parliament, or a modern type of legislature.

Just as perplexing as this confusion of powers was the ability of the officers to hide behind the principle of divine-right absolutism. One would think that this weapon of the king could not have been

[13] The comments on the officers' adherence to correct governmental forms, in d'Avenel, *Richelieu* IV, 137, and the emphasis on the legal-judicial nature of the medieval-early modern French government, in Shennan, *The Parlement of Paris*, come closest to my interpretation on this point.

[14] W. F. Church, *Constitutional Thought in Sixteenth-Century France*, Cambridge, 1941, pp. 137-139, 145. Antiabsolutist scholars of the so-called "liberal school" have attacked the sovereign courts for usurping the role of the Estates General, thereby completely confusing nineteenth- and twentieth-century notions of government with those of an earlier age. See, e.g., G. J. de Cosnac, *Souvenirs du règne de Louis XIV*, 8 vols., Paris, 1866-1882, I, 164, 172-173, 242-244; C. Normand, *La Bourgeoisie française au XVIIe siècle*, Paris, 1908, p. 320. Historical apologists of absolute monarchy, understandably, have criticized opposition by either the Estates or courts.

[15] Such was the interpretation of E. Lavisse, ed., *Histoire de France depuis les origines jusqu'à la Révolution*, 9 vols., Paris, 1900-1911, VII, pt. i, p. 34.

deflected by the officials' corporations, for the officers thought of themselves as royal representatives, or, more precisely, as an integral element of the "Crown." This peculiar position of the courts and bureaus as inseparable from the monarchy has led at least one distinguished scholar to the brilliantly expounded, but untenable conclusion that the officials' brand of royalism made them weak threats to royal absolutism.[16] The truth is that the officers deftly fashioned their role as "part of the Crown" into a flexible, double-edged weapon of offense and defense. On the one hand, they had developed the technique of acting against royal interests by feigning ignorance of the king's wishes, thereby giving their own rebellious *arrêts* and judgments the prestige of being acts of the Crown. On the other, they never broke formally with the principle of royal absolutism, thereby making it difficult for the monarch to tar them with the brush of rebellion or treason.[17]

To be sure, the officials were maintaining a difficult, ambivalent position. Even if successful, it threatened to place them in the position of antagonizing the king, at the same time preventing them, by their avowed royalism, from attempting any fundamental changes in the political structure of France. Assuming the fact that they were only moderate, almost reluctant, opponents of royal authority, one can accept the thesis that the officers were not true revolutionaries. But they maintained a great deal of maneuverability, and could force the monarchy into concessions it might never have granted if they had broken cleanly with the principle of absolute monarchy. Then, too, their position as part of the Crown made them very desirable allies in the monarchy's conflicts with subjects, however strong the king's aversion to their elusive opposition might be. After all, the officers were defenders of law and order, and had helped monarchs subdue overmighty subjects in the past. The Parlement of Paris, for example, also had played a major role in placing and keeping Henri IV on the throne in the 1590's (by ruling that a foreigner or a female could not become ruler of France), and had been even more royalist than the king in defending the rights of the secular state against the Papacy.[18] Louis XIII's first minister, Cardinal Riche-

---

[16] E. H. Kossman, *La Fronde*, Leiden, 1954, especially chap. 1.

[17] Mme Cubells, "Le Parlement de Paris pendant la Fronde," *XVIIe Siècle*, no. 35 (1957), 173-177, gives an excellent analysis of the parlementarians' political thought.

[18] P. Blet, *Le Clergé de France et la monarchie, 1615-1666*, 2 vols., Rome, 1959, especially II, 34, fn. 134, 54, 406-413.

lieu, was to urge that the parlementarians must not be dealt with too harshly, admitting that they were "on many occasions . . . necessary for the maintenance of the state," in defending royal interests against the clergy.[19] All things considered, it seemed best for a monarch to court the parlementarians and other officers, whenever the issue of law and order arose.

As an opposition, hiding behind the principle of royal absolutism, the French officials were a unique force in seventeenth-century Europe. For all the unfavorable comparisons historians make between the institutional opposition of the mid-century rebellions in France and England, the fact remains that England's Long Parliament was unable to survive the revolution when caught between the forces of Charles I and the rebel army of Roundheads, whereas the Parlement of Paris was to outlast the civil wars of the Fronde. Although the comparison takes us ahead in our story, it is a point well worth emphasizing. The English House of Commons lost control over the course of the revolution partly because it openly defied the king whose approval alone made its acts legal. That situation was prevented in France during the Fronde because the parlementarians knew how to employ the governmental confusion of powers, so that they could act independently of the monarch and still remain part of the Crown.

3

THE MAJOR weakness of the officiers was the existence of divisions and rivalries within their ranks. A member of the Parlement of Paris, for example, was most concerned with the affairs of his tribunal, somewhat less interested in the interaction of parlementary and royal power, and least concerned with the affairs of officiers in other corporations. The same could be said of members of all other judicial and financial bodies, large or small. The compartmentalization of the officiers into distinct corporations reflected the structure of early modern French society, which was composed of separate, almost self-contained groups, such as guilds and religious orders. Just as each guild or other professional group had its *esprit de corps*, so, too, did each court or financial bureau. Ironically, the very legalism that made the officiers as a whole such a formidable rival of

[19] Cardinal de Richelieu, *Mémoires*, ed. Société de l'Histoire de France, 10 vols., 1907-1931, v, 336.

royal authority also helped nourish the isolation of their individual corporations. Each was concerned with preserving its legal powers to the fullest. Despite serious differences of opinion and quarrels within a corporation, its members agreed on one thing: the perpetuation of their institution could not be sacrificed by internecine feuds. When they looked beyond their narrow world to the broader world of the officers as a whole, it was usually to defend their own corporation against another which might seem to be encroaching on their territory or their functions.

The institutional history of early modern France is replete with examples of such wrangles.[20] Not even the quasi-hierarchical arrangement within a region prevented this legal warfare of pen and *arrêt*. Each parlement sought to prevent inferior *présidial* courts from judging suits which it felt were within its competence. Courts of *baillis* were suspicious of the *présidiaux*'s encroachment on their functions. Similar quarrels turned chambres des comptes against bureaus of *trésoriers,* and *trésoriers* against *élus*. The parlement, chambre des comptes, and cour des aides in the same area were equally hasty to compete for control over financial matters that were so complex that they were partly within the jurisdiction of them all. And where legalism did not envenom relations, geographic separation did. A provincial parlement was not likely to understand the quarrels which pitted the Parlement of Paris against the royal administration, or to sympathize with a comparable struggle involving another provincial parlement (unless their jurisdictional territories bordered on each other).

Fratricidal struggles, geographic separation, and narrow vision within the family of officers threatened to turn governmental dualism into self-defeating pluralism. Obviously, the greatest corporations could survive, although even their narrow *esprit de corps* gave the monarch an opportunity to play the game of dividing and ruling, keeping corporations from uniting against royal policies by encouraging their family squabbles.[21] The lesser corporations were

---

[20] See, inter alia, Boislisle, *Chambre des Comptes,* intro.; Charmeil, *Les Trésoriers de France,* pp. 274-355; P. Goubert, "Les Officiers royaux des présidiaux, bailliages et élections dans la société française au XVIIe siècle," *XVIIe Siècle,* nos. 42-43 (1959), 59-60.

[21] R. Mousnier, *La Vénalité des offices sous Henri IV et Louis XIII,* Rouen, 1945, stresses the royal tactic of dividing and ruling. That interpretation probably merits reexamination as a result of the discovery of numerous instances where the royal

not so likely to survive without support. Their functions were far more restricted, the territory within their jurisdiction much smaller, and their prestige far less. They had to watch both the encroachment of the sovereign courts on their functions and the constant attempt by the king, ministers, and councils to place them more firmly under royal control. By 1610, the *baillis* and *sénéchaux* had already lost many of the functions they had held in the Middle Ages, although some of those powers had simply been transferred to the *présidial* courts and the *trésoriers*. The *élus* and *trésoriers*, in turn, were beginning to lose prestige and power in the face of unrelenting encroachment by the financial branch of the central administration headed by the *surintendant*. All the officers were threatened by the gradual emergence in recent decades of special royal commissioners, sent to individual provinces, *généralités*, or *élections*, to supervise their work.[22] And there was also the disturbing rise of tax farmers (*partisans* or *traitants*), who loaned money to the king. Whether these private financiers drew their interest from state revenues or actually collected the money themselves, they were deeply interested in the assessment and collection of royal taxes. There was a very real possibility that they might take the place of local financial bureaus and sovereign courts in all matters related to taxation and fiscal litigation.[23]

Yet, despite these numerous problems, the officers had the ability to overcome their divisiveness if the need arose. That they would ever act as a united force against the monarchy was very doubtful. That they could find ways to cooperate against encroachments by the royal administration, or to follow one another's lead in the midst of a major conflict with the central administration, was much more likely.[24] Subordinate courts could swallow their pride and appeal

---

administration tried to be an impartial mediator. See Charmeil, *Les Trésoriers de France*, passim, and my review, *American Historical Review* LXX (1965), 861-862.

[22] Pagès, "Essai sur l'évolution des institutions administratives," has an excellent treatment of the previous points.

[23] There are fresh studies of this bewildering subject: A. D. Lublinskaya, *French Absolutism: The Crucial Phase, 1620-1629*, trans. B. Pearce. Cambridge, 1968, chap. 5, "The Financiers and the Absolute Monarchy"; and A. Chauleur, "Le Rôle des traitants dans l'administration financière de la France de 1643 à 1653," *XVIIe Siècle*, no. 65 (1964), 16-49.

[24] To document the points in the following two paragraphs would require a needlessly extended footnote crammed with a mass of citations. Some notion of a few

for help from the sovereign tribunal above them. Sovereign courts within the same area could also communicate easily, especially if they resided in the same city. Communication between courts or bureaus with the same rank and functions, however, was rarer, since they were geographically separated. Nevertheless, parlements had occasionally appealed to each other for assistance against the royal administration.

The form of assistance varied considerably, but the most common type was one in which a superior court helped an inferior one within its jurisdiction. The sovereign tribunal would place the prestige of its name behind the grievances of the appellant, and perhaps issue *arrêts* against the interfering royal council if the law was clearly on the side of the beleaguered corporation. Between corporations of the same rank, relationships were more complicated. No parlement had the right to pass an *arrêt* binding on another parlement, or the authority to order a chambre des comptes or cour des aides to resist the king. What could be done, however, was more dramatic. A sovereign court would send a letter of sympathy, or even an *arrêt* of union, to a comparable tribunal within another area of the realm. "Union" implied that the assisting tribunal pledged its full support, and would use all its influence with the royal administration to bring redress of grievances. The letter of sympathy, vaguer than outright union, acted as a warning to the monarch and an announcement to subjects that the tribunal might issue an *arrêt* of union if the situation worsened. Most dramatic of all were exchanges between different sovereign courts within the same region. This rallying of the highest officers in an area to a common cause was a frightening prospect for the royal administration. (Henri IV had been forced in 1597 to cut short his absence from the capital in order to prevent such brazen cooperation.) Although the form of this common protest might be limited to letters of mutual sympathy, or *arrêts* of union, it could also include joint sessions. At Paris, since the Chambre des Comptes, Cour des Aides, and Parlement shared the Palace of Justice, under extreme provocation each could send delegates to a special assembly in the building's Chambre Saint Louis.

sources can be found in A. L. Moote, "The Parlementary Fronde and Seventeenth-Century Robe Solidarity," *French Historical Studies* II (1962), 330-348. That article was written at a time when the author was more interested in the weakness of the officers' legendary *esprit de corps* than in analyzing their means of overcoming the problems of separatism and rivalry.

The officiers had one common interest overshadowing all traditional divisions: a determination to perpetuate officeholding and the numerous benefits it bestowed on every official, from petty collector of taxes to a parlementary president. Their offices were becoming virtual private property through the practice of venality of offices (*vénalité*).[25] During the sixteenth century, the French monarchy had ceased to exercise its right to choose officials, preferring to turn the selection into a financial transaction. A person with wealth offered to buy an office; the monarch readily accepted, and the individual was installed with only a perfunctory examination of his qualifications or his loyalty to the monarch. In 1604, Henri IV took *vénalité* to its logical conclusion. The famous *paulette*, renewed every nine years, permitted judicial and financial officials to bequeath their offices at will in return for an annual fee (*droit annuel*). The fee was modest—one-sixtieth of the estimated value of the office; the prize was a handsome one: the assurance that the office could be kept within the family. Sale of offices and the privilege of the paulette may have helped increase natural jealousies and rivalry between the sovereign courts and the lower echelons of officiers, since holders of offices in financial bureaus or petty courts could not aspire to the much more costly judgeships of the sovereign tribunals. Yet, all officiers had a common interest in holding their offices and in protecting them through the paulette. Any attack by a monarch on the principle of the paulette or the suggestion that sale of offices be ended was bound to cause anxiety throughout the ranks of the officiers, regardless of what specific institution was threatened.

The salaried income (*gages*) from the "investment" in most offices was not as significant as the fringe benefits which had accumulated in recent times. Officials were exempt from many taxes, the most important being the basic land tax (*taille*). Then, too, officiers collected fees for their services, and these were sometimes quite lucrative. Perhaps the greatest advantage of officeholding was the opportunities it gave for further acquisition of wealth and land. Judges were in an excellent position to know when local landowners were in financial distress, and could either use this information to purchase property at low prices, or press landowners into selling cheaply by harassing them with legal action in their tribunal. Tax officials could manipulate assessments so that they were excessive for their

---

[25] Mousnier, *Vénalité des offices*, is an exhaustive study of the subject and has not yet been fully utilized by historians.

enemies, and light for their servants, tenants, or themselves (if the officers paid directly). Administrative *arrêts*, court decisions, and judicial review could also be employed to manipulate the law to the advantage of officials, as property owners or litigants. It is difficult to determine just how self-seeking and corrupt the officers were as a group.[26] In the early seventeenth century all civil services fed on such unsavory transactions, but in France, because of the number of officials, the vested interest in officeholding was far more significant than elsewhere.

This vested interest reinforced the connections and common concerns existing between individual corporations. But even the sale of offices and the paulette could not provide the judicial and financial officials with the means to act as an all-inclusive unit. It was the Parlement of Paris which exploited the common bond of officeholding, providing a degree of leadership and coordination which otherwise would not have existed. That tribunal could not dictate to its sister courts in Paris or any of the remaining sovereign tribunals of the realm, and its legal control over lesser officials was limited to the subordinate courts within its district. Nevertheless, it was so superior to all other corporations that its actions could influence the most distant sovereign court or the least significant bureau, regardless of the jealousies the rest of the officers had toward its members. And even the legally restricted connections it had with other courts and bureaus provided a network of communications far greater than those between any other corporations in the realm. Royal control over the officers clearly depended to a large degree on the administration's relations with the parlementarians in the capital city. If the Parlement of Paris became engaged in a conflict with the king over a grievance common to several corporations, its resistance might encourage the others to take similar action. If that sovereign court

---

[26] Historians have tended to defend the particular group of officials which they have studied, while engaging in polemics against rival officials. Unfortunately, it is difficult to discover precise documentation on the alleged malpractices, and one should not take too seriously the irresponsible, if sincere, accusations of persons sympathetic to the early modern French monarchy. For varying interpretations, see Charmeil, *Les Trésoriers de France*, chap. III, "Pourquoi l'on devenait trésorier de France"; R. Mousnier, "Recherches sur les syndicats d'officiers pendant la Fronde. Trésoriers généraux de France et élus dans la révolution," *XVIIe Siècle*, nos. 42-43 (1959), 76-117; M. Venard, *Bourgeois et paysans au XVIIe siècle. Recherches sur le rôle des bourgeois parisiens dans la vie agricole au sud de Paris au XVIIe siècle*, Paris, 1957.

clashed with the absolute monarchy over the common issue of office-holding, the entire world of officials might follow its lead and join in the struggle—each corporation in its own way. [27]

As sovereign court for civil and criminal suits in central France, the Parlement of Paris decided an immense number of disputes, either in the first instance, or by appeal. No provincial parlement could claim so large a territory as it held within its jurisdiction. None of the other types of sovereign tribunals could rival its functions; they were too specialized. It is no exaggeration to say that the Parlement of Paris was *the* court of the realm. It was the court of peers, judging suits involving the "dukes and peers" of the realm—the highest ranked nobles of France. Its police decrees were binding on the entire realm, and most royal legislation found its way into the parlementary registers. During the sixteenth century, the Parlement of Paris had started a campaign of encroachment on the functions of the other sovereign courts of Paris. According to a distinguished scholar, it wished to have no superior, at least in fiscal legislation, with the exception of the king himself.[28]

Through the pageantry and ceremony that were such an important aspect of the *ancien régime*, the Parlement of Paris received added luster. Kings' wills were deposited with it (and in these same chambers their successors broke those wills with parlementary approval). The peers of the realm—great nobles and distinguished ecclesiastics—had the privilege of sitting in its sessions when major affairs of state were discussed. International treaties involving France were solemnly registered in that august tribunal. The king, himself, visited the Parlement when he wished to override its judicial review (the other sovereign courts had to be satisfied with royal princes as representatives of the monarch). There was scarcely a public event in the life of the *ancien régime* that was not in some way noted at the Parlement of Paris.

This was the institution which sprang from the medieval *curia regis*, the original king's council, and the parlementarians never forgot their heritage. If all courts and bureaus were integral elements of the Crown, the Parlement of Paris was preeminently so. At times,

[27] On the history of the Parlement of Paris, see the admirable synthesis of older studies by Shennan, *The Parlement of Paris*. Maugis, *Histoire du Parlement de Paris* is still indispensable for the details, and Glasson, *Le Parlement de Paris*, can be used to supplement Shennan, although it is to be used with caution.

[28] Zeller, "Parlements et gouverneurs," p. 197.

19

its members spoke and acted as if they were the king's council. They naturally also saw themselves as superior to the Estates General, while it still survived, and as the symbolic center of royal government; they contended that all measures proposed in the Estates General "must be verified in the [Parlement] in which lies the seat of the royal throne and the bed of royal justice."[29] During the Fronde, one judge had the audacity to stress an argument for parlementary authority which made the king himself look inferior by comparison: the Parlement acted without interruption as an institutional arm of the monarchy, while the monarch was a mortal being who eventually had to transmit his personal authority to an heir.[30]

A glance at the early seventeenth-century institutional map will illustrate the important position of the Parlement of Paris. Within the capital, it had direct surveillance over the important lesser court known as the *châtelet*, and could quickly communicate with the Cour des Aides, Chambre des Comptes, and Grand Conseil in Paris. It also frequently corresponded with the other parlements of the realm over common issues concerning criminal justice and the maintenance of law and order. Its orders to inferior civil and criminal courts within its jurisdiction could not easily be ignored, and in matters such as the royal domains and law enforcement it had some claims to superiority over the financial bureaus of its area. In short, it had wide connections outside and within its own territory, an area encompassing a major section of France, including the capital.[31]

Because the Parlement of Paris was to play a major role in the Fronde, its internal organization is of more than passing interest.[32] All told there were ten parlementary chambers, and some two hundred judges.[33] Five *chambres des enquêtes* and two *chambres des*

---

[29] Quoted by M. Marion, *Dictionnaire des institutions de la France aux XVIIe et XVIIIe siècles*, Paris, 1923, p. 423.

[30] Archives Nationales, U 336, pp. 47-48.

[31] Its *ressort* encompassed the Ile de France, Picardy, Orléanais, Touraine, Maine, Anjou, Poitou, Angoumois, Champagne, Bourbonnais, Berry, Lyonnais, Forez, Beauplais, and Auvergne.

[32] The only way to understand the Parlement's organization is to read its records. However, there is a good outline in Cardinal de Retz, *Oeuvres*, ed. A. Feillet et al., 10 vols., Paris, 1870-1896, I, 304, fn. 4.

[33] Numbers and personnel changed constantly through royal creation of new offices and deaths or resignations. I have found no foolproof figures for the early seventeenth century, but there are fairly complete lists for the late 1640's in A.N. U 336 and Cosnac, *Souvenirs* I, 441-451.

requêtes carried on preliminary work, the latter hearing subjects' requests for justice, and the former inquiring about the facts of a suit. These chambers were composed of junior judges. Above them were three senior chambers. Most prominent of all was the *grand chambre*, staffed with senior judges and theoretically having final authority in judicial matters coming before the Parlement. In practice, it cooperated with a criminal chamber (*chambre de la tournelle*), and a *chambre de l'édit*, which judged suits involving Huguenots in accordance with the terms of the Edict of Nantes. Both chambers were composed of officials from the other parlementary chambers on a rotating basis, but senior judges predominated. When the Parlement was recessed in autumn, a skeleton body of parlementary judges (*chambre des vacations*) conducted the business that could not await the return of the full court. All chambers met together in plenary sessions whenever the Parlement had occasion to install new judges or to discuss internal disciplinary matters. Matters of political importance, such as judicial review or administrative decrees, could also lead to plenary assemblies, but the three senior chambers had the right to decide if this was to be done, and for years such meetings might be avoided. However, during a prolonged political crisis such as the Fronde, the regular judicial functions of the Parlement were overshadowed, or even totally neglected, as plenary sessions on state affairs consumed the judges' working hours.

In terms of personnel, the Parlement of Paris was equally complex. Each chamber had its councilors, both lay and clerical, as well as its presidents. The eight presidents in the great chamber (*présidents à mortier*)—who towered above the other presidents in prestige and importance—were, in turn, headed by the first president; the latter acted as both speaker and head of the Parlement during plenary sessions, taking a leading role in discussions and controlling debating and voting procedures. There were three royal representatives or attorneys (the *procureur général* and two *avocats généraux*, called collectively the *gens du roi*)—in essence members of the Parlement rather than royal agents—who presented legal opinions and read royal messages to their fellow judges, usually through the senior *avocat général*. Formal membership in the Parlement was also granted to the maîtres des requêtes, who were best known for their prominent role within the royal councils. The maîtres' relationship with other parlementarians was clearly an awkward one, since only four were permitted to attend the Parlement's plenary sessions at one time, and they usually defended the interests of king and councils against parlementary criticisms.[34] Plenary sessions could also be attended by numerous honorary councilors, and by the dukes and peers of the realm. Like all other courts, the Parlement of Paris had many lawyers to plead cases before the judges, and an army of scribes, pages, and clerks.

The Parlement was thus a mixture of elements—clergy and laymen, judges and royal attorneys, presidents and councilors, older and younger men. The most likely to initiate action against royal interests were the junior judges of *requêtes* and *enquêtes*. Their tendency toward political radicalism was balanced by the conservatism of the three senior chambers, which were traditionally less inclined to oppose the king's policies except under extreme provocation. At times, the older judges who dominated the senior chambers verged on obsequiousness to royal commands. The first president and the royal attorneys were in a peculiar position because of the way in which they were chosen. *Vénalité* applied to their offices, but the paulette did not. The royal administration handpicked the candidate, and then subsidized his purchase of the position. Usually, this gave the administration a staunch ally within the Parlement, although such was not always the case. The king might choose an individual he thought he could rely on, only to find that either he became independent once in office or the monarchy's own policies shifted direction and the incumbent became a political liability.

Plenary parlementary sessions on political issues brought the court's internal divisions and rivalries into the open,[35] and voting was a complicated process. The junior judges had the advantage of superiority in numbers and every judge had the right to debate. But the three senior chambers decided whether a plenary session should be held in the first place, and the junior judges could only request a favorable decision. Henri IV drafted a decree prohibiting the junior chambers from even attending plenary sessions, and Louis XIII was to renew it in 1642, but that heavy-handed measure was not

[34] The maîtres des requêtes are not to be confused with the councilors and presidents in the *chambres des requêtes*.

[35] The treatment of plenary sessions is based on a close reading of parlementary debates during the early seventeenth century.

22

enforced—it was simply a royal threat to keep the junior judges under control.[36] During a plenary session, debate proceeded from the recommendations voiced by the *gens du roi* through speeches by the *présidents à mortier*, dean, and councilors of the *grand chambre*, to the presidents and councilors of *enquêtes* and *requêtes*. If this procedure gave the senior judges the advantage of speaking first, voting was arranged to effect a compromise between conservative and radical opinions. A first count reduced all opinions to two or three, and another tally decided between or among these. Where three opinions were in question, conservatives could shift to the middle position to turn aside the most radical of the three proposals. Conversely, some radicals would tend to shift to the center in order to arrive at a decision acceptable to the entire Parlement.

Though cumbersome in procedures and troubled by divisions, the plenary sessions of the Parlement of Paris were a frightening prospect for the monarchy, and their complex workings made the Parlement highly unpredictable. Under extreme provocation by the administration, the tribunal could very easily prove a formidable opponent of royal policies; rivalries could be smoothed over, compromises achieved, and a true corporate identity attained. Its internal weaknesses, its unrepresentative nature, and the fact that it was neither English Parliament nor French Estates General are far less significant than its members' ability to act as a body, their prestige and strategic position among the many judicial and financial corporations of the realm, and their claim to be the symbolic center of the Crown of France.

4

ALTHOUGH judicial and financial officials were set apart from the rest of French society by their common bond of officeholding and their position within the government, they did have connections with all kinds of outside groups. No matter how hard they tried to keep those connections separate from professional interests, their relationship with the royal administration was bound to be affected by the social setting. They had helped the monarchy overcome opposition by *les grands*; they stood firmly for royal absolutism against

[36] Mathieu Molé, *Mémoires*, ed. A. Champollion-Figeac, 4 vols., Paris, 1855-1857, II, 321-324, and 470, fn. 1; Omer Talon, *Mémoires*, Michaud and Poujoulat collection (ser. III, vol. VI), Paris, 1839, pp. 45-46, and 45, fn. 1.

the Papacy and clerical privileges; they knew that it was their duty to impose the king's will on peasants, artisans, merchants, and vagabonds (*gens sans aveu, gens de néant*) by collecting taxes and maintaining law and order. But they also had economic and social interests—and occasionally a social conscience as Christians—which made it difficult for them to hold to their past role as defenders of the Crown.

The social structure of France in 1610 was almost as complex as the organization and relations of the various corporations of officiers. Owing to the corporative nature of society at the time, individuals gave their greatest loyalty to their limited professional group rather than to their town, province, or country. There was really no such person as a Parisian or a Breton, and, in a modern sense, not even a Frenchman. Legal compartmentalization and deeply ingrained hierarchical instincts led to rivalries even among the six major guilds of Paris merchants (drapers, grocers, mercers, furriers, hatters, and silversmiths), set them above and apart from the would-be seventh guild of wine merchants, and placed them at some distance socially from the inferior craft guilds. Divisiveness could also be detected within early modern France's most exclusive social group, the nobility: the uncle or cousin of the king was a prince, unrivaled even by a duke and peer; a prince, duke, count, or marquis—collectively *les grands*—was certainly incapable of treating a mere *gentilhomme* as an equal.[37]

There were, nonetheless, connections cutting across these professional, social, and legal boundaries. These connections led to constant alignments and realignments among the various corporative groups of society. Neither the emphasis by Marxist historians on broad class conflicts nor non-Marxist scholars' stress on patron-client relations provides a satisfactory explanation of what was happening; but, together, they give us some clues.[38] General socioeconomic dif-

[37] The corporative nature of early modern France is lucidly illustrated in O. Ranum, *Paris in the Age of Absolutism*, New York, 1968, especially pp. 25-31.

[38] B. Porchnev, *Les Soulèvements populaires en France de 1623 à 1648*, Paris, 1963 (for the Marxist "horizontal" argument); R. Mousnier, "Recherches sur les soulèvements populaires en France avant la Fronde," *Revue d'Histoire Moderne et Contemporaine* v (1958), 81-113 (for the "vertical" patron-client thesis); and for critiques: R. Mandrou, *Classes et luttes de classes en France au début du XVIIe siècle*, Florence, 1965; W. F. Church, "Publications on Cardinal Richelieu Since 1945. A Bibliographical Study," *Journal of Modern History* xxxvii (1965), 421-444;

ferences divided society along horizontal lines, pitting a broad group against those which were either their social superiors or inferiors. Peasants could not help feeling some common hostility toward their noble lords, who treated them as inferior and exacted heavy rents. And the division between town, *faubourg*, and countryside was not sharp enough to preclude the uniting of poor wage earners and peasants against merchants, especially during market days or economic recessions when peasants swarmed to the local towns. The wealthier merchants could sometimes forget their interguild rivalries in the face of rioting and looting by poorer persons, who were driven by hunger and fear into attacks on property. *Les grands* could agree with the *hobereaux*, or lesser noblemen, that both were threatened with a watering down of their privileged position by the upward social thrust of lawyers, guildsmen, and officiers into noble status. It would seem, however, that vertical connections between a patron and a client of different status were stronger than "class conflict" at the end of Henri IV's reign and during the following decades. In the absence of an all-powerful central government that could maintain order, such private connections were frequent, *les grands* being the most adept at forging alignments with individuals in all socio-economic groups. Despite the growing decay of provincial assemblies, the three estates of clergy, nobles, and commoners retained that vehicle of common action in several provinces (notably in Brittany, Languedoc, Provence, Burgundy, and Dauphiné). And the multiple role of *les grands*—as commanders of royal armies, governors of provinces, relatives of bishops or abbots, or patrons of other nobles who were governors of provinces or fortresses—also broke down barriers throughout the realm and within every social group.

The complex compartmentalized nature of early seventeenth-century French society, and the latent distrust between broad social groups, made a massive, coordinated revolution against royal absolutism impossible. Such an occurrence was as unthinkable as a unified revolt by the officiers, even if antagonism toward the king's policies became acute as a result of a grave political crisis, fiscal oppression, or economic recession (all of which developed in the

E. H. Kossman, "Een Blik op het Franse absolutisme," *Tidj. voor Gesch.* LXXVIII (1966), 52-58; A. L. Moote, "The Parlementary Fronde," pp. 348-354; and the same author's review of Mandrou's book in *American Historical Review* LXXI (1966), 970.

succeeding decades leading up to the Fronde). The pathetic conclusion of the last early-modern meeting of the Estates General in 1615, amid bitter words between clergy and commoners and between commoners and nobles, underscores that fact.

But the threat of several simultaneous group protests was very real. Such upheavals could be drawn together by the leadership of a provincial governor, by temporary bonds within a town between rich and poor forged by intimidation from below or tax-weariness from above, or by a network of patron-client relationships. Therefore, if French rebels could not fully unite, they could at least cause such confusion throughout the realm that a decisive military repression of all the rebellious elements would be impossible. In France, the townspeople, peasants, and clergy were not as obsessed with the hatred of nobles as they were in central and eastern European countries. The possibility of the French monarchy turning the antinoble estates against nobles, as was to be done in mid-seventeenth-century Sweden and Denmark, was very remote. Nor was France as sharply divided into hostile geographic areas as Spain, whose mid-seventeenth-century rebellions by Portuguese and Catalan separatists failed to arouse sympathy within the central, Castilian region. One suspects, also, that the vertical connections in French society were stronger than those in either the Dutch republic or England. Certainly the involvement of the lesser social orders in England's Great Rebellion was minimal by comparison with the "popular" role in the Fronde. The apparent relative detachment of the urban and rural poor from the Dutch quarrel of 1647-1650 between the House of Orange and the "regent class" of landowners, great merchants, and officials, reinforces the impression of France's unique potential for widespread upheaval.[39]

What was the place of the officiers in this uncertain social picture? They were clearly ambivalent toward the fluctuations and strains within contemporary society. In 1610, the judicial and financial officials were neither truly nobles nor commoners, but rather most often bourgeois in background and noble in aspiration. In the Estates General, they sat with commoners as the Third Estate, yet the members of the sovereign courts and the bureaus of *trésoriers* had the privileges of noblemen by virtue of their offices (and in some cases by

[39] See A. L. Moote, *The Seventeenth Century: Europe in Ferment*, Lexington, 1970, pp. 174-185, 197-230.

noble birth or acquisition of noble lands). Contemporary writers on officeholding, such as Charles Loyseau, also asserted that after two generations in the same office in one of these high corporations, this "personal nobility" became hereditary or true nobility. By the 1640's, the monarchy was actually conferring hereditary nobility on first-generation members of the parlements of Grenoble and Paris, and on officials in some chambres des comptes and bureaus of *trésoriers*.[40]

Despite jurisdictional disputes between judicial corporations and municipal governments (*bureaux de ville*), and a tendency for officiers to treat merchants as social inferiors, there were connections between town and court which could forge ties of sympathy, if not outright unity, in a political crisis. Judges and merchants invested in semistate bonds (municipal *rentes*). Both had property in the same town quarters and in some cases rural estates as well. Individual officiers were chosen as frequently as merchants to high positions in the *bureau de ville*, although the highest municipal positions of *prévôt des marchands* and *échevins* were frequently conferred by the monarch on proroyalist, antiparlementary persons. And the guildsman, *prévôt des marchands*, and officiers all had a common interest in maintaining order, protecting property, and preventing new royal taxes on their towns. While jurisdictional rivalry continued to pit the *bureau de ville*, as a body, against the officials' corporations, even at the height of a royal-official conflict over taxation, the well-to-do merchants realized that this type of tax dispute could be turned to their own advantage. These so-called *bons bourgeois* not only relished royal repression of the socially superior officiers, but, at the same time, lobbied for royal concessions to their guilds under cover of the separate quarrels between officials and monarch.[41]

The social gulf between officiers and peasants or artisans was greater, and relationships were very uncertain. Judges and tax collectors obviously did not have the same fiscal grievances as these social inferiors because of their own tax-exempt status. They were clearly terrified at the prospect of a popular uprising, or *émeute*, fearing that it might threaten their lives and property. But the mem-

[40] Charmeil, *Les Trésoriers de France*, pp. 72-73.

[41] On urban society and politics, see J. L. Bourgeon, "L'Ile de la Cité pendant la Fronde. Structure sociale," *Paris et Ile de France, Mémoires* XIII (1962), 23-144; L. Lecestre, *La Bourgeoisie parisienne au temps de la Fronde*, Paris, 1913. Normand, *La Bourgeoisie française*, is now outdated.

bers of the sovereign courts and many lesser officials had personal relations with peasants in their capacity as rural landowners. They were almost as eager as their peasants to prevent an increase in the *taille*, since this would reduce the peasant's capacity to pay his rent. Within the town and in its *faubourgs* there was a comparable relationship between official as slumlord and worker as tenant. The *élus* and *trésoriers* had to weigh carefully the advantage of permitting urban or rural tax riots, against their duty to act as the king's financial agents. The parlementarian had to decide whether in vetoing fiscal legislation he might become a popular hero or a victim of an uncontrollable riot.[42]

Relations between officers and nobles are the best documented, but they, too, are difficult to evaluate. Officials in petty positions were not, and often could not become, nobles. But the higher officials were closing the gap between personal and hereditary nobility. In either case, many officers were the personal servants or agents of great nobles, managing their finances, giving legal advice, or even serving as advisers in political matters. Occasionally, hereditary nobles treated parlementarians as equals. The member of the Third Estate who claimed in 1615 that the nobles and clergy should accept the officers as "brothers" was treated with verbal abuse; but a prince, Henri de Condé, was pleased to treat judges as his honored guests at a ball the same year.[43] Nobles detested *vénalité* because it often placed judgeships beyond their means; yet they had no intention of letting that irritant prevent them from lobbying in the courts for favorable judicial and administrative decisions.[44]

The Parlement of Paris had a peculiar place in French society. Its members could not dominate that society, just as they could not claim to have any legally binding power over most of the other corporations of officers. Nevertheless, all social groups, whether they came under the Parlement's jurisdiction or resided outside its territory, followed its political activities with intense interest. Its quarrels with the royal administration could touch off independent revolts by *les grands*, peasants, merchants, towns, or entire provinces. Or, conversely, parlementary opposition to the king's policies could

[42] On the officers' relations with peasants and wage earners, see above fns. 26 and 41.

[43] Blet, *Le Clergé de France* I, 33-34.

[44] On noble-official relations, see, inter alia, P. Goubert, "Les Officiers royaux."

lead to bitter disputes between parlementarians and other men of property, who were terrified at the "bad example" the Parlement was setting for rebel-prone peasants and wage earners by its institutional attacks on higher authority.

The relationship between the Parlement of Paris and *les grands* was a particularly important one. As noted earlier, that parlement was the court of peers for the realm, judging suits involving *les grands*. And the princes and great lay and ecclesiastical peers had the right to attend its ceremonial sessions, even to take part in the political debates of its plenary sessions. *Les grands* knew that it was in their interest to influence this most prestigious body, and they thought they had the means to achieve this. Though they normally ignored the Parlement's plenary meetings, during a political crisis they were sure to attend those sessions, sitting on a special bench set aside for the dukes and peers.

The role of the Parlement of Paris in the affairs of the capital was equally important. It is true that it had to contend with the rival jurisdiction of the other sovereign courts, and could never count on the support of the municipal government housed in the Hôtel de Ville (since jurisdictional disputes were compounded by the *prévôt des marchands'* inclination to serve the king, who virtually appointed him). Nevertheless, no other institution in the capital had the Parlement's prestige and powers. Its judges censored the press, kept a watchful eye on ecclesiastical matters, defended public morals by regulating stage performances, supervised the work of the University of Paris, and were responsible (along with the other sovereign courts and the *bureau de ville*) for the maintenance of order, the upkeep of the city, and the administration of the Hôtel de Ville's rentes. In times of crisis, it had coordinated the city's efforts, taking a lead in levying taxes for defense against approaching foreign armies, and in providing supplies for the inhabitants. Even if the *prévôt des marchands* blocked cooperation by the *bureau de ville*, the Parlement could overpower that proroyalist corporation by its hold over laboring Parisians and some merchants who welcomed the judges' opposition to new royal taxes on the city. Through its judicial and police powers, the Parlement also directly affected the lives of all subjects within the vast central provinces of the realm. As holders of country estates scattered throughout much of the kingdom, as priors, abbots, and other leading ecclesiastical figures in many areas, its members could add their personal influence to the *arrêts* of their court. In short, the Parlement of Paris would be a major factor in any upheaval within French society as instigator, mediator, or defender of royal order.[45]

5

How COULD Louis XIII be sure of loyalty from the parlementarians in Paris and his other officers? The role they would play in the coming decades was less certain than it had been in previous centuries. While royal officials had established a tradition of serving the Crown, they had, at the same time, and somewhat paradoxically, turned their positions into virtual private property as the result of the paulette (with the rise of royal absolutism they had grown in numbers and in stature), and constituted an element within the French state which had no parallel elsewhere. To be sure, no monarch could be content with a governmental structure which gave the corporations of officials such freedom from royal control, or potential for obstructing the king's will on major issues. Yet the monarchy's means of overcoming these inherent weaknesses were limited. Henri IV's weapons had been, on the whole, precisely those which had been utilized time after time by his predecessors. His uniqueness, however, lay in his restraint from viewing every evasion of his will as a major challenge to his administration,[46] and in his ability to work with the officers during a difficult period of civil war and reconstruction. It was questionable whether his successors would show such restraint and ability.

The most enduring and satisfactory solution for a monarch was to let the royal councils go into direct competition with courts and bureaus.[47] Confusion of powers, which so often permitted the king's

[45] On the social connections of judges in the Parlement of Paris, see Mme Cubells, "Le Parlement de Paris," pp. 177-198; and J. L. Bourgeon, "L'Ile de la Cité."

[46] See Maugis, *Histoire du Parlement de Paris* II, 51-92, 216-228, 243-276; Shennan, *The Parlement of Paris*, 227-241.

[47] On the potential power of the councils and commissaires, see R. Mousnier, "Le Conseil du roi de la mort de Henri IV au gouvernement personnel de Louis XIV," *Etudes d'Histoire Moderne et Contemporaine* I (1947), 29-67; Mousnier, "Etat et commissaire. Recherches sur la création des intendants des provinces (1634-1648)," *Forschungen zu Staat und Verfassung. Festgabe für Fritz Hartung*, Berlin, 1958, pp. 325-344; E. Esmonin, "L'Origine des intendants jusqu'en 1665," *Etudes sur la France*, pp. 25-31; Pagès, "Essai sur l'évolution des institutions administratives," and Pagès, *La Monarchie d'ancien régime en France (de Henri IV à Louis XIV)*,

officials to expand their functions, at the councils' expense, could just as easily justify a more active conciliar role in justice, taxation, and police. Individual councilors of state, maîtres des requêtes, or *intendants des finances* could also be specially commissioned to investigate and report to the councils on the actions of local courts and bureaus. However, the officers looked suspiciously on the possibility of such activities, sensing that the king might be trying to transfer their regular functions to quasi-permanent commissaires acting in his name. The courts and bureaus could see no reason for obeying a royal commissioner or a conciliar *arrêt* unless the king had personally taken part in the decision; after all, they could argue that they, too, represented the Crown and had no superior except the monarch himself.

Moreover, the royal councils had a much less well-defined position within the French government than the tribunals and bureaus. Even the *conseil d'état*, as one historian pointed out over a century ago, "did not form a distinct body with a clearly defined rank in the administrative hierarchy."[48] Any parlementary lawyer could present cases before the royal councils without taking a special oath, other than the one he made before a parlement. Councilors of state required a special summons before they could actually take part in the work of a royal council, but honorary councilorships were often given to individuals, including some members of sovereign courts, and these judges were even invited by the king to enter the royal councils for important discussions. Some had the nerve to demand precedence over career councilors in seatings, discussing, and voting on such occasions. Between reporting maîtres des requêtes and voting councilors of state there was much rivalry and confusion of functions, and between councils there were quarrels over personnel and the division of duties. Nor was it entirely clear whether the loyalties of maîtres des requêtes lay with the royal councils or the Parlement of Paris, since they reported to both and held purchased offices and the paulette. To be sure, their work was most frequently within the

---

Paris, 1946. In Mousnier's article on the intendants, he returns to many points made by Esmonin at the beginning of the twentieth century, but overlooked by succeeding generations of scholars.

[48] P. A. Chéruel, *Histoire de l'administration monarchique en France depuis l'avènement de Philippe-Auguste jusqu'à la mort de Louis XIV*, 2 vols., Paris, 1855, I, 287.

royal councils or as special commissioners, and hence they tended to side with the king against other officers in courts and bureaus. But *vénalité* and the paulette could conceivably place them on the opposite side if either practice were suddenly challenged by a ruler.

The position of special, or "extraordinary," commissioners was particularly nebulous. Their job within the central administration could not be regular or clearly defined, given the temporary nature of their assignments to investigate and try to solve the problems in particular regions created by local rebelliousness or maladministration on the part of permanently entrenched officiers. Still, the historian of early seventeenth-century France cannot help being amazed at the degree of informality and imprecision of orders that existed. Vague or blanket authority to investigate, report to the councils, perhaps to take action against a local rebellion or irregularities in justice and taxation was warranted when commissioners were dealing with unusual incidents in the realm, but it was unworkable if the commissioners were to exercise day-to-day control over the judicial and financial officials.

The potential of extraordinary commissions became somewhat clearer in the late sixteenth century, as temporary, special commissioners were supplemented by a peculiar type of commissaire called the "intendant." Intendants were employed to look after the judicial and financial problems of the royal armies, to supervise tax assessment and collection by the tax bureaus, or to spy on the judicial work of local judges and tax agents. Their commissions were relatively clear, and were registered at the local *présidial* court or bureau of *trésoriers de France*. Yet it was never quite clear how these intendants were to act in relation to the existing judicial and financial officials—whether to cooperate with the latter, to bypass them, to make unilateral decisions, or to investigate and report to the councils for action. Their functions still resembled the emergency role of traditional commissioners, yet they were destined for a regular position within the French government. It was far from certain how they were to fit into the regular governmental structure.

No matter how hard a monarch tried to transfer his authority to councils and special commissions, or to clarify their position within the government, past laws continued to be on the side of the judicial and financial officials. Indeed, the sixteenth century introduced new legal sanctions against interference by councils and commissioners.

Three great royal ordinances—Orléans (1560), Moulins (1566), and Blois (1579)—were originally meant to clarify relationships between officiers and commissaires; but, strangely enough, the officials gained far more than the royal administration. The councils, and particularly the *conseil des parties*, could suspend the judicial decrees of a sovereign court in two instances only: on an appeal from one of the parties "in proposition of error of fact," and on "civil request" that the judges' decision should be considered prejudiced due to fraud and deceit by the other party. Even then, the intervening council could do no more than order a retrial by the court in question. Suits could be evoked from court to council while in process, but only when one of the parties formally complained of judicial partiality due to a conflict of interest or solicitations by the other party. If the charges proved true, the council had to send the suit to another court. Extraordinary commissions were equally restricted by the ordinances. By law they were limited to investigating and reporting to the councils on abuses by judges and tax officials. Where commissioners happened to be maîtres des requêtes, they had the right to attend sessions of courts and bureaus and even take part in decisions; but they could not make decisions on their own. The specialized executive tribunal of the maîtres, known as *requêtes de l'Hôtel*, could judge certain suits, but appellate jurisdiction belonged to the sovereign courts of the realm.[49] An adept chancellor or keeper of the seals might argue with judges over the interpretation of these procedural points, and councils and extraordinary commissioners could try to evade the law, but courts would be likely to order the cases back to their chambers, and the judicial process would degenerate into a flood of *arrêts* and counter-*arrêts*, leaving justice in chaos. In legislative matters, it was still more difficult to bypass the courts.[50] Occasionally, conciliar *arrêts*, which required only signing by king and a secretary of state and sealing by the chancellor, introduced new laws without the formality of judicial review. Normally, a monarch thought it best to have legislation registered

[49] See articles 91, 92, 97, 98, and 99 of the Ordinance of Blois, and article 70 of the Ordinance of Moulins, in F. A. Isambert et al., eds., *Recueil général des anciennes lois françaises depuis l'an 420 jusqu'à la révolution de 1789*, 29 vols., Paris, 1822-1833, XIV, 404-405, 208; and Mousnier, "Le Conseil du roi," pp. 49-50, 64-65.

[50] See Olivier-Martin, *Histoire du droit français*, especially pp. 349-350, for the involved legislative process and differences in terminology between *ordonnances*, *édits*, *déclarations*, *arrêts*.

in the appropriate tribunals, since this enhanced subjects' respect for the new laws. The only way to ensure registration, if a court rejected or amended such legislation, was to fall back on the king's personal authority. *Lettres de jussion*, declaring that the king demanded immediate and unqualified registration, were the first step in employing the king's personal will. If a court still delayed, the king had the right to enter the Parlement of Paris in person, symbolically taking the place of that court during this *lit de justice*. His brother or uncle represented him at similar ceremonies in the Chambre des Comptes or Cour des Aides of Paris. Paradoxically, the employment of the king's personal will was more often a tell-tale sign of royal weakness than a demonstration of royal absolutism. As Colbert noted late in the seventeenth century, the *lit de justice* was held most frequently by kings who were so ineffective as rulers that they had to make a major crisis out of conflicts within their government, staking their personal authority and prestige on every issue between themselves and their tribunals.[51] At the very least, repeated use of the *lit de justice* diminished respect by officials and other subjects for that ceremony and the royal person who presided over it. Moreover, the wily officers had the means and the ability to blunt or turn aside this weapon. In the presence of the king or a prince, the officers had no choice but to bow before royal commands and register the legislation in question, but they had the right to append the phrase "by the very command of the king," thereby removing much of the respect subjects were supposed to have for registered laws. When the king or prince departed, the officers could still argue their right to present remonstrances. Until those remonstrances were drafted, presented to the king, and answered by him, the legislation was set aside. *Lettres de jussion* were less effective than a *lit de justice*, because an offending court might table the letter, or commence an endless debate on how it should be obeyed.

In their efforts to halt this brazen institutional opposition, Henri IV and his predecessors had occasionally singled out the most obstinate members of a recalcitrant court or bureau for exemplary punishment. The king signed *lettres de cachet* consigning the political offenders to exile or imprisonment; armed agents promptly took these sealed letters to the guilty parties and, backed by this particu-

---

[51] Colbert, *Lettres* vi, 16. Colbert's incisive comments on the officers' relations with the royal administration are worth reading in their entirety.

lar expression of the king's will, carried out the royal orders. This weapon, too, failed to subdue the officers when brandished recklessly. Courts and bureaus had been known to go on strike in protest against arbitrary removal of their members. Tax collection or the judicial process came to a halt, and the king was forced to compromise, perhaps to yield completely before the demands of the officers.

A more subtle royal tactic was the intentional leaking of news that the king contemplated abolishing the sale of offices. Of course, after 1604, the renewal of the paulette every nine years gave the administration an additional opportunity for periodic bargaining. In 1610, it was still too early to tell whether the officers would reduce their opposition to the king in order to keep the privilege of bequeathing their offices, or increase pressures on the monarch in order to force him into retaining the paulette. At best, tampering with *vénalité* and the paulette was exceedingly risky, for it struck at the very roots of the officers' independence and position in society. Here was an issue that might lead to intensified opposition, not just from an isolated court and bureau, but the rank and file of royal officials, including the maîtres des requêtes who were so important as defenders of royal authority against their fellow officers.[52]

In 1610, the direction relations would take between king and officers was uncertain. It was not clear whether the latter would drift from independence and occasional opposition into deep-seated hostility toward royal policies; nor was it certain how Louis XIII would deal with his officials. A major revolt by officers against the royal administration was still inconceivable to the king, his officials, and his other subjects. What made that revolt finally possible were the drastic governmental policies forced on a hesitant monarch and his consummate politician-minister by internal strife and foreign war. Without knowing or willing it, Louis XIII and Cardinal Richelieu prepared the Fronde by undertaking an administrative revolution which profoundly changed the way in which the government of France functioned.

[52] The brilliantly expounded thesis that the monarchy used *vénalité* and the paulette to subdue the officers (Mousnier, *Vénalité des offices*) has been accepted too readily by historians. While no serious scholar could now revert to the simplistic thesis that the paulette placed the officials outside royal control, the rest of this book should demonstrate that royal-official clashes over the mode of office-holding contributed greatly to the crisis of the Fronde.

CHAPTER TWO

THE REIGN OF LOUIS XIII:
GOVERNMENTAL "REVOLUTION"
AND THE *OFFICIERS*

THE POLITICAL climate of Louis XIII's long reign was charged with tension, frequent rebellion, and deepening crisis.[1] To be sure, no threat to the monarchy's existence confronted the successive administrations of the reign: the regency of Marie de Médicis and her favorite, Concino Concini (1610-1617), the uncertain rule of the young Louis (1617-1624), or the royal-ministerial partnership of Cardinal Richelieu and the mature Louis XIII (1624-1643). And no single issue divided Frenchmen into irreconcilable factions like those of the religious wars of the late sixteenth century. Many rebellions were little more than poorly planned and badly executed attempts by *les grands* to win back the prestige and independence of their medieval forebears. Prince Henri de Condé's opportunistic move to force concessions on Marie through the Estates General of 1614-1615 ended in the collapse of the Estates. Palace conspiracies against Richelieu during the 1620's and 1630's stopped short of opposing the king's person. Huguenots could no longer rally the large forces they had maintained during the religious wars, and many Huguenot nobles were actually willing to see the monarchy crush rebellions by their more militant coreligionaries. Catholic prelates were determined to hold the line against secular encroachments on the First Estate's remaining ecclesiastic privileges and fiscal immunity, but they had no reason to rebel against a Catholic ruler, and their opposition was confined to peaceful negotiations with royal agents at the clerical estate's periodic national assemblies. Yet the conditions that produced the Fronde five years after Louis XIII's death were without doubt developing during his reign, and gradually those conditions threatened to turn isolated revolts into a major rebellion.

Some of the reasons for the growing crisis are easy to detect, others

[1] See especially V.-L. Tapié, *La France de Louis XIII et de Richelieu*, Paris, 1952, which can be supplemented with the more specialized Porchnev, *Soulèvements populaires*.

36

have never been fully understood. In part, the problems which faced other European states in the seventeenth century plagued the French monarch and his subjects. Short-run economic cycles and frequent crop failures caused prices to fluctuate wildly and undermined the relative prosperity of the sixteenth century. In their desperate struggle for existence, poverty-stricken *petits gens* in town and country-side lashed out at any scapegoat, including the royal tax collector or tax farmer whose exactions seemed less justifiable than the traditional payments to their noble landlord, *bureau de ville*, or local clergy.[2] The monarchy was equally hard-pressed to meet its normal expenses. Successive *surintendants des finances* were understandably angered by the tax rebellions which depleted the already inadequate treasury, and they responded with attempts to increase taxes. Thus the royal treasury and taxpayers competed for their share of the uncertain national wealth.

Another major cause of friction was the royal administration's determination to overcome twin challenges: noble-Huguenot rebelliousness from within, and territorial encirclement by the encroaching Austrian and Spanish Hapsburg states after Hapsburg victories in the early years of the Thirty Years' War (1618-1648). Whether internal rebellion and external aggression were as serious threats as Louis XIII and his ministers believed, the king was drawn into a militaristic policy which escalated beyond his intentions. French attempts to neutralize the Rhineland in 1620 were followed by subsidization of the anti-Hapsburg armies of Sweden and the Dutch republic, and finally resulted in open war with Spain and Austria after 1635. Marie's efforts to buy internal peace through monetary bribes in the early 1610's gave way to clashes with noble rebels during the rest of the reign, and royal attacks on Huguenot strongholds which did not end until the royalist victories of the 1630's. Military repression of noble revolts and arbitrary executions of their ringleaders incited new rebellions. The costs of war had to be met by increases in levies on non-nobles, and by the imposition of indirect taxes such as *aides* and *gabelles* on provinces or social groups previously exempt. A staggering increase in loans from *partisans*, or tax farmers, placed new burdens on taxpayers because of the high interest rates and the tax farmers' extortionate methods of collecting taxes

[2] See J. Meuvret, "Comment les Français du XVIIe siècle voyaient l'impôt," *XVIIe Siècle*, nos. 25-26 (1955), 59-82.

assigned to them.[3] In addition, troops stationed inside France exacted contributions from all social groups in the form of quartering, supplies, and money.[4]

France was affected by inexorable demands of war and peace-making similar to those that turned Charles I's difficulties with Scotland and Ireland into an English civil war, that expanded the Bourbon-Hapsburg conflict into a combined civil and foreign war for Spain, and that caused severe political crises in the Dutch, Swedish, and Danish states. Unlike Philip IV and Olivares in Spain, Louis XIII's military-fiscal policies antagonized the entire geographic spectrum. And, in apparent contrast to England's Charles I, the French king's financial program alienated all social groups. Because of France's complex social structure, these policies threatened to ignite an internal conflagration dwarfing the upheavals that were erupting in other countries.[5] Even without the intrusion of disputes between the monarchy and its officers, Louis XIII's reign would have been a critical period for France. Urban *émeutes*, peasant attacks on royal fiscal agents, tax revolts by assemblies of provincial Estates, the conspiracies of *les grands*, and even demonstrations by propertied holders of rentes became more numerous, frequent, and violent. There was an ever-increasing possibility that as uprisings coincided, they might converge in a general melee. No single element of opposition to royal policies could emasculate royal authority on its own, but the cumulative effect threatened chaos, even as the monarchy was gradually winning the war against Hapsburg Austria and Spain, and solving the Huguenot problem by combining military-political repression with religious toleration.

One has only to glance at the major clusters of revolts during the reign to see how close Louis XIII came to inciting a general rebellion. The best example is the group of rebellions that erupted between 1628 and 1632.[6] The focal point of that particular crisis was the abortive palace revolt against Richelieu, culminating in the "Day of Dupes." Eased out of influence in the *conseil d'état* by Louis XIII and his chief minister, the queen mother's Devout party of rival min-

---

[3] See Lublinskaya, *French Absolutism*, pp. 229-271.

[4] There is a good analysis of these unrecorded "taxes" in Porchnev, *Soulèvements populaires*.

[5] On the social structure in France, see chap. 1.

[6] See especially Tapié, *La France de Louis XIII*, pp. 263-295.

isters, clerics, and great nobles tried unsuccessfully to secure Riche-lieu's dismissal.[7] Their inability to force the king to dismiss the hated first minister on the Day of Dupes precipitated a military clash. After a hasty flight from France by Marie and the king's brother, Gaston, Duke of Orléans, the duke boldly reentered the kingdom with a small army. Meanwhile, royal attempts to impose fiscal inno-vations in the southern provinces had aroused peaceful opposition from provincial Estates in Burgundy, Provence, and Languedoc. This resistance touched off further violent protests by peasants and indigent town dwellers. Wealthier inhabitants of some towns turned against the urban rioters out of fear for their property, but in some instances they supported the uprisings. Civic governments wavered between countering rebellion, letting it get out of hand, or covertly supporting it. Parish priests and the most poverty-stricken nobles occasionally led peasant bands bent on looting and plundering. Then the princely and local revolts converged. Gaston trooped across the rebellious provinces. Local military governors, who were great nobles in their own right and in sympathy with the princely rebels, flirted with, or actually raised troops in support of, the provincial tax revolts. The Duke of Montmorency openly joined the rebellion as governor of Languedoc, while the Duke of Bellegarde and Duke of Guise proved to be unreliable upholders of royal authority in Bur-gundy and Provence.

Historians have unanimously viewed the Day of Dupes and its aftermath as the crucial turning point in Richelieu's rise to power, and as the symbol of the emerging modern state's triumph over the old nobility. But it was also a prelude to the Fronde, signaling a warning to the monarchy of the dangers implicit in policies which antagonized both *les grands* and entire provinces. True, swift mili-tary intervention by Louis XIII, Richelieu, and a loyal prince, Henri de Condé (father of the *Grand* Condé of the Fronde), swept aside the threat from the military governors and popular rebellions, and tactful compromises over the issue of provincial taxation helped pacify, but Louis XIII barely won out in the crisis. Granted, he was able to isolate and repress a major rebellion in Normandy in 1639 and a revolt by Parisian *rentiers* (holders of rentes) the previous

---

[7] The *dévots* combined a religious interest in peace between the Catholic states of France and Spain with hatred toward Richelieu as their political rival and the pro-ponent of war against Spain.

year, just as the regent and he had contained revolts by *les grands* in the 1610's and early 1620's, but a few false steps, such as unwillingness to compromise or military indecision, could well have brought a major upheaval to France by 1640, as it did in Spain and England.

The political role of the judicial and financial officials in the midst of these crises did not disturb Louis XIII as much as the constant threat posed by noble rebelliousness and popular revolt between 1610 and 1643. Still, the officers demonstrated during the course of the reign that they could be a significant factor in the conflicts between king and subjects. Indeed, they could spell the difference between containment of rebellion and its expansion into a general uprising. Richelieu was particularly aware of the importance of the kingdom's sovereign tribunals, "those great and sovereign companies being the primary cause of the people's contentment or dissatisfaction."[8] Hence there was irony in Louis XIII's treatment of his officers; by alienating them, he unwittingly fostered a political climate which encouraged their approval of rebellions.

Louis XIII's relations with his judicial and financial officials were highly complex. Neither he, nor Richelieu, nor any other influential minister of his reign intended to undertake comprehensive, sweeping measures against the courts and bureaus.[9] Time and again, royal *règlements* (regulatory memoranda) tried to prevent the king's councils from taking an inordinate number of suits out of the hands of sovereign court judges.[10] Several persons who had some influence with Louis XIII and Richelieu tried to avoid clashes with the courts over financial legislation. Henri de Condé, who had tried to lure the Parlement of Paris into his rebellious princely camp in the first decade of the reign, and therefore knew how much peace depended on its members, strongly urged the king not to use his personal authority to override free judicial review.[11] The Marquis d'Effiat, *surintendant des finances* in the mid-1620's, was so conscious of the poten-

[8] Cardinal de Richelieu, *Lettres, instructions diplomatiques, et papiers d'état*, ed. M. Avenel, 8 vols., Paris, 1853-1877, II, 197.

[9] Richelieu's rival and *garde des sceaux* in the late 1620's, Michel de Marillac, came closest to advocating fundamental changes. But his famous, unenforced *Code Michau* must be compared with his insistence that reform of the officers be undertaken within the framework of existing customs and procedures. See his unpublished notes, B. N. Ms. Fr. 7549, especially fol. 148v.

[10] See R. Mousnier, ed., "Les Règlements du conseil du roi sous Louis XIII," *Annuaire-Bulletin de la Société de l'Histoire de France* (1948), pp. 92-206.

[11] Richelieu, *Mémoires* VII, 33.

tial for resistance within the Parlement of Paris that he repeatedly avoided a confrontation. He met the soaring costs of Louis XIII's major internal and external commitments by trying to curb other expenses, instead of resorting constantly to new taxes which would be sure to draw criticism when presented for parlementary registration. D'Effiat was actually willing to jeopardize the state's credit with its *partisans*, or *traitants*, rather than antagonize the Parlement of Paris—hence his temporary reduction of royal interest rates from the normal level of 18 or 20 per cent to a niggardly 10 per cent.[12]

Cardinal Richelieu was particularly aware of the need to compromise with the realm's leading tribunal. While insisting that crimes of high treason, or *lèse-majesté*, be judged by special commissions, and despite his stern opposition to parlementary sabotaging of Louis XIII's campaign against noble duels, Richelieu nevertheless kept royal-parlementary relations from reaching the breaking point. Often, when the tempers of king and judges got out of control, Richelieu worked behind the scenes to placate the Parlement of Paris. The chief minister's firsthand knowledge of recent French history gave him added incentive for his tactic of flattering the parlementarians, and his realistic policy of protecting them against a diminution of prestige or authority. He knew the story of the aftermath of Henri IV's assassination by a religious fanatic, an act which had unleashed an hysterical parlementary counterattack against all pro-papal pamphlets and clerical pronouncements, as the Parlement sought to save Louis XIII from his father's fate. During the rest of the reign, Richelieu watched that tribunal and others assiduously uphold the judicial authority of the Crown against clerical immunities and the rights of the Pope. Writing in his *Mémoires* about parlementary-ecclesiastical relations in 1626, Richelieu stated his conclusions forcefully and clearly. The Catholic clergy's authority must be maintained, but the king must be careful not to violate the authority of the Parlement of Paris, "which, on many occasions is necessary for the maintenance of the state."[13]

Louis XIII was far more hostile to the Parlement of Paris and the other judicial and financial corporations than Richelieu, but he tried to keep the problem in its proper perspective. Only when he became

[12] *Mercure François*, 25 vols., Paris, 1605-1644, XIV, pt. ii, 589-590. See also Lublinskaya, *French Absolutism*, pp. 305-306.

[13] Richelieu, *Mémoires* v, 336.

exasperated did he exclaim to the parlementarians in a *lit de justice*:
"You are here solely to judge between Master Peter and Master John,
and I intend to put you in your place; and if you continue your
undertakings, I will cut your nails to the quick."[14] This outburst,
which was an emotional amalgam of distrust, fear, and pride, shows
only one side of the strange and fascinating king who presided over
the prelude to the Fronde. The other side of his character, manifested
on many occasions, reveals a monarch who considered himself the
father of his people, and was, appropriately, called Louis *le Juste*.
Louis XIII wanted his judges to obey his paternal authority, but he
wished to act within the framework of the laws of France. He firmly
believed that whenever he overruled his officiers he was not overriding, but applying, existing laws. He was furious with the parlementarians in Paris when they accused him of disregarding legalities.[15]
His legal advisers, especially his chancellors and keepers of the seals,
time and again argued with the law courts over the interpretation of
laws, rather than simply falling back on the principles of *raison
d'état* (state needs) and the king's personal will as a justification for
actions against the officiers.[16] It should also be remembered that Louis
XIII was the son of Henri IV, who had made compromises with the
sovereign courts, and of Marie de Médicis, who had relied on the
Parlement of Paris to establish her authority as regent in 1610 when
Henri IV had been assassinated without providing for an orderly
succession. Henri IV had informed Marie of his own, frequent quarrels with the parlements, and, according to Richelieu's reconstruction of the conversation, the king had admitted "that he had not
been more successful than his predecessors in handling them, and
that neither she nor her son could expect to do any better."[17] While
regent, Marie de Médicis had been advised to keep the Parlement
of Paris satisfied; and she had actually entrusted its members with

---

[14] Molé, *Mémoires* II, 143-144.   [15] Talon, *Mémoires*, p. 65.

[16] For example, the ministers argued with representatives of the Parlement of
Paris over the king's right to override article 428 of the Ordinance of Moulins (limiting royal punishment of judges to a five-year suspension of their functions, pending
the appearance of the defendants for a trial). The ministers argued that article 183
of the Ordinance of Blois (which called for harsher penalties in the case of crimes
against the state) took precedence and permitted the king to remove from office
anyone charged with *lèse-majesté*. Ibid., pp. 20-21.

[17] Richelieu, *Mémoires* I, 30.

the task of keeping Paris quiet and loyal while she and the young Louis XIII had ventured into distant provinces to put down princely revolts in 1615-1616.[18] Louis XIII was thus schooled in the knowledge that he must watch his officers carefully, and that he should pay particular attention to the Parlement of Paris. So by background, temperament, and the influence of those around him, Louis XIII had as many reasons to temporize with his officers as to run roughshod over their privileges and powers.

What, then, explains the attacks which that monarch unleashed against his judicial and financial officials—an assault historians have come to describe as a "revolution in government"?[19] As an explanation, we must fall back largely on the same broad factors which embittered relations between Louis XIII and his other subjects. If the king did not consciously unleash such a revolution, he was unwittingly drawn toward it by the conditions of early seventeenth-century France and Europe. Costly wars, uncertain economic conditions, and shaky royal finances necessitated a sharp increase in taxation and other fiscal legislation. This inevitably brought about clashes with the courts over verification. Moreover, the imperious demands of foreign war could not permit dilatory and corrupt tax collection by financial bureaus. A monarch who was equally determined to subdue *les grands*, put down tax revolts, and maintain internal order while royal armies were battling with France's external enemies, could not allow courts and bureaus to let rebelliousness get out of hand. Under the circumstances, neither lax enforcement of royal laws and policies nor judicial decisions and regulatory *arrêts* running counter to the will of the monarch could be tolerated. Hence, in spite of his desire to reign as Louis *le Juste*, and in contradiction to the desire of his advisers to placate his officers, Louis XIII constantly clashed with law courts and taxing bureaus. No grand design was involved, but by striking out against the officers with short-run expedients and specific actions, he set in motion long-range tendencies which can collectively be called a governmental "revolution."

[18] Duc de Rohan, *Mémoires*, Michaud and Poujoulat collection (ser. ii, vol. v), Paris, 1837, pp. 517-518.

[19] The thesis of a governmental "revolution" was first developed by the late Georges Pagès in his "Essai sur l'évolution des institutions administratives." The theme reappears in Mousnier's article, "Le Conseil du roi."

2

As THE REIGN progressed, the royal revolution began to take shape as a many-sided attack on the prestige, functions, and wealth of the judicial and financial officers. Royal councils, special judicial commissions, and quasi-permanent intendancies assumed many of the judicial, financial, and police functions of the officers. A flood of fiscal measures was rushed through the courts arbitrarily, and some legislation was enforced simply by issuing conciliar *arrêts*. The position of councils and commissaires within the governmental structure of the state was clarified, while the personal freedom, wealth, and even offices of the officers were repeatedly placed in jeopardy by royal policies.

The increased use of the royal administration's inherent powers during Louis XIII's reign was spectacular. A leading member of the Parlement of Paris, who was as sympathetic to the king's problems as any of his colleagues, lamented on one occasion that "there are more affairs in petty justice decided by commissions than by ordinary judges." The strongly royalist presidents of the same tribunal were even more bitter and sarcastic in their complaints. Near the end of the reign they cried out that Louis XIII was so arbitrary and powerful that he could have any subject tried, by any person he designated as judge, if he felt offended in any way. Both statements were exaggerations, but they did underline what was happening.[20]

To Louis XIII's subjects, the most visible aspect of this royal offensive was the monarchy's excessive use of special commissions to try crimes of *lèse-majesté*. Despite the regent's initial conciliatory gesture of announcing the suppression of fourteen judicial commissions established by Henry IV,[21] by 1618 the king's chief adviser and favorite, the Duke of Luynes, was tampering with the regular course of justice for his own advancement. After engineering a *coup d'état* which brought exile to the regent and death by assassination to her minister-favorite, Luynes vindictively pursued the remaining leaders of Marie's administration. Avoiding the Parlement of Paris, he put his enemies on trial before the more pliable judges of the Grand Conseil, virtually dictating sentences which ensured political obliv-

[20] Molé, *Mémoires* II, 102-103; Talon, *Mémoires*, p. 65.
[21] Richelieu, *Mémoires* I, 108-109.

ion for Marie's followers.[22] After 1624, the new royal favorite, Cardinal Richelieu, put the law to work for his own advancement, but also used irregular judicial procedures in the service of his king.[23] Hand-picked royal commissions dealt with alleged treason, meting out the death penalty to an agent of the king's own brother, Gaston d'Orléans (Puylaurens), a marshal of France (Louis de Marillac), a member of a great French family (Henri de Montmorency), and finally a king's favorite-turned-conspirator (Cinq-Mars). Similar commissions were established to judge other crimes that endangered royal policies. The *chambre de l'arsenal* tried counterfeiters, and gained an odious reputation for cloak-and-dagger operations by prescribing executions in the dark of night.[24] During the Norman uprisings in 1639-1640, executive justice was reduced to the informality of oral decisions by the chancellor. But Richelieu and Louis XIII were not above making use of the regular courts, employing the Grand Conseil because of its tendency to oppose the parlements, and provincial parlements when they seemed more likely to pronounce desired sentences than the Parlement of Paris. There was even an attempt, although quickly withdrawn, to give all members of the Grand Conseil the functions and titles of maîtres des requêtes; the objective was to expand the number of judges who could be used as instruments of executive justice.[25]

These special commissions were a serious threat to the regular officers. They did not assume charge of most suits normally tried in the criminal or financial courts, and their members were sometimes drawn from the ranks of those tribunals. Nevertheless, the regular courts were deprived of major lawsuits, and their members lost legal fees. When judges sat in commissions, they acted as commissaires, not as officers controlled by the rules and authority of their own

[22] Phélypeaux de Pontchartrain, *Mémoires*, Michaud and Poujoulat collection (ser. II, vol. v), Paris, 1837, pp. 400; Richelieu, *Mémoires* II, 217-222, 287-303.

[23] Richelieu's interference with lawsuits involving his personal interests and wealth is documented in a University of Paris dissertation by Catherine E. Holmes, *L'Eloquence judiciaire de 1620 à 1660: Reflet des problèmes sociaux, religieux et politiques.*

[24] See d'Avenel, *Richelieu* IV, 22-28; Talon, *Mémoires*, p. 7; Molé, *Mémoires* II, 70-76. The *chambre de l'arsenal* was staffed by two councilors of state, six maîtres des requêtes, six councilors from the Grand Conseil, and an acting *procureur général* who was a maître des requêtes.

[25] See Molé, *Mémoires*, especially II, 38-39; and N.C.F. de Peiresc, *Lettres aux frères Dupuy*, ed. P. T. de Larroque, 7 vols., Paris, 1888-1898, I, 815, 820, 826-827.

tribunals. And in most commissions, the majority of commissaires were maîtres des requêtes, or persons without any office. Thus the commissions were an extension of the royal councils, not appendages to the regular courts. There were good reasons for Louis XIII's extreme use of commissions, since he was more determined than his predecessors to bring criminals to justice, and he could not depend on the regular courts to judge in his favor. But the officiers, especially in the Parlement of Paris which had traditional claims to jurisdiction over major crimes, saw only that they were losing prestige, power, and income.

At the same time, the officiers were threatened by the emergence of a far more formidable instrument of royal authority: the intendancies. While the special commissions for major state crimes were limited to a single incident, intendancies were a much broader type of commission, with the potential to replace judges and tax collectors on a permanent basis. Richelieu did not create the intendants, but it was during his ministry in the 1630's that they came of age. Throughout the earlier years of Louis XIII's reign, individual intendants were employed, as in the past, for rather specific and temporary purposes: to negotiate with Huguenot dissidents, to enforce collection of a new tax in a troublesome corner of the realm, to stamp out a local rebellion, and occasionally to oversee the lower echelons of officials in the *trésoriers'* fiscal districts (*généralités*) or the *baillis'* judicial ressorts (*bailliages*) for several months or years. Sometime between 1634 and 1637, the use of intendants sharply increased. Intendants were sent to most of the kingdom's *généralités*, given commissions which placed them over all local officials, and left in the locality for extended periods. When their commissions were revoked, they were quickly replaced by other commissaires. It is certain that neither Louis XIII, nor Richelieu, nor other members of the *conseil d'état* expected the intendants to become permanent replacements for officiers, but that was what happened. Desperate for money to wage war against the Hapsburgs, the Bourbon ruler took drastic, emergency measures: the intendants were given authority to see that taxes were collected, tax revolts put down, and subjects' appeals against impositions decided efficiently and quickly. If local officiers were willing to cooperate, the intendants would act in conjunction with them and through their tribunals and bureaus. If not, intendants acted independently, assessing, collecting, judging without going through regular judicial and taxing channels. Often they cooperated with tax farmers, and used troops to enforce their decisions.

In 1643, it was still uncertain whether the intendants would outlast the emergency which had led to their transformation into serious rivals of the officers. But as the Bourbon-Hapsburg war continued year after year, without hope of an immediate conclusion, the intendants looked more and more like a permanent fixture in the institutional life of France. They assumed the most important functions of the *trésoriers, élus,* and other local officials formerly in charge of tax assessment, collection, and litigation. Although the counterparts of these officials in civil and criminal affairs were less affected, their control over litigation within their *présidial, bailliage,* and *sénéchaussée* districts was reduced. The parlements and cours des aides also suffered indirectly, since their appellate jurisdiction was affected. Whereas appeals from decisions by lesser tribunals and bureaus had normally been made to these sovereign courts, the intendants acted as sovereign commissioners, and their decisions could be reviewed only by the royal councils. There was virtually no officer who was unaffected by the emergence of the intendants: most lost prestige, legal fees, functions—and opportunities for corrupt practices.[26]

While the intendants were tightening the king's control over regional corporations, the central elements of his administration were also being strengthened by internal reorganization. The process was far from complete in 1643, but Louis XIII, Richelieu, and other ministers made the royal councils far more efficient instruments of the Crown than had been the case in 1610. Richelieu was most effective in making the traditional inner council of the king's most trusted advisers the center of royal activity. His ability to mold a team of trustworthy servants who could work with both the chief minister and the king was one of his greatest achievements. Without altering the functions of ministers, he gave far greater duties to the individuals whom he and the king could trust. After 1635, his team consisted of Chancellor Pierre Séguier, *Surintendants* Claude le Bouthillier and Claude Bullion, and two of the secretaries of state, Sublet

---

[26] Esmonin, *Etudes,* pp. 25-26, 28-31. For the more specialized commissions of the early years of the reign, see the examples in *Mercure François,* IV, pt. ii, 351; pt. iii, 20-23.

des Noyers for war, and Léon le Bouthillier, Count of Chavigny, for foreign affairs.[27] Both before and during the period of Richelieu's ministry, some important formal changes were also made by nameless bureaucrats and important ministers. The most important formal council, or *conseil d'état* (which legalized the acts of the informal council and was often indistinguishable from it), was placed more firmly over the specialized financial and judicial councils. The term "administration" can most appropriately be applied to the select group composed of king, chief minister, inner council, and formal *conseil d'état*, rather than to the entire body of councils and commissaires, in describing the governmental structure that emerged from this reorganization. For the most vital decisions were made and authorized by that inner circle, by the end of Louis XIII's reign. To be sure, after 1630, whenever one of the formal councils issued an *arrêt* that caused conflicts with the sovereign courts, the *conseil des parties*, or judicial council, was given the function of mediating the dispute. But this merely strengthened the control of the working administration and the formal *conseil d'état* over the officiers. The administration, in the broadest sense of the word, was also set above the corporations of officiers by a ruling in 1643 that all lawyers serving the Parlement of Paris had to take a separate oath when acting inside a royal council. Finally, the traditional rivalries within the councils between councilors of state and maîtres des requêtes were reduced by written *règlements* clarifying their respective duties.[28]

The extensive use of commissaires to judge state crimes, the emergence of intendants, and the streamlining of the councils gave the king some control over his officiers in judicial, police, and financial affairs. But Louis XIII had greater difficulty in purely legislative matters. In some instances, notably the creation of salable offices and new fees in the chancellery, he was able to avoid judicial review by simply issuing conciliar *arrêts*. And, when he raised the *taille* (a royal prerogative), the sovereign courts followed tradition and registered the increases. At times, he was able to avoid clashes with the parlements by sending controversial tax measures to the cours des aides and chambres des comptes, contending that the legislation was within the jurisdiction of the more amenable financial courts. Yet

27 O. A. Ranum, *Richelieu and the Councillors of Louis XIII*, Oxford, 1963.
28 Mousnier, "Le Conseil du roi," especially pp. 37-40, 49, 57-58, 61.

he could not be sure that a cour des aides or chambre des comptes would register without difficulty any piece of financial legislation, and he was far less certain of the parlements, which still had to review most fiscal measures. Hence, he invoked his personal authority more frequently than his predecessors to stifle free discussion and verification in all sovereign courts. He came frequently to the Parlement of Paris to hold *lits de justice*, and occasionally traveled to a hostile provincial parlement for the same ceremony. The Chambre des Comptes and Cour des Aides of the capital received similar visits by royal princes. *Lettres de jussion* were even more common during his reign.[29] Sovereign court judges grumbled, and even the conservative (proroyalist) *avocat général* of the Parlement of Paris was shocked at Louis XIII's frequent personal intervention to cut off free discussion. That judge concurred with his colleagues' opinion that a king's personal appearance during a *lit de justice* should be used as an opportunity to hear his officiers' objections, rather than as a weapon to enforce royal commands.[30] From the parlementarians' viewpoint, Louis XIII was breaking with tradition and, in the process, making a mockery of their interpretation of the parlement as the center of the Crown.

Near the end of the reign, in 1641, Louis XIII took a bolder step to contain opposition to legislation. At a *lit de justice* held in the Parlement of Paris, he issued a declaration setting forth restrictions on parlementary review of all types of legislation. No parlementary objections were to be permitted where state affairs were involved. In the case of other laws registered at a *lit de justice*, objections were to be limited to one remonstrance, though financial legislation was allowed two successive remonstrances.

By making state affairs the legislative prerogative of the Crown, by prohibiting any legally binding modification or rejection of other new laws, and, in general, by permitting only remonstrances, the king hoped to reduce parlementary verification to a relatively innocuous procedure.[31]

---

[29] There are many references in the *Mémoires* of Talon and Molé. See also d'Avenel, *Richelieu* II, appen. VIII, "Refus d'enregistrement d'un édit par la cour des aides," pp. 435-437.

[30] Talon, *Mémoires*, pp. 57-59.

[31] Isambert, *Anciennes lois françaises* XVI, 534.

The greatest assault on Louis XIII's officers came in the shape of attacks on their personal freedom and offices. The most recalcitrant members of a court or bureau were singled out for punishment by temporary imprisonment or exile to family estates. Occasionally, an entire corporation had its functions suspended; at other times, one of its chambers was singled out for punishment as a warning to the others. Parlements, cours des aides, bureaus of *trésoriers*, and *présidial* courts all experienced such humiliations. Usually, Louis XIII permitted the punished officials to return to work after a few weeks, but during the last decade of his reign, he resorted to harsher tactics. Unrepentant officials were banished permanently from their corporations, and an attempt was made to deprive them formally of their offices. Only when the approach of death brought pangs of remorse to the king did he restore those exiled officers to their functions.[32]

These attacks on individual officials and entire corporations were combined with threats to abolish the sale of offices and the paulette. The reign began with a wave of noble protests against *vénalité*. The possibility that the monarch might give in to these pressures terrified the officiers, individually and collectively. And even after it became apparent that the practice of selling offices would continue, the king retained considerable influence over his officials because the paulette was subject to renewal every nine years. Whenever that privilege of bequeathing offices was about to expire, his administration hinted that it might not be renewed. If the officials wished to retain the paulette, they would have to agree to pay more for it than they had in the past. King and officiers also understood that the latter's acceptance of tax legislation and executive justice, and their cooperation in collecting taxes, would greatly improve the prospect of retaining the paulette. To be sure, this privilege was suspended only once during the reign; and that interruption, from 1618 to 1621, was obviously a temporizing gesture by Louis XIII to appease *les grands*, who had so forcefully opposed the broader system of purchasable officeholding, or *vénalité*, during the previous four years. Yet the officiers were never sure that the offices in their possession would be preserved as family property.[33]

Vénalité and the paulette were preserved, although with difficulty;

---

[32] The controversies over the officiers' immunity from punishment can be followed in the *Mémoires* of Molé and Talon.

[33] Mousnier, *La Vénalité des offices*, especially pp. 286, 561-562, 623.

their fringe benefits were not.[34] In addition to the loss of functions, fees, and occasionally personal freedom, judicial and financial officials suffered from the extortionate financial policies of Louis XIII's successive administrations. While officiers were exempt from most taxes, Louis XIII's financial advisers found means to tap the financial resources that had placed them among the wealthiest groups in French society. One of the most common types of financial legislation during Louis XIII's reign was the creation of new offices. These brought a windfall to the royal treasury: in effect, the king was taxing his officials. Revenue from sales of offices, paulette fees, and closely related sources became the largest single source of income for the *épargne*, or treasury. By permitting the creation of additional offices, existing officials subsidized the incoming colleagues' payments to the treasury, since they now had to share their corporation's functions and fees with these intruders. The administration was willing to abolish new offices, but only in return for what was euphemistically called a gift, equal to the lost income from the sales. Salaries, or *gages*, were also arbitrarily raised, but since *gages* were really an interest-charge on the capital sum originally paid for offices, that capital was increased proportionally at the same time. Hence the incumbents were actually providing the king with a forced loan. In the last years of the reign, the royal treasury also began the practice of withholding a portion of the salary or interest. If one adds the many other ways by which Louis XIII dipped into his officiers' pocketbooks, by requisitioning supplies, quartering troops, and subjecting officials to taxes, all without even the formality of conciliar *arrêts* or royal orders, it becomes evident that all officiers were suffering severe financial losses by the end of the reign. Members of the lesser courts and bureaus faced financial disaster. The *élus* claimed that they had contributed 140 million *livres* to the treasury between 1620 and 1640.[35]

Louis XIII's constant efforts to divide and rule were a natural

---

[34] M. Göhring, *Die Amterkauflichkeit im ancien Regime*, Berlin, 1938, pp. 108-157, is a convenient source for the following two paragraphs. However, the basic work is Mousnier, *La Vénalité des offices*. See also Charmeil, *Les Trésoriers de France*, pp. 11-15, 84-87, 418-422; and the list of royal laws for Louis XIII's reign, A.L.P. Isnard and S. Honoré, eds., *Catalogue générale des livres imprimés de la Bibliothèque Nationale: Actes Royaux*, Paris, 1938, II, 2-647.

[35] See especially Bibliothèque Mazarine, Ms. 2239, fol. xiv ("Etat au vray des élections"); Charmeil, *Les Trésoriers de France*, p. 422.

complement to these frontal assaults on the officials' power, offices, wealth, and personal freedom. This tactic of playing on the already deep-seated animosities between corporations and between different types of officials was employed most openly during negotiations for the paulette's renewal. Capitalizing on the sovereign courts' attitude of superiority toward the weaker, lesser corporations, the monarchy set higher renewal fees for the vulnerable *élus*, *trésoriers*, *présidial* judges, and the rest of the lesser judiciary, than for the high courts' members. The administration's tendency to fall on its easiest prey was demonstrated even when the paulette was not in question; for it was the *trésoriers* and *élus* who suffered far more than the sovereign courts from the expansion of the intendants' functions. However, the king's councils did not let slip any opportunity to isolate the most powerful corporations in the realm, as was demonstrated by the repeated transfer of judicial review and criminal suits from the Parlement of Paris to the more amenable financial tribunals in the capital, or even to distant provincial parlements. Whether it was the mighty or the lowly corporations which bore the brunt of such attacks, the effect was the same. The administration's maneuvers engendered distrust between *trésoriers* and parlementarians, between fiscal and criminal tribunals, even between one parlement and another. What the king could not accomplish by transferring the officials' functions to councils and commissions, or confronting them with his personal authority, he sought to achieve by turning officiers against officiers.

3

ON THE SURFACE, Louis XIII's governmental revolution was relatively successful, but, in reality, it was its weaknesses more than its achievements that set the stage for the revolt of the judges in 1648. How else can we explain the officials' resiliency after three decades of eroding power and prestige? Clearly, historians have exaggerated the monarchy's accomplishments in depicting the officials during the events of 1610-1643 as disunited, subdued, and desperate men kept in check by the king's governmental changes and his clever manipulation of the paulette. Had the balance of governmental power been tipped irrevocably in favor of king, councils, and commissaires, the eventual parlementary Fronde would have been little more than a feeble protest by the officiers, and the Frondes of the nobles, peasants, and townspeople a faint echo of the rebellions and riots of Louis XIII's reign. Scholars who have been surprised by the vigorous nature of the mid-century reaction to the previous governmental revolution need only look beneath the surface of royal-official relations between 1610 and 1643 to discover the factors which made the Fronde such a potent movement. The officiers' status as representatives of the Crown was, in itself, not impaired during the royal-official conflict of 1610-1643, and the way in which the courts and bureaus resisted royal attacks on specific aspects of their power within the king's government strengthened them in important respects.[36]

Governmental revolution acted as a catalyst, preparing the officiers for the Fronde by placing them on the defensive. As they defended themselves, the courts and bureaus of the realm began to develop effective, obstructionist tactics. Instead of educating the officials to the desirability of passively accepting his will, Louis XIII inadvertently schooled them in the habit of seeking new means to preserve their traditional role within the French government. Instead of rendering them hopelessly divided and demoralized, Louis XIII's tactics tended to unite them despite the increased bitter feelings between corporations. And instead of isolating them from outside social groups, the king unwittingly encouraged the courts and bureaus to collaborate with outsiders to a greater degree than social divisions and animosities would normally have permitted.

Even as separate corporations, the royal courts and bureaus resisted the pressures brought to bear on their members by the governmental revolution. Opposition was greatest when an individual corporation was threatened with an increase in membership by the creation of new offices, since all existing members were equally involved in the potential loss of powers and income. The most spectacular resistance of this kind came from the Parlement of Paris. Its members not only continued to block that type of financial legislation after several

---

[36] J. Caillet, *De l'administration en France sous le ministère du Cardinal de Richelieu*, Paris, 1863, is a scholarly representation of the thesis of the officiers' demoralization. The Mousnier thesis on the administration's effective use of the paulette to divide and rule is examined critically but without fundamental revisions by Porchnev, *Les Soulèvements populaires*; and M. Prestwich, "The Making of Absolute Monarchy (1559-1683)," *France: Government and Society*, ed. J. M. Wallace-Hadrill and J. McManners, London, 1957, pp. 122-123. Shennan, *The Parlement of Paris*, pp. 250-254, provides a good analysis of that tribunal's legal power under Louis XIII, but this is only one aspect of the officiers' complex reaction to that king's offensive.

lettres de jussion and the ceremony of the *lit de justice*, but filibustered against the seating of new members for years after the creation of parlementary offices had been formally accepted by them.[37] And no matter whether new offices were accepted, reduced in number, or rejected, the Parlement took so long in reaching a decision that the treasury had trouble using the offices as collateral for securing loans from *traitants*. These men usually loaned the king ready cash in return for the privilege of pocketing the profits from the actual sale of offices. They became increasingly less willing to administer such transactions, knowing that the parlementarians' obstructionist delays would frighten away purchasers.[38] Almost as disconcerting for the treasury and *traitants* was the sullen resistance to new offices and taxes by provincial parlements, particularly the southern ones which justified their rejection on the ground that the local populace had longstanding exemption from most of the projected charges. The contagion of tax rebellion spread to the various chambres des comptes, cours des aides, and bureaus of *trésoriers* and *élus*, although none of these corporations objected as consistently as did the parlements, and their obstructionism was usually overcome by the king's administration.[39]

Arbitrary removal of a corporation's radical members, the emergence of the intendants, and the creation of special judicial commissions were also opposed, although with less success. The Parlement of Paris failed to suppress a single judicial commission established by Richelieu and Louis XIII, although there was a good deal of obstructionism until halted by a series of conciliar decrees and royal letters.[40] That high court was more effective in combating royalist detention of its members. By remonstrating repeatedly for clemency, by threatening to halt all normal judicial work, and by arguing strenuously over the interpretation of past laws regarding the right of judges to trial by their colleagues, the parlementarians usually

[37] Peiresc, *Lettres* I, 815-836, 894, 897; Molé, *Mémoires* I, 493-494; II, 318-343, 475-481, 481, fn. 1; Talon, *Mémoires*, pp. 41-58.

[38] Molé, *Mémoires* II, 309-310; Talon, *Mémoires*, pp. 57-58.

[39] See Charmeil, *Les Trésoriers de France*, especially pp. 11-15 (text and footnotes); *Mercure François* IV, pt. ii, 126-128; Caillet, *De l'administration en France*, pp. 215-221.

[40] Molé, *Mémoires* II, 32-34, 38-43, 62-148; Talon, *Mémoires*, pp. 5-11, 64-67. The parlementarians drafted remonstrances, called commissioners before the bar, and issued *arrêts* halting the work of commissions.

secured the release of their colleagues after a few weeks of imprisonment or exile.[41] Little is known about royal conflicts with other corporations over commissions and arbitrary justice, but what we do
know fits the pattern of relations between the king and the Parlement of Paris. Even the most docile sovereign court, the Grand Conseil, resorted on occasion to opposition.[42] Sometimes, local corporations of officials resisted the intendants so strenuously that the latter
had to restrict or suspend their activities.[43] Occasionally, conservative
members of an individual sovereign court were willing to support
their radical colleagues' opposition to royal encroachments, staking
their political future on the outcome. Thus, when the chancellor or
other representative of the king tried to divide the Parlement of
Paris by praising the presidents in the *grand chambre* and blaming
the *enquêtes* judges for the court's actions, the presidents came to
their colleagues' defense, contending that the Parlement acted as a
body.[44]

In the face of simultaneous royal attacks, an entire echelon of corporations occasionally closed its ranks; and unusual circumstances,
such as royal tampering with the paulette, were capable of breaking
down divisions between the most bitter corporate rivals. Since the
most consistently oppressed officials were the *trésoriers* and *élus*, each
of these groups was active in organizing collective resistance. Thus
a permanent syndicate of *trésoriers* at Paris, representing all their
bureaus, presented general remonstrances to the king, along with the
customary protests by their individual bureaus. The *élus* followed
suit, establishing a similar syndicate in 1641, although using it spar-
ingly during the period of organization coinciding with the last two
years of the reign.[45] The much broader collaboration between different types of corporations during royal-official negotiations on the
paulette requires closer examination, because the final terms of the
renewal leave a one-sided and incomplete impression that the monarchy had subdued and divided the corporation. To look exclusively
at the conclusion of these crises is to miss an important phenome-

---

[41] The administration was able to detain President Le Jay in 1615, on the argument that his detention was punishment for treasonable relations with noble rebels,
not because of obstructionism as a judge. Molé, *Mémoires* I, 72-84.

[42] Molé, *Mémoires* II, 42-43.

[43] Mousnier, "Etat et commissaire," pp. 330-334; d'Avenel, *Richelieu* IV, 211.

[44] Molé, *Mémoires* II, 332-342, 377, fn. 2.

[45] Charmeil, *Les Trésoriers de France*, pp. 247, 247, fn. 85, 422, 422, fn. 798.

non: the temporary intensification of hostility by officials toward the central administration at the outset of the disputes, and the widespread cooperation among their corporations in the face of a common enemy. This evidence that the courts and bureaus were capable of casting aside normal rivalries, if only for a brief time, suggests that the monarchy was playing a dangerous game. For the sake of wringing new concessions from the officials, the regent (and later the king and his ministers) placed the officiers' corporations in a situation which nearly resulted in a Fronde.

While each confrontation over the paulette was slightly different from the preceding one, the general pattern was the same. First the royal ministers threatened to abolish the privilege, or implied that this would occur unless financial gifts were made to the treasury. Corporations in one area after another reacted, first by individual and then collective refusals. After publicly matching this intransigence with equally firm insistence on compliance, the king's administration would then strike a bargain with individual corporations. A central feature of these compromises was a discounted price for the paulette's renewal, in return for the resumption of normal activities by the officiers, and a tacit agreement by each corporation to reduce its attacks on intendants, financial legislation, and other encroachments by councils and commissaires.

The first showdown over the paulette, since its establishment in 1604, merits special consideration because of its timing.[46] Not only was it the first serious test of the officials' attitude toward that privilege, but it coincided with the last days of the reform-minded Estates General of 1614-1615. Hence the officiers had an unusual opportunity to link a personal grievance with the broader issue of state reform. Somewhat ironically, the royal-official dispute stemmed from the only proposal by the national assembly which displeased the officiers: the abolition of *vénalité*. Acting on the Estates General's request, the regent agreed to abolish the paulette as well as the broader practice of selling offices. At Paris, the Parlement, Cour des Aides, Chambre des Comptes, and the local bureau of *trésoriers*, all protested against this reform, which threatened their members' offices. The Parlement of Rouen followed suit, asking its sister court in Paris to work on

[46] Mousnier, *La Vénalité des offices*, pp. 570-590, contains an excellent account, but stresses what is believed to have been a royalist victory at the conclusion of the controversy.

its behalf. Then the parlementarians in the capital abruptly changed tactics, taking advantage of the regent's decision to dismiss the Estates General abruptly without implementing its other reforms. The judges made the national assembly's program their own, calling on all princes, dukes, peers, and officials of the Crown who were then in the capital to attend a plenary session of the Parlement. At this assembly of notables, these dignitaries were to "give their advice on propositions which will be made [i.e., which the Parlement will make] for the king's service." This pronouncement was vague on the precise nature of the projected reforms, but the parlementary debates preceding the summons and the remonstrances eventually drafted by the Parlement of Paris show what the judges had in mind. The parlementarians were determined to halt royal attacks on their own court, all other sovereign tribunals, and even the lesser courts and bureaus of the kingdom. The judges opposed the evocation of suits to royal councils, and the councils' claim to override the *arrêts* of courts by their own *arrêts*. Extraordinary commissions were also condemned. Tenure of office was upheld against arbitrary removal of judges by exile or imprisonment, and judicial review of taxation was strongly defended. The Parlement also attacked the regent's close advisers, particularly Concini, for alleged misuse of royal revenues.[47]

Outwardly, Marie and her closest advisers remained unruffled; the *conseil d'état* issued an *arrêt de cassation* quashing the parlementary decree which had called for an assembly of notables. But the regent soon learned that such a heavy-handed act only made matters worse. To prevent the officers from carrying through their threats to unite against governmental abuses, she agreed to retain the practice of *vénalité*, and postponed action on the paulette's revocation. She also had to retreat from the explicit principle of conciliar superiority over the Parlement of Paris. The parlementary judges insisted that their tribunal represented the Crown just as fully as the councils did, and they were infuriated at the *arrêt de cassation*. Marie would not formally revoke that offensive conciliar decree, but she did not carry out its provision for the suppression of the Parlement's own *arrêt*, thereby implying that the decrees of sovereign courts were

[47] *Mercure François* IV, 25-26, 76-77; C. J. Mayer, ed., *Des Etats Généraux et autres assemblées nationales*, 18 vols., The Hague, 1789, XVII, 130-143; Molé, *Mémoires* I, 28-51.

equal in authority to those of the royal councils. The officers of the realm were mollified by retention of *vénalité* and the tabling of action against the paulette; the Parlement of Paris was pleased with the diplomatic resolution of the confrontation with the *conseil d'état*; the protesting sovereign courts and *trésoriers* stopped corresponding; the Parlement of Paris dropped its plans to convoke the notables; and any lingering parlementary hostility to the administration found a harmless outlet in remonstrances, which the regent wisely allowed the parlementarians to make to her administration.[48] Obviously, Marie gained something. Her concessions had prevented the episode over the paulette from turning into a major crisis. But she also lost something by failing to impose conciliar supremacy over the most powerful sovereign court, and by allowing rival corporations of officials to grope toward a degree of cooperation which almost resulted in disaster for royal power.

When Louis XIII assumed personal direction of royal policies in 1617, he discovered that his interference with the paulette also aroused opposition in the courts and bureaus. However, it was fortunate for him that the Estates General no longer met, and hence the officers could not make the national assembly's program an excuse for demanding major governmental reforms. The timing of the young king's first dispute with his officials over the paulette was another stroke of luck, for negotiations began immediately after a widely acclaimed *coup d'état* by the king in 1617, which had resulted in the exiling of Louis' mother and the assassination of her favorite, Concini, the *bête noire* of the officers. While the officers were still trying to adjust to the fact that a popular king rather than a universally hated minister-favorite was now challenging their powers, the king took advantage of their confusion and announced the outright abolition of the paulette. Nevertheless, that decision brought a storm of protest from the officials, led by the parlementarians at Paris. While the Parlement of Rouen was soliciting their support and the Chambre des Comptes of Paris waited to see how they would react, the Parlement of Paris sent its *procureur général* to warn the chancellor that civil strife would erupt unless the king restored the paulette. Then, in a dramatic demonstration of solidarity, the *trésoriers*, Parlement of Rouen, and sovereign courts at Paris all protested

---

[48] Molé, *Mémoires* I, 52-57.

to the king. Thanks to the officers' initial confusion and the king's popular act of eliminating Concini, Louis XIII was able to withstand this tempest and keep the paulette suppressed for three years. But by 1621, the lingering bitterness of the officers (along with the treasury's need for paulette fees) caused the monarch to restore that privilege. Even this did not mollify the officers, since Louis insisted on onerous financial conditions. After months of threats and objections by the kingdom's tribunals and bureaus, the king restored calm by awarding the paulette to the sovereign courts without exorbitant fees, and for the lesser financial officials on terms which were far more lenient than Louis had originally set.[49]

As the reign progressed, the acceleration of Louis XIII's governmental revolution added new causes for provocation in the negotiations over the paulette. Officials became increasingly alienated by royal attacks on their power and their purses, and were therefore all the more determined to use the issue of the paulette as an excuse for countering these attacks. The officers fought back in 1629-1631 (in the midst of a broader political crisis to be discussed shortly), again in 1636, and toward the end of the reign, from 1640 to 1641. To be sure, each time they eventually made concessions for the retention of the paulette without high fees, notably by registering increases in taxes and salable offices. But before they resigned themselves to such compromises, they placed enormous pressure on the king. During the negotiations of 1629-1631, the Parlement of Paris not only threw its support behind all the realm's officers, but reverted to its tactics of 1615 by threatening to convoke a reformist assembly of notables. The parlementarians in the capital were bolder in 1641, going so far as to initiate a parlementary investigation of fiscal disorders and corruption within the royal administration. Even after the judges agreed to stop these attacks and to accept new offices in return for the paulette's renewal, they pared down the number of offices and thus deprived the treasury of most of the income it had anticipated.[50]

---

[49] See *Mercure François* vi, pt. iii, 32-42; Richelieu, *Mémoires* iii, 128; and for facts (but an interpretation which conflicts with mine), Mousnier, *La Vénalité des offices*, pp. 592-597, 255-260.

[50] See Mousnier, *La Vénalité des offices*, pp. 269-283, 609-617, for the facts; also Molé, *Mémoires* ii, 336, 342, 390, 390, fn. 1, 395-396, 505.

Just as shocking to the king and his ministers was a totally unpredicted coalition of parlementarians and maîtres des requêtes during the paulette negotiations in 1631 and 1641. The maîtres were normally the judges' bitter enemies, since they acted as intendants and advised the royal councils on ways to undermine the officers' powers. But they were alienated temporarily by the king's creation of additional maîtres, and by his decision to use other persons in intendancies and judicial commissions which the maîtres des requêtes considered their preserve. While the Parlement of Paris criticized the maîtres for their role in the king's administration, it did not miss the opportunity to exploit the administration's internal troubles. In 1631, the parlementarians drafted remonstrances when some of the maîtres were deprived of their functions for opposing the king. In 1640, the judges refused to register the legislation establishing new offices of maîtres des requêtes, and agreed to let the offended maîtres come to the Parlement and present their case. The king finally brought the maîtres back to the royalist camp by jailing one maître des requêtes, forbidding his colleagues to appeal before the Parlement, and eliminating four of the sixteen new offices.[51]

Quite clearly, disputes over the paulette that provoked such attacks on the king's administration were far more perilous for the monarchy than historians have recognized. The dangers implicit to periodic near-rebellions by the Parlement of Paris and other corporations outweighed the advantages of concessions wrung by the king from the officers at the conclusion of each negotiation over the paulette. For the sake of temporarily reducing the officers' opposition to royal fiscal programs, Louis XIII was courting political disaster.

Royal interference with the paulette also had a profound impact on relations between the officers and outside social groups. By comparing the chronology of disputes over that privilege with the timing of urban *émeutes*, provincial uprisings, and revolts by *les grands*, we can see that the two broad sources of opposition to the royal administration coincided frequently. Even where movements by officers and *les grands* remained separate, they clearly influenced each other. In 1615 Henri de Condé launched a spirited campaign to turn the Parlement of Paris against the regent while the parlementarians asked all the great nobles to attend its assembly of notables. Marie's

[51] Molé, *Mémoires* II, 38-39, 43, 475-481, 475, fn. 1.

hasty reconciliation with the officers ended that particular flirtation. The regent was luckier than she realized at the time. A year later, Condé combined a noble revolt with a manifesto crammed with precisely those grievances that had highlighted the Parlement's remonstrances of 1615.[52] Had Marie mishandled the conclusion of the earlier controversy over the paulette, parlementary and princely opposition might well have united in 1616. The dangers for the royal administration were much greater during the explosive period of 1628-1632, when the question of the paulette became connected with the great political crisis involving the Day of Dupes. The Parlement of Paris refused to throw its unqualified support behind the complex noble and courtly opposition to Richelieu, but it took advantage of the minister's difficulties by rejecting legislation. And at one crucial point in the crisis, the parlementary judges delayed registration of royal declarations that condemned the rebel followers of Orléans and Marie.[53]

The events of 1615-1616 and 1628-1632 illustrate the social dangers implicit in every royalist tampering with the paulette.[54] Circumstances differed from region to region, but the underlying role of the paulette as a catalyst of widespread opposition was always present. In 1629, the southern provinces had their peculiar version of the broader controversy of 1628-1632. Popular agitation against new fiscal measures coincided with opposition by local judges, who seized on the chance to force a satisfactory renewal of the paulette on the king, by blocking the passage of the unpopular levies. The precise role of Norman officials during the revolt of the so-called "Barefooted Ones" a decade later is not as clear. However, the central administration was convinced that local officers were lax in maintaining order.

[52] *Mercure François* IV, pt. ii, 45-53.

[53] See G. Pagès, "Autour du grand orage. Richelieu et Marillac, deux politiques," *Revue Historique* CLXXIX (1937), 63-97; and scattered references in G. Hanotaux and Duc de La Force, *Histoire du Cardinal de Richelieu*, 6 vols., Paris, 1933-1947, especially IV, 158-168.

[54] This does not mean that the officers were docile between the periodic confrontations over the paulette. For example, in 1634 and 1638, the Parlement of Paris supported the rentiers' protests against the reduction of interest rates. Parlementary opposition was halted after *lettres de jussion* were issued in 1634. The *chambres des enquêtes* were prevented from forcing a plenary parlementary session on the senior chambers in 1638 by the suspension of their functions. Molé, *Mémoires* II, 207-214, 211, fn. 2, 397-399, 397, fn. 1; Talon, *Mémoires*, pp. 59-61.

There was every reason for the courts and bureaus to wink at rebellion, since popular disturbances hampered the royal ministers' efforts to impose a renewal of the paulette on unsatisfactory terms.[55]

The most complex of all the regional disturbances involving officials and outside groups occurred at Paris in 1631. At precisely the time when the issue of the paulette was disturbing judges in the Palace of Justice, a poorly timed tax on wine brought taxpaying demonstrators into the nearby streets. Before long, legalistic resistance by judges converged with popular agitation. The Cour des Aides in Paris employed judicial review against the unpopular tax, and crowds of poor Parisians, tavernkeepers, and *marchands de vin* made an ugly scene at the *bureau de ville*. Partly from fear of mob reprisal if they backed down, partly due to the social conscience of the judges concerning "the poverty and necessity of the people," and with the question of the paulette uppermost in their minds, the members of that tribunal held firm. Not even the presence of a royal prince, who commanded them to register the fiscal measure, brought obedience to the king's explicit orders. The royal administration unwittingly drew the *petits gens, bons bourgeois*, and members of one high court together, and then united several sovereign courts by injecting a new issue into the raging controversy. The tactic of punishing the Cour des Aides by replacing it with a special commission was enough to evoke joint protests by that court's lawyers and judges, along with the Chambre des Comptes and Grand Conseil.

Before the Parisian crisis of 1631 faded, many of the ingredients of the mid-century Fronde were in full evidence. There was violent opposition to taxation by poor and rich alike, evasion of the king's will by a sovereign court on a legislative issue, cooperation by several tribunals in the face of punitive action against one of their corporations, complicity between law-enforcing judges and rioting Parisians, and the underlying threat to officeholding. But 1631 was not 1648, partly because the king's ministers compromised. Predictably, Paris returned to normal when the Cour des Aides was reinstated and the paulette renewed.[56]

While popular and princely opposition continued to capture the attention of subjects and administrators down to the end of the reign,

[55] The uprisings in the provinces can be followed in Tapié, *La France de Louis XIII*; and Porchnev, *Les Soulèvements populaires*.

[56] D'Avenel, *Richelieu* II, 434-445.

the overlapping issue of royal-official relations remained a constant source of trouble for Louis XIII. Indeed, the king seems to have handled noble revolts and popular uprisings far more effectively than he did the less violent, legalistic opposition from his officiers. Revolts by particular regions or individual great nobles were rarely repeated, but the same officials agitated year after year against the erosion of their functions and prestige. The reactions of officiers, whether calculated counterattacks, or instinctive, could not be ignored by Louis XIII. No matter how successful Louis XIII's handling of other internal problems would prove to be in the long run, his governmental revolution and the relative control it gave him over his kingdom was bound to founder unless the officiers were controlled. The officiers might well turn from an issue like the paulette to an attack on all aspects of the governmental revolution, thereby crippling royal power temporarily, and giving the princely and popular opposition a new lease on life. Louis XIII had barely escaped such an occurrence on several occasions. Probably the political wisdom of Richelieu was as responsible as any factor in preventing a Fronde during the last years of the reign. He knew when to compromise with the officiers, particularly parlementary judges in Paris. He could sense when it was essential to suppress a provincial revolt before the contagion could spread. He was also trusted by the parlementarians in Paris, who knew that when he made a bargain he would stand by it.[57] But in 1642 he died, and the following year the death of his king placed the burden of containing the Parlement of Paris, the other corporations of the realm, and outside social groups, squarely on the shoulders of a regent and a minister who lacked the political experience and common sense of Louis XIII and Richelieu. Within five years, French subjects discovered that Anne of Austria and Cardinal Mazarin were unable to prevent the holocaust which their predecessors' actions had helped to prepare.

[57] Hanotaux and La Force, *Richelieu* IV, 154-174, notes Richelieu's moderation at the outset of his ministry, but reverts to the stock image of an intransigent cardinal-minister when discussing the closing years of the reign. It is illuminating to see how Richelieu retained his ability to compromise and reconcile at the end of his life. In 1641, he and Chancellor Séguier attacked presidents de Novion and de Nesmond for criticizing the king's enforcement of his will by a *lit de justice* in the Parlement of Paris. Both ministers tried to soften the blow by saying that they had persuaded Louis XIII to moderate his hostility toward the parlementarians. The presidents called Séguier a liar, but knew that Richelieu was telling the truth and showed no antipathy toward him. Talon, *Mémoires*, p. 75.

CHAPTER THREE

ANNE OF AUSTRIA AS REGENT:
FALTERING LEADERSHIP
AND THE CONTINUING
GOVERNMENTAL REVOLUTION

FROM THE MOMENT Louis XIII's widow assumed charge of the royal administration in 1643, there was a subtle but unmistakable change in the political climate of France. As regent for her son, Louis XIV, who could not legally act on his own until his thirteenth birthday, in September 1651, Anne of Austria was expected to encounter internal turmoil. If Louis XIII had had trouble containing his officers and other subjects, how much harder would it be for someone not ruling on her own authority? Moreover, Anne was a member of the Spanish royal house, which was at war with France, and the intimate friend of most of the great nobles who had intrigued and rebelled against Louis XIII and Richelieu. No one believed that she could suddenly adapt to her new role, or that she would continue the internal and external policies of her late husband and his chief minister. At best, subjects hoped for a period of restraint by the new administration. At worst, they feared that the country might drift into anarchy or, as one contemporary said, an "era of disorder and conflagration."[1] But the combination of new internal conditions and old administrative policies made the political climate of the first five years of the regency even more explosive than the gloomiest prognosticators had predicted.

Lacking confidence in the royal family, Louis XIII had drawn up a will greatly restricting the powers of his wife, brother, and cousin. To be sure, he designated Anne as regent for the young Louis XIV, made his brother Gaston d'Orléans *lieutenant général* of the realm, and chose his cousin, Henri de Condé, as head of the royal household. However, his will stipulated that basic state policies must be

[1] O. L. d'Ormesson, *Journal*, ed. P. A. Chéruel, 2 vols., Paris, 1860-1861, I, 277, fn. 1.

64

approved by majority vote in the formal *conseil d'état*, where Anne, Orléans, and Condé shared power with precisely those administrators who had been the strongest members of Louis XIII's government. Claude le Bouthillier continued as *surintendant des finances*, his son Chavigny as a secretary of state, and Séguier as chancellor. They were joined in the *conseil d'état* by Jules Mazarin, an Italian who had impressed Richelieu so much that Louis XIII's chief minister had used him as a confidant. In 1643, he was already a cardinal, a naturalized French subject, and an important figure within the inner circles of the royal administration. He entered Anne's council as a minister, a position which gave him no special duties but the right to deliberate and vote as an equal with Anne, Orléans, Condé, and the other former servants of Louis XIII. This will was the greatest humiliation a king could inflict on his widow, and Louis XIII had given it the sanctity of law by registering it with the prestigious Parlement of Paris. Anne was determined that her late husband would not dictate to her from his grave, and therefore asked the help of the parlementarians.

It was ironical that the first great ceremony of the regency was a royal session of the Parlement, at which the regent's absolute authority within the realm was made possible by the votes of the very judges who had so often obstructed royal policies in the recent past. The Parlement solemnly nullified Louis XIII's will, transformed the *conseil d'état* from a ruling body to an advisory board, and enabled the regent to choose ministers and set policies on her own authority. In return, Anne invited the parlementarians to give her advice about "the welfare of the state" during the rest of her regency. There can be no doubt that the regent gained more than the Parlement at that session, but the *mariage de convenance* underscored dramatically the historic position of the Parlement as an integral element of the Crown, and countered much of the humiliation it had suffered as a byproduct of Louis XIII's governmental revolution. At the ceremony, President Barillon even dared to suggest that the Parlement should assume immediately the advisory role Anne had promised it, and be empowered "to discover means of relieving the state and to make remonstrances on the conduct observed in past affairs." Behind the indirect language of the wily judge was the threat that the Parlement would use all its legal powers to overturn the governmental innovations of Louis XIII's reign, unless the regent undertook such action herself.[2] Barillon's words indicated the role many of his colleagues wished to play in the future, at the same time making it clear to Anne that she would have to conciliate the parlementarians and other officiers if she hoped to have a harmonious regency.

For the moment, the possibility of future conflicts with the Parlement of Paris was overshadowed by the reshuffling of the royal administration which immediately followed that royal session. An inner group of ministers henceforth made the basic state decisions. Mazarin became Anne's closest adviser and chief minister—the political relationship being strengthened by a strong personal bond between the two. He was assisted by Séguier, the expert in judicial matters, Particelli d'Emery, a brilliant finance minister, and Michel Le Tellier, the able and trustworthy secretary of state for war. Although the *conseil d'état* was a party to official decisions by the regent's administration, that formal council could do little more than ratify the policies which Anne, Mazarin, and the other members of the inner council had formulated in advance. The remaining career councilors and other ministers (such as Chavigny) became something less than administrators and something more than mere clerks. Anne and Mazarin also tapped the prestige of the *conseil d'état*'s princely element without admitting *les grands* to the inner circles of the regency. Thus, Orléans and Condé were retained as heads of the military and the royal household, and continued to sit in the *conseil d'état*, but only occasionally were they seriously consulted on basic state decisions made by the regent and her chief advisers. This policy of associating illustrious names with the regency without granting a corresponding responsibility was continued during the next few years. On Condé's death in 1646, his son Louis (the *Grand* Condé) inherited the family seat in the formal *conseil* as well as the headship of the royal household, and in 1648 Louis de Condé's brother-in-law, the Duke of Longueville, was admitted to the same *conseil*.[3]

The most striking characteristic of Anne's revised administration was its lack of capable leadership. The conciliar rearrangements of 1643 gave the regent the authority she wanted and the advisers she

[2] Ibid. I, 52-53.
[3] On Mazarin's rise to power, see G. Dethan, "Mazarin avant le ministère," *Revue Historique* ccxxvii (1962), 33-66.

could trust, but her administration lacked the cohesion and sense of direction of Louis XIII's. Mazarin was a clever diplomat, but in foreign affairs he lacked Richelieu's ability to distinguish between desirable goals and attainable objectives. His chief weakness, however, was his incredible ignorance about internal affairs. He settled on policies aimed at securing money for the continuing war with the Hapsburgs and preventing *les grands* from dislodging him from power, but did not know how to run the intricate governmental machinery required in those tasks.[4] Lacking the interest to remedy that basic flaw, he had no choice but to leave the complex judicial and financial arrangements to specialists like Séguier and d'Emery while he concentrated on foreign affairs and purely personal relations with *les grands*.[5] Thus, in contrast to Richelieu who kept in touch with his fellow ministers and thereby anticipated crises, Mazarin repeatedly discovered that his ministers of justice and finance were so deeply enmeshed in quarrels with privileged groups or institutions that his last-minute maneuvering could not snatch victory from the jaws of political disaster. Moreover, Mazarin's method of combating potential troublemakers, which he had learned in the military and diplomatic service of the Papacy, was not applicable to France in 1643. Anne of Austria needed an adviser who could combine principle, firmness, and tact, but her chief minister—again in contrast to Richelieu—could not be trusted by princes or parlementarians. For him, internal politics was a complicated set of business transactions, in which, simply by holding out hopes of preferment to each, he could turn one man against another and make both beholden to himself.[6] In the long run, government by diplomacy and intrigue was to pay political dividends, but in the short run it was disastrous.

As the years went on, Mazarin's foreign birth, his apparently untrustworthy nature, and the growing impression among subjects that he placed personal advancement and family wealth above the

---

[4] See Ormesson, *Journal* I, 250, 533.

[5] Chéruel, *Histoire de l'administration monarchique* II, 14.

[6] The best character sketch of Mazarin is to be found in the work of an intimate of the Duke of Longueville: B. Priolo, *The History of France under the Ministry of Cardinal Mazarine*, trans. C. Wase, London, 1671, especially pp. 13, 28. For the traditional, flattering picture, see P. A. Chéruel, *Histoire de France pendant la minorité de Louis XIV*, 4 vols., Paris, 1879-1880. Chéruel did acknowledge Mazarin's neglect of internal affairs (see vol. III, 517), but the first serious reappraisal did not appear until Kossman's book on the Fronde. There is no satisfactory biography.

plight of an overtaxed and war-weary people, turned suspicion into hatred. Ironically, his policy of bribing—and, at most, jailing or exiling—instead of employing the death penalty as Richelieu and Louis XIII had done, turned hatred into contempt. Mazarin not only provided poor leadership for the monarchy, but gave French subjects of every walk of life a personal symbol of royal tyranny on whom to vent their rage, and a scapegoat for the country's troubles. During the Fronde the flood of anti-Mazarinist pamphlets, called *"Mazarinades,"* would play on this popular theme.[7]

Given Mazarin's duplicity and disastrous method of governing in combination with Anne's authoritarianism, harmony within the state and the administration was virtually impossible. For Anne added another negative factor to the governing process in her determination to uphold the authority of her son as a trust, and to pass it on unimpaired to Louis XIV. Anne did not have the perseverance, patience, or intelligence to direct the French government, but she did have intense pride in being the formal head of state. Her fierce temper boiled when her authority or her ministers' policies were questioned, and for all his personal influence, Mazarin could not prevent her outbursts of temper at precisely the times when tactfulness was essential. She called some maîtres des requêtes upstart *"belles gens"* for questioning her authority, and even told judges in the most vulgar terms to hold their tongues. The regent's temperament, and her Spanish background which Frenchmen never forgot, cannot be overlooked in accounting for the growing tenseness within France after 1643. Though Anne was never hated with the animosity subjects felt toward Mazarin, she came to be disliked, and during the Fronde was to be lampooned in pamphlets and insulted on the streets of Paris.[8]

The ministers who were left on their own by Mazarin and Anne were competent as specialists and dedicated to the strengthening of royal authority. However, they could not coordinate their activities, and each had weaknesses as an administrator. Chancellor Séguier's relentless prosecution of rebel peasants and artisans during the previ-

[7] See M.-N. Grand-Mesnil, *Mazarin, la Fronde et la presse, 1647-1649*, Paris, 1967, pp. 83-84, 138-154, 199-209.

[8] For glimpses of Anne's character, see Talon, *Mémoires*, p. 142; Ormesson, *Journal* I, 419; J. Vallier, *Journal*, ed. H. Courteault et al., 4 vols., Paris, 1902-1918, I, 11; Kossman, *La Fronde*, p. 70; J. B. Wolf, "The Formation of a King," *French Historical Studies* I (1958), 41-42, 48-50, 61-62, 68-71; and Wolf, *Louis XIV*, New York, 1968, pp. 3-62.

ous reign passed on an unfortunate legacy to the important ministry of justice in Anne's administration. His apparent insensitivity to the real grievances which fomented popular revolts had made for mutual distrust between subjects and administration. Séguier had also gained the reputation of being deferential to *les grands*, thereby increasing the suspicions of the rural and urban poor toward the administration. Nor were his relations with the officers cordial. Lacking Richelieu's firmness and tact, he had acquired, as Louis XIII's chancellor, the image of a dissembler, the sovereign court judges considering his conciliatory words to be mere flattery and lies. After Richelieu's death, he tried to continue the cardinal's moderation in judicial matters, but the officers remained suspicious despite their respect for his grasp of French law and his refusal to become rich through shady financial arrangements with *traitants*.[9]

D'Emery equaled Séguier in intellectual ability and was a much more skillful politician. He had proved his competence in fiscal matters as an *intendant des finances* during Louis XIII's last years, and soon dominated the other members of Anne's financial ministry, even though he was not formally made *surintendant* until 1647. D'Emery quickly reached the conclusion that the staggering annual expenditure, which spiraling costs of foreign war drove as high as 124 million *livres* in 1643, could be maintained only by outwitting large numbers of reluctant taxpayers. Rejecting as visionary all schemes to overhaul the cumbersome and overburdened fiscal machinery, he gambled on his ability to trick the sovereign courts into accepting stopgap tax legislation, and on the use of troops to force its imposition on subjects. And, while he awaited the outcome of these battles, he sought to stave off bankruptcy by using the expected new income as collateral for fresh loans from *partisans*, or *traitants*. However, the finance minister's immense self-confidence made him underestimate the problem of achieving his goals; officers and other subjects respected his cleverness, while stiffening their resistance to his schemes. His close association with the state's creditors also made him the most hated person in the realm, with the possible exception of Mazarin. In the past, Richelieu and other min-

---

[9] See above, chap. 2, fn. 57; and Charmeil, *Les Trésoriers de France*, pp. 254-255, 255, fn. 117, 336-337. Séguier's economic and social status is discussed briefly in R. Mousnier, ed., *Lettres et mémoires adressés au Chancelier Séguier (1633-1649)*, 2 vols., Paris, 1965, I, 26-38.

isters and courtiers had assumed a similar dual capacity as servants of the state and private subjects, amassing huge personal wealth by underhanded deals with the state and its creditors. But they had been discreet in their profiteering, and—in the case of Richelieu—desirous of curbing the *partisans'* appropriation of state wealth. D'Emery saw nothing wrong with turning the state over to these private financiers, and he made no secret of his personal role as a profiteer. His very cleverness and his unashamed corruption were to bring odium to his financial administration and to cause his fall from power in 1648.[10]

In addition to Séguier and d'Emery, Mazarin relied heavily on three personal agents—Le Tellier, Servien, and Lionne. Each was considered the chief minister's *créature*, a seventeenth-century term indicating the strong bonds of friendship, loyalty, and obligation which tied an individual to the fortunes of his patron. Of the three creatures, Le Tellier alone held an important governmental post, as secretary of state for war. Mazarin permitted him to dominate the other three secretaries, thereby reducing Henri de Guenégaud and Henri-Auguste de Loménie de Brienne to the level of mere letter writers, and keeping Louis Phélypeaux de la Vrillière in a similarly perfunctory position, despite his family connections with d'Emery. Le Tellier was called *le fidèle* in the correspondence between Anne and Mazarin, and his trustworthiness was demonstrated by his constant attention to the personal interests of the chief minister, as well as by Mazarin's confidence in his administration of the military. However, neither the regent nor her confidant were influenced by his advocacy of a conciliatory policy toward princes, parlementarians, and taxpaying subjects, until late in the Fronde. Abel Servien and Hugues de Lionne were also important as Mazarin's confidential informants and trouble shooters, but they had to follow the cardinal-minister's orders explicitly. In Lionne's case, this was unfortunate since he shared Le Tellier's approach to politics.[11]

[10] The best appraisal of d'Emery is by F.V.D. de Forbonnais, *Recherches et considérations sur les finances de France depuis 1596 jusqu'en 1721*, 6 vols., Liège, 1758, II, 77. See also Charmeil, *Les Trésoriers de France*, pp. 266, fn. 156, 273, fn. 186.

[11] The roles of Le Tellier, Servien, and Lionne are amply revealed in Chéruel, *Minorité de Louis XIV*, passim. For the moderate views of Le Tellier and Lionne, see G. Dethan, *Gaston d'Orléans, conspirateur et prince charmant*, Paris, 1959, especially pp. 376-378; Porchnev, *Les Soulèvements populaires*, pp. 646-647; Esmonin, *Etudes*, p. 81.

While the underlying weaknesses of the regent's reorganized administration were not immediately apparent, the problem of governing the state while the king was still a minor was evident to all. Despite the fact that Anne had freed herself from the tutelage of a formal *conseil d'état*, she could not remove the connotation of weak authority implicit in her title as regent. During Marie de Médicis' shorter regency of four years, the Parlement and Chambre des Comptes of Paris had raised the question whether a regent had the same legal powers as a king. That issue was debated much more intensely during the first years of Anne's regency, and in the process her authority was badly damaged. Pamphleteers, princes, and members of the Parlement, Chambre des Comptes, and Cour des Aides of Paris all urged the view that Anne could act merely as a caretaker, with no right to use either her own authority or the will of her son to impose innovations on the realm; in particular, the boy king was not to hold a *lit de justice* to override opposition by the Parlement of Paris or to send Orléans and Condé to the other sovereign courts of the capital in similar ceremonies. These proponents of a limited regency declared that even *lettres de jussion* were illegal.[12] Actually, tradition sided with the opposition, for no *lit de justice* had in fact ever been held during a royal minority. (Marie de Médicis had been fortunate in being able to put off the Estates General of 1614 and the dispute over the paulette in 1615 until after her son came of age.) Even the mature Louis XIII and Richelieu had been criticized for using *lettres de jussion* and *lits de justice* to halt opposition to royal policies, though there was little question of their legal right to do so. Their task had been to turn a legal right into a moral one acceptable to courts and subjects; Anne's far greater problem was trying to make judges and taxpaying subjects accept the very legality of a *lit de justice*.

Though it is an exaggeration to say that the regent, chancellor, and courtiers found no satisfactory reply to the proponents of a limited regency,[13] her regime took time to formulate a response. Hampered by their own ignorance and Anne's impatience with legal niceties, Séguier and his colleagues proceeded cautiously. The regent kept

---

[12] Talon, *Mémoires*, pp. 124, 128-129; Ormesson, *Journal* I, 173-174, 212; II, 869; Boislisle, *Chambre des Comptes de Paris*, p. 415; and for pamphlets, Doolin, *The Fronde*, pp. 148-152.

[13] See the arguments by Doolin, *The Fronde*, p. 148; and Kossman, *La Fronde*, p. 43.

insisting that her powers were unlimited, but when *Avocat Général* Omer Talon of the Parlement of Paris broached the same subject with a secretary of state in 1644, the befuddled functionary could only answer evasively that his colleagues had not thought about it.[14] The following year, royal circles began serious debates on the question, spurred on by the ministers' decision to hold a *lit de justice* and the necessity to find arguments to support this test case of the regent's authority. To their surprise, courtiers and ministers discovered that they were badly divided. At one extreme, Prince Henri de Condé threatened to boycott any *lit* held during the regency, contending that there was no example of a regent calling such a ceremony. Other courtiers tried to counter that argument with the suggestion that the question of precedents was irrelevant: if no *lit de justice* had been held during a previous regency, this merely signified that no regent had found it necessary to exercise that power, not that she did not have it. But the most extreme and persuasive argument in defense of holding a *lit* was expressed by Chancellor Séguier. Invoking the principle of *raison d'état*, he declared that the state's welfare required that a regent must have the same authority as a reigning monarch: just as a king had to hold ultimate authority inside the state to keep it from disintegration, so, too, should a regent who was acting on his behalf.[15]

The rival camp of sovereign court judges was more united in opposing a *lit de justice* than royal circles were in supporting it, but there, too, heated discussions clouded the issue. Séguier's reasoning was actually expressed more elaborately and precisely by a conservative, proroyalist judge in the Parlement of Paris, President Henri de Mesmes, who was reported as declaring that:

> In France, kings were not minors in respect to sovereignty; that authority was always joined to the king's person as its center. The distinction [was] that [as a] major he acted without a council [whereas while a] minor he was assisted by the council or the regent; and that it was important not to diminish the authority of kings during their minority, for an occasion might arise when the establishment of such a maxim would be prejudicial to the state.[16]

[14] Talon, *Mémoires*, p. 124.
[15] Ormesson, *Journal* i, 297, 306; Talon, *Mémoires*, p. 129.
[16] Ormesson, *Journal* ii, 869-870.

The radical *chambres des enquêtes* and many members of other sovereign courts persisted in holding to their view of a limited regency, while others could see both sides of the argument. The parlementary *avocat général*, Talon, wished to keep *lits de justice* to a minimum, but he admitted that a regent had the right to use that ceremony to curb the restiveness of *les grands*, or to force registration of fiscal measures essential to the state.[17]

While the debates raged within royal and judicial circles, valuable time was lost. No parlementary *lit de justice* or comparable ceremony in the other sovereign courts was held until 1645, and in 1647 the administration was uncertain whether it dared hold a second *lit*; so strong was the opposition by the officiers that the ministers thought it best to use such a ceremony only to enforce past fiscal practices, pending a definitive decision on their legality when the king came of age.[18] Only at the beginning of 1648 was the second *lit de justice* of Anne's regime actually held. For five crucial years at the beginning of the regency, she was thus virtually deprived of a major weapon against opposition by the sovereign tribunals.

The foreign war which Anne inherited from Louis XIII added to the organizational and "constitutional" problems of the new administration. A spectacular victory by the future *Grande* Condé over the Spaniards at Rocroi marked the beginning of the regency. However, that battle and the previous success of French arms over the Spanish and Austrian Hapsburgs had an unfortunate impact on Mazarin. Military triumphs increased his ambitions, and he threw away the chance for an honorable peace in his quest for more substantial territorial gains. Thus an increased necessity for income forced d'Emery to rely all the more heavily on those fiscal expedients which had triggered popular revolts and involved repeated clashes with the officiers in the 1620's and 1630's. Louis XIII's financial advisers had exhausted the most obvious expedients, so the untapped resources left for d'Emery after 1643 were largely controlled by entrenched, tax exempt groups in sensitive areas of the realm. Louis XIII and Richelieu had compromised with deep-rooted fiscal immunities, or left them intact, in order to keep rebellions from spreading. D'Emery either did not realize the danger or felt that he had to take the risk. He failed to take note of tax rebellions by the Catalans and Portu-

[17] Talon, *Mémoires*, pp. 129, 132-133.
[18] Ibid., p. 202.

guese against Spain's Philip IV in 1640, and the resistance to taxation under Charles I by Englishmen in the 1630's, which culminated in the Great Rebellion. Nor was he particularly moved by a violent and highly publicized tax revolt in Naples which temporarily toppled Spanish rule in that city at the end of 1647. The finance minister simply dismissed the possibility that he might be courting the same disaster which was overwhelming these other countries.

The victory of French arms between 1643 and 1648 had another unfortunate effect on the fortunes of Anne's regency. As French forces began to penetrate deeply into the Spanish Netherlands, the grand alliance which Richelieu had forged with the Dutch Netherlands and Sweden began to crumble. Franco-Swedish forces continued to coordinate their attacks on Austria, but the Dutch now feared France more than they did Spain. At the beginning of 1648, a Spanish-Dutch settlement deprived Mazarin of Dutch support. At precisely the time when internal problems were reaching their most critical phase, the cardinal-minister was distracted by the imperious demands of European diplomacy. Mazarin managed to counter the Dutch withdrawal by the Treaties of Westphalia with Austria in October 1648, thereby detaching Hapsburg Austria from its alliance with Hapsburg Spain. But the war with Spain continued, and many Frenchmen began to question a diplomatic maneuver which ended one aspect of the foreign war only to intensify the other. Suspicions were raised that Mazarin was continuing the Franco-Spanish conflict in order to make himself indispensable to the regent, and that his greed for further gains from Spain blinded him to the misery which war brought to French taxpayers. Hence the prestige and popularity of minister and regent were further undermined.

2

ANNE, Mazarin, Séguier, and d'Emery had little time to reflect on the conditions which made the regency vulnerable to criticism and attack from within France. They had to concentrate on specific day-to-day problems: how to finance the war, evade judicial review, crush tax revolts, and prevent conspiracies by *les grands*. Money continued to trickle into the treasury, officiers and taxpayers resisted fiscal policies without launching major insurrections, and *les grands* intrigued without revolting. But beneath the relatively calm surface were the potential forces of overt opposition; subjects were becoming increasingly disenchanted with the regency, having expected a break with Louis XIII's governmental revolution rather than its continuation and escalation. Anne and her ministers may have thought they were winning the struggle to control and discipline her son's subjects; but they were simply postponing the Fronde, and at the same time helping to make the revolt, when it did come, far more serious than the opposition Louis XIII had faced.

Like Louis XIII, Anne was most concerned about the restiveness of *les grands*. She was quite willing to free her old friends and Richelieu's political enemies from imprisonment and exile, and even to shower them with gifts and pensions. But when it became apparent that they intended to take Mazarin's place in her government and to subject her to humiliating demands and controls, her friendship turned to hostility. Mazarin was naturally more fearful than Anne of princes and leading nobles, for *les grands* wanted his position, and if it became necessary, his life. But despite the cardinal-minister's obsession with fears of assassination, he was fascinated with the game of counterintrigue which he played with his political foes. His tactic of dividing and ruling through duplicity was successful in keeping *les grands* in check for six years, preventing their attempt at a major revolt until after the parlementary Fronde of 1648-1649. Nevertheless, Mazarin's tactics antagonized *les grands*, who grumbled, continued to intrigue, and waited for an opportunity to strike back.

The nobles' first challenge to Anne and Mazarin came from the so-called *cabale des importants* in 1643-1644, a conspiracy organized by relatively important subjects having great ambitions. The Vendôme family, headed by an illegitimate son of Henri IV, wanted to recapture the positions which Richelieu had wrested from their control. The Duke of Vendôme demanded the admiralty and the governorship of Brittany for himself, and promises of preferment for his son, François, Duke of Beaufort. Augustin de Potier, Bishop of Beauvais and relative of influential judges in the Parlement of Paris, coveted a cardinal's hat and Mazarin's position. Charles de l'Aubespine, Marquis of Châteauneuf, had been keeper of the seals and creature of Richelieu, only to lose his post and his personal freedom due to that minister's suspicion of his untrustworthiness. He wanted to be restored to favor. When Anne made promises without fulfilling them, the *cabale* plotted revenge. Convinced that Mazarin was behind Anne's evasiveness, its members tried to bring the regent under their control by plotting the assassination of the cardinal-minister.

Mazarin discovered the plot, and broke up the *cabale* by imprisoning Beaufort and frightening others into voluntary exile from Paris. However, these men were not resigned to their fate. Beaufort escaped from prison in mid-1648, and Châteauneuf and Potier, though kept politically impotent, continually tried to turn other nobles and Parisian judges against the regency's leadership. So Mazarin was kept in constant fear.[19]

Mazarin even had difficulty securing the support of the prominent courtiers who had remained aloof from the *cabale des importants*, including the *Grand* Condé, the dukes of Orléans and Longueville, and the Count of Chavigny. The minister's way of soliciting them did not gain their real loyalty, merely their temporary acquiescence to his leadership. He was too openly eager to court them, too prone to play them off against each other, and too forgetful of his casual promises to reward them for their submission.

All these prominent persons were to join the ranks of the Fronde in time. But during the first years of the regency, they bade their time, sitting in the *conseil d'état* where they had little influence. Orléans had already dabbled in plots against Richelieu, and he was to become Mazarin's enemy. Yet his firm belief in monarchy and the fact that he was a prince led him to support Anne during the first years of her regency, even though he grew critical of Mazarin's underhanded intrigues and neglect of internal problems. Consequently, the regent was to use him as her chief negotiator with the Parlement of Paris in 1648, and later as a mediator between herself and Condé, while never fully trusting him to stand firm against the judges or to resist siding with dissatisfied nobles. The *Grand* Condé was too busy winning battles against the Spaniards to play a prominent role in internal affairs until late 1648, and too proud of being a Bourbon to plunge immediately into revolt against the regent and cardinal-minister. Indeed, at the outset of the Fronde he was very hostile to Anne's parlementary opponents, and in 1649, he was to lead the royal armies against the parlementary Fronde. On the other hand, his love of danger, his reputation as a victorious general after the battle of Rocroi, and his haughty manner made him someone to be handled with care by Anne and Mazarin. His break with Anne

[19] See Chéruel, *Minorité de Louis XIV* i.

did not come until 1650, but when it did, he proved to be a powerful foe.

The Duke of Longueville and the Count of Chavigny, though bearing less prestigious names than these princes, were just as unpredictable. The weak-willed Longueville was dragged into the Fronde in 1649 by his domineering wife, whose addiction to adventure and intrigue surpassed that of her brother, Condé. Chavigny, one of Richelieu's ablest and most influential creatures, thought that he and not Mazarin should have inherited Richelieu's position. He was persuaded to resign as secretary of state, then somewhat placated by being made minister, but he continually schemed to undermine the cardinal-minister's position. He became a close friend of Condé, and by 1648 was secretly negotiating with Mazarin's enemies in the sovereign courts of Paris. In the summer of 1648, he apparently gave Mazarin bad advice on how to handle a popular insurrection in Paris, was temporarily imprisoned afer that *émeute*, and later joined the noble Fronde.[20]

While Mazarin concentrated on the war and kept an eye on *les grands*, d'Emery was left to find the money for the chief minister's ambitious foreign policy.[21] There was scarcely a social group or geographic region that escaped his clutches, whatever its privileged status had been in the past. The *taille* was reduced by ten million *livres* in 1643, but the next year the peasants discovered that at least half that amount had been replaced by a complementary tax called *subsistances*. Requisitioning of supplies and quartering of troops continued unabated. Indirect taxes on wine and meat were sharply increased in the towns, and most noticeably in the capital. These *aides* fell heavily on the urban poor, but they also threatened merchants with loss of sales, and in some cases affected the pocketbooks of officers and the *bons bourgeois* who sold the produce of their country estates in town markets. Forced loans in the form of new rentes were levied on the wealthiest city groups, including the six

---

[20] For Mazarin's relations with these persons, see ibid. I and II. There are brief character sketches in Priolo, *Ministry of Cardinal Mazarine*, pp. 16-18. Orléans has been rehabilitated by Dethan, *Gaston d'Orléans*, pp. 351, 355-358, 363-369, 382, 385. There is an old but very sound study of the *Grand* Condé: P. Coste, *Histoire de Louis de Bourbon, second de nom (1646-1686)*, The Hague, 1748.

[21] On financial affairs under d'Emery, see especially Forbonnais, *Finances de France* II; and H. Martin, *Histoire de France depuis les temps les plus reculés jusqu'en 1789*, 17 vols., Paris, 1855-1860, XII.

great merchant guilds of Paris. At the same time, interest payments on existing rentes, already poorly and irregularly paid, were frequently suspended. A fine (*toisé*) was levied on illegal housing on the outskirts of Paris, thereby reviving a long-forgotten and unenforced law. That levy threatened both the wealthy slumlords from Paris and their desperately poor tenants. In order to secure income from alienated and untaxed royal domains, d'Emery demanded a year's income from their leaseholders in return for an extension of their leases and tax exemptions. If d'Emery had deliberately attempted to throw divergent social groups together against the regent's authority, he could not have found a more effective means than these diverse taxes which fell indiscriminately on individuals of every social and economic background. Peasants, petty nobles, and urban proprietors of country estates were equally concerned by the demands on rural incomes. Wage earners, small shopkeepers, well-to-do guildsmen, and officiers had common interests in opposing indirect taxes and levies on urban and suburban property. Parisians of all conditions were antagonized by the treasury's demands on the capital city of the realm.

D'Emery's disregard for the fiscal privileges of the officiers was particularly reckless. Already hard-pressed under Louis XIII, the officiers were virtually invited to rebel against Anne of Austria by her finance minister's demands. In 1643 salaries of judges in the Parlement of Paris alone were twelve hundred thousand *livres* in arrears. D'Emery officially cut back sovereign court salaries by one-quarter in 1645, while the *trésoriers* and *élus* complained, in 1648, that they were virtually without income due to salary arrears and other demands on their wealth. Not content with that fiscal brigandage, he had the nerve to raise the official rate of the unpaid salaries—a paper transaction which merely increased the principal which officiers advanced to the treasury in return for the interest payments, or salaries.[22] Moreover, the practice of creating new offices and forcing old officiers to share their functions and fees with the newcomers continued under d'Emery. While he refrained from subjecting the sovereign courts of Paris to that expedient, he tried to reimpose Louis XIII's plan to double the number of parlementary judgeships

[22] Talon, *Mémoires*, pp. 271-300; Charmeil, *Les Trésoriers de France*, p. 422; B. M. Ms. 2239, fol. xiv ("Etat au vray des élections"); Bibliothèque Nationale, Actes Royaux, F 23611 (royal decrees), nos. 685, 736, 748.

in the rebel-prone provinces of Provence and Normandy, as well as adding members to several lesser courts and bureaus throughout the realm.[23]

D'Emery might have reduced some of the inevitable tensions over taxes by permitting flexibility in handling complaints, but he tightened the administrative machinery in fiscal matters instead of using it as a safety valve. Specially constituted royal commissions assessed and collected taxes of dubious legality such as the *toisé*, and subjects could not even take complaints to the sovereign courts, since the commissioners tried suits without appeal except to the royal councils.[24] Enforcement of a royal *arrêt* issued just before Louis XIII's death placed the more regular forms of taxations, such as the *taille*, more firmly than ever under the control of intendants.[25] D'Emery was equally firm in suppressing tax revolts, sending royal troops to stamp out provincial opposition and using royal guards instead of the *bureau de ville*'s militia in the capital. Appalled by his measures, Hugues de Lionne and the intendant of Dauphiné, Lozières, pleaded—in vain—for moderation. A tax revolt had erupted in that province in 1645, and a *gentilhomme* had been apprehended. Lionne was convinced that the culprit should not be tried, as this would intensify the hostility of the local populace, and Lozières requested that royal troops be kept out of the area until calm was restored. But d'Emery insisted on punishment and the use of force as a warning to other rebel-prone subjects. The incident is a clear illustration of the finance minister's mishandling of political-fiscal issues, the confusion which was prevalent within royal circles, and the inability of those in power to distinguish between measured authoritarianism and ruthless suppression of all opposition.[26]

The relation between d'Emery and the *traitants* helps explain the finance minister's necessity for such harsh policies. If these state creditors were unable to reimburse themselves by collecting taxes, they would cease to lend money to the state. Hence, with d'Emery's backing, intendants and other commissioners worked side by side

[23] Actes Royaux, F 23611, nos. 702, 703, 735; Kossman, *La Fronde*, pp. 119-120, 139-140.

[24] Talon, *Mémoires*, p. 113; Molé, *Mémoires* III, 104-105.

[25] Charmeil, *Les Trésoriers de France*, p. 156; Mousnier, "Etat et commissaire," pp. 336-337.

[26] Esmonin, *Etudes*, p. 81; Porchnev, *Les Soulèvements populaires*, pp. 122-134, 646-647.

with the *traitants*, judging suits arbitrarily, using troops to see that taxes were paid, and preventing the local tax officials from interfering with assessments and collection. It did not take long for the most ignorant peasant to realize that he was the victim of a cruel system which lined the pockets of *traitants*; and bitter hatred of these state creditors merged with hostility toward the intendants. It was well known that some intendants were not only aiding the *traitants*, but were actually *traitants* in disguise, secretly lending money to the royal treasury on the security of taxes. *Traitants* and intendants became known collectively as *voleurs publics*.[27] D'Emery was so committed to the tax-farming system that in 1645 he farmed the *taille*, the last major tax still officially controlled by the regular officiers.[28] No one knew the precise details of agreements between d'Emery and the *traitants*, because contracts were awarded by the royal councils instead of the *trésoriers de France*, who were legally responsible for the task. Even if the contracts had been known, there was no way to determine whether creditors were actually paid more than had been stipulated. The chambres des comptes audited the accounts of state officials, but they were not authorized to pry into the secrets of most treasury expenditures. Moreover, the central administration could bypass its treasury officials as well as the chambres des comptes, by assigning disbursements directly from revenues. Legally, these special *comptants* covered payments which could not be made known without endangering state security. By 1643, one-third of royal expenditures were made through *comptants*.[29] Subjects were naturally suspicious, believing, correctly, that illicit reimbursements were involved, and that the *comptants* were protecting the security of the *traitants* rather than that of the state.

The tightening of fiscal machinery was particularly offensive to the officiers. Increased control by councils, intendants, and other special commissions meant a corresponding decrease in the functions and power of officiers. The lesser taxing bureaus and petty criminal tribunals were particularly hard hit, and with the farming of the *taille* in 1645, the *élus* and *trésoriers* were shorn of their most important duties—the assessment, collection, and litigation of suits con-

[27] Ormesson, *Journal* I, 231; Vallier, *Journal* I, 5-7, 49-50; Bibliothèque de l'Université de Paris, Ms. 64 (Lallement's journal), fols. 35-36; *Catalogue des partisans*, Paris, 1649 (a *Mazarinade*).

[28] E. Esmonin, *La Taille en Normandie au temps de Colbert (1661-1683)*, Paris, 1913, pp. 46-48; Forbonnais, *Finances de France* II, 82-83.

[29] Martin, *Histoire de France* XII, 178.

nected with that important tax. The *trésoriers* were also disgruntled by conciliar usurpation of their right to award tax farms. Sovereign courts, though to a lesser degree, also continued to lose functions. The parlements knew that many taxes were imposed without registration in any court, and others after verification in the tribunals least likely to resist their registration. By mid-1648, it was contended by parlementarians in Paris that unverified fees in the chancellery were almost equal to those which were registered in the courts.[30] The chambres des comptes were unable to audit even the direct loans between the treasury and state creditors, except for municipal *rentes*; and the parlements discovered that state borrowing, with the exception of *rentes*, was never submitted to them for judicial review. Tax farming was also beyond the control of the chambres des comptes and cours des aides. Traditionally, they were responsible for registering such contracts, but now only the farming of the *gabelle* (salt tax) was subject to judicial review by their members.[31]

Though there were some officers who were implicated in loans, and others who acted as intendants' aides, most refused to accept these corrupt practices which were stripping every corporation of its functions.[32] Even the maîtres des requêtes became outraged by d'Emery's policies. As intendancies became more important, the administration turned increasingly to private individuals rather than to the maîtres in its quest for totally "reliable" intendants. Along with their fear of this indirect attack the maîtres cried out against the direct threat posed by royal creation of new masterships, declaring that they would not suffer the fate of the *élus* and other aggrieved officers.[33] Still more ominous was the alienation of the Parlement of Paris, whose functions were affected by most of d'Emery's expedients. All in all, maîtres, parlementarians, and other officers saw a common enemy in the *traitants*, or *partisans*, who were assuming their duties, amassing huge fortunes at their expense, and pocketing revenues set aside for their own salaries.[34]

[30] B. N. Ms. Fr. 23319 (Parlement of Paris debates), fol. 39r.

[31] A. N. U 336 (Parlement of Paris debates), pp. 380-384; B. U. P. Ms. 64, fol. 60; Talon, *Mémoires*, pp. 154, 206-207.

[32] See the refusal by the Parlement of Rennes to allow its members to act as intendants, Ormesson, *Journal* i, 443.

[33] Ibid. i, 154-155, 344, 404-406.

[34] Again, the example of the maîtres des requêtes is a graphic illustration. In 1648, they threatened to try a *traitant* in charge of selling new offices of maîtres. Ibid. i, 407-409.

D'Emery's efforts to dupe the officiers into accepting his fiscal policies made a bad situation worse. By treating judicial review and the
officiers' personal privileges as objects of barter and legalistic haggling, he encouraged his opponents to outwit him at his own game.
This was at best a bad gamble, since the officiers were much more
knowledgeable in such matters.

The finance minister used several techniques to control judicial
review. In some cases, such as the *toisé* of 1644-1645, he invented
taxes which by his interpretation were justified by laws from previous reigns that had not previously been enforced, and did not explicitly call for those impositions. Arguing that the original legislation
had long ago been registered by the law courts, d'Emery insisted that
he could impose what amounted to a new tax without submitting it
to judicial review. Another tactic was to ask the courts to approve
fiscal measures which should have been registered when they had
been first imposed, during Louis XIII's reign. In effect, the judges
were now asked to give the finance minister a free hand to continue
or expand the use of these taxes in return for the meaningless honor
of exercising a belated judicial review. For example, d'Emery wanted
the Parlement of Paris to register past alienations of royal domains
and approve a tax on the proprietor equal to one year's income from
the land, in return for a thirty-year extension of their leases.[35] What
d'Emery failed to foresee was that the officiers would neither accept
his interpretation of laws which had been registered, nor be satisfied
with winning the principle of judicial review at the expense of giving him *carte blanche*.

More complicated than either of these tactics was the finance minister's manipulation of indirect levies. His tariff on Paris in 1646-1647
was a combination of several types of taxes on wine and meat. Some
were based on the permanent domainal rights of the Crown and
were not subject to judicial review; others went back to tax laws
previously registered by the Parlement of Paris. Still others were
temporary excise taxes—hence, as such, verifiable by the Cour des
Aides of Paris, rather than by the Parlement. But d'Emery asserted
that the taxes as a group were an *aide*. Reasoning that the Cour des
Aides would register the package legislation, and that the Parlement
could have no legal reason to intervene, he failed to take into account
the fact that both courts were highly suspicious of such a tax becom-

[35] Talon, *Mémoires*, pp. 111-113, 154-156; Actes Royaux, F 23611, no. 751.

ing permanent, and establishing precedence for the imposition of similar tariffs on other cities in the realm.[36] If he thought the sovereign court judges would be enticed into accepting his scheme, he badly misjudged these legalistically minded officials.

D'Emery was equally naïve in thinking he could pass off as a concession the granting of "perfect," or hereditary, nobility to members of some regional sovereign courts and bureaus of *trésoriers*. In many instances, these officers had already risen from personal nobility to hereditary nobility, either by the fact of being the third generation in office or by purchasing noble property.[37] Moreover, the attribute of tax-exempt status traditionally granted to hereditary nobles meant nothing to these officials, since in their case it was offset by other fiscal measures which deprived them of their salaries, fees, and private wealth. On the other hand, lesser officials failed to secure the privilege of noble status, and were in the process of losing what tax exemptions they had. For example, in 1646, a host of minor officiers saw their immunity to the costly salt tax, or *gabelle*, lost by royal decrees.[38] Perhaps d'Emery hoped that he would make the petty officials jealous of their superiors by such tactics. Whether he did or not, he convinced the sovereign court judges that they could not desert minor officials, whose fate was linked to their own. Added to this frightening situation was the fact that many officiers were being forced into quartering and supplying other services for the army, despite their legal exemption. All this reaffirmed the now obnoxious fact that Anne's administration did not honor its agreements.[39]

D'Emery's most glaring error was his ill-timed and heavy-handed interference with the paulette at the beginning of 1648. Instead of renewing the privilege, he threatened to suspend it unless the Parlement of Paris approved a bloc of financial expedients which he was preparing for registration. While Mazarin knew of the negotiations, he did little to curb the vindictiveness of his fellow minister. The cardinal made conciliatory gestures in secret conferences with the leading parlementarians, but the finance minister undid all Maza-

---

[36] A. N. U 28 (Parlement of Paris register), fols. 64-69; Talon, *Mémoires*, pp. 196-199; Forbonnais, *Finances de France* II, 86-88.

[37] Actes Royaux, F 23611, no. 681; Boislisle, *Chambre des Comptes*, pp. 417-418. See also F. L. Ford, *Robe and Sword: The Regrouping of the French Aristocracy after Louis XIV*, Cambridge, 1953, p. 63.

[38] Actes Royaux, F 23611, no. 782; Charmeil, *Les Trésoriers de France*, p. 99.

[39] Actes Royaux, F 23611, no. 736.

rin's work by continuing to threaten them with the loss of the paulette. Perhaps d'Emery sensed the importance of the occasion—he
surely must have been aware of Louis XIII's troubles over that issue—
but he seems to have been totally unaware that his acceleration of
Louis XIII's governmental revolution had made the officers far less
willing to compromise than they had been in the 1630's.[40] Also, one
is led to believe that he thought he could succeed with his blackmail.

Financial issues were not the only ones which led to the revolt of
the judges. But d'Emery's handling of the officers was probably the
most important factor in unleashing the Fronde. His career as finance
minister under Anne of Austria, and his curious combination of self-
confidence, cleverness, and naïveté, deserve far greater emphasis and
study than historians of the Fronde have given them.

There was another, less conspicuous, side to the increasing tensions
between officers and monarchy between 1643 and 1648. While many
concentrated their attention on financial grievances, Chancellor
Séguier undermined the officers' already shaky control over criminal
justice and police. Although Anne and Mazarin gave him their backing, they usually knew only the general outlines of his policies.
Nevertheless, Mazarin ventured into the judicial sphere with his decision to imprison and exile the *importants* without referring the matter to the Parlement of Paris. Anne, too, was forced to make a decision, right at the outset of the regency, when that court asked her
to abolish all special judicial commissions established by Louis XIII.
The regent was less cooperative than Marie de Médicis had been in a
similar situation in 1610: Marie had abolished all commissions, but
Anne suppressed only the most infamous of her husband's commissions, the *chambre de l'arsenal*.[41] Soon, the royal exercise of judicial
authority was increased. During the first five years of the regency,
new commissions were created, royal councils quashed judicial and
police decisions made by the sovereign courts of the realm, and conciliar *arrêts* evoked suits while in process. The intendants broadened
their control over general criminal justice and police matters as well
as tax litigation.[42]

Meanwhile, Séguier continued Louis XIII's reorganization of the

[40] Priolo, *Ministry of Cardinal Mazarine*, p. 91; Talon, *Mémoires*, p. 208.

[41] Molé, *Mémoires* iii, 84, fn. 1.

[42] B. N. Ms. Baluze 291, fols. 8-15 (papers on evocations belonging to the parlementary councilor, Pierre Broussel); and scattered references in A.N. U 28.

royal councils. In 1643 and 1644, the minister of justice rigorously applied recently established regulations concerning the place of lawyers and maîtres des requêtes in the royal councils. The following year, Séguier strengthened one of the most important links in the chain of executive authority by resolving the question: who should investigate subjects' interference with the implementation of conciliar *arrêts*, royal ordinances, intendants' decisions, and decrees by other commissaires? In a landmark decision, a royal decree specifically empowered the primarily judicial *conseil des parties* to probe all such "violences, excesses, imprisonments and rebellions," thereby serving notice that the administration's own machinery would move into a field which traditional governmental confusion had allowed a host of law courts and tax bureaus to dominate.[43] However, the minister of justice was not successful in all his efforts to streamline the executive machinery, for he could not reduce the numbers in the royal councils, as he had planned. As was the custom during all regencies, throngs of honorary councilors tried to take advantage of Anne's uncertain position as a caretaker regent and clamored to sit in on the sessions of councils, which under a mature king were reserved for career councilors and maîtres des requêtes. Despite Séguier's vigilance, several persons holding honorary councilorships—including a few sovereign court judges—managed to slip into the councils, thereby blurring the lines of authority between executive and judiciary which that minister was trying to clarify.

Like d'Emery, Séguier tried to outwit the officers. In conferences with the judges of the Parlement of Paris, the chancellor went so far as to disguise the fact that councils, intendants, and other commissioners were steadily encroaching on the courts' powers. According to him, the regent had no intention of allowing her agencies to assume functions which past laws had given to the judiciary: if any royal agents had done this, it had been without her knowledge. And, while feigning royal ignorance of any new wrongdoing, Séguier drew on the principle of *raison d'état* to defend the regent's continuation of Louis XIII's previous tampering with the regular course of justice; in his view, such activities had originally been undertaken not as deliberate violations of the law, but rather as emergency devices necessitated by the long Bourbon-Hapsburg war. He also sought to allay the judges' fears that these emergency powers would continue

---

[43] Mousnier, "Le Conseil du roi," especially pp. 37, 50.

indefinitely—arguing that they would be suppressed as soon as that foreign conflict ended. That Séguier had no intention of carrying out his promises was shown by his very different stand at council sessions, where he declared flatly that the royal councils should be placed firmly above the Parlement of Paris. The distrust the officiers had felt toward Séguier earlier, under Louis XIII, was naturally now intensified by such tactics.[44]

The combination of new circumstances, faltering leadership, and questionable management of financial and judicial affairs made the regent's administration far weaker in 1648 than it had been in 1643, despite the continuation of Louis XIII's governmental revolution. Historians have been aware that something was sapping the strength of the regency during its first years, but none has placed sufficient emphasis on the tensions and difficulties that worked from within the administration. The personalities, attitudes, and policies of Anne, Mazarin, d'Emery, and Séguier were particularly important as contributing factors to the outbreak of the Fronde. Their rare attempts to coordinate their activities showed an almost hopeless confusion and lack of direction.

This confusion was first demonstrated within the administration during a series of disputes between Anne's ministers and the maîtres des requêtes. While the maîtres repeatedly assailed the ministers for robbing them of their historic role as council members, commissioners, and intendants, Séguier alternated between a policy of ridiculing them and making vague promises, and d'Emery seemed determined to reduce their powers sharply, wishing, according to some observers, "to reestablish the order in [financial] affairs which existed in M. de Sully's time" (i.e., to rival the almost legendary control Henri IV's finance minister held over finances). In keeping with her character, Anne simply told the maîtres to obey her ministers, and, characteristically, Mazarin flattered the maîtres, while candidly admitting to them that he did not even know what functions and powers they had a right to claim within the administration.[45]

Then, in 1648, the administration virtually collapsed because of such inner contradictions. In the face of unprecedented opposition from the sovereign courts of Paris and the popular backing of the judges, each member of Anne's team canceled out the strengths of

[44] Molé, *Mémoires* III, 118-119; Ormesson, *Journal* I, 246.
[45] Ormesson, *Journal* I, 154-155, 166-170, 176-177, 199-202, 344, 389.

the others. Mazarin totally lost control due to his ignorance and inattention, d'Emery pressed for a concerted counterattack, Anne became the victim of temper tantrums, and Séguier was too afraid of offending d'Emery to suggest a moderately measured response.[46] It is not surprising that the officiers were able to take advantage of the situation and sought revenge for the humiliations begun under Louis XIII. Anne and her ministers encouraged the upheaval, just as Charles I of England and Spain's chief minister, the Count-Duke of Olivares, had incited revolution in their countries. The officiers seized the opportunity and brought about the revolt of the judges known as the "parlementary Fronde."

[46] Ibid. I, 533.

PART II

THE PARLEMENTARY FRONDE
1643-1649

CHAPTER FOUR

THE DEVELOPMENT OF AN
EFFECTIVE OPPOSITION

THE FRONDE began in the summer of 1648 when the sovereign courts of Paris assembled in the Chambre Saint Louis and imposed crippling reforms on the regent's regime. In their eagerness to examine the dramatic collapse of Anne's authority, historians have failed to grasp the connection between that formal revolt of the judges and the preliminary skirmishing of 1643-1648.[1] To some extent, this oversight is understandable, since the timing of the Fronde was a surprise to the very individuals who experienced it. Just before, there had been a brief period of calm which had allowed many persons to forget the numerous tax revolts of the immediately preceding years. Superficially, it had even appeared that the regent was winning her struggle against fiscal obstructionism by the Parlement of Paris: on January 15, 1648, she had brought the king to that high court and compelled the judges to register fiscal measures during the *lit de justice*; then in the course of a two-month dispute over their implementation, she had forced the judges to admit that they could neither amend nor veto these expressions of the king's will. However, the silence was ominous and the regent's victory was an illusion. How else can one explain the spectacular success of the sovereign courts a few weeks later? The fact is that there was a logical progression from the first signs of parlementary resistance in 1643 to the convocation of the Chambre Saint Louis in mid-1648, and the debates and maneuvering after the *lit de justice* of January 1648 constituted a major aspect of that evolution. During the first five years of the regency, the Parlement of Paris proved itself to be a mature opposition to Anne's administration, developing and perfecting the tech-

---

[1] Even the latest treatment of the subject assumes that the administration won legal victories during the first years, although it recognizes that the Parlement of Paris continued to attack royal policies with some legal backing. See Shennan, *The Parlement of Paris*, pp. 260, 262. Doolin, *The Fronde*, has become the source for many accounts of the "constitutional" aspects of the Fronde, but that study omits all the events of 1643-1647, and hedges on the outcome of parlementary disputes with the administration during the first months of 1648.

niques of legislative and judicial obstructionism which were to be employed so effectively when the Fronde erupted.

The development of that leading court as an effective opposition must, of course, be placed in its proper context as part of the general reaction against the policies of Louis XIII, and against the regent as the symbol of his governmental revolution. What we know of the activities of the various courts and bureaus after 1643 reveals a far more aggressive attitude toward the royal administration than was evident under Louis XIII, with leading members of the Chambre des Comptes and Cour des Aides of Paris, for example, being just as vocal as the parlementarians in asserting that their tribunals would not allow judicial review to be overridden. In 1644, the mere rumor that the royal princes might come to their chambers to force registration of contentious legislation brought sharp protests. The *procureur général* of the Chambre des Comptes made a personal appeal to the administration; and members of the Cour des Aides asserted that they considered the entry of a prince illegal, and would therefore oppose it even if this resulted in their interdiction.[2] Although those courts failed to go beyond verbal criticism when princes actually came to their chambers with legislation in 1645 and 1648, on other occasions they were bolder. For example, at the beginning of the regency, the Cour des Aides at Paris attached important amendments to one of Louis XIII's last regulatory decrees, thereby hampering that king's design to place the realm's lesser financial officials more firmly under the intendants. That high court and the Chambre des Comptes of Paris also modified some important financial legislation drafted during the early years of the regency, and even the Grand Conseil, the most docile sovereign court in the capital, occasionally obstructed the passage of new laws.[3]

The provincial parlements, chambres des comptes, and cours des aides were equally bold. The most celebrated acts of defiance occurred in Normandy and Provence, where the parlements at Rouen and Aix successfully resisted d'Emery's attempt to double their membership. In Provence, the judges' resistance degenerated into a minor civil war with the provincial governor, who was friendly to the regent.[4] In addition to such attacks on financial legislation, the pro-

[2] Boislisle, *Chambre des Comptes*, p. 415; Ormesson, *Journal* I, 173-174.

[3] Actes Royaux, F 23611, nos. 720, 744, 749, 795, 806, 810, 819, 823.

[4] Kossman, *La Fronde*, pp. 120-121, 140.

vincial sovereign courts began to quarrel with local intendants immediately after Louis XIII's death, and intensified their harassment as
time passed; early in 1648, the Parlement of Aix forced the local
intendant to leave the area, while the Parlement of Rennes forbade
one of its members to act as an intendant and implied that it would
no longer tolerate intendancies.[5]

Even the *trésoriers* and *élus* made far greater use of their representative assemblies in Paris than they had under Louis XIII, being
in a much more desperate situation than even the sovereign courts.
The syndicate of the *trésoriers de France*, for example, demanded the
suppression of the intendants, during a conference with Mazarin in
1644. The effectiveness of such lobbies is questionable, but the fact
that the *élus* and *trésoriers* were at least using their machinery for
collective action indicates a change in attitude. Opposition by individual corporations of *élus* and *trésoriers* to the encroachment of
intendants and the projected sale of new offices was much more successful. At least three attempts by d'Emery to create new bureaus of
trésoriers were blocked by neighboring bureaus during the first years
of the regency. Intendants in several districts also failed to secure
the cooperation which they had come to expect from the *élus*, dis-
covering in some cases that they could not even use the facilities or
records of those financial officials. Still more significant was the willingness of some sovereign courts to support the cause of these inferior bureaus, despite traditional animosities.[6]

Lacking the officials' legal weapons, other subjects resorted to violence in their efforts to avoid taxation. The tax revolts of the 1620's
and 1630's were probably more frequent and serious than those of
Anne's first years, but insurrections in her time were common
enough to rob the treasury of badly needed revenue and disrupt the
work of intendants. One suspects that in many areas the absence of
revolts was due to the hesitation of intendants and *traitants* to collect
taxes. As in the past, virtually every social and economic group was
represented in these violent protests. When an intendant began to

[5] N. Goulas, *Mémoires*, ed. C. Constant, 3 vols., Paris, 1879-1882, ii, 266-267;
Ormesson, *Journal* i, 443.

[6] Charmeil, *Les Trésoriers de France*, pp. 14, 247-248, 375-376; Mousnier, "Etat et
commissaire," pp. 338-340; Esmonin, *Etudes*, pp. 86-87; Porchnev, *Les Soulèvements
populaires*, p. 501. There is a wealth of material on the opposition from many corporations of officiers, in Mousnier, *Lettres et mémoires adressés au Chancelier
Séguier*.

strike out against local tax evasions or disregarded traditional exemptions, as in the Rouergue in 1643, a massive protest was almost certain to follow.[7] In some instances, all local officials, from sovereign court judges to members of *bailliage* courts and taxing bureaus, were directly or indirectly implicated. In fact, a protest in 1645 against royal efforts to create a *présidial* court at St. Quentin spread throughout the entire community, gaining the support of the mayor, aldermen, and inhabitants of Laon and St. Quentin, the Bishop of Laon and the regular clergy, the *bailliage* court of Vermandois, and the *présidial* tribunal at Laon, as well as the more distant Parlement of Paris. In this case, as in many others, the opposition achieved its objective.[8]

The most dangerous tax revolts occurred in the city and *faubourgs* of Paris. During the 1630's Louis XIII had witnessed ugly demonstrations by Parisian rentiers and wine merchants, but, in general, the capital had been kept quiet by his preferential treatment of its inhabitants. By contrast, riots and nonviolent demonstrations became a common occurrence on the streets of Paris during the mid-1640's, since Anne's finance minister decided that Parisians should share the financial burdens of the provinces. Included in the ranks of the protestors were the wealthiest merchants (*bons bourgeois*) and other propertied Parisians—whose hostility toward the regency underscores the explosive background of the simultaneous agitations against taxation by the Parlement of Paris.

Historians have badly distorted the roles of these very diverse bourgeois groups by categorizing them as a distinct social element— a "middle class," comparable to the postindustrial bourgeoisie. From this rigid classification emerges the stereotype of a fervently royalist Parisian bourgeoisie, committed to law and order, and wary of protesting against taxes for fear of encouraging attacks by social inferiors on their own property.[9] In reality, even the *bons bourgeois*, who come closest to fitting that stereotype, were far from being unswerv-

---

[7] M. Degarne, "Etudes sur les soulèvements provinciaux en France avant la Fronde. La Révolte du Rouergue en 1643," *XVII Siècle*, no. 56 (1962), 3-18.

[8] Actes Royaux, F 23668 (*arrêts* of the Parlement of Paris), no. 631.

[9] Bourgeon, "L'Ile de la Cité," is a superb study which comes closest to a repudiation of the thesis of a royalist bourgeoisie, especially during the early stages of the Fronde. Kossman, *La Fronde*, is an articulate defense of the *thèse royale*, but it equates the royalist *bureau de ville* with the not-so-royalist merchants, and selects incidents of merchant docility to the exclusion of hostile acts by bourgeois groups.

ing royalists, for they combined their dislike of violence with an equally deep-seated determination to oppose exorbitant taxes by peaceful means. Since they needed public order as much as the regent needed their support, they rarely demonstrated in public against taxation, and even then they avoided willfully destructive acts. But, having protected themselves with this image of law-abiding subjects, the six merchant guilds of Paris were quick to engage in behind-the-scenes lobbying which frequently degenerated into shouting matches with Anne's ministers. The mercers and drapers were especially vocal when the six guilds took issue with a royal council's decision to raise the Paris tariff in 1644. This was the first of a series of confrontations between guildsmen and ministers, during which each side bargained and tried to outwit the other. After the first session, d'Emery converted the tariff into a *taxe des aisés* (forced loan), which fell exclusively on one hundred and twenty members of the six guilds. In contrast to merchants slightly lower on the social scale—who threatened insurrection at the very rumor that they too would be included in the imposition—the six guilds tried to convince Anne and members of her councils that the hated *traitants* could better afford to pay the loan. Then, in 1646-1647, d'Emery resorted to a broad tariff plan, which fell on the Parisian guilds just as had the tariff of 1644. Guildsmen tried a variety of tactics to oppose the tax, sometimes rejecting it without suggesting alternatives, sometimes requesting that they be permitted to administer the levy without royal supervision. D'Emery's persistent efforts to tax the six guilds helped make relations between the wealthiest merchants of Paris and the regent very uncertain by 1648, and his eventual admission that he could not accomplish this encouraged other Parisians to resist fiscal extortions.[10]

It would appear that the lower they were on the economic scale, the more prone bourgeois Parisians were to open violence. We know that wine merchants and tavernkeepers (slightly beneath the six guilds), the less affluent butchers, and the still poorer craftsmen and dealers in the wood trade lobbied more openly against tariffs than did the six guilds—their lobbying occasionally verging on ugly mob scenes.[11] In January 1648, an entire street of some two or three

[10] B. N. Ms. Fr. 18367, fols. 95-107, 109; Ormesson, *Journal* I, 155-156, 232-235.
[11] Actes Royaux, F 23611, nos. 810, 819; Goulas, *Mémoires* II, 130; Chéruel, *Minorité de Louis XIV* II, 105; B. U. P. Ms. 64, fols. 184-185, 201.

hundred shopkeepers from the rue Saint Denis erupted in a demonstration.[12] The riots, triggered by the *toisé* fine on illegal buildings in 1644 involved many elements of the bourgeoisie, and, according to a well-informed and highly reputable observer, one day four hundred persons "of every condition, age, and sex" demonstrated; he reported to the regent that property owners as well as their tenants were agitated by the *toisé*. The slumlords probably did not take part in the attempts by laborers to burn down d'Emery's house and lynch his son, but they were able to show their fury at the finance minister's efforts to tax their property in less extreme fashion.[13]

By comparison with these bourgeois groups, it is easy to document the acts of violence committed in Paris between 1643 and 1648 by the city's lowest social elements. Unfortunately, scholars have been so captivated by the superficial contrast between the relatively law-abiding bourgeoisie and the violence-prone poor that they have overlooked an intermediate group of Parisians: carpenters, masons, boatmen, water carriers, and other laborers who were sufficiently skilled to be placed in distinct corporations of artisans. As property-less laborers, they bear some resemblance to the many vagrant types which swelled the population of Paris and other seventeenth-century cities. But as members of corporations with particular functions or skills, they were much closer to the corporative, property-owning bourgeoisie. Even the most affluent bourgeois of the capital drew a distinction between these lesser, corporative Parisians and the lowest groups on the social scale. The latter, including the chronically unemployed, as well as beggars, thieves, and mere drifters, were considered dangerous threats to the rest of society. They were denounced as *gens de néant, gens sans aveu,* or even *la canaille*—all disparaging terms which were not usually applied to poor, but socially respectable Parisian workers. Therefore, when the records left by wealthy Parisians refer pointedly to corporative laborers as participants in a demonstration against the central administration, we should not conclude that this was merely another senseless riot. To the contrary, what was involved was a warning to the monarchy that men on the fringes of the Parisian bourgeoisie were angry enough to risk their lives—

[12] Vallier, *Journal* I, 2-9, 3, fn. I.
[13] Talon, *Mémoires*, pp. 111-113; Ormesson, *Journal* I, 194-196; Molé, *Mémoires* III, 104-106.

a political protest which the *bons bourgeois* understood well and followed closely. Of course, rioting by these artisans might easily turn into attacks on bourgeois property, frightening the well-to-do *"gens de bien"* into siding with the monarchy against that wave of lawlessness. On the other hand, demonstrations by the corporate Parisian poor could, by combining intimidation and encouragement, draw some of the wealthier inhabitants into the laborers' tax revolts.

Early seventeenth-century demonstrations acknowledgedly included many drifters, the chronically unemployed, and peasants who came to market or wandered into Paris seeking relief from rural poverty. But between 1643 and 1648, it was the participation of masons, carpenters, turners, joiners, carters, porters, and boatmen—ordinary semiskilled and unskilled laborers who normally shunned violence—that was particularly noted. In the 1640's these workers were trapped by the high price of bread, which consumed half their daily wages, and by d'Emery's relentless increases in taxes on the capital. Their disenchantment with the regency, their bitter hatred of d'Emery, and their willingness to risk death or injury in riots reveal all too clearly why Anne of Austria was losing control after 1643. No matter whether the wealthier inhabitants of Paris joined their less fortunate neighbors or not, the regent was virtually incapable of handling the explosive situation in the city by 1648.[14]

2

WHILE Parisians and provincials were revolting against taxes, and individual courts and bureaus obstructed the regent's programs, the Parlement of Paris held tenaciously to its position as the most persistent and successful opposition to the regent's policies. There was little coordination of its activities with the actions of other corporations of officers, either in Paris or elsewhere, and connections with uprisings by outside social groups were limited to the area within its jurisdiction, and unpredictable. The six great guilds usually bypassed the Parlement in their negotiations with the administration, although concern by guildsmen and parlementarians over the same issues certainly had the effect of stiffening each group's opposition. Less affluent elements within the Parisian bourgeoisie, and the city's laborers, appealed frequently to the Parlement as well as to the

[14] There is a wealth of information in the Actes Royaux, F 23611, and a good analysis in Bourgeon, "L'Ile de la Cité," pp. 115-120.

administration; but their demonstrations before the Palace of Justice often bore the implied threat that the judges would become victims of the rioters rather than their heroes unless they backed their demands. Those individual parlementarians who were known for their unflinching hostility to royal "tyranny" were far more popular than the conservative royal attorneys and *présidents à mortier* who attempted to reconcile royal needs, parlementary rights, and popular demands. Yet despite all these uncertain relations, the parlementarians as a body became the heroes of rich and poor, the envy of *les grands*, and the de facto leaders of all the scattered forces which were hostile to the regency's policies.

The Parlement's opposition after 1643 can be divided into three categories: clashes over finances from 1644 to 1648, the dispute over the *lit de justice* during the first months of 1648, and a recurring debate on judicial affairs throughout the first five years of the regency. The conflicts over taxation brought the administrators and parlementarians close to an open breach, but ended with the administration yielding. This led directly to a confrontation on the issue of royal and parlementary authority, at which time the judges strengthened their position as a formidable opposition working within the context of royal absolutism. Meanwhile, the discussion of judicial affairs brought into the open all the grievances the officiers of the realm had felt since 1610, and underscored the seriousness of the regent's troubles with the chief tribunal of the kingdom.

The conflicts over finances centered on three major taxes: the *toisé* of 1644-1645, the fee on alienated domains in 1645, and the Paris tariff of 1646-1648. Together, these disputes had several important results. Anne's regime lost prestige as well as income, thus frightening her ministers and inducing them to take drastic punitive measures against the judges. This vindictiveness, in turn, brought the parlementarians closer together, forcing them to subordinate traditional internal animosities to their common interest in defending their corporation. And then the tenuous, but unmistakable, bond of judges and taxpayers made the parlementarians all the more determined to resist unpopular financial legislation.

The *toisé* was the first major issue which reflected all these developments. As introduced in March of 1644, it was a tax of some four to ten million *livres* on the owners of houses, built in defiance of a sixteenth-century law, in the Parisian *faubourgs*. It was to be administered by the petty *châtelet* court, but all appeals were to come before the royal councils, rather than the Parlement of Paris which normally had appellate jurisdiction over that tribunal. The property owners, however, did appeal to the Parlement against the tax, not trusting conciliar judicial decisions. At stake, then, was a potential windfall in revenue, the Parlement's jurisdiction, and the loss of income to property owners (or their tenants, if landlords added the tax to their rental fees). While the *toisé* need not inevitably have been a controversial issue, only skillful handling could have prevented trouble. Mazarin, d'Emery, Anne, and Séguier all share the blame for mishandling the situation. The Parlement of Paris stepped in and took advantage of their blundering.

When the property owners first appealed to the Parlement, the royal attorneys of that tribunal went directly to Mazarin to suggest a way to avoid the crisis. Their spokesman, the very conservative *avocat général*, Omer Talon, requested royal authorization of parlementary hearings on appeals against the tax. This would, he thought, contain the restiveness of his colleagues, and act as a peaceful outlet for the emotional opposition of property owners. Talon warned of the consequences which any affront to the Parlement would bring. The opposition to the tax would spread to tenants who might riot; and any conflict of authority between regent and Parlement might encourage provincial parlements to stiffen their own resistance to royal policies. Séguier insisted that urgent financial necessity required the regent to bypass the slow-moving Parlement, despite the warning, but he was overruled. Mazarin placated the judges somewhat by asking Talon to make a conciliatory report to them. Then, to prevent the Parlement from submitting a remonstrance which it had already drafted, the objectionable tax was withdrawn.[15]

Since that conciliatory gesture left the financial problem unsolved, d'Emery resumed the collection of *toisé* fees three months later—this time through openly authoritarian methods. Instead of the *châtelet*, a special commission of three councilors of state and one maître des requêtes was placed in charge, with all litigation to be handled by the royal councils. Moreover, the commissioners were assisted by two companies of royal guards when they started to assess the property fines in the *faubourgs* of Saint-Antoine and Saint-Germain. Immediately tenants rioted in those areas, while additional demonstrations

[15] Talon, *Mémoires*, pp. 111-113.

by tenants and property owners took place in the heart of the city, near the Palace of Justice. Inside, the parlementarians were adding to the confusion with their own dispute. Conservative and radical judges, alike, resented the heavy-handed way in which the *toisé* had been reimposed, but the conservative senior chambers decided to oppose the regent as diplomatically and indirectly as possible, without listening to the radical chambers' pleas for direct parlementary action. On their own, the senior chambers sent Anne the mild remonstrance which had been tabled when the *toisé* collections had ceased, asking that the Parlement be authorized to hear appeals against assessments. The radicals responded by clamoring for a plenary parlementary session, hoping to control such a meeting by sheer weight of numbers and dictate bolder terms to the senior chambers. Among their aims were a parlementary *arrêt* suspending the *toisé*, and the arrest of the royal commissioners by parlementary order.[16] In turn, the regent's informal council of advisers was thrown into confusion. Mazarin wished to be conciliatory to the Parlement (although no one believed him), but he also wanted money for the war against the Hapsburgs. While he vacillated, the regent and the chancellor made matters worse by taking a much more belligerent stand. Séguier tried to turn the senior and junior parlementarians against each other by flattering the former for their moderate position and accusing the latter of antiroyalist tactics. Anne simply accused the *chambres des enquêtes* and *requêtes* of being the cause of all the disturbances and rioting in Paris, and told one radical to "shut up" when he replied.[17]

The chancellor might have succeeded in splitting the Parlement had Anne held her tongue, but her ill-considered remarks infuriated the senior judges as well as their junior colleagues. Even the most conservative and royalist member of the Parlement, First President Mathieu Molé, was swept along by the current of events. Although he managed to prevent the plenary session which the junior chambers desired, he vigorously defended them in personal conferences with the regent and her ministers, insisting that the Parlement acted as a body, not as individual groups, and that it was slanderous for Anne and Séguier to single out any group within it for censure.

[16] Ibid., pp. 113-116; Ormesson, *Journal* I, 192-196; Molé, *Mémoires* III, 104-106.
[17] Talon, *Mémoires*, pp. 114-117; Goulas, *Mémoires* II, 85; B. N. Ms. Fr. 18367, fol. 77 (draft of a speech by Séguier).

Emboldened by Molé's stand, the *enquêtes* and *requêtes* judges became even more critical of the regent, accusing her of prodigal use of royal revenues and of being too submissive to her advisers. Whether or not the radical judges were directly involved in the rioting which continued in the city and *faubourgs*, those riots became uglier with each passing day. The Parlement closed its ranks against the regent, shifted more and more toward an open break with royal authority, and encouraged the rioters by its opposition to the *toisé*. Anne had to concede defeat. At a special session of the formal council of state, attended by the elder Condé and two of the *toisé* commissioners, as well as Anne's inner group, the tax was drastically altered. Exemptions were granted to religious communities, indigent families, and owners of buildings that had been constructed with royal permission. Still, the modified levy of one million *livres* was too unpopular to be enforced. It was suspended, just as had been the case earlier in 1644.[18]

The dispute over the *toisé* had a bizarre conclusion. In March, 1645, the tax was revived once more, and a single royal commissioner tried to administer the modified levy quietly. Immediate protests in the *faubourgs* of Paris and by senior and junior parlementarians at the Palace of Justice brought an end to its collection. The *toisé* was never revived after this final rebuff, but of course no one could predict at the time. The senior parlementary chambers decided to let the matter rest, but the junior *chambres des enquêtes* and *requêtes* wanted assurances from Anne. President Barillon and Gayant led this new movement. The former tried unsuccessfully to force a plenary parlementary session on the senior chambers, arguing that the Parlement must press for the formal revocation of the *toisé*, rather than accept its informal suspension. Barillon also wanted a statement from the regent that in the future no tax like the *toisé* would be imposed without verification and registration in the Parlement. Gayant chaired a special afternoon session of ninety-four junior judges who discussed how they could force their senior colleagues to authorize the plenary session. The regent responded by having Barillon, Gayant, and two other radical judges arrested and exiled from Paris.[19]

It proved to be a Pyrrhic victory for Anne. She won the principle

[18] Ormesson, *Journal* i, 195-198; Talon, *Mémoires*, pp. 116-117.
[19] Talon, *Mémoires*, especially pp. 139-141.

that the *toisé* should not be formally revoked, but she lost far more. Eventually all the exiled judges except Barillon were released, and his death in a prison far from Paris made him a martyr. She dared not reimpose the tax, and the Parlement was unlikely after such a spectacular achievement to approve future fiscal expedients. The combination of taxpayers' revolt and parlementary obstructionism was sure to be repeated in future, and it was a combination which the regent would find difficult to withstand, short of sheer military reprisals which might cause civil war. The judges did not have to coordinate their activities with those of taxpaying subjects; the mere coinciding of grievances and opposition was enough to endanger the regent's fiscal program.[20]

The most important setback for the administration was its failure to exploit divisions within the Parlement. To be sure, the arrests of leading radical judges helped prevent the special session which they had demanded, but the remaining radicals went on strike to protest the action against their colleagues (though after three months they returned to work). It is particularly noteworthy that Talon and Molé sympathized with the radicals' ultimate aims, despite the first president's disapproval of their strike and their attempts to force a plenary session against the will of the senior parlementarians. In the Parlement, Molé and Talon criticized the radicals; in discussions with Anne and her ministers, they insisted that the punishment of any judge, however radical, was an affront to the entire Parlement. Moreover, the dispute within the Parlement over tactics led to a remarkable informal agreement a few months after the episode of the *toisé* came to an end. The senior chambers remained opposed to convoking plenary sessions automatically when requested by their junior colleagues, but they agreed to settle any future disagreements over convocation through conferences with the judges of *enquêtes* and *requêtes*.[21]

This growth in solidarity was in sharp contrast to the deterioration of relations within administrative circles. One of the councilors of state who had been a member of the *toisé* commission bluntly told Anne that she should have been more conciliatory toward the

---

[20] There is an excellent appraisal of the mood of officiers and Parisians in Goulas, *Mémoires* II, 85-86.

[21] Talon, *Mémoires*, pp. 141-150, 159-161.

Parlement.[22] The fact that this commissaire was Omer Talon's brother and had connections with the parlementarians is less significant than his courage to risk the loss of lucrative positions as councilor and commissaire. Obviously, the possibility of fraternization between councilors and officers was a bad omen for the administration. But the ministers did not know how to deal with either the broadening of the Parlement's *esprit de corps* or the confusion within the administration. Séguier did analyze the problem of parlementary solidarity, but his notes betray his inability to find any foolproof method of dividing and ruling.[23]

As the controversy over the *toisé* died down, d'Emery attempted to make up for the loss of revenue with the tax on alienated royal domains. His hopes for quick parlementary registration were dashed, however, as the judges refused to take any action. Two successive *lettres de jussion* requesting registration by the personal order of the king had little effect. The Parlement evaded the king's will by appending conditions to the legislation. The basic amendment, suggested by the Parlement's royal attorneys, amounted to a veiled veto of the compulsory tax by converting it into a voluntary levy. Not content with that legal chicanery, the parlementarians added a clause requesting that the *conseil d'état* write the voluntary-payment provision into the original tax bill. The judges were, by this clever request, seeking to place their amendment in an impregnable position. So long as the voluntary clause remained a parlementary amendment, it could be overridden by a conciliar *arrêt*; but once the highest council incorporated that amendment into royal legislation, it would bear the stamp of the regent's approval.[24]

Sensing that he could not defeat the parlementarians at their own game of legalistic maneuvering, d'Emery fell back on the use of a *lit de justice*, hoping to end the Parlement's evasions on the tax, once for all. This was a gamble, since Anne's ministers had not yet confronted the judges on the touchy issue of the regent's right to hold such a ceremony. But there seemed to be no other way to overcome the parlementary opposition. The *lit de justice* was held on Septem-

[22] Ibid., p. 149.
[23] B. N. Ms. Fr. 18367, fol. 89. Ranum, *Paris in the Age of Absolutism*, pp. 206-210, has an astute analysis of the controversy over the *toisé*.
[24] See Talon, *Mémoires*, pp. 154-155.

103

ber 7, 1645, one day before the autumn parlementary recess, to ensure that there could be no parlementary debate. The Parlement was thereby outmaneuvered. At the ceremony, Talon and Molé denounced the use of the *lit* to prevent free parlementary suffrage, and the *avocat général* went so far as to claim that his tribunal was a necessary check on tyranny, which he thought was not suited to France, but only to what he termed "oriental" and "southern" lands. However, the Parlement gave way to royal absolutism and registered the contentious tax on domains and some eighteen other fiscal expedients.[25]

This time, opposition outside the Palace of Justice accomplished what the judges had been unwilling to attempt. Indirect taxes enacted at the *lit de justice* were stubbornly resisted by Paris merchants, who threatened to close their shops rather than pay. The tax on royal domains was suspended before organized opposition came to a head. Thus, d'Emery discovered that even the king's personal will was no substitute for free parlementary review of legislation. The Parlement had come to the assistance of taxpayers over the *toisé*; now taxpayers had provided the Parlement with a victory in defeat, showing, by their refusal to pay, that parlementary review alone could convert the king's will into law.[26]

The controversy over the Paris tariff of 1646-1647 was still more damaging to d'Emery's reputation. To avoid parlementary interference, he contended that the tax was a temporary levy or *aide*, subject only to registration by the Cour des Aides of Paris. The finance minister thought that subjects would find the tax equitable and that the Cour des Aides would be compliant. But that tribunal blunted the tax bill's effectiveness, initially by rejecting it on the first reading, and finally, at the end of 1646, by ruling that it could be enforced on a temporary basis only (as d'Emery had said but not intended) and with a sweeping exemption for the produce of the Parisian bourgeoisie's country estates. D'Emery had barely recovered from the shock of that setback when the Parlement began to claim

---

[25] Ibid., pp. 155-159; Ormesson, *Journal* I, 311-312. See the list of financial measures in Forbonnais, *Finances de France* II, 83-84.

[26] See Chéruel, *Minorité de Louis XIV* II, 105 (based on the Venetian ambassador's report); A. N. U 28, fol. 48; and B. N. Ms. Fr. 18367, fols. 95-107. Agitation by the Parlement's junior chambers for a plenary session after the autumn recess may have played a role in the administration's decision to withdraw the edict on the alienated domains. Molé, *Mémoires* III, 158.

that the tariff could not be imposed without its authorization. Significantly, it was the conservative presidents in the *grand chambre*, led by Molé, who directed the parlementary campaign.[27]

One need not examine in detail the maze of technical arguments or the bewildering series of conferences held in the administration's vain effort to defend the tariff. Anne and her ministers were even more confused by this new challenge than they had been during previous clashes with the parlementarians, and the regent was so angry that when she finally agreed to seek a compromise, she refused to see the parlementarians, letting Orléans and her ministers negotiate for her. Mazarin was of little help, wanting to avoid an impasse but not knowing how to conciliate the judges without sacrificing the tax. And d'Emery advocated the use of another *lit de justice*! When Talon made it clear that the parlementarians would reject that expression of royal absolutism, the finance minister tried one ruse after another in a vain effort to avoid parlementary review. First he tried to give the judges just the general tenor of the tariff, but they insisted on seeing the entire declaration. Then he took them into his confidence and gave them an elaborate account of the state's financial situation, but this merely showed them how vulnerable the treasury was and they continued to press for judicial review of the tariff.[28] In desperation, d'Emery tried to steer past the Parlement a group of fiscal measures which included the controversial tariff in disguise. (Technically, the Parlement was asked simply to register the creation of petty police officials, but in fact this new machinery was designed to administer tariff collections.) The finance minister's plan went awry, as parlementary conservatives and radicals took advantage of the fact that they now had an actual body of legislation in their hands, and proceeded to amend or remonstrate against each part.[29] Their most damaging and brilliant attack by far was against

[27] The conflict between administration and Cour des Aides can be followed in Actes Royaux, F 23611, no. 819; and A. N. U 28, fols. 64, 67. The arguments of the parlementarians are in the *Mémoires* of Molé and Talon.

[28] See B. N. Ms. Fr. 18367, fols. 111-128; Talon, *Mémoires*, pp. 197, 200-206, 205, fn. 1.

[29] A tax on the lesser judges, known as *prévôts généraux des maréchaux*, was modified to give the Parlement the right to verify the creation of such offices, and restricted the functions of those officials in accordance with past royal ordinances. New controllers of weights and measures were permitted for two years only and with restricted powers. Remonstrances were made against a forced loan on wealthy merchants and against the creation of a second *châtelet* court in Paris; in Talon's

the disguised tariff. A parlementary amendment reconverted the creation of police officials to the original tariff bill, thereby reasserting the judges' right to register tariffs. Then the parlementarians added a clause stipulating that in future all indirect taxes of a permanent nature must be registered by the Parlement as well as the Cour des Aides of Paris. Finally, the judges placed a two-hundred-thousand-*livre* ceiling on this modified tariff of 1647, thereby virtually vetoing a tax which had an estimated potential of 450 thousand *livres* per annum.[30]

The obstructionism of the judges in 1647, accompanied by lobbying and rioting by merchants, virtually eliminated d'Emery's most promising source of revenue. The *toisé* and the fee on alienated royal domains were both temporary, while the tariff was meant to be permanent. The dispute over the Paris tariff was also a test case for the imposition of tariffs on other cities. In the seventeenth century, indirect taxes were major items in the budgets of most states. They were instrumental in helping the Great Elector of Brandenburg-Prussia build a strong state, and they allowed Charles I of England to rule without Parliament for eleven long years before the Long Parliament was called in 1640. At the end of 1647, d'Emery tried to overrule the Parlement's amendments to his tariff by issuing a conciliar *arrêt*, but that decree, in turn, was countermanded by a parlementary *arrêt*.[31] A belated effort to revive the tax on alienated royal domains at the beginning of 1648 triggered more riots in the capital and unleashed a new storm of protest by radicals in the Parlement. The fact that a few parlementary conservatives agreed to act as tax assessors with the support of royal French and Swiss guards made no impression on taxpayers and *enquêtes* judges. The troops were withdrawn, and the tax was suspended.[32]

By 1648, parlementary emasculation of d'Emery's fiscal program had become so serious that the finance minister was encountering

opinion, these remonstrances amounted to a veiled rejection. In any case, the regent withdrew the edict on the *châtelet* without putting it to the test. Talon, *Mémoires*, p. 207; cf. A. N. U 28, fols. 109-111; Actes Royaux, F 23611, nos. 839, 840. The original creation of *maréchaux* officials in 1641, referred to in the parlementary modification of 1647, is in P. Néron and E. Girard, eds., *Recueil d'édits et d'ordonnances royaux*, 2 vols., Paris, 1750, I, 918-923.

[30] A. N. U 28, fols. 106-109.

[31] Talon, *Mémoires*, p. 207.

[32] Vallier, *Journal* I, 2-9; *Histoire du temps*, 2 vols., Paris, 1649, I, 22-31.

difficulties with the tax farmers and other *traitants*. In 1644, the Parlement had amended a *taxe des aisés*, so that in effect it taxed the hated *traitants* rather than the wealthiest merchants of Paris. The state's creditors naturally threatened to withdraw their loans to the treasury unless the administration stopped this vindictive action of the judges. But every time the finance minister tried to reconvert the *taxe des aisés* to a levy on the merchants, parlementary legalism and merchant lobbying blocked his efforts. D'Emery's practice of borrowing on the security of expected tax revenue therefore also ran into difficulties. The *traitants* knew that the Parlement would probably amend or veto his fiscal legislation and that they would have no way of recovering their investment. They began to withhold advances until the parlementarians accepted the taxes that backed their loans. D'Emery continued to squeeze loans from the *traitants*, but the amount of money they were willing to risk became less and less, and the interest rates they charged became almost prohibitive. When d'Emery tried to regain the confidence of these creditors by having them take their grievances directly to Anne without consulting Mazarin, he offended the chief minister. Mazarin did not watch financial affairs closely, but he would not tolerate any maneuvering which placed a fellow minister between himself and the regent.[33] Outwitted by the parlementarians, estranged from the *traitants*, and suspected by Mazarin, the finance minister was rapidly becoming expendable. He needed a dramatic victory over the parlementarians, and in January 1648, he sought to achieve that goal by combining the suspension of the paulette with another *lit de justice*.

3

ON JANUARY 15, 1648, the nine-year-old Louis XIV held his second *lit de justice* at the Parlement of Paris. There, in the company of his mother, her ministers, and the dukes and peers of the realm, he invoked his personal will and forced the judges to register several financial edicts.[34] As a bloc, these measures were as objectionable to the parlementarians as any of d'Emery's previous expedients. Indeed, they included three proposals which had already been opposed by both judges and taxpayers: the Paris tariff, in the disguised form of

---

[33] See, inter alia, Talon, *Mémoires*, pp. 121-122; Ormesson, *Journal* I, 214-215, 215, fn. 1; Actes Royaux, F 23631 (*arrêts* of the *conseil d'état*), no. 405.

[34] The edicts are in A. N. U 28, fols. 144-147.

new officials in the capital; the sale of new offices in provincial police districts, or *maréchaussées*; and the tax on alienated royal domains. The other edicts were just as controversial. There were to be twelve new maîtres des requêtes, a host of additional offices in the chancellery, and a complicated fee (*franc-fief*) on feudal property acquired by non-nobles. The existing *maîtres* had already joined the Parlement in opposition to Louis XIII's attempts to add to their numbers. The roturier holders of fiefs were bound to complain because the *franc-fief* had not been collected since 1634, and now they were asked to pay all arrears and prepay the fees for an additional eleven years. The sale of offices in the chancellery was anathema to the parlementarians, since that practice had been employed several times in recent years without any judicial review in the sovereign courts. To be sure, a final edict revoked the *taxe des aisés* of 1647, but parlementary remonstrances and opposition by the wealthy merchants had already made its collection impossible; d'Emery was merely making a meaningless formal retraction look like a gracious concession. The use of the controversial *lit de justice* to force registration made these taxes all the more objectionable to the parlementarians, and the *surintendant*'s decision to withhold the renewal of the paulette until the edicts were registered and enforced needlessly provoked them to stiffen their resistance to the taxes all the more, in the hope of forcing him to renew the paulette unconditionally.[35]

Nothing could dissuade Anne and her advisers from injecting so many issues into the ceremony of January 15. Talon denounced the use of the *lit de justice*, itself, but his words fell on deaf ears.[36] He had also warned Mazarin in advance against withholding the paulette, but d'Emery had apparently converted the regent to an uncompromising stand on that issue.[37] Anne never seems to have considered what would happen; that the judges would question her son's authority was unthinkable to this proud Spanish princess. Formal registration was accomplished on January 15, but opposition did emerge. Historians seem to have been unable to understand the con-

---

[35] Molé, *Mémoires* III, 201; Talon, *Mémoires*, p. 222; Ormesson, *Journal* I, 428-429, 433.

[36] Talon, *Mémoires*, pp. 209-212; Chéruel, *Minorité de Louis XIV* II, 500-502 (including footnotes); and H. Mailfait, *Un Magistrat de l'ancien régime. Omer Talon, sa vie et ses oeuvres*, Paris, 1902, p. 230, which notes that the actual speech was harsher than the version in the judge's diary-memoirs.

[37] Talon, *Mémoires*, p. 208.

troversy that erupted in the succeeding weeks, because the Parlement never made an unqualified break with the principle of the king's personal will; after coming precariously close to defiance, its members appeared to resign themselves to the forced registration. What scholars have missed is the fact that parlementary compromising over the principle of royal absolutism obscured their actual victory over the regent. The judges went far enough in opposing the taxes of January 15 to make them unenforceable, while remaining so deferential to royal absolutism that they could not be incriminated as rebels or traitors. This was the great strength of the Parlement in the early months of 1648, and it was to be the key to parlementary actions and successes during the course of the Fronde.

The difficulties encountered by the parlementarians were not dissipated by their arrival at this *via media*. Internal dissension, jealousies, and suspicions (particularly between the senior and junior chambers) never completely disappeared. But the experience gained in earlier controversies, along with the blundering of the regent and her ministers, drew the Parlement more closely together than ever.

Instrumental in achieving that limited *esprit de corps* were the two judges First President Mathieu Molé, and councilor Pierre Broussel of the *grand chambre*. Molé repeatedly tried to outmaneuver his more radical colleagues, and render innocuous their demands for measures which would have utterly denied the principle of royal absolutism, but he was also ready to compromise enough to curb their intransigence. He was a confirmed royalist, but knew that to serve the king he must not lose control of his fellow judges and let them break with absolute monarchy. The first president also knew that monarchy could survive in France only if the king or regent acted in the interest of subjects, and was therefore horrified by the callous and frequent use of arbitrary judicial procedures and taxation which he felt was becoming all too common. In one of his lectures to Anne on her responsibilities, Molé told her eloquently:

One can say to Your Majesty that the greatest advantage a sovereign can possess on earth consists in reigning always by love over his subjects . . . that he cannot commit a graver mistake than to have himself continually obeyed through terror; it is a fatal moment when the majesty which is graven on his countenance, which alone separates him from common men, is not respected for the tender and true sentiments which it conveys to the hearts of the people, but is regarded as the means to obtain what is desired, just or unjust.

Molé was equally convinced that the Parlement of Paris had a right to require responsibility in the actions of the administration. He particularly stressed his tribunal's police authority, and its obligation to advise the king or regent against actions which might incite rebellion.[38] As first president, Molé had immense influence within the Parlement, and he knew how to wield it.

Pierre Broussel, more radical in his views, had no official capacity within his tribunal, but he was just as influential as Molé. He has been universally depicted as a feeble-minded and senile man, though honest and incorruptible. However, a close look at the parlementary debates of early 1648 shows that he had a keen grasp of the legal rights of the Parlement, making him as respected within the Palace of Justice as he was idolized by Parisians outside its walls. Broussel, like Molé, was aware of the legal and practical limits of the rights of the Parlement. Just as Molé moderated his conservatism, Broussel tempered his radicalism. He managed to bring many of his still more radical colleagues around to a compromise with persons like Molé, and persuaded them to abandon outright defiance of the king's will. He was equally effective in dissuading conservatives like Molé from being more deferential to royal authority than was healthy for parlementary authority. Time and again, Broussel would make a ringing speech in favor of parlementary rights, asserting that the king's will could be not only questioned, as Molé believed, but rejected: the commands of God and the welfare of the state stood above loyalty to king or regent. Along with this, the venerable judge knew how to modify his demands sufficiently to sway his more conservative colleagues to his side.[39] Many other parlementary judges were as eloquent and forceful as Broussel and Molé: Talon and Henri de Mesmes, for example, on the conservative side, Le Meusnier and Laisné on the radical side. But it was the first president and the councilor of the *grand chambre* who were to persuade and manipulate in such a way that they achieved the compromises which made the Parlement a formidable opponent of Anne of Austria.

[38] B. U. P. Ms. 64, fols. 16-19; Molé, *Mémoires* III, 225-230.
[39] See the debates in A. N. U 336, especially pp. 29-31, 39.

It did not take long for the Parlement to take up the challenge posed by the *lit de justice* of January 15. While leading members of the Chambre des Comptes and Cour des Aides confined themselves to verbal criticisms of similar ceremonies in their tribunals, the parlementarians began to examine the contents of the legislation which they had been forced to register. This was harmless on the surface, and Molé had personally authorized the investigation—probably thinking that it would provide an outlet for his more radical colleagues who wanted to reject the laws outright, and act as a stiff warning to Anne that she should in future avoid imposing controversial taxes in such highhanded fashion. He managed to persuade the regent that his decision was a proper one, pointing out to her that Louis XIII's *règlement* of 1641 on judicial review permitted remonstrances after a *lit de justice*, and that remonstrances were obviously impossible without a preliminary scrutiny and debate.[40] But actually Molé's decision was a fateful one, since it opened the way for much greater radical parlementary action. *Avocat Général* Omer Talon, writing in his diary-memoirs, noted what would happen: "Freedom to debate," he said, "will result in the option of modifying [laws] and appending conditions which will render void their execution."[41]

This investigation was fateful also because of the involvement of outside interests. Appeals had come in from many groups directly affected by the edicts of January 15. A request by the maîtres des requêtes was particularly urgent. Like the parlementarians, they were incensed by the suspension of the paulette and critical of forced registrations during a minority. Molé chided these archrivals of the Parlement for their previous activities in the councils and intendancies, but the parlementarians were delighted to join forces with a major element within the administration.[42] Astute observers knew that this almost unprecedented coalition was an ominous sign for the regency.[43] The combined resistance of maîtres and parlementarians was soon broadened to include councilors of state and conciliar

---

[40] Molé, *Mémoires* III, 201; A. N. U 28, fols. 134-135.

[41] Talon, *Mémoires*, p. 214.

[42] Ormesson, *Journal* I, 405-414.

[43] F. B. de Motteville, *Mémoires*, Michaud and Poujoulat collection (ser. II, vol. X), Paris, 1838, pp. 146, 149-150; Vallier, *Journal* I, 16; F. A. d'Estrées, *Mémoires*, ed. P. Bonnefon, Paris, 1910, pp. 239-240.

lawyers, who refused to assume the maîtres' functions in the councils when the latter were deprived of them in March.[44]

Outside the Parlement's chambers, Parisians followed its debates with rapt attention, and some news of its actions and reprints of a few speeches reached the provinces. But apart from the continuation of festering opposition by the parlements of Aix and Rouen, most officers outside the capital awaited word of the outcome of the *lit de justice* quietly. The rioting inside Paris, which had occurred as late as early January, came to a halt. The short-lived rebellion in Naples, which had inspired the Parisian rioters to use the rallying cry "*Napoli, Napoli,*" was all but forgotten. Even the civil war in England seems to have been pushed into the background by the Parlement's actions, although the sudden collapse of Charles I's cause during these months would later cast its shadow over the Fronde. Surprisingly, the Spanish-Dutch peace of January 1648, and Mazarin's feverish negotiations to bring an end to the war against Austria, failed to hold the attention of Frenchmen. The Parlement of Paris was the center of attention in France, and every one of its members knew it.

The Parlement of Paris began its attacks on the legislation of January 15 with relatively moderate decisions, then became bolder as its members sensed the ministers' indecision and their own potential power. Parlementary radicals wished to suspend or modify the first edict that came before them, involving royal domains, but conservatives refused to vote for any censure stronger than a remonstrance. Broussel threw his support to the latter, and remonstrances were voted.[45] The regent's advisers sensed trouble, since a remonstrance implied a rejection of the king's will. However, they decided to postpone action and waited for the judges to make the next move.[46] Thinking that the regent accepted the principle of remonstrances, the Parlement decided to see how she would react to an outright modification. After considering milder forms of protest, it decreed that the *franc-fief* should be collected for the fourteen years in arrears alone, forbidding advances on the next eleven years' dues.[47]

[44] The activities of the maîtres des requêtes can be followed in d'Ormesson's *Journal*.

[45] A. N. U 336, pp. 23-31, 37.

[46] Ormesson, *Journal* 1, 441.

[47] A. N. U 336, p. 38. Some judges had wished to limit opposition to remonstrances, while others desired a request for a royal declaration in conformity with

This time, the regent could not avoid replying to the parlementary decision. Unless she acted, the parlementary *arrêt* would become law and take the place of the royal edict.

Anne was no match for the judges. Her demand to see the offensive parlementary decree led to the evasive reply that the Parlement had not meant to modify the king's will, but simply to request an amendment by the regent.[48] Knowing full well that what was meant and what was done were entirely different, the regent tried to make the judges change their modification to a remonstrance. Her aim was politically sound, but her tactics were naïve. Instead of simply insisting that the judges rephrase their modification in the form of a remonstrance, she angrily demanded to know whether they meant to deny the principle of royal absolutism. Anne, Mazarin, the proud Condé, and the well-intentioned Orléans all failed to detect the danger of phrasing Anne's ultimatum as a question;[49] but several contemporaries saw that it might prompt the parlementarians to show that royal authority was not absolute in fact, thereby undermining subjects' obedience to the king. The later Frondeur, Archbishop-Coadjutor Paul de Gondi, expressed the possible consequences succinctly when he said that the stability of the state depended on the myth of royal absolutism. If the Parlement admitted that the monarch's authority was limited, this would tear asunder the "veil" which surrounded the "mystery of the state." Subjects would no longer stand in awe of monarchy; civil war and anarchy would result.[50] The conservative maître des requêtes, Olivier Lefèvre d'Ormesson, was naturally even more horrified at the regent's apparent willingness "to push the Parlement into committing itself to extreme action, if it avowed that it could modify edicts verified in the king's presence."[51]

Ironically, the judges' own hesitation to give Anne an unequivocal answer deepened the crisis caused by her blundering. As the Parle-

---

the parlement's modification. Both proposals were veiled denials of the principle of the king's personal authority, but they left the regent the option of changing the *franc-fief* edict by royal authority. Ibid., pp. 39-40.

[48] Ormesson, *Journal* I, 445-446; A. N. U 336, pp. 42-43.

[49] Talon, *Mémoires*, p. 215, fn. 2; Ormesson, *Journal* I, 417.

[50] P. de Gondi, Cardinal de Retz, *Oeuvres*, ed. A. Feillet et al., 10 vols., Paris, 1870-1896, II, 105-106.

[51] Ormesson, *Journal* I, 448.

ment debated, day after day, the radical judges' speeches became increasingly hostile to royal authority, and their moderate colleagues were drawn further to the left in a desperate attempt to satisfy the radicals and still keep them from a complete break with royal absolutism.[52] Realizing the direction of parlementary debate, First President Molé used one pretext after another to suspend discussion indefinitely.[53] Anne was too emotionally upset to let the issue drop, and demanded an immediate answer to her question.[54] The judges finally found one which combined their customary cleverness with their new-found intransigence. On March 3, 1648, they declared that modification of the *franc-fief* was "subject to the king's good pleasure"—but this statement was merely oral; the modification itself remained on paper and in law.[55] The parlementarians had eluded the regent's pointed question. It was obvious that they had also evaded the king's will.

When Omer Talon notified the regent of this oral statement, he did his best to camouflage its underlying meaning. In a deliberate falsification, the *avocat général* told Anne and her ministers that the Parlement had opposed the king's will only by remonstrances,[56] and did not inform her that "remonstrances" meant modifications; nor did he tell them that a bare majority of judges had adopted the statement of March 3 over the objections of radical colleagues who had opposed even an oral concession.[57] Talon's oratory satisfied Anne either because she really believed him or, more likely, because she wanted to. In any case, she and her ministers decided against repris-

---

[52] A. N. U 336, pp. 44-53.

[53] Talon, *Mémoires*, pp. 215-216; Ormesson, *Journal* I, 452. Molé's tactics included feigning illness, limiting the number of speeches per day (a relatively simple matter, since the Parlement normally met for two hours only, from 8 A.M. to 10 A.M.), and then placing legal business on the agenda without setting a date for resumption of the debate.

[54] Talon, *Mémoires*, pp. 216-217; Ormesson, *Journal* I, 448.

[55] Ormesson, *Journal* I, 455.

[56] Talon, *Mémoires*, p. 217. President de Mesmes later attacked Talon's speech to the regent as being too obsequious. The *avocat général* tried to have the portion of his report referring to remonstrances deleted from the Parlement's registers to avoid further attacks from his colleagues. The episode is indicative of the radical trend within the Palace of Justice. See A. N. U 336, pp. 53-54.

[57] After a parlementary deadlock (70-70), Molé persuaded a few extremist judges to change their votes on a third ballot. The decision avoided an extreme proposal to reject any change, oral or written; it also set aside a more moderate suggestion that written remonstrances be voted. A. N. U 336, pp. 53-54.

als. Chancellor Séguier was able to save some face for the regent by replying to Talon that the regent would consider the parlementary "request" for a royal declaration (i.e., the parlementary modification). He concluded by declaring that it was "advantageous to the welfare of the state that matters of that nature be studied and discussed in the Parlement; and [provided] authority remained with the king, he would willingly receive parlementary counsel."[58] The chancellor meant what he said; but he was too knowledgeable not to know that he was expressing a royalist ideal, not the reality of the moment.[59]

The parlementary judges then turned to the next edict, and by an overwhelming majority (79-39) issued another objectionable decree. The wording of the parlementary decision was more subtle than that of the outright modification of the *franc-fief*. But the effect was the same. The ever-contentious Paris tariff substitute was once more subjected to conditions that destroyed its effectiveness.[60] The regent saw through the judges' action, and this time she was more astute in her response. Rather than raise the question of authority, Anne let it be known that she was contemplating punitive action.[61] This sobered the judges somewhat. First President Molé helped the royal

[58] Talon, *Mémoires*, pp. 217-218.

[59] The Venetian ambassador, as well as Molé, realized that the Parlement's concession was a mere formality. Chéruel, *Minorité de Louis XIV* II, 506, fn. 4; Molé, *Mémoires* III, 206. Kossman's observation that the Parlement's final decision was "a conciliatory proposition," although accurate in describing its effect on the regent, fails to show that the substantive victory belonged to the judges. Cf. Kossman, *La Fronde*, p. 46.

[60] Talon, *Mémoires*, p. 219; A. N. U 336, pp. 63-69; Ormesson, *Journal* I, 459-460. The Parlement's decree was divided into two parts. In the first, the judges substituted their decree of 1647 which had modified the original Paris tariff. That modification included the principle of parlementary verification of all indirect taxes, or *aides!* The second portion was a parlementary request for the regent to revoke the tariff of January 15, 1648. The judges did not include in the decree of 1648 the saving clause "subject to the king's good pleasure." Molé, *Mémoires* III, 206. Rather than drawing back in the face of royal pressures, the parlementarians were becoming more sophisticated, and in a sense more determined, in their opposition.

[61] In order to give the judges every chance to make a gracious surrender, the regent first stated that she would not consider their decree injurious to royal authority until she was able to examine it. When this failed to bring about the desired change, Anne ordered them to come to the royal palace in a body. Behind both royal statements was the obvious threat of force. The regent planned to have the offensive decree torn from the Parlement's registers if the judges dared to bring it unaltered, and to exile the most radical officials of the court. Talon, *Mémoires*, p. 219.

cause by drawing on every resource at his command to make the parlementary decision as palatable to the regent as possible. On one occasion, he put off a parlementary vote which he knew would be unfavorable to royal authority, and had the royal attorneys tell the regent that their colleagues meant to remonstrate against, not modify, the tariff. Later, Molé decided to risk a vote. To ensure a moderate decision, the first president called for balloting before the radical backbenchers in the Parlement could voice their propositions. In addition, he permitted only one vote on all opinions expressed in debate, rather than calling for the customary preliminary poll which reduced all propositions to two or three leading ones. By these unorthodox but shrewd tactics, Molé overpowered his most radical colleagues, and persuaded the Parlement to make an important concession to the regent. On March 17, the amendment to the tariff edict was rephrased so that it became a written remonstrance.[62]

It was a dramatic moment when the parlementarians marched in a body to announce their decision at the nearby Palais Royal. A throng of curious courtiers had gathered to enjoy the climax of the dispute over the *lit de justice*. The regent and her ministers greeted the judges with icy silence. The parlementarians were outwardly calm but inwardly fearful that their capitulation might prove too limited to save them from punishment. But obviously they satisfied Anne and her advisers, for as soon as they notified the regent of their decision to remonstrate instead of insisting on the amendment, the hostile atmosphere vanished from the reception hall.[63]

But how justified was the regent's joy? She had won a formal victory for the principle of royal absolutism, but the shift from modification to remonstrances actually left the tariff edict unenforced. It was the same with edicts increasing the numbers of maîtres des requêtes and other officers, which were subjected to a similar mild form of protest during the last days of March.[64] Until the remonstrances were actually read to the regent and the Parlement accepted her reply, the edicts were not legally binding on subjects. The Parlement had merely notified the ministers that it *would* remonstrate;

---

[62] A. N. U 336, pp. 82-84, 87-91; Ormesson, *Journal* I, 462-463; Talon, *Mémoires*, p. 220.

[63] Ormesson, *Journal* I, 464.

[64] A. N. U 28, fols. 150, 156; Talon, *Mémoires*, p. 221.

time alone would tell what the maneuvering over remonstrances would produce. Moreover, the formal modification of the edict regulating the *franc-fief* was not changed by the judges' decision to limit attacks on the other edicts to remonstrances; as has been seen, the chancellor had merely said that he would treat that amendment as a remonstrance. It was certainly the intention of the parlementary radicals and the hope of their more conservative colleagues that their wishes would still prevail. Both groups in the Parlement wanted the edicts to be modified along the lines they had suggested, but they were willing to let the regent have the honor of making the changes as the act of an absolute ruler. The parlementarians' concession was thus a diplomatic one. There was, to be sure, a motive of fear as well as one of hope: the Parlement had yielded ground in order to prevent recrimination. But this halting exercise in legalism was to be the basis of successful opposition by the Parlement during the Fronde. Couching their demands in royalist language and hiding behind the ruse that formal decisions were made by the monarch rather than by themselves, the parlementarians had discovered that they could oppose the king's will and still avoid the type of punishment reserved for rebels and traitors.

The judges had stumbled unconsciously on this combined offensive and defensive tactic. Even the first president reacted more out of desperation than coolheaded Machiavellism as he outmaneuvered the parlementary radicals and tempered their self-defeating extremist position. After the original decision for an outright amendment to the tariff edict, Molé had lamented: "Messieurs, this will be our last debate, and we are depriving ourselves of the means to serve the people."[65] The junior *avocat général*, Jérome Bignon, predicted that this dispute would start a chain reaction of parlementary intransigence, tyrannical royal response, and finally sedition by subjects on behalf of the embattled judges.[66] Yet, out of the fearful reaction of parlementary conservatives was born a potent and positive weapon of the parlementary Fronde.

The aftermath of the Parlement's delicately balanced position of March 17 on judicial review was a fitting, if inconclusive, ending to the dispute over the principle of royal absolutism. Early in April

[65] Ormesson, *Journal* 1, 462.
[66] Ibid. 1, 464.

1648, Molé presented the Parlement's remonstrances to the regent. On April 23, the chancellor gave her answer: pressing state needs made any royal modification or withdrawal of the edicts impossible.[67] The Parlement did not respond immediately to this rejection of its stand against taxes, but only because its first president deliberately delayed his report of Séguier's reply. Molé knew that as soon as he made that reply official, the *chambres des enquêtes* would raise a storm of protest. In fact, the *enquêtes* judges grew tired of waiting for Molé to speak, and on May 4 stormed into the *grand chambre* to demand a plenary session on the chancellor's reply, which had leaked out.[68]

This sequel to the conflict over the *lit de justice* has never been brought out by historians, because nothing actually happened during the uncertain days of April and early May. But the regent's administration realized what was transpiring, and what was likely to be the ultimate result, as a remark in the unpublished papers of Pierre Broussel shows. The royal family had planned to leave Paris on May 3 for a customary spring vacation in the countryside. Preparations were abruptly halted, and the regent, princes, and courtiers stayed in Paris in order to "try to bring the Parlement around to changing part of what it has done."[69] When this remark is placed side by side with the well-known fact that Anne's regime was resurrecting the issue of the paulette at precisely this time, it becomes clear what the regent's strategy was. Having failed to subdue parlementary resistance to the edicts of January by temporarily suspending the paulette at the beginning of the year, Anne's advisers decided in April to renew that privilege in such a way that the parlementarians would be more cooperative: they were granted the paulette on relatively traditional terms, while it was offered to the other sovereign courts of Paris on condition that their members pay an exorbitant fee, and withheld from the maîtres des requêtes. Parlementary judges were thus being tempted with a bribe in return for a real, rather than nominal, capitulation on the issue of the taxes of January 15. Moreover, the Parlement was being invited to remain aloof from the other officiers of Paris. The regent sought in particular to detach that sovereign court from the maîtres des requêtes, who

[67] Molé, *Mémoires* III, 207-214; Ormesson, *Journal* I, 478-479.
[68] A. N. U 336, pp. 97-98.
[69] B. N. Ms. Baluze 291, fol. 114r.

had stiffened their opposition when the Parlement agreed to make a remonstrance against the creation of additional maîtres.[70]

Thus "mere" remonstrances had already proved to be a very potent weapon against the regent. If her advisers thought that they could override the remonstrances by employing the weapon of the paulette, they received a disagreeable surprise. While the ministers looked back to the issue of the taxes of January, the parlementarians looked ahead to the new issue of the paulette. Radical members of the Parlement immediately changed their tactics. They now insisted that they did not want a plenary session to debate the chancellor's rejection of the remonstrances. Instead, they demanded a full parlementary assembly to discuss the paulette![71] They did not treat the issue of remonstrances lightly, but they saw in the paulette a far more attractive controversy. That issue would, in fact, lead to the parlementary Fronde, the defeat of the taxes of January 15, and, ultimately, the collapse of the governmental revolution which had been in process since 1610.

Molé was horrified at the radicals' change in tactics, for he was trying to bridge the widening chasm between regent and Parlement—to make the monarchy responsible, but not to undermine its powers. Indeed, he sought in vain to turn the radicals' attention from the paulette to the remonstrances![72] Nevertheless, the first president, avocats généraux, and other parlementary conservatives were not as far apart from their militant colleagues as Molé's anguish suggests. In tactics, conservatives and radicals still parted company; the former wanted to save the fiction of royal absolutism, while many of the latter had voiced opinions in recent weeks which denied the regent's right to override parlementary arrêts.[73] But the conservatives were almost as disturbed by so-called royal "tyranny" as by the inflammatory language of their colleagues. In delivering the Parlement's remonstrances to Anne in April, Molé had shocked the regent and delighted his colleagues with an untempered, almost intemperate, attack on her administration's policies. He pleaded against the rising level of taxation, but he denounced the forced registration of January 15. To suppress free parlementary voting on royal legislation, he

[70] See chap. 5.
[71] A. N. U 336, pp. 98-104.　　　[72] Ormesson, *Journal* I, 485-486.
[73] The debates can be followed in detail in A. N. U 336. Doolin, *The Fronde*, contains excerpts from several speeches recorded in that journal.

thundered, was not only contrary to tradition but might lead to rebellion, since it deprived subjects of their only means of making their grievances known to the king.[74] There was a limit to the patience of responsible conservatives like Molé, Talon, Bignon, and de Mesmes. They had managed to keep the Parlement united during the past weeks, both by outwitting and yielding to their junior colleagues. Mazarin certainly erred in accusing Molé and Talon of letting the radicals run rampant.[75] In the emotionally charged atmosphere of the spring of 1648, it would be easier for these conservatives to be swept along by the current of protests in the Palace of Justice and on the streets of Paris than to stand firmly for the principle of responsible absolutism, which was being attacked by their colleagues and undermined by the regent's intransigence.

4

DURING these first years of Anne's regency, the tax controversies of 1644-1647 and the furor of 1648 were accompanied by an equally important, but quieter, debate on judicial affairs. The Parlement of Paris again took the lead, assuming a much more aggressive posture than it had under Louis XIII. As early as 1644, its members investigated alleged sovereign judgments by an intendant named Favier, at Alençon. We know nothing of the results, but the incident was followed immediately by a similar parlementary challenge. A maître des requêtes had angered the parlementarians by handing down a sovereign judgment in the conciliar tribunal known as the *"requêtes de l'hôtel."* Despite several conciliar *arrêts*, the Parlement insisted on overruling this rival body. By perseverance, the administration finally overcame the parlementarians' opposition. However, the incident so shocked one knowledgeable contemporary that he predicted the collapse of royal authority unless the regent remained firmly in support of the councils on such matters. This was no idle chatter; before the year ended, the parlementarians were discussing the possibility of presenting comprehensive remonstrances on all grievances related to justice.[76]

By 1645, the Parlement had decided to prepare those remonstrances. Chancellor Séguier tried in vain to dissuade the judges from

[74] Molé, *Mémoires* III, 207-214.
[75] Talon, *Mémoires*, pp. 200-201; Ormesson, *Journal* I, 464-465.
[76] Ormesson, *Journal* I, 140, 150, 217-220.

making such a sweeping investigation, but the Parlement was adamant. When he held a conference with the parlementary *gens du
roi* in an effort to delay the investigation, those royal attorneys simply gave an oral version of their tribunal's remonstrances. They
denounced general evocations of suits to the councils, pointing out
that these permanently deprived the Parlement of all litigation falling within the categories evoked. The evocation of specific suits was
subjected to a milder but equally determined attack. The attorneys
also criticized conciliar *arrêts* which quashed parlementary decisions,
arguing that they delayed justice and caused financial hardship for
the litigants. Finally, intendancies and other special agencies of the
councils were bitterly assailed. The *gens du roi* conceded that maîtres
des requêtes could act as commissioners and even hand down judgments, but they demanded that the maîtres make their decisions as
officiers, not as commissaires. This meant that litigants could appeal
to the Parlement for a reversal of the maîtres' judgments. It also ruled
out any preliminary or sovereign judgments by those intendants who
had no formal judicial office (such as a mastership); these individuals could only suggest criminal proceedings by local courts in the
bailliages or *présidiaux*. It is obvious that the parlementarians were
acting through self-interest with these remonstrances. However, the
attorneys were able to back up their attacks on the loss of functions
and fees with specific references to the great sixteenth-century ordinances which had guarded against the misuse of conciliar *arrêts*,
evocations, and special commissions.[77]

The royal attorneys did not impress Séguier with their knowledge
of French law, or obtain any real concessions from him. However,
Séguier took particular care to discuss the legal niceties of each point
at issue.[78] He must have felt that his knowledge of law, backed by
royal authority and power, was sufficient to hold the parlementarians
in check. Instead, his willingness to employ legal arguments encouraged the parlementarians to do the same. Immediately, the Parlement ordered the enforcement of all royal laws restricting the cassation of parlementary decisions, evocation of suits from its chambers,
and creation of extraordinary commissions encroaching on its jurisdiction. To be sure, such a general pronouncement meant nothing
by itself. However, the parlementarians placed direct pressure on the

---

[77] Molé, *Mémoires* III, 117-119; Talon, *Mémoires*, pp. 135-137, 135, fn. 1.
[78] Talon, *Mémoires*, pp. 137-138. See also chap. 3.

persons most involved in such activities by forbidding entry to any maître des requêtes who usurped parlementary functions.[79] In 1647, the parlementarians became bolder: they forbade litigants to bypass the Parlement and appeal to the councils or special commissions, if the suits were within the parlementarians' jurisdiction. At the same time, they decreed that all trials which had been evoked to conciliar bodies, and were still in process, should be returned immediately to the Parlement. We do not know the results of these decisions, but they were a dramatic indication of the Parlement's growing impatience and its willingness to move from mere words to action.[80]

As in the case of financial legislation, parlementary agitation over purely judicial matters after 1643 involved the older, most conservative judges as well as their junior colleagues. Indeed, one suspects that where executive justice was in question, the royal attorneys and the first president were the leaders of attacks by the Parlement. Certainly they were highly vocal. In 1645, Molé bitterly denounced the arbitrary exiling of parlementary judges, even though he knew that Anne's actions were based on the suspicion of treasonable activities by these men. What offended the first president most was the implication that the regent did not trust his tribunal to mete out justice to its own members on matters of state concern. Although he received no satisfaction, Molé pointedly told Anne and Séguier that the Parlement did not approve of factions and rebelliousness, and challenged them to let the exiles stand trial in that high court if they wanted to prove their guilt.[81]

In 1647, the first president showed still more clearly that his sympathies lay with his fellow judges and the king's subjects on the issue of conciliar justice. In a conference on tariffs, he reminded Anne that at the beginning of her regency, in 1643, she had resolved "to stop the disorderliness which reigned everywhere [and] to begin restoring to the Parlement its original lustre." Molé argued that the Parlement and other courts of the realm held the keys to internal peace, but only if their authority was respected by the Crown could the officers "keep everyone obedient." He took up the themes the royal attorneys had expounded so eloquently in 1645 concerning the toisé, and challenged the regent to return to the spirit of 1643. As

[79] Ibid., p. 138; Ormesson, *Journal* 1, 252-253.
[80] A. N. U 28, fol. 91; Ormesson, *Journal* 1, 389-390.
[81] Talon, *Mémoires*, pp. 144-145.

was the case at the time of Talon's appeal to Mazarin in 1645, Molé feared the imminence of disorders and widespread rebellion by the king's subjects.[82] So disenchanted was Molé with the regent's polarizing policies that he exclaimed to her, later that year, in the midst of a bitter speech: "What ravages, what violence is committed in the exacting [of taxes]! It is harder . . . to pass [safely] from province to province, even to leave one's house, than to enter the [Spanish] enemy's homeland."[83]

As the summer of 1648 approached, the Parlement of Paris found itself in a stronger position than at the beginning of the year, and far stronger than it had been in 1643. Through skillful leadership and internal compromises it had taken advantage of the weaknesses and blunders which were so characteristic of Anne of Austria's administration. Without directly allying itself with other sovereign courts or uniting fully with taxpayers, it had done much to undermine the bases of royal attacks on officiers and subjects, just as their related opposition had helped, in turn, to make the Parlement's resistance more effective. By the spring of 1648, d'Emery's financial program was at a standstill; the Parlement was highly critical of the finance minister's handling of fiscal problems, and subjects were in no mood to pay even customary taxes. The councils and intendants remained in a relatively strong position in matters of criminal justice, but Chancellor Séguier was hard-pressed to justify their actions to the parlementarians. In external affairs, the normal winter truce had been followed by the resumption of campaigns between French and Spanish forces, particularly in the Spanish Netherlands, even as the German phase of the international war was coming to a close. The regent was thus left without any assurance that troops could be recalled to Paris, if popular rioting and parlementary obstructionism resulted in further deterioration of royal power.

The situation had come about without a civil war, without even a categorical denial of royal absolutism by the parlementary judges. Try as she did, the regent could not come to grips with an opposition which cloaked its every act with the mantle of legalism. On Louis XIV's accession, Anne had actually been unable to secure a loyalty oath by parlementarians to the new monarch; it was argued that since their loyalty and their offices were perpetual, these did not

[82] Ibid., pp. 199-200; Molé, *Mémoires* III, 170-172; A. N. U 28, fol. 77.
[83] Molé, *Mémoires* III, 186-187; A. N. U 28, fols. 99-100.

require confirmation on the death of a king.[84] Then, in 1645, the Parlement had argued without rebuttal that it was the equal of royal councils, except for the occasions when the king personally authorized conciliar encroachments on parlementary functions.[85] Finally, as the Parlement was in the process of evading the king's will, itself, after the *lit de justice* of January 1648, *Avocat Général* Talon had the effrontery to tell Anne that his tribunal never really acted as a sovereign body, since its decisions were always reversible if the king wished to exercise his "good pleasure" and override them.[86]

At this critical moment in the history of Louis XIV's minority, the regent was still in a position to reach an accord with the Parlement of Paris, her other corporations, and ordinary subjects. If her regime satisfied the Parlement and other sovereign courts on the new issue of the paulette, it might avoid civil war, which had undermined royal authority in Spain and was on the point of destroying the monarchy in England. The Parlement of Paris had not yet attempted to overthrow major elements of the administration's machinery, and its members still hesitated to unite with other dissident corporations or with outside social groups. But the new controversy over the paulette was precisely the issue which could lead to such developments, if Anne and Mazarin mishandled the delicate situation.

[84] Talon, *Mémoires*, pp. 88-90, 90, fn. 1.
[85] Talon, *Mémoires*, pp. 150-154; Ormesson, *Journal* 1, 298-301. See also Mousnier, "Le Conseil du roi," p. 66.
[86] A. N. U 336, pp. 82-84; Ormesson, *Journal* 1, 462-463; Talon, *Mémoires*, p. 220.

CHAPTER FIVE

THE CHAMBRE SAINT LOUIS
AND STATE REFORM

POLITICAL EXPEDIENCY called for unconditional renewal of the paulette by Anne of Austria and her ministers in the spring of 1648. D'Emery's temporary suspension of the privilege in January had proved futile; instead of frightening the Parlement of Paris into accepting the *lit de justice* of January 15, the finance minister had stiffened its resistance. Why, then, did the regent think that she could gain anything by bargaining in March and April? Why were petty officers offered that privilege in March on financial terms which turned past hardships into economic disaster? Why were the sovereign courts asked at the end of April to sacrifice their salaries for the following four years in return for the paulette, while the maîtres des requêtes were deprived of the paulette itself? And why was the Parlement of Paris alone in having no condition imposed beyond the traditional one of paying a special fee?[1] Such offers were unlikely to pay either financial or political dividends. The officials who were asked to waive future payment of salaries had already suffered the partial suspension of this income in the early 1640's; and the *trésoriers* had virtually no salary payments by 1648. Income from these lost salaries in mid-1648 would add very little revenue to the treasury. On the contrary, such conditions would be more likely to goad officers into demanding payment of arrears (which amounted to some five million *livres* since 1644 in the case of the *trésoriers* alone). Moreover, the attack on salaries was bound to turn the officers' wrath on the *traitants*, who had been paid the tax revenue set aside for officers' salaries. In the case of the maîtres, it was foolhardy to assume that the outright loss of the paulette would force them to end their four-month feud with the administration. It was also naïve to believe that the judges of the Parlement of Paris, who had been the most vociferous critics of Anne's administration, would stand by

---

[1] For the renewal, see Actes Royaux, F 23611, nos. 882, 887; F.N.B. Dubuisson-Aubenay, *Journal des guerres civiles*, ed. G. Saige, 2 vols., Paris, 1883-1885, I, 13, 18; Talon, *Mémoires*, p. 222. The administration's strategy can be followed in Talon, *Mémoires*, pp. 271, 300.

in the spring of 1648 and let other corporations accuse them of being bribed into silence by special treatment over the paulette. Even if the parlementarians were tempted to remain aloof from the controversy, they had little reason to consider Anne's treatment of them benevolent. In their case, the traditional fee entailed a greater financial sacrifice than the loss of their very low salaries.[2] Any parlementary judge who took a moment to compute the difference could tell that the regent was helping her treasury, not his pocketbook. All one can say in defense of the administration's manipulation of the paulette is that Louis XIII had attempted the same thing, and that persons like d'Emery and Séguier thought it might, in the long run, coerce the officiers into submission. But if that was their contention, they must have had extreme *sang-froid*, or the compulsive gambler's urge, given the political climate which had developed during the first five years of the regency.

At any rate, the regent and her ministers were surprised by the nature and extent of the reaction. The usually proroyal Grand Conseil joined the Chambre des Comptes and Cour des Aides of Paris in a common effort to lobby for better terms. On May 4, representatives of the three courts met at the Cour des Aides—without the usual wrangles over the ranking of each tribunal—and decided to ask the Parlement of Paris to join them. At the Parlement, there was strong support for these sister courts, and in preliminary discussions several parlementarians urged that their tribunal support not only the other sovereign courts of Paris but also the lesser officiers within their jurisdictional boundaries. The four maîtres des requêtes who represented their colleagues in the Parlement also made an emotional appeal for protection. They were warmly received, and President de Mesmes told his fellow judges that they should continue the support they had been giving to the maîtres since the previous winter.[3]

The most significant development took place in the Parlement of Paris on May 13, 1648, when parlementary radicals joined with their conservative colleagues in issuing an *arrêt de union*. This act of union called for special meetings by representatives of the four sovereign courts of Paris in the Chambre Saint Louis of the Palace of Justice—ostensibly to discuss the related issues of salaries and the

---

[2] A. de R. Bazin, *Histoire de France sous Louis XIII et sous le ministère du Cardinal Mazarin*, 4 vols., Paris, 1846, III, 390-391. See also Charmeil, *Les Trésoriers de France*, p. 267, fn. 160; Actes Royaux, F 23611, no. 887.

[3] A. N. U 336, pp. 98-119; Ormesson, *Journal* I, 482-491.

paulette.[4] The parlementary decree dramatically changed the nature of the dispute between officers and administration. On the surface, the *arrêt* of May 13 was not a revolutionary pronouncement—the sovereign courts of Paris had occasionally combined to organize the defense of the capital against foreign invaders or to protest alleged mistreatment by a monarch. However, the background of royal-official relations since 1643 and the current dispute over the paulette made this latest *arrêt de union* a unique act. There could be no doubt that a special assembly of the four courts at this time could easily lead to the reversal of the governmental revolution undertaken by Louis XIII and his widow. And the fact that the prestigious Parlement of Paris had advocated joint sessions in the Chambre Saint Louis made the administration's position especially precarious. No one in the administration had entertained the slightest thought that the parlementary judges would join their fellow officers, and even when the parlementarians had started to discuss the issue, Anne's ministers confidently believed that the Parlement would never unite with the other tribunals and, if this were so, that they could handle any united resistance by the other officiers.[5]

The most obvious fear in royal circles, now, was that the four courts in the capital would undermine royal absolutism by the very fact of their agreement to meet in special assembly. Chancellor Séguier told members of the Parlement that "to establish in Paris an assembly of fifty or sixty persons, to transform four sovereign companies into a fifth without legitimate authority ... can be dangerous and prejudicial to the order of public government."[6] A conciliar *arrêt* against the parlementary *arrêt de union* stated the issue more explicitly:

> Officials have no authority beyond what is given them by kings to be exercised according to strict rules prescribed for them.... Royal authority cannot permit, without being weakened, that officials exercise their [delegated authority] by means of a violent usurpation with the object of opposing the will of their king and master. ... To permit any extraordinary assembly without the king's consent and will would be tantamount to creating a new power.[7]

[4] A. N. U 336, p. 120; A. N. U 28, fol. 163v.
[5] Ormesson, *Journal* 1, 488-489.
[6] Talon, *Mémoires*, pp. 224-225.
[7] *Journal contenant tout ce qui s'est fait et passé en la cour de Parlement de Paris*, Paris, 1649, pp. 5-6.

Naturally, the regent and her ministers did not care to disclose their personal reasons for objecting to the assembly, even though everyone knew that their fears stemmed most of all from the vulnerability of d'Emery's financial administration and person. So many individuals in high political and courtly positions were plundering the treasury that no one could predict what heads might fall if the sovereign courts investigated finances. Some courtiers even thought that Mazarin's position as chief minister could be challenged (on the ground that he was a foreigner). It was widely rumored, also, that the Chambre Saint Louis might go beyond such attacks on individual ministers and courtiers, and condemn intendancies, conciliar authority over the courts, special criminal commissions, unverified taxes, and fiscal expedients of dubious legality. It was even thought possible that all the realm's tribunals and bureaus might appeal to the Chambre Saint Louis for redress of past and present grievances.[8]

From mid-May to the end of June 1648, the administration fought a losing battle to place the various corporations on the defensive, unable even to control the courts and bureaus in the most poorly informed outlying provinces. (A sketchy, garbled report of a "League and Junction" at Paris was enough to incite seditious pamphleteering in Guienne and to inspire the Parlement of Bordeaux to demand royal concessions for its members.)[9] The difficulties posed by widespread provincial agitation were compounded by the central administration's miscalculation of the tactics of the provincial officials. Assuming that the outlying sovereign courts would lodge appeals or send delegates to the Chambre Saint Louis, Anne's ministers instructed the provincial governors to prevent this. Consequently, the governors wasted time and energy devising schemes to block a provincial-Parisian union which most local courts did not seek, while the officiers in their area set as their goal the more realistic objective of assailing the local machinery of the regent's administration. What the ministers in Paris had failed to perceive was the provincial courts' parochialism: regional judges were willing enough to take advantage of the regent's troubles in the capital—even to the point of accepting any reforms which their Parisian counterparts

---

[8] Talon, *Mémoires*, pp. 222-223; Ormesson, *Journal* I, 492-493; J. B. Perkins, *France under Mazarin, with a Review of the Administration of Richelieu*, 2 vols., New York, 1886, I, 400 (based on the Venetian ambassador's reports).

[9] Mousnier, *Lettres et mémoires adressés au Chancelier Séguier* II, 878.

could wring from Anne—but they avoided, for the most part, any formal connection which would restrict their freedom to bargain over local reforms and perhaps reduce them to ciphers of the Paris judges. Moreover, when governors tried to deal with local grievances, they rarely knew how to handle the contagion of opposition. The most prestigious governors were somewhat more successful than others, but we know little about their specific efforts and less of the results. The Duke of Longueville rushed to Normandy in a frantic effort to placate the Parlement of Rouen. The *Grand* Condé was busy with the campaign against the Spaniards and had to hope that his messages and offers of concessions would contain the Parlement of Dijon. The Duke of Orléans made a concerted effort to win royal concessions for the Parlement of Toulouse.[10] (That tribunal did respond by helping to put down an uprising against the *gabelle*.) However, Orléans was an absentee-governor of the province of Languedoc, and his absence weakened the efforts by lesser royal agents to keep the local parlementarians from agitating for their own tribunal's interests. Other governors who had far less illustrious names ran into one misfortune after another. The Duke of Epernon tried to keep his province of Guienne quiet by offering to mediate between the Parlement of Bordeaux and the regent, but his offer was construed as an insult to the tribunal's junior members. In Brittany, the Parlement of Rennes had a fiscal agent of the administration hanged, despite contrary orders from the *conseil d'état*.[11]

The *trésoriers* and *élus* reacted somewhat differently from the provincial parlementarians since they had permanent representatives in the capital as well as their local machinery. Ten days after the parlementary *arrêt de union*, the syndicate of *trésoriers* published an open letter to the Parlement of Paris, requesting authority to seize five million *livres* from the *traitants* who had pocketed the revenues allotted for their salaries. At the same time, that assembly sent a circular to all bureaus of *trésoriers*, stating that it would take appropriate measures, and asking them to assist its efforts. The local *trésoriers* were requested to unite quickly with the other officials in their localities, and to forward to Paris any documents which revealed "the bad conduct of the intendants . . . and *traitants*." The response from

---

[10] B. N. Ms. Baluze 291, fols. 106-110.

[11] Ibid., fol. 110v; Mousnier, *Lettres et mémoires adressés au Chancelier Séguier* I, 828, 830, 878; Ormesson, *Journal* I, 493.

the provinces was not entirely favorable—one *trésorier* promptly handed his copy of the circular to a local intendant. The movement was serious enough to disturb the regent's administration, however, and on receiving the copy from the intendant, d'Emery arrested six officiers who had signed the original circular. This repressive action, instead of intimidating the syndicate in Paris, led that assembly to send new copies to the provinces, with the names of the signatories discreetly omitted.[12] Meanwhile, the syndicate of *élus* continued to press its own case and to appeal to the Paris Cour des Aides.[13]

Anne's administration, however, was disturbed most of all by the union of the sovereign courts in the capital. The ministers' first response was an oblique attack on the *arrêt de union* of May 13. Five days after that parlementary decree had been voted, the regent withdrew her conditional offer of the paulette to the sovereign courts. This meant that the officials' salaries would no longer be subject to forfeiture, but it also meant that the paulette was being withheld. The ministers thought that this double-edged tactic would bring the judges to their senses. The sovereign courts would no longer have any justification for convoking the Chambre Saint Louis, since salaries were no longer in question. It was assumed that the judges could not use that extraordinary assembly to secure the paulette since this was a privilege, and not a right as in the case of salaries. If the sovereign tribunals wanted the paulette, they had only to make a new financial offer in lieu of the loss of salaries. The underlying assumption of the ministers was that the sovereign courts would now be forced to bargain separately, thereby engendering distrust between them.[14]

This was clever reasoning, but it failed to influence the sovereign courts of Paris. They were more determined than ever to force the regent to renew the paulette on customary terms, and they had no intention of discarding the Chambre Saint Louis as a vehicle for collective bargaining. Moreover, the ministers blundered in including the Parlement of Paris in the new arrangement. Anne's ministers intended to punish the parlementarians for their *arrêt de union*. Instead, they strengthened the bonds between the Parlement and the

---

[12] Charmeil, *Les Trésoriers de France*, pp. 268-271; Talon, *Mémoires*, p. 233, fn. 1.

[13] Esmonin, *La Taille en Normandie*, pp. 110-112.

[14] Ormesson, *Journal* I, 492; Dubuisson-Aubenay, *Journal* I, 20. The revocation is in Actes Royaux, F 23611, no. 890.

other courts, since the parlementarians were now asked to bargain for the paulette instead of receiving it in return for a customary fee. Predictably, the radicals in the Parlement began to press the first president to execute the decree of union immediately, and just as predictably, the other three courts agreed not to make separate arrangements with the administration. For a few days there was speculation that the regent would break the impasse by compromising on the paulette. Then the *conseil d'état* made the fatal mistake of arresting members of the Grand Conseil and Cour des Aides for delivering messages between their tribunals. The sovereign courts were shaken by this arbitrary act, but nevertheless, all exchanged messages of sympathy and renewed support. Even the maîtres des requêtes joined in the emotional display of solidarity, sending their condolences to the Grand Conseil and Cour des Aides.[15]

It is difficult to say who was responsible for the heavy-handed tactics of the administration, or whether there even was one single person who coordinated the counterattack. Mazarin was becoming more and more concerned about the possible effect of the internal troubles on the European war and the negotiations for peace with Austria. On June 2, the chief minister wrote to Longueville of his bewilderment, saying that he did not know what the sovereign courts really wanted, but that he was determined to halt their activities.[16] Séguier echoed the chief minister's concern when he conferred with a delegation from the Parlement of Paris two weeks later, speaking gravely of the appearance on the frontier of Hapsburg forces which had "come to evaluate the disaffection of the people and to discover if the news which had been written to them about the divisions [among Frenchmen] was accurate."[17]

Anne's ministers persisted in trying to halt the officers' movement, but the Parlement of Paris stood in the way of repression. That court had changed the character of the crisis with its *arrêt de union.* Now, in early June, its members forced Molé to call a plenary session to discuss the advisability of insisting on the Chambre Saint Louis' meeting in defiance of the administration. The first president had been desperately avoiding such a debate for weeks, although his motives differed from those of Anne's advisers. He simply did

[15] Ormesson, *Journal* I, 492-507.
[16] J. Mazarin, *Lettres,* ed. P. A. Chéruel, 9 vols., Paris, 1872-1906, I, 127.
[17] Charmeil, *Les Trésoriers de France,* p. 270.

not want a direct clash of royal and parlementary authority, and had attempted to entice his colleagues into negotiations over the paulette.[18] They had refused, just as had members of the other sovereign courts; and when the parlementary debate began, they vented their rage against the administration in speech after speech. On June 10, the *conseil d'état* quashed the parlementary *arrêt de union*, but the debate on its implementation continued. One conservative judge, Hilerin, was viciously criticized for supporting an "unlimited monarchy" when he exclaimed, "What do you want to do, Messieurs, draw the sword against the king and measure it against his own?" The Parlement concluded its debate with a majority of thirty-two voting for immediate sessions of the Chambre Saint Louis.[19]

Courtiers and ministers were stupefied. After considering the extreme punishment of exiling the parlementarians *en masse* from Paris, the regent decided to call the entire court to the Palais Royal and tear the *arrêt de union* from the parlementary register while the judges watched. The confrontation was just as dramatic as the similar encounter over the tariff edict in March. But this time the parlementarians refused to make the slightest concession. As they marched to the royal residence on June 16, thousands of Parisians lined the streets and shouted encouraging words. And when the regent met the judges, she discovered that they had left the register in the Parlement! She could not destroy the offensive decree of May 13, and the presence of a hostile crowd outside the palace made punitive measures against the judges an impossibility. She and her ministers had to be satisfied with threatening the most radical judges with punishment unless the conciliar *arrêt* forbidding the Chambre Saint Louis was obeyed. Anne must have known that these stern words were useless. Molé answered her charge that the radicals were rebels with the retort that the Parlement was indivisible, and its members must all be treated as loyal subjects or as enemies of the king.[20]

What Anne construed as a question of authority, and Mazarin viewed as a blow to his foreign policy, was both more and less than those two vital issues. It was less, because in the realm of foreign

---

[18] B. N. Ms. Fr. 18367, especially fols. 172r, 211.

[19] A. N. U 336, pp. 139-161. The conciliar decree is in *Journal contenant tout ce qui s'est fait*, p. 4.

[20] A. N. U 336, 131-169; Ormesson, *Journal* I, 517-518; Vallier, *Journal* I, 140, fn. 2.

affairs the parlementarians were more indifferent than hostile to state interests, and in internal matters they had no intention of raising openly the question of monarchical absolutism which they had already evaded in March. At the same time, it was more than Anne and Mazarin realized, since the parlementary judges had set as their goal the redressing of the balance of governmental power, and were determined to do this in such a way that the regent could not accuse them of undermining subjects' obedience or of usurping royal authority.

The mood of the parlementarians is best illustrated by the shifting of their debates from the topic of the paulette, which held their attention in May, to the broader issue of state reform, which increasingly dominated their discussions in June. Without realizing where their deliberations were leading, the parlementarians began to evoke deep-seated grievances from the distant and immediate past. The original question of the paulette was almost forgotten and normal judicial duties were ignored as the plenary sessions continued day after day. Gradually, some judges began to see that the Chambre Saint Louis could be used to implement the reforms which the administration had originally feared in May. Radicals and a few conservatives joined in suggesting that royal finances be investigated, the intendancies abolished, the power of the councils curbed, the functions of all of France's officers fully restored, and subjects relieved of the burdensome weight of wartime taxes. Such proposals were bound to excite the interest of parlementarians, since they combined the altruistic goal of helping subjects and the principle of self-interest.[21]

The parlementarians were also in virtually unanimous agreement that their right to call the Chambre Saint Louis should be vigorously defended, but conservatives and radicals argued sharply over the best way to force that extraordinary assemblage on the regent. Conservatives like Molé and Talon believed that their tribunal must remonstrate to the regent for royal approval, rather than convoking the special chamber by parlementary decree as the radicals desired. *Avocat Général* Talon was sickened by the radicals' tactics, this feeling being heightened when a *président à mortier* told him that the *chambres des enquêtes* were willing to risk sedition in Paris and victories by the Hapsburgs in their determination to override the

[21] See, e.g., A. N. U 336, pp. 147-149.

regent's wishes. Talon made an eloquent plea to his fellow judges, reminding them that attempts to convoke similar assemblies without royal authorization had been followed by civil strife in the 1580's and 1610's. He compared the radicals' tactics to medical prescriptions which were "excellent in themselves and conforming to nature," but often produced an effect contrary to the intention of the physician. The royal attorney's speech was interrupted three times, and he finally stalked out of the Parlement without finishing.[22] His radical colleagues were pleasantly surprised when someone read his concluding statement which condemned the conciliar revocation of the *arrêt de union*. However, they could not agree with his opinion that remonstrances were the only defense against that act. Talon seemed to imply that the Chambre Saint Louis was not a legitimate assembly, but one which had to be justified by arguments and pleas to the regent. A few days earlier, a perusal of the parlementary registers had shown that such meetings had frequently taken place with tacit royal approval, a fact which undermined Talon's position that a formal request, in the form of a remonstrance, was a prerequisite. And, as Broussel had noted at the time, the Chambre Saint Louis could not be construed as usurping the king's right to enact legislation, for it would merely present proposals for the consideration of the individual courts.[23]

When Broussel rose to challenge Talon's position, he was able to convince many of his colleagues that remonstrances were degrading and unnecessary. And, by a clever interpretation of royal absolutism, he suggested that the Parlement could actually safeguard the monarchy by tempering the king's will, whenever it was unjust and susceptible to popular attacks. The venerable judge concluded by calling on his colleagues to place the *fleur de lis* on their hearts and save the monarchy by convoking the Chambre Saint Louis.[24]

After Broussel's speech, it was clear to the regent that the Parlement would summon the Chambre Saint Louis without explicit royal authorization. She tried to convince the *conseil d'état* that the insolence of the judges should not be permitted, but arguments on behalf of duplicity overcame her inclination for sheer authoritarianism. Mazarin helped persuade Anne that she should make temporary concessions in return for a parlementary agreement to call off

---

[22] Talon, *Mémoires*, pp. 237-239; A. N. U 336, pp. 171-173.
[23] A. N. U 336, pp. 145-147.   [24] Ibid., pp. 173-177.

the Chambre Saint Louis. He argued that whatever the regent granted now could be rescinded during the following winter with the aid of troops, which could be released from duty during the customary seasonal lull in fighting.[25] Anne sent Orléans to ask for a parlementary recess so that he and the regent's ministers could confer with parlementary representatives. The Parlement agreed to postpone voting on whether to implement the *arrêt de union*, and on June 21 the two sides conferred. Orléans tried to woo the judges with concessions which would interest them personally: restoration of the paulette on traditional terms, release of imprisoned *trésoriers* and members of the Grand Conseil and Cour des Aides, and the possibility that the maîtres des requêtes would be restored to the conciliar functions which they had lost in March. Séguier made less firm assurances that the farming of the *taille* would soon be ended, the intendants' powers curbed, and the *trésoriers, élus,* and lesser criminal courts restored to their normal duties. As the parlementarians argued for more sweeping and basic reforms, Orléans countered with the suggestion that the Chambre Saint Louis could meet if it promised to deal only with the interests of the sovereign courts.[26]

The ultimate result of the conference was a royal declaration on June 27, which went far beyond the promises of Orléans and Séguier, and included many of the reforms which the Chambre Saint Louis was to propose in July.[27] However, the declaration came too late. The parlementary delegates at the conference of June 21 believed that the administration had no intention of honoring its proposals or broadening them in accordance with the judges' demands. Without waiting for the declaration, the Parlement resumed the debate which Orléans had interrupted.

Immediately, it became clear that the parlementarians would reject the proposals of June 21. They believed that they could obtain even more by acting through the Chambre Saint Louis, and they dared not desert the other sovereign courts of Paris or their ever-increasing supporters among the other inhabitants of the capital. The parlementary debates also revealed the sincere desire of many judges to place the relief of indigent subjects, and what they described as "reforms of the state," above personal interests. Molé was mercilessly

[25] Ormesson, *Journal* I, 524-525.
[26] A. N. U 336, pp. 180-185; Molé, *Mémoires* III, 222-223.
[27] See B. N. Ms. Fr. 23319, fol. 13; *Journal contenant tout ce qui s'est fait,* p. 9.

condemned for suggesting that the *arrêt de union* referred only to the paulette and salaries, and that the promised restoration of both benefits canceled the need for the Chambre Saint Louis. He should have known that this was a futile argument, since he himself had predicted that the administration's manipulation of the paulette would cause the officers to turn from personal interest to the broader issues of corruption and reform.[28] One parlementarian, Laisné, stated the problem most clearly when he said that the Parlement had survived the exiling of members, the imprisonment of the *trésoriers*, and the death of Barillon; and that it would now survive the temptation to renounce broader concerns for the sake of securing personal benefits. A maître des requêtes, Le Gras, reminded the Parlement that the maîtres had rejected similar temptations, and that the Grand Conseil and Cour des Aides had refused the administration's offer to return their imprisoned members and to restore the paulette. The parlementary judge Blancmesnil declared that an "act of God" had turned the officers' selfishness into a means to help desperate subjects who were tortured and killed for smuggling salt or evading the *taille*. After a five-day debate, the Parlement voted on June 26 to assemble the delegates of the four sovereign courts. By a slim majority of some half-dozen votes, the parlementarians added the slight concession that they would notify the regent before the Chambre Saint Louis actually met.[29]

Having been persuaded against her better judgment to let Orléans negotiate a settlement, the regent now had to make the ultimate concession of permitting the sovereign courts to hold the Chambre Saint Louis. She had no choice. The financial situation was desperate. Until the officers actually presented their demands for reform, no one could tell what sort of budget the *surintendant* would have, or what financial machinery the administration would be able to salvage. Subjects throughout the realm knew enough of events in Paris to suspect that massive tax relief was in sight, and they were unwilling to pay any taxes while the controversy over reform continued. The *traitants* were equally uncertain of the outcome and were afraid to continue loans since their contracts might be repudiated. They were already sending money to the treasury on a month-to-month basis instead of prepaying the entire sum of their loans. It

[28] Molé, *Mémoires* III, 215-216.
[29] A. N. U 336, pp. 185-204.

would be better for the regent to gamble on the moderation of the Chambre Saint Louis than to continue the present confusion which was destroying the tax and credit system of the monarchy.[30]

Mazarin had more personal reasons for capitulating to the Parlement. The decline of the administration's fortunes made him increasingly vulnerable to intrigues by *les grands* and a possible coalition of officiers and nobles. To be sure, the notes of plottings and intrigues which he recorded in his personal notebooks, or *carnets*, were based more on rumor and imagination than on fact.[31] Apart from the arch-conspirator of the old *cabale des importants*, Beaufort, who had recently escaped from prison, *les grands* were reasonably loyal to Anne and Mazarin at this time. And precisely those persons whom Mazarin suspected of intriguing with the parlementarians were actually trying to moderate the officiers' opposition. This was especially true of the Duke of Longueville, who had tried to keep the sovereign courts of Normandy in check. It also applied to Orléans, who sought to keep the Languedocians loyal and to contain the reformism of the Parisian courts. Mazarin's conviction that the parlementary opposition to taxes in 1647 had been masterminded by the imprisoned Beaufort and the ex-minister Châteauneuf was sincere enough; but it merely reflected his tendency to see a hidden conspiratorial hand behind any opposition to the regent's administration. It was equally preposterous for Mazarin to have placed a spy outside President de Mesmes' house during the debates over the *arrêt de union*. De Mesmes was personally alienated by the recall of his brother, Count d'Avaux, from his post as plenipotentiary in the Franco-Austrian negotiations for peace, but de Mesmes was no radical, and certainly no advocate of parlementary union with *les grands*. Mazarin treated him as a criminal and conspirator simply because this exasperated conservative judge echoed Molé's charges that the administration was blindly pursuing self-defeating policies. The only parlementarian who might have engaged in outright conspiracy with

[30] For an assessment of the financial situation by the administration, see B. N. Ms. Fr. 23319, fols. 16-18; Molé, *Mémoires* III, 222-223.

[31] Mazarin's carnets are almost unreadable. Fortunately, portions have been deciphered, and the chief minister's almost paranoic fear can be seen in the excerpts by V. Cousin, *Madame de Chevreuse*, Paris, 1886, p. 289, and by P. A. Chéruel, ed., "Les Carnets de Mazarin pendant la Fronde," *Revue Historique* IV (1877), 103-138. See Chéruel, *Minorité de Louis XIV* II, III, for an informative but uncritical treatment of Mazarin's views.

les grands was President Barillon, whose imprisonment in 1645 was based largely on his uncompromising opposition to the *toisé*, and partly on the suspicion of collusion with *les grands*. But Barillon had died in prison—and, it might be noted, without being given the opportunity to answer the latter charge in a hearing or formal trial.

While the chief minister was hasty in accepting rumors of past and present intrigues as fact, he did have grounds for anticipating conspiracies if the internal situation worsened. An anonymous letter to Broussel from one of *les grands* sometime before 1648 proves that at least one great noble or prince was waiting for an opportunity to strike at Mazarin. The writer hinted at possible support for the parlementarians at some later date, if they could hold out against the administration.[32] Vague offers like this were to be translated into noble-official cooperation and intrigues during the Fronde—although this was caused as much by the regent's mishandling of the Chambre Saint Louis as by diabolical efforts of *les grands* to woo judges to their cause. For the moment, Mazarin continued his ceaseless efforts to play nobles against nobles; and he hoped that by allowing the Chambre Saint Louis to meet, the regent could divert the officiers from aligning more closely with *les grands*.

For Mazarin, the critical military-diplomatic situation was an even stronger reason for yielding temporarily to the judges. Apart from his fears that an irreparable breach with the sovereign courts would cause the Austrians to stiffen their demands at the peace conferences, he was very concerned about the condition of France's military forces. By mid-1648, even Condé's army was in difficulty because of the lack of food and clothing. Swiss mercenaries had not been paid for three months, and they were threatening to break their contract with the French monarchy. The Catalan rebels against Spain were reluctant to aid France, since French subsidies were in arrears. The French forces in Italy were on the verge of breaking up due to the lack of money. But if the Chambre Saint Louis were permitted to assemble, and then made only minor recommendations for fiscal retrenchment, royal finances might be stabilized and the French military machine could resume its work of forcing peace on Austria.[33]

[32] B. N. Ms. Baluze, fols. 3-4.
[33] See the references in fn. 30; and Forbonnais, *Finances de France*, p. 93. There are comments on the various reasons for the administration's capitulation in the accounts by Motteville, Dubuisson-Aubenay, Ormesson, and Vallier.

On June 27, Anne heard Molé's report of the Parlement's decision to convoke the Chambre Saint Louis, in which he made an astonishingly strong and uncompromising defense of his tribunal's stand.[34] Making no reference to his personal efforts to prevent the Chambre Saint Louis, he stressed that assembly's legitimacy. He ignored the grave financial and diplomatic problems of the administration, preferring to attack the evil influence of foreigners on the regent (an obvious reference to Mazarin), and denouncing the administration for trying to override all laws by its attacks on the Parlement—the last barrier against tyrannical government. Instead of mutely accepting the recent charges that the parlementarians were treasonous, Molé accused Anne's advisers of the criminal act of turning subjects against their monarch. Most astounding of all his statements was his conclusion. He simply informed the regent that the Chambre Saint Louis would meet. The first president could have couched this statement in diplomatic language, making it sound like a request; instead, he virtually repudiated the very principle of royal absolutism by implying that the king's personal will could not override the decisions of the Parlement of Paris. The regent was so shocked by this eloquent repudiation of her administration's policies that she was unable to reply to his charges, other than saying that her council would discuss the matter and announce its decision.

The regent must have wondered whether Mazarin had been overly optimistic in allowing the parlementarians to play at reform, for Molé's attitudes reflected the feelings of the Parlement's most conservative members. The first president had been the strongest supporter of the administration within the Parlement during the previous weeks, and had almost lost all credit with his radical colleagues by putting off debates and working for a *rapprochement* with the regent. If one accepts the charges and rumors that abound in contemporary accounts, Molé and several of the *présidents à mortier* had actually tried to betray their corporation, in return for financial bribes and offers of sinecures for their friends and relatives.[35] Probably no historian will be able to evaluate the role of royal bribery at this stage of the regency, on the eve of the Fronde. All that can

---

[34] A. N. U 336, p. 207; Ormesson, *Journal* I, 530; Vallier, *Journal* I, 45-56; Talon, *Mémoires*, p. 240; *Histoire du temps* I, 136. The speech is recorded in B. N. Ms. Fr. 23319, fols. 9-13r; the parlementary reports of A. N. U 336 and B. U. P. Ms. 64; and Molé, *Mémoires* III, 225-230.

[35] See especially the radical judges' speeches and a commentary by the anonymous writer of A. N. U 336 during May and June; and B. N. Ms. Fr. 18367, fol. 177.

be said is that many parlementary conservatives must have been torn by conflicting interests. They wished to preserve monarchical authority, but they also wanted to make the administration responsive to the needs of subjects. They were lured by pensions, sinecures, and possible advancement to positions within the administration, but they also had to work with colleagues who would not countenance any open betrayal of parlementary interests. Certainly the honorary position of councilor of state and the accompanying fee of fifteen hundred *livres*, which were given to almost every parlementarian who sought them in 1648, did not buy the votes of most recipients, whatever their political leanings were. This was true even of the archconservatives in the usually proroyal *grand chambre*. At this time, all but four members of that chamber had royal pensions; yet many were almost as hostile to the regent's administration as the most radical judges in the *chambres des enquêtes*. Mazarin could count on only one sure dividend from royal investment in pensions and other gifts—he acknowledged that he received a written account every day of the Parlement's supposedly secret work from friends in that high court who disregarded the oath of secrecy which bound each member.[36] But regardless of the effects of royal bribery, it was a bad omen for Anne's regime that the conservatives could not control their radical colleagues, and that the first president, himself, was now defending the Parlement's stand in the most uncompromising manner.

The *arrêt de union* of May 13 had radically altered the parlementary-royal conflict which had been initiated by President Barillon's dramatic request, in 1643, for a reform of the state. The Parlement's decision on June 26, 1648, to convoke the Chambre Saint Louis immediately was another landmark in royal-parlementary relations during Anne's regency, for it marked the formal beginning of the Fronde. And Molé's oral defense of that decision, on June 27, under-

---

[36] On the administration's attempts to bribe parlementarians, see Ormesson, *Journal* I, 424, 467; A. N. U 336, pp. 236-245. The ministers were shocked by their failure to control parlementary conservatives, despite d'Emery's distribution, in June, of 25,000 *livres* to members of the *grand chambre* and to twelve judges in each of the other chambers. Ormesson, *Journal* I, 492. Although Molé had actually handled the bribery for the *surintendant*, the first president immediately sent the royal attorneys to the regent in an effort to secure royal approval of the Chambre Saint Louis (which he had previously been opposing!). And the chancellor accused the most conservative judges, as a group, of secretly supporting their radical colleagues. Ormesson, *Journal* I, 492; Talon, *Mémoires*, pp. 231-234; A. N. U 336, pp. 173-174.

lined the serious intentions of the officiers, conservatives as well as radicals. Two days later, the chancellor gave the regent's reply to the royal attorneys of the Parlement.[37] Séguier's speech was a pathetic commentary on the regent's tragic plight; he had to give the regent's official approval of the Chambre Saint Louis in order to save the fiction of royal absolutism. He also touched on the delicate military and diplomatic situation in a vain effort to gain the parlementarians' sympathy for the administration's difficulties, and tried to flatter the judges by saying that the regent hoped the sovereign courts would serve the monarchy as faithfully in the Chambre Saint Louis as they had in the past! He concluded with the forlorn hope that this extraordinary assembly would be able to finish its work within a week. The speech was certainly not a true reflection of the regent's bitterness toward the parlementarians—it reflected only the misplaced optimism of Mazarin, who probably wrote it. Séguier's words did little to smooth over the serious, now almost irreconcilable, differences between the administration and the officiers of the realm, and his pleading made no impression on the Parlement, which received it secondhand from the royal attorneys the following day.

2

THIRTY-TWO members of the Chambre Saint Louis held afternoon sessions from June 30 to July 29, 1648. There was no serious disagreement between the fourteen parlementary delegates and six representatives from each of the other sovereign courts in Paris. By July 17 they had drafted twenty-seven proposals, an achievement which apparently left the delegates nothing to do during the last sessions apart from clarifying these hastily written suggestions for royal legislation. The harmonious atmosphere among the delegates was demonstrated not only by the speed of their work, but by their ability to draft thorough and complex reforms, in language general enough to antagonize neither the individual courts they represented nor any of the other tribunals and bureaus in the kingdom.[38] The trésoriers were angry with the Chambre des Comptes for rejecting their request to send representatives to the special assembly, but this was an insult

[37] Talon, Mémoires, p. 240; A. N. U 336, pp. 206-207.
[38] There is no record of the Chambre Saint Louis' discussions. Its twenty-seven recommendations and the actual legislation which stemmed from them are discussed in pt. 3 of this chapter. The assembly's procedures are noted in B. U. P. Ms. 64, fol. 56; and Dubuisson-Aubenay, Journal I, 32.

rather than an injury. The sovereign courts did not intend to make the symbolic gesture of raising these inferior officials to their own level, but they took pains to produce reforms specifically related to the *trésoriers'* grievances. The Parlement of Paris rejected a similar plea by the maîtres des requêtes, on the argument that separate representation would jeopardize the maîtres' position as members of that sovereign tribunal.[39] The maîtres were more than amply paid for their tactful acceptance of this ruling. It was to be expected that the Chambre Saint Louis would look after the interests of the other petty officers within the jurisdiction of the Parisian courts; but even the provincial sovereign courts and the officials beneath them were included in the sweeping reforms.

The regent's plans to return quickly to government as usual were not easily executed. She could not hastily implement the reforms by new laws, without destroying much of the financial, military, and administrative machinery of the state, nor could she easily evade the proposals for reform without becoming involved in a time-consuming conflict with the officers. Faced with equally distasteful alternatives, Anne and Mazarin procrastinated—and instead of saving time or power, they lost both. By offering no legislative enactment of the Chambre Saint Louis' recommendations during the first days of July, the administration lost control over the revolt of the judges and caused unnecessary confusion. Then, when the regent tried to regain the initiative, she badly mismanaged. By drafting legislation which was vague and incomplete, Anne's advisers merely encouraged the officials to hold out for the Chambre Saint Louis' broad reforms.

The administration's plight, however, was not entirely due to its ineptitude. Anne could not negotiate the implementation of reform directly with the Chambre Saint Louis because that special assembly lacked the regular courts' right to review and register legislation. Any royal legislation on reform had to go through the regular channels, a delicate operation at best and one which was all but fated to degenerate into a series of squabbles with individual sovereign courts. This legislative process was all the more complex because the very reforms suggested by the Chambre Saint Louis were designed to apply to all officers, and hence were too broad and vague to

[39] Charmeil, *Les Trésoriers de France*, p. 268, and 268, fn. 164; A. N. U 336, p. 208; Archives des Affaires Etrangères, Mémoires et Documents, France, 861, fol. 221.

satisfy all the special interests of any one corporation. Even if the regent's ministers succeeded in translating the general reforms into specific laws satisfying all sovereign courts there was bound to be some temporary confusion until the laws reached all the appropriate authorities. Rumor spread faster than law, and while one tribunal was deliberating on a declaration, another would be suspiciously waiting to see whether the version destined for its own scrutiny conformed to advance reports.[40]

There was additional confusion at the lower governmental levels. Most of the petty courts and bureaus had very limited control over legislation, and even the reforms that were sent to them for registration had to be submitted first to the appropriate sovereign tribunals. However, there was nothing to prevent them from lobbying with those higher courts or the administration. One could compose a long list of little-known officials who clamored for the attention of their superiors in a desperate effort to avoid being overlooked. To this could be added the almost as lengthy list of officials who appealed *against* reforms which threatened to suppress their newly created offices. Naturally, the Parlement of Paris was the tribunal most frequently besieged by requests for aid, the *trésoriers* in the capital making a particularly dramatic appeal in person,[41] and the maîtres des requêtes seeking that court's support at the same time that they were in constant contact with the ministers and councils.[42] Occasionally, regionally based corporations managed to combine in imitation of the Chambre Saint Louis; in Dauphiné the *trésoriers*, Chambre des Comptes, and Parlement held joint conferences at Grenoble to discuss their common grievances.[43]

Thus the revolt of the judges became a many-sided scramble for redress of diverse grievances and a legal nightmare for the administration. The combination of governmental complexity and tactical errors by Anne's ministers would have turned France into indescribable chaos had not the Parlement of Paris decided to intervene. This action had two major results: it gave the movement for reform a degree of cohesion, which would otherwise have been nonexistent

---

[40] The provincial situation can be followed in Mousnier, *Lettres et mémoires adressés au Chancelier Séguier* II.

[41] A. N. U 336, pp. 256-263.

[42] See, inter alia, Ormesson, *Journal* I, 556, fn. 2 (notes of André d'Ormesson).

[43] Mousnier, *Lettres et mémoires adressés au Chancelier Séguier* II, 847; Charmeil, *Les Trésoriers de France*, pp. 288-289.

as soon as the initiative passed from the temporary Chambre Saint Louis, and it frustrated the administration's attempts to divide and rule through separate agreements with individual corporations. In a literal, if incomplete sense, then, the revolt of the judges in the summer of 1648 can be called the "parlementary Fronde."

From the very beginning of the Chambre Saint Louis' sessions, the Parlement of Paris seized the initiative which the administration refused to take. Its members decided after a brief but heated debate to discuss and act on each article of reform as it was drafted, rather than waiting for the entire program to take shape. Their boldness was in sharp contrast to the timidity of the other sovereign courts at Paris and the uncertainty that pervaded the poorly informed provincial halls of justice. The Chambre des Comptes and Cour des Aides of Paris voted to do nothing until the Chambre Saint Louis' work was completed.[44] The Grand Conseil was even less aggressive, probably because its largely ecclesiastical functions had given it few grievances against the administration other than the loss of the paulette and arbitrary detention of some members; and it apparently would have waited until the regent actually responded to the Chambre Saint Louis' proposals for reform. The maîtres des requêtes were active in negotiating their own settlement with the administration, but they were too closely identified with the councils to act as a unifying force for the officers. Indeed, the danger was that they would be so successful in their own negotiations that they would completely desert the other corporations, and resume their normal role as administrative agents. The lesser officers were too restricted in functions and territorial jurisdiction to take the lead, despite frantic lobbying by the *trésoriers* at Paris. In the provinces, sovereign courts tried to keep abreast of events in the capital, but their distance from the center of activity precluded any possibility of leadership; some decided to wait for royal legislation, a few, notably the parlements of Bordeaux and Toulouse, started to investigate specific abuses as soon as they heard that the Parlement of Paris or royal administration was acting on these grievances. The Parlement of Aix in Provence merged its old stand against the creation of judgeships with new activities on behalf of state reforms. And the sovereign courts and *trésoriers* at Grenoble became so frustrated that they planned to send a delegation to Paris (although this apparently never

[44] A. N. U 336, pp. 233-235.

came about).[45] Thus there were provincial parlementary Frondes in the making, but the real revolt of the judges in the provinces got under way only when the Parlement of Paris forced the regent to send legislation for the consideration of those local corporations.

The Parlement of Paris turned out to be not only the sole possible leader of reform, but an excellent one. The prestige behind every parlementary decision gave encouragement to wavering sister courts in Paris and to bewildered provincial courts. The vastness of the Parlement's jurisdictional area also made those decisions automatically binding on much of the kingdom, and the employment of techniques which its judges had developed from 1643 to 1647, and perfected during the debate after the *lit de justice* of January 15, 1648, made them an elusive target for counterattacks by the administration.

As in the past, compromises made between parlementary conservatives and radicals avoided the fatal extremes of obsequiousness to royal authority and outright rejection of monarchical absolutism. Radicals urged the Parlement to implement reforms on its own authority; conservatives were deferential to royal authority, a few opposing any type of parlementary opposition, however minimal. In the course of debates on specific reforms, Broussel and Molé continued to find ways to reconcile the extremists on both sides. As a rule, the Parlement decided that it could unilaterally issue *arrêts* to enforce any existing laws which had been evaded by the administration.[46] Hence the Parlement abolished the intendancies, whose functions violated the limitations outlined in sixteenth-century royal ordinances, and whose commissions had not been registered with the sovereign courts as the law required.[47] By contrast, however, the Parlement agreed that remonstrances were the only legitimate vehicle for implementing those reforms which went beyond existing laws or lay within the monarch's exclusive jurisdiction. Consequently, the parlementarians refused to use *arrêts* to alter contracts between the treasury and *traitants*. (Broussel accepted Molé's ruling that the granting of state leases was a royal prerogative.) The same moderate stand was taken when the judges discussed the reform calling for a reduc-

---

[45] Mousnier, *Lettres et mémoires adressés au Chancelier Séguier* ii, 839, 847-850, 852-856, 864-865, 890-891.

[46] A. N. U 336, pp. 233-234; B. N. Ms. Fr. 23319, fol. 39r.

[47] A. N. U 336, pp. 238-245; *Journal contenant tout ce qui s'est fait*, p. 23.

tion in the *taille*; it was agreed that this permanent tax was not subject to parlementary review. In both cases, the Parlement merely
drafted remonstrances urging the regent to implement the reforms
through royal legislation.[48] Occasionally, the parlementarians avoided
taking unilateral action even though the law clearly gave them the
right to issue *arrêts*. The motive behind this surprising exercise of
restraint was purely practical: the judges knew that it would be
futile to reiterate legal limitations on conciliar interference with the
judicial work of the officiers, since the councils would disregard such
arrêts. Casting aside their usual mania for legalism, the parlementarians merely remonstrated with the regent to curb the councils'
powers.[49] It is interesting to note that the Parlement also hesitated
to draft a comprehensive royal declaration on all the Chambre Saint
Louis' articles. The judges knew that this was an encroachment on
the king's legislative preserve. They agreed to assume that task only
when the desperate regent pleaded with them in October to cooperate, and thus cut short the interminable disputes over reform which
were disrupting the kingdom.[50]

This tactic of alternating between *arrêts* and remonstrances,
according to legal or practical considerations, was a devastating
weapon against the administration. The regent could not prove that
the Parlement was antimonarchical, even though she knew its members were subverting royal authority, nor could she ignore parlementary *arrêts*, since they had the force of law. Sometimes, she tried to
modify the parlementarians' stand by having Orléans negotiate with
them. However, the duke was no match for the judges, who forced
him to admit that such innovations as intendancies were illegal and
could be revoked by parlementary decrees. Not even his pleas that
the foreign war and desperate financial situation required the continuation of intendants halted the revolt of the judges. Their only
concession was to suspend a few parlementary *arrêts* which seemed
to tarnish the image of royal absolutism, a concession which was
more than offset by the Parlement's insistence that the *arrêts* be
replaced with royal declarations granting exactly what the judges
had decreed. Then, if the regent submitted unsatisfactory or evasive
declarations, the Parlement promptly appended modifications which
turned the legislation into very specific and sweeping reforms.[51]

---

[48] See especially A. N. U 336, pp. 262-263, 305-306, 308-309, 363-365.
[49] Ibid., pp. 247-256.   [50] Talon, *Mémoires*, p. 285.
[51] See, inter alia, ibid., pp. 245-252.

The Parlement's ability to pry legislation from an unwilling regent had far-reaching implications. In effect, the parlementarians were drawing the other courts at Paris and elsewhere into the center of the movement for reform. Once news of the administration's legislative concessions to the Parlement of Paris leaked out, the regent could not avoid sending similar declarations to the other sovereign tribunals. If she delayed, she ran the risk of letting those courts implement the same reforms through their own *arrêts* in imitation of the Parlement of Paris. The situation in the outlying areas of the realm was more critical than in the capital because poor communications with Paris thwarted the hapless military governors' attempts to persuade Séguier to send appropriate legislation without delay. And when legislation did arrive at the provincial courts (or at the nonparlementary tribunals in Paris), those corporations promptly amended the declarations to suit their interests, or delayed registration while they engaged in time-consuming debates over appropriate action.[52]

The existence of cooperation between the Parlement of Paris and corporations under its jurisdiction also frequently forced the regent's hand. The Parlement did not need to issue *arrêts* on behalf of the maîtres des requêtes or *trésoriers*, although it occasionally did. All that was needed was a favorable parlementary reception of appeals from those officers. For example, the very evening after the *trésoriers* at Paris appealed to the parlementarians for redress of grievances, the regent freed those *trésoriers* and sovereign court judges who had been placed in the Bastille in May and June; and the following day, the treasury set aside funds for payment of delinquent salaries to the *trésoriers* of central France.[53] The parlementarians' attitude toward the maîtres des requêtes was more restrained, however, because of traditional rivalry. Nevertheless, they did officially support the maîtres' demands for the restoration of the paulette and their positions in the councils. The maîtres were so impressed with this good will that they hesitated to negotiate a separate settlement with the administration. They succumbed to tempting offers by Secretary of State Le Tellier, and pressures by a few maîtres who were obsequious to the administration, only when the Parlement sanctioned their negotiations. Even then, the maîtres made a point of informing the

---

[52] Mousnier, *Lettres et mémoires adressés au Chancelier Séguier* II, especially 840, 886-891.

[53] Dubuisson-Aubenay, *Journal* I, 36-37; Vallier, *Journal* I, 59; *Journal contenant tout ce qui s'est fait*, p. 25.

Parlement of the actual settlement. They also made it clear that they had thanked only the regent, and had refused to pay their respects to the universally disliked Mazarin.[54] This spectacular display of solidarity was complemented by parlementary support for minor judicial corporations—which could easily have been ignored. Instead of forgetting petty officiers, for example, when the administration craftily restored the paulette and partial payment of salaries for the sovereign courts in Paris, the Parlement kept insisting that those concessions were to be made to all officials under its jurisdiction. This parlementary intransigence eventually forced the administration to offer the paulette unconditionally to the petty officiers. And similar parlementary support for the provincial sovereign courts helped to secure the belated restoration of the same privilege for their members.[55]

Preliminary skirmishes between the Parlement of Paris and the administration lasted throughout the entire month of July. Anne, Mazarin, and other ministers finally awoke to the necessity for drastic measures to end these quarrels. The opportunity came after July 29, when the Parlement presented some remonstrances on a few articles which it favored but could not legally implement on its own authority. Anne's reply to the remonstrances came in the form of a *lit de justice*. At this solemn ceremony on July 31, the king, regent, and state dignitaries presented a major declaration of reforms for registration. That declaration cleverly omitted many articles of the Chambre Saint Louis which had not yet been considered by the parlementarians, and, by substituting vague measures, aimed at overriding parlementary *arrêts* and remonstrances on other articles. In an effort to prevent further parlementary reforms, the declaration of July stated that wartime conditions did not permit a thorough revamping of the French government; this would be done through an assembly of notables as soon as external affairs permitted. It was also thought that the recent victory by Marshal Schomberg over the Spaniards at Tortosa would divert attention from internal reform.[56]

The *lit de justice* of July 1648 was no more effective than the previous ceremony in January. The judges did not challenge the king's

[54] There is an excellent account in Séguier's papers, B. N. Ms. Fr. 23319, fols. 22v-24r, 96v; cf. Ms. Fr. 18367; fols. 312r-314r.

[55] See especially Talon, *Mémoires*, p. 261; A. N. U 336, pp. 266-267.

[56] Talon, *Mémoires*, 256-259, contains the declaration.

personal will in his presence, but they knew how to evade it after the *lit*. At the ceremony itself, First President Molé warned the regent that if the king insisted on shirking his duty to initiate basic reforms on behalf of subjects, he would endanger the throne itself. And the equally conservative Talon pointedly declared that "although kings are of the race of Gods, [they] are nonetheless equal to the children of men according to nature's common precepts." Talon's fear of an antimonarchical revolution was even more marked in his conclusion. He exclaimed that kings were "indebted for their fortune and the grandeur of their crown to the diverse qualities of the men who obey them." Then he noted that the interests of *les grands* were less urgent than the plight of magistrates, artisans, peasants, and soldiers. "Without [prosperous and loyal] people," he intoned, "states would not exist and monarchy would be only an idea."[57]

After registering the declaration in the king's presence, the Parlement resumed its discussion of the original reforms during the first days of August. The judges justified their evasion of the king's will by a variety of legalistic arguments. Broussel led the way in forcing even such parlementary conservatives as Molé to admit that the debate should continue. The most clever argument by the radicals stated that the declaration of July 31 had not quashed the parlementary *arrêt* of early July, which had outlined parlementary procedure on reforms. Since that decree called for continuous plenary sessions until the Chambre Saint Louis' entire program was examined, the Parlement decided that it could legally continue its discussions. Anne hastily sent Orléans to stop the debate, but the duke's angry defense of royal absolutism had no effect. He asserted that the *lit de justice* had obviously overridden the parlementarians' right to debate, even though the original parlementary *arrêt* had not been explicitly revoked. The judges saw the trap and refused to be drawn into a debate over the principle of absolute monarchy. Their only concession was to delay their reexamination of the articles of reform for a few days, in deference to royal authority. When they resumed their discussions in mid-August, the old legalistic devices were employed against the new royal declaration of July. One of its clauses was unceremoniously modified: in place of a vague royal promise to halt arbitrary taxation, the Parlement inserted a series of *arrêts*, promul-

[57] The speeches are in B. U. P. Ms. 64, fols. 68-71, 81-84. See also Molé, *Mémoires* III, 237-239; Talon, *Mémoires*, p. 259.

gated originally in 1647, stating that certain types of taxation could not be collected until registered at the Parlement. Orléans tried to make the judges change the modification to a remonstrance, but he was outwitted. The Parlement blandly declared that its amendment was "subject to the king's good pleasure." By making this concession, the judges again saved the principle of royal absolutism; but by insisting (as they had temporarily in March) that the admission be oral rather than written, they kept the amendment on their register.[58] This *de facto* victory for the Parlement was followed by a much bolder decision a few days later, on August 22, concerning contracts between the treasury and *traitants*. Though the judges could not legally interfere, they found a way to get around that obstacle. Arguing that they had jurisdiction over their own income, they began an investigation of three notorious *traitants* who had advanced loans in return for state income which should have been used for judges' salaries. It was a clever way of launching a full-scale investigation of financial corruption within the state.[59]

The Parlement's leadership of the movement for reform in July and August had thus thwarted every attempt by the administration to return to government as usual. Absolutist arguments had no effect on the parlementarians, who simply countered with legal measures which forced the regent to make further concessions. The *lit de justice* of July 31 had been a dismal failure. Moreover, parlementary intransigence, and the spread of reformism to the provinces, brought taxpaying subjects into the revolt of the judges as powerful allies of the movement. Not every subject was involved, to be sure; leading members of the *bureau de ville* of Paris, and many provincial town councils staffed with royal appointees, were conspicuously silent on the issue of tax relief. The Parisian Hôtel de Ville actually tried to put down a massive uprising in the capital during the so-called "Days of Barricades," in late August.[60] Many merchants were hesitant to become involved in the reform movement, fearing that reformism could lead to violent attacks on property. The six major guilds of Paris declined to testify before the Chambre Saint Louis,

---

[58] B. U. P. Ms. 64, fols. 87-97; A. N. U 336, pp. 331-378.

[59] B. U. P. Ms. 64, fol. 99; A. N. U 336, pp. 385-389. The Parlement had undertaken a preliminary investigation early in July, and had been trying to prosecute the *traitants* since 1646. See Actes Royaux, F 23668, no. 656.

[60] See Kossman, *La Fronde*, pp. 64-70; B. U. P. Ms. 64, fols. 102-103.

although they had been invited.[61] Then, too, the urban and rural poor had mixed feelings about the parlementary Fronde. Ironically, Pierre Broussel was hailed as a hero in Paris, while conservative judges like Molé were in danger of being physically attacked because they tried to temper their more militant colleagues' radicalism. As parlementary debates continued and political maneuvering over tax relief became the order of the day, many Parisians became impatient with the due process of law.[62] Yet there can be no doubt that most subjects welcomed the revolt of the judges, in spite of its baffling legalism and annoying slowness. Conversely, the parlementary Fronde raised popular expectations and led to a massive taxpayers' revolt which diverted the administration's attention from its quarrel with the officiers. Copies of the Chambre Saint Louis' articles were distributed in many provinces, rumors of major tax cuts became common, and some subjects were convinced that soon they would not have to pay any taxes to the state.[63]

Parisians and peasants from surrounding areas played a major role in this "popular" phase of the parlementary Fronde. On July 20, some six thousand peasants streamed into Paris from Meudon and its environs. For four days, they demonstrated in favor of the reform which called for drastic reduction in the *taille*, the major tax on the peasantry. The crowd was relatively orderly in urging its views on the Parlement, Orléans, and Condé (who had returned briefly from the Franco-Spanish front). But the peasants shouted to Orléans that he was trying to prevent the Parlement from securing tax relief. In September, Parisian merchants and workers in the wine, meat, and wood trades made similar demonstrations in favor of reforms which advocated a reduction of tariffs on goods entering the capital. In both instances, the fury of the mob forced the Parlement to demand new tax cuts, and compelled Anne's ministers to accept the judges' recommendations.[64]

Between those two minor *émeutes* there was the major Paris upheaval of August 26-28, known as the "Days of Barricades." On

[61] B. N. Ms. Fr. 18367, fol. 197r. The account in Séguier's papers concludes with the mystifying statement that the six guilds had been forbidden to speak at the Chambre Saint Louis; but no one knew who had issued the warning.

[62] Talon, *Mémoires*, p. 301.

[63] See, inter alia, ibid., p. 250; Molé, *Mémoires* III, 257; Mousnier, *Lettres et mémoires adressés au Chancelier Séguier* II, 841-842, 849-850, 887, 891.

[64] Talon, *Mémoires*, pp. 254, 278-285; Dubuisson-Aubenay, *Journal* I, 40-41.

August 26, the immensely popular Broussel and other parlementary radicals were arrested. Immediately, barricades were erected in the heart of the capital near Broussel's home on the *Ile de la Cité* near the Palace of Justice, and also in the marketing district of *les Halles* on the right bank of the Seine River. The arrests came right after Broussel had secured parlementary decrees against tariffs and the *traitants*; it was clear that the regent intended not only to punish the people's hero but to obstruct some of the reforms which appealed most to Parisians. This time, the *bons bourgeois*, as well as less afflu-ent Parisians, were directly involved in the disturbance. In *les Halles*, the well to do were coerced into demonstrating by intimidation from social inferiors, but in the elite shopping and residential area of the *Cité* there were few workers and virtually no acts of intimi-dation. There, the merchants took the lead. On August 27, the silver-smiths, members of one of the six major guilds, organized mass opposition to Chancellor Séguier when he tried to get past their shops with royal orders to the nearby Parlement. Later a clockmaker tried to kill Marshal de La Meilleraye, when he brought royal guards into the area. Although the man's pistol failed to fire, the marshal had to retreat. Then, the Parlement walked en masse to the royal palace, followed by a huge throng. The regent sent the judges away with vague promises, but the crowd forced the parlementarians back to secure firmer concessions. Anne had to release Broussel and his fellow judges, and agreed to terms which, in effect, allowed the Par-lement to continue its work on reform.[65]

If the French and Swiss guards in charge of arresting Broussel had been able to prevent the first barricades, they might well have con-trolled the situation. But the erection of those barricades turned the heart of Paris into an antiroyalist fortress. Punishment of the Parle-ment became impossible. The French and Swiss guards could barely defend the royal palace; some guardsmen actually fraternized with the demonstrators. There were, at that time, several hundred cavalry

[65] On the Days of Barricades, see especially B. N. Ms. Baluze, 291, fols. 45-48 (Broussel's papers); B. N. Ms. Fr. 23319, fols. 129-159 (Séguier's papers); and A. N. U 336, pp. 391-422 (an excellent account by a parlementary judge whose information is very precise). The registers of the Hôtel de Ville and Kossman's account (see above, fn. 60) are accurate for the *bureau de ville*, but both equate the pro-Maza-rinist royal appointees in the civic government with the *bons bourgeois* which played an active role in the riots. See the excellent analysis by Bourgeon, "L'Ile de la Cité," pp. 127-136.

in Marshal de La Meilleraye's horse regiment at Etampes. But to use them in the narrow, barricaded, and populous *Cité* district around the Palace of Justice would have been suicidal. Instead, they were brought to the Boulogne woods, ready to escort the royal family to safety in the countryside. Mazarin was so unnerved by the mob scenes that he was prepared to leave the capital at a moment's notice. Anne remained calm throughout the *émeute*, and her tearful concessions to the judges calmed Parisians. By August 28, relative quiet had returned to the capital, and royal plans to leave the city were discarded.[66]

The role of *les grands* in the parlementary Fronde, although complex and indirect, was no less important. Both Condé and Orléans helped Anne by remaining loyal, despite their belief that Mazarin was an inept chief minister. The *Grand* Condé continued to win military victories on the Franco-Spanish frontiers, and occasionally made secret visits with Mazarin to discuss the parlementary Fronde. Condé had no love for the parlementarians, whose reforms were diverting money from the military campaign; in fact, he would have used his troops to put down the revolt of the judges if they could have been freed from active service. Orléans' attempts to conciliate the parlementarians made Mazarin and Condé suspect his motives, but Anne certainly did not question the duke's loyalty, and continued to use him as a mediator.[67]

Secondary figures among *les grands* lacked the scruples of Condé and Orléans, but none of them committed a punishable crime during the first weeks of the parlementary Fronde, and their roles in the Days of Barricades remain too shrouded in mystery to invite a judgment. The most mysterious figure was the archbishop-coadjutor of Paris, Paul de Gondi, who combined a desire to act the part of a master conspirator with boastful writings of his supposed role in mediating between irate subjects and a vengeful regent during the "Days." Mazarin suspected Gondi of encouraging the riots, but his hypothesis cannot be proved any more than Gondi's contradictory

---

[66] See especially B. N. Ms. Fr. 23319, fols. 154v-158r; Ms. Baluze, 291, fols. 45-46r; and the first-rate commentary by Mousnier, "Quelques raisons de la Fronde: Les Causes des journées révolutionnaires parisiennes de 1648," *XVIIe Siècle*, nos. 2-3 (1949), pp. 38, 41-42, 44-45, 49, 51-53.

[67] See Dethan, *Gaston d'Orléans*, pp. 347-348; and the views of a friend of the princes, Priolo, *Ministry of Cardinal Mazarine*, pp. 110-112. Condé's secret visits to Mazarin are noted in B. N. Ms. Baluze, 291, fols. 36v, 38r, 45.

stands can be reconciled. There is more credence to rumors that the disgruntled minister Chavigny was trying to undermine Mazarin's authority. Some thought that he maliciously advised the chief minister to arrest Broussel on August 26, hoping to receive the credit if this succeeded and let Mazarin take the blame if it failed.[68]

After the Days of Barricades, some of *les grands* actively opposed Anne's regime. They were led by Chavigny, Gondi, and the ex-minister Châteauneuf—all of whom coveted Mazarin's position. These men tried to help their cause by renewing old friendships with a few radical parlementarians and probably made contacts with other judges. It was a strange coalition. The nobles mistrusted each other as much as they envied Mazarin. The parlementary members of the *cabale* were attracted by a variety of concerns which made them uncertain allies of *les grands*. Judges like *Président à Mortier* Novion, President Viole, and Councilor Blancmesnil did support the nobles' immediate aim of ousting Mazarin, hating the cardinal because he had failed to give them and their relatives courtly positions and governmental sinecures. Yet these disgruntled judges opposed the chief minister's policies as well. Other judges were drawn by the genuine bond of friendship with individual nobles. Some, like Broussel, were simply well-intentioned reformers who though they could serve subjects and officiers by throwing their support to *les grands*. Broussel had clearly been driven into the arms of these noble conspirators more by Mazarin's maladministration than by any genuine desire to serve the peculiar interests of *les grands*.[69]

How much of a threat was this fragile alliance, held together by common dislike of Mazarin? Its noble members could accomplish little without the support of prestigious figures like Condé or

[68] See especially Priolo, *Ministry of Cardinal Mazarine*, pp. 98-99, 110; Talon, *Mémoires*, pp. 274-275. Gondi's account in Retz, *Oeuvres* ii, 12-55, is corrected in the articles by Bourgeon and Mousnier cited in fns. 65, 66.

[69] On the *cabale* and its motives, see P. R. Rapin, *Mémoires sur l'église et la société*, ed. L. Aubeneau, 2 vols., Paris, 1865, i, 205-239; Goulas, *Mémoires* ii, 373-378; F. Annibal, Maréchal d'Estrées, *Mémoires*, ed. P. Bonnefon, Paris, 1910, pp. 251-261; Marquis de Montglat, *Mémoires*, Michaud and Poujoulat collection (ser. iii, vol. v), Paris, 1838, 200-201; Retz, *Oeuvres* ii, 55-60; and Mazarin's *carnets*, printed in Chéruel, *Minorité de Louis XIV* iii, 73-74, 397-402; Chéruel, "Les Carnets de Mazarin," pp. 108, 114-117. President de Novion and councilors Blancmesnil and Broussel solicited positions for their relatives, but they also rejected offers which would have compromised their independence, B. N. Ms. Fr. 25025, fol. 3.

Orléans. The parlementary group was a mere handful of judges, who could not dominate the Parlement unless their colleagues allowed themselves to be whipped into an anti-Mazarinist frenzy. The *cabale* became important only because Mazarin took the plotting seriously and attempted repressive measures. Alarmed by the growing hatred of nobles, Parisians, and pamphleteers, the chief minister fled on September 13 with the royal family to the nearby royal residence of Saint-Germain-en-Laye. Then Chavigny was arrested and Château-neuf sent into exile. The *cabale* now had a cause, which it had previously lacked. Its parlementary wing played on rumors that Paris was about to be besieged by royal forces, and on September 22 they openly accused Mazarin of arbitrary justice and military repression.[70] Mazarin had, indeed, planned to besiege Paris. But the parlementary threats to summon the dukes and peers to a special session and invoke an *arrêt* of 1617 against foreigner-ministers forced him to compromise in order to save his political career.[71] There is also very strong evidence that Orléans and Condé drew back from a military showdown. Orléans yearned for harmony within the state. Condé was intelligent enough to realize that internal disruptions were now a greater danger to the state than anything else, including military setbacks at the hands of the Hapsburgs. He also knew that the siege could not succeed. He had rushed to Saint-Germain to discuss the latest internal crisis, but had been forced to leave his army behind.[72] So the siege of Paris had to be postponed until the following winter. The administration agreed to free Chavigny and Châteauneuf, and resumed negotiations with the parlementarians. Thanks to Mazarin's mismanagement of the episode, *les grands* had helped the cause of reform in spite of their weaknesses. The Parlement was only too happy to postpone the issue of Mazarin's right to govern, and sent delegates to Saint-Germain to bargain over the remaining articles of reform.

Thus the convergence of popular rebellion, noble intrigue, and the revolt of the judges, in mid-1648, completed the debacle which had

[70] The excellent account in A. N. U 336 concludes with the comment that no more than 14 judges actually made the accusations (pp. 432-437).

[71] See Bazin, *Histoire de France* III, 436-437.

[72] See Kossman, *La Fronde*, p. 73; Chéruel, *Minorité de Louis XIV* III, 85-88, and 88, fn. 1; P. Lenet, *Mémoires*, Michaud and Poujoulat collection (ser. III, vol. II), Paris, 1838, pp. 515-516 (the account of a close friend of Condé).

started in 1643. Anne and her ministers had tried in vain to slow down, delay, and even halt the movement for reform. Royal obstruction of reforms made the parlementarians all the more popular with taxpayers, and rendered Anne and Mazarin highly unpopular. The flood of scurrilous pamphlets, called *"Mazarinades,"* intensified popular hatred of the regent and her chief minister, and at the same time publicized the popular aspects of the parlementarians' reforms. Royal obstructionism had also given *les grands* their chance to raise the specter of noble revolt.

Above all, the administration's fitful opposition to reform caused the state's financial plight to become graver with every passing week. On July 9, the finance minister, d'Emery, had to be dismissed because of popular hatred for him, and a potential parlementary investigation which threatened to bring other corrupt politicians into disrepute along with him. His successor, La Meilleraye, was thoroughly incorruptible, but his appointment in mid-1648 was a disaster for the monarchy. La Meilleraye's main task was to keep the flow of money from *traitants* running smoothly, so that the troops could be paid and the Austrian Hapsburgs forced to sign a peace treaty with France. However, the new finance minister had no personal connections with *traitants*. They had retained some respect for d'Emery, who was one of them; they neither knew nor trusted La Meilleraye.[73] Then, too, parlementary persistence in investigating the *traitants'* profiteering continued under La Meilleraye. This completely destroyed the finance minister's effectiveness. In July a number of *traitants* refused to subscribe to a loan of one million *livres*. Parlementary proceedings against three notorious *traitants*, on August 22, made other *traitants* declare that they would advance no further loans until assured of royal protection.[74] Parlementary attacks on irregular contracts unwittingly helped the treasury, but only temporarily. Taking advantage of the judges' attack on *traitants*, the treasury declared a state of bankruptcy and then arbitrarily reduced its interest rates from 15 to 5½ per cent. Mazarin estimated that this measure would save the treasury some fifty million *livres*, which would otherwise have gone to the *traitants*. However, would-be creditors were so angry that they

---

[73] B. N. Ms. Baluze 291, fol. 36; Ms. Fr. 23319, fol. 26; Vallier, *Journal* 1, 53-54.

[74] B. N. Ms. Baluze 291, fol. 106r; Ormesson, *Journal* 1, 556, fn. 2 (André d'Ormesson's account).

refused to make new loans, while taxpayers continued to block all efforts to collect impositions. Without those two sources of revenue, the treasury could barely function, even with the windfall resulting from reduced interest.[75]

Even the parlementary-royal conferences which followed the administration's flight to Saint-Germain in September brought little solace to the regent. It had been hoped that they would cut through the red tape which had overwhelmed the movement for reform. However, the conferences dragged on into October. After placing a ceiling on tax reductions, the regent permitted the Parlement to make further cutbacks by unilateral decrees—just to save time! This type of capitulation, in such sharp contrast to Anne's earlier delaying tactics, reveals how desperate she was by September and October of 1648.[76]

The conferences finally came to an end after Anne's ministers conceded enough to satisfy the Parlement. On October 22, a royal declaration, drafted by the parlementarians in accordance with the terms of this settlement, was officially approved by the regent. Two days later, it was registered by the Parlement. By coincidence, the treaties which ended the Franco-Austrian conflict were signed the same day. However, the war with Spain continued without interruption; and internal peace was as elusive as a Franco-Spanish settlement. The Chambre des Comptes and Cour des Aides of Paris did not register the Declaration of October 22 until several days later, and only with crippling amendments.[77] Ratification by provincial courts and lesser corporations was much slower. The Chambre des Comptes in Normandy, for example, issued *arrêts* on December 15 which modified the articles of reform; and the battle of conciliar *arrêts*, further modifications by that court, *lettres de jussion* by the king, and still more amendments by the tribunal, continued into 1649 and 1650. This legalistic war in Normandy did not come to an end until well after the Fronde formally ended in 1652-1653.[78] Records of conciliar decisions indicate that this long-term Norman dispute was typical of royal relations with the regional parlements, chambres des comptes,

---

[75] On the bankruptcy, see Kossman, *La Fronde*, pp. 57-60; Perkins, *France under Mazarin* I, 416-417; and Actes Royaux, F 23631, no. 420.

[76] B. U. P. Ms. 64, fol. 200. [77] See below, fn. 82.

[78] Actes Royaux, F 23611, nos. 955, 1011.

and cours des aides.[79] Reports from provincial governors to the chancellor are sketchier, but the Duke of Epernon's alarming letter of November 29, 1648, was an accurate reflection of the provincial troubles. He noted that the Parlement of Bordeaux had used ratification of the Declaration of October as an excuse for attacking local taxes which were left untouched by that legislation.[80]

3

It is difficult to evaluate the achievements of the Chambre Saint Louis. The original twenty-seven articles were highly technical, and there are minor discrepancies between the original draft and the final proposals.[81] They were followed by a veritable flood of royal declarations, and additional *arrêts* by the various corporations of officials. No exhaustive study has been made of the regional variations of the reforms. Until scholars undertake that task, province by province, we will have an incomplete picture of the parlementary Fronde. Fortunately, the original program of reform provides an excellent basis for determining what the officers of France were trying to accomplish. The subsequent pronouncements by royal councils and individual sovereign courts in Paris are equally valuable sources, for they show precisely how the initial program was implemented in the sprawling central region of France. The decrees and amendments of the Parlement of Paris are especially noteworthy, since they frequently included concessions for the outlying areas of the realm.[82] From this mass of documents emerges a detailed, but clear picture, which becomes still clearer when viewed in the context

[79] See, inter alia, ibid., nos. 914, 921, 926, 927. The bureau of *trésoriers* at Paris amended the same declaration on December 30, 1648. Ibid., no. 939. As late as 1653, the Parlement of Grenoble defended the entire Declaration of October, 1648, in a letter to Séguier. See Bibliothèque de l'Institut, Collection Godefroy, Ms. 274, fol. 236.

[80] Mousnier, *Lettres et mémoires adressés au Chancelier Séguier* II, 892-893.

[81] The numbered version of the articles in the *Journal contenant tout ce qui s'est fait*, pp. 9-19, appears to be the final draft. There is a reprint in Isambert, *Anciennes lois françaises* XVII, 72-84. Talon, *Mémoires*, p. 241, fn. 1, contains a much rougher version, with unnumbered and haphazardly arranged clauses. The slight deviations from Talon's version in *Histoire du temps* I, 158-176, cannot be trusted because of the author's habit of altering facts to enhance the image of the parlementary Frondeurs.

[82] The all-important royal Declaration of October 22 is in Talon, *Mémoires*, pp. 293-297. The amendments by the Chambre des Comptes and Cour des Aides of Paris are on pp. 307-311 and 313-314.

of the royal-official conflicts between 1610 and 1648. Given the opportunity to strike back at the governmental revolution of the previous thirty-eight years, the officiers of France reclaimed functions which had been undermined or wrested from their control. At the same time, they fulfilled their promise to provide relief for outside social groups, since many of their reforms curbed the very institutions which had subjected taxpayers and privileged subjects to financial extortion and vindictive justice.

Although several reforms dealt exclusively with the officiers' personal interests, the original *raison d'être* of the union of mid-1648 was not mentioned by the Chambre Saint Louis. The omission of the paulette from the long list of articles was not an oversight, however. The officiers left that issue to the end of their deliberations, in order to underline their commitment to less selfish reforms which benefited outside social groups as well as themselves. Then they decided not to include an article on the subject at all, assuming that the regent's ministers would have to concede the paulette in order to bring the reform movement to an end.[83] The administration did, indeed, make offers to the sovereign courts in Paris; and relentless pressure by the Parlement, Cour des Aides, and Chambre des Comptes of Paris finally secured the unconditional restoration of the privilege to all officiers in the realm.[84]

The complementary struggle over investment in offices was brought into the open from the very beginning of the judges' revolt. This was a logical move, since the officials' income was considered a valid remuneration for services, and not a special interest like the paulette. The Chambre Saint Louis called for the restoration of salaries to all officials and the abolition of recently created offices. It also sought promises that any new sales would be submitted for approval by the appropriate courts. The rough draft of the articles was more specific, demanding the revocation of recent additions to the maîtres des requêtes, and the abolition of many offices in the provincial sovereign courts and other corporations.[85] Bargaining with the administration was an involved process; but the Parlement of Paris was

---

[83] See, inter alia, Ormesson, *Journal* 1, 556, fn. 2.

[84] Talon, *Mémoires*, pp. 294, 309, 313-315; Actes Royaux, F 23611, nos. 916, 917, 922.

[85] Articles 4, 15, 19, 21 of the proposals by the Chambre Saint Louis (see above, fn. 81); and Talon, *Mémoires*, p. 241, fn. 1 (dated July 14).

able to lead the courts in forcing the administration to satisfy one bureau and court after another. The sovereign court judges throughout the realm were promised three-fourths of their salaries, and full payment after the conclusion of the Bourbon-Hapsburg war. The grievance-ridden *trésoriers* were offered the same terms, while the weaker *élus* had to settle for half pay. Thanks to their peculiar position as conciliar agents and members of the Parlement of Paris, the maîtres des requêtes received special consideration. They regained the positions in the councils which they had lost in March, and they also managed to have the new masterships revoked. A host of other offices were abolished, including many petty positions in the chancellery. Moreover, the administration temporarily slackened its longstanding efforts to double the judgeships in the parlements of Rouen and Aix. The regent was also forced to agree that no new offices or reduction in salaries would be introduced for four years. Thereafter, such innovations would be subject to verification without coercion by *lits de justice* or similar expressions of the king's personal will.[86]

These highly personal reforms were combined with efforts to protect the functions of the officiers. The most spectacular of all the original articles was a proposal to suppress the administration's "extralegal" agencies. Specifically, the reform called for abolition of all special commissions except those which had been verified by the appropriate courts. This measure was even more sweeping than it appeared on the surface. Most judicial commissions had been formed without approval in any court, and it had become the practice to send the intendants' papers to minor local officials without even informing the sovereign courts. The attack on intendancies and other special agencies complemented another reform which condemned the practice of farming the *taille*. With a stroke of the pen, the delegates at the Chambre Saint Louis intended to return the *taille*'s supervision to the *trésoriers* and *élus*. A less spectacular assault on the illegal activities of the royal councils rounded out the Chambre Saint Louis' program for basic administrative readjustments. Its members called for strict enforcement of sixteenth-century royal codes, particularly the Ordinance of Blois, which had severely limited the right of councils to evoke suits from the regular courts or to overrule their judicial decisions.[87]

---

[86] Talon, *Mémoires*, pp. 258-259, 261, 294-295, 313-314; Kossman, *La Fronde*, pp. 121, 140-141.

[87] Articles 1, 2, 10, 17.

The prospect of handing over control of major crimes and basic taxes to thousands of officials appalled the administration and delighted officiers and taxpayers. The Parlement of Paris abolished the intendancies within its *ressort* without awaiting royal legislation; the regent replied by instructing the governors and intendants to disregard the parlementary *arrêt*.[88] Taxpayers' implacable hostility to local intendants destroyed the effectiveness of that royal directive. The Duke of Orléans could do nothing more than bargain with the Parlement over the reform's implementation. In the end the administration compromised, issuing declarations which abolished all intendancies except six in the militarily vulnerable areas of Lyonnais, Champagne, Picardy, Languedoc, Burgundy, and Provence, and at the same time allowing the *trésoriers* and *élus* to resume charge of the *taille*.[89] This still did not satisfy any of the sovereign courts. The Parlement of Paris amended these royal concessions in such a way that the remaining intendancies were deprived of all control over civilians. In effect, the six intendants were restricted to the task of supplying and disciplining the French armies fighting against the Hapsburgs. To guarantee compliance with that provision, the parlementarians insisted on scrutinizing the commissions of these military intendants. The Chambre des Comptes and Cour des Aides of Paris also rewrote parts of the royal declarations to guard against any extralegal restoration of intendancies or other unverified commissions.[90]

The administration's response to the judges' attacks on the royal councils was less direct; a royal declaration accepted the principle of the reforms but avoided any specific concessions. This angered the Parlement of Paris, and its members remonstrated for a detailed implementation of the program, citing one article after another from the sixteenth-century ordinances. The regent then capitulated to the judges' demands and offered legislation so comprehensive that the courts in Paris raised no further objections.[91]

[88] There is an extremely interesting reprint of the parlementary *arrêt* with a commentary, dated 1651. Actes Royaux, F 23668, no. 720. Dubuisson-Aubenay, *Journal* I, 33, notes the administration's defensive action.

[89] See A. N. U 336, pp. 250-273; Talon, *Mémoires*, pp. 245-252; Dubuisson-Aubenay, *Journal* I, 37.

[90] The amendments of the courts can be followed in Talon, *Mémoires*, especially pp. 250-252, 311, 313. See also Actes Royaux, F 23611, nos. 892, 902.

[91] A. N. U 226, pp. 247-256; *Journal contenant tout ce qui s'est fait*, pp. 58-59; Talon, *Mémoires*, p. 296.

The reforming judges were also determined to stop the arbitrary detention of subjects. However, their professed concern for the poor and wealthy, who had been victims of royal reprisals for tax revolts and suspected anti-Mazarinist plots, was surpassed by their determination to protect their own corporate interests. Remembering that the parlementary radical Barillon had been arrested in 1645 for defending the Parlement's functions, and, in 1648, members of other sovereign courts and a few *trésoriers* had been summarily punished for supporting the Chambre Saint Louis, the delegates at that assembly knew that if they could guarantee personal liberty they would be striking a blow at royal encroachment on their corporations' functions. Hence they recommended that all political prisoners be released immediately, and called for the trial of all subjects within twenty-four hours of their arrest.[92]

Those proposals were among the most controversial submitted by the Chambre Saint Louis. The regent had no intention of relinquishing her right to suspend regular judicial procedures, and Mazarin was determined to use arbitrary punishment as a weapon against his noble enemies. The detention of Chavigny and Châteauneuf in September brought the explosive issue into the open, necessitating extensive conferences between Anne's representatives and the Parlement of Paris. Orléans, Condé, and Séguier all defended the administration's position—a stand which Condé was later to regret when he, himself, was arbitrarily imprisoned in 1650. While that prince defended Anne's responsibility to God alone for her actions, the chancellor engaged in a detailed argument with the parlementarians. His points were brilliantly expressed, but they also revealed his total disregard for human suffering. For Séguier, *raison d'état* always took precedence over individual rights. He icily declared that Anne could not be deprived of the discretionary power to detain, which had been "exercised throughout the ages." That option must be used against "persons who could disturb the tranquility of states by cabals, conduct, intrigues and other evil means [even though their] crimes could not be proved." He went on to state that "in such cases, formalities are useless." In Séguier's words, it was better to have a hundred innocent individuals suffer along with the guilty than exercise restraint and allow the state to perish. Naturally, the parlementarians raised violent objections to this appraisal, and First President

[92] Article 6.

162

Molé made an impassioned plea for individual rights. Despite his conservatism and his sincere desire to buttress royal authority, Molé could not accept Séguier's heartless brand of *raison d'état*. Adroitly exploiting the weakness in the chancellor's defense of that principle, the first president replied that "there was a great difference between rare and singular occasions when legal provisions were unnecessary and the many normal and common occasions when [legal protection] was desirable." What Molé wanted was a guarantee that the regent would not abuse the principle of *raison d'état*.[93]

There was virtually no way of reconciling Molé's and Séguier's views. All the administrators and judges could do was draft a law so vaguely worded that it might be interpreted to suit either the monarch or his subjects, depending on circumstances. This was no solution at all, but merely a postponement of a settlement. The Declaration of October 22 reiterated the monarchy's right to detain subjects, but stated also that the restrictions placed on this right by "past laws" were to be observed. Interpreting "past laws" to include Louis XI's provision for trial within twenty-four hours of an arrest, the parlementarians believed that they could enforce that specific legal restriction. On the other hand, royal ministers could argue in future that the twenty-four-hour clause was not explicitly mentioned in the declaration of 1648, while many past laws authorized arbitrary detention. The parlementarians tried to protect themselves by inserting a special clause in the declaration: no official was to be deprived of his functions or freedom by such an arbitrary device as sealed letters (*lettres de cachet*), authorized by the king's personal will. However this special-interest clause was no more airtight than the general provision for other subjects. Anne might arrest an official and argue that the detention was for crimes committed as a private citizen against the state rather than acts committed as an officier. Realizing this, the Parlement and Chambre des Comptes of Paris issued secret *arrêts* establishing machinery for resisting arbitrary arrests. As soon as a judge was arrested, his colleagues would hold a plenary session to discuss appropriate action. If a private subject were detained without cause and appealed to one of those two courts, it would discuss his case in a similar assembly.[94]

[93] B. U. P. Ms. 64, fol. 169; Talon, *Mémoires*, pp. 282-283.
[94] The final law is in Talon, *Mémoires*, p. 296. The secret *arrêts* are in ibid., pp. 290-291; B. U. P. Ms. 64, fols. 220-221; Boislisle, *Chambre des Comptes*, pp. 430-431.

All the foregoing reforms were primarily concerned with the grievances of officers, although many concessions, by coincidence, protected other subjects against repressive use of the state's administrative machinery. The Chambre Saint Louis' proposed changes in state taxes and loans reversed that set of priorities. Taxpaying subjects of every social description were to benefit most, while officials were incidentally helped, because they had been subjected to financial extortion despite their tax-exempt status. In addition, proposed restrictions on arbitrary fiscal activities by the administration would automatically restore many traditional functions of the courts and bureaus.

The Chambre Saint Louis sought to relieve a major tax burden on the peasantry by demanding a 25 per cent reduction in the *taille*, and a broad segment of urban society stood to benefit from a complementary proposal to suppress many indirect levies. (Unregistered tariffs, and some that had been verified by inappropriate courts, were scheduled for abolition.) The reforming judges also called for closer supervision of Paris tariffs by the city's sovereign tribunals and the *bureau de ville*, nor did they overlook two old impositions falling on well-to-do and poor commoners. The Parlement of Paris had already made enforcement of the *toisé* and tax on alienated domains impossible; the special reformist assembly added its own request that those discredited levies be formally revoked. The Chambre Saint Louis paid particular attention to wealthy subjects' grievances concerning state borrowing. It opposed forced loans on merchants and demanded close judicial supervision of state-directed loans floated officially by the Parisian *bureau de ville* (rentes). Rentiers of bourgeois or officier background were to be guaranteed partial payment of their interest, pending full payment at the close of the foreign war.[95]

By contrast, the hated *traitants* were threatened with severe punishment for their corrupt practices. Farming of the *taille* was to cease. The remaining tax farmers were to send their revenue to the treasury as long as the war lasted, instead of pocketing it as repayment for loans to the state. Moreover, existing leases were to be replaced by

---

The attitudes of both sides are amply illustrated in the parlementary-royal negotiations, B. U. P. Ms. 64, fols. 169-220.

[95] Articles 2, 3, 5, 9, 11, 13, 26.

new contracts, awarded on a competitive basis to the highest bidders. To prevent other fraudulent practices, the judges declared that the special funds known as *comptants* were not to be used to reimburse *traitants* underhandedly. This meant that the Chambre des Comptes would regain its function of auditing some of these transactions. The delegates also wanted to fine professional speculators who purchased depreciated rentes and then redeemed them at the treasury for their original value. Finally, a special *chambre de justice* of judges was to be formed for the purpose of investigating all questionable financial dealings between the state and its creditors.[96]

These fiscal proposals were totally unacceptable to Anne's administration. For example, the regent had no intention of carrying out the judges' request for suppression of every indirect tax which had been imposed without registration anywhere, and her ministers were outraged by the additional parlementary position declaring these levies illegal unless registration had taken place at the Parlement of Paris. The administration's intransigence was understandable: the first proposal would override many impositions approved by the chancellor's office or authorized merely by conciliar *arrêts*, while the second would also nullify the registration of all *aides* and *gabelles* with the Cour des Aides of Paris, including all tariffs enacted since 1606. Equally offensive was a parlementary assertion that all indirect taxes in future must be registered freely (i.e., without *lettres de jussion* or *lits de justice*) at the Parlement. Only a timely formula, suggested by Pierre Broussel, made any agreement on indirect taxes possible. The administration was conceded the right to collect any tariffs which had been registered in the Cour des Aides, but only until the end of 1649. Other tariffs which had never been approved by any court were to be immediately revoked. A parlementary committee, headed by Broussel, and authorized by the regent to draw up a revised list of legitimate tariffs, cut back taxes still further. Although the regent was shocked that the committee members dared to exclude from the list of legitimate tariffs some which had been verified by the Cour des Aides, parlementary insistence and popular demand forced her to accept the decision. The Parlement of Paris, by simply restating a parlementary *arrêt* of 1647, also preserved the principle that future sales taxes were to be subject to its approval,

---

[96] Articles 2, 5, 7, 8, 11, 12, 22; and Talon, *Mémoires*, p. 241, fn. 1 (rough draft on the *comptants*).

and resisted all efforts by the administration to quash their decree.[97] The Cour des Aides appended similar amendments to royal concessions, thereby strengthening the claim to register all fiscal measures lying within its specialized jurisdiction.[98]

Anne and her ministers were equally appalled by the reformist judges' assault on direct taxes, and many issues of municipal rentes, including some which had served as forced loans. Yet, after resisting as best it could, the regent's regime conceded as much as it had in the case of indirect taxation. A royal declaration reduced the *taille* by 20 per cent and canceled most overdue payments on that basic land tax. The regent also formally revoked the *toisé*, along with fees on alienated domains.[99] Existing forced loans were abolished *in toto*, since all rentes imposed on subjects without parlementary approval since 1630 were abruptly revoked. Parisians' voluntary investments in other rentes were placed under the protection of the *bureau de ville* and sovereign courts of the capital. Under the supervision of those authorities, taxes were to be set aside for partial payment of interest to rentiers, with a provision for full interest as soon as the war came to an end. To guard against future abuses, new rentes were to be sent to the Parlement of Paris for verification.[100]

The *traitants* escaped the harsh punishment envisaged by the Chambre Saint Louis, but their powers were severely restricted, nonetheless. Farming of the *taille* came to an abrupt end, and *Surintendant* La Meilleraye began to award other leases to new and more generous contractors. It was even conceded on paper that the *trésoriers* would be placed in charge of auctioning many new leases. Reforms undertaken unilaterally by the Chambre des Comptes and Cour des Aides of Paris added further controls. In amending the Declaration of October 22, the Chambre des Comptes restricted the *comptants* to a mere three million *livres*, and the Cour des Aides added a modification preventing the state from floating loans on the security of future revenue from the *taille*.[101] The *traitants* were fortunate that the administration seized control of fiscal investiga-

---

[97] See Talon, *Mémoires*, especially pp. 249-250, 262, 283-287, 293-294; *Journal contenant tout ce qui s'est fait*, p. 37; A. N. U 336, pp. 299-300.

[98] Talon, *Mémoires*, p. 313.

[99] Ibid., pp. 258, 293.

[100] Ibid., pp. 267, 294.

[101] Ibid., pp. 294, 310, 312; Dubuisson-Aubenay, *Journal* I, 89; A. N. U 336, p. 383 (de Mesmes' report on new state leases).

tions from the less kindly parlementarians. Since the Parlement's plan to establish a special *chambre de justice* composed of radical judges was shelved in favor of a state-controlled chamber packed with conservatives, the *traitants* were not prosecuted, and the parlementarians could only wait for some future opportunity to press charges on their own authority. Equally unsatisfactory to the Parlement was a semiprivate agreement between the ministers and *traitants* to alter interest rates, since this took the place of a more drastic parlementary scheme. Nevertheless, the threat of parlementary interference had taken its toll. As noted earlier, the administration declared a state of bankruptcy and then reduced the interest rate to 5½ per cent.[102]

The foregoing analysis shows clearly the specific losses sustained by the central administration in the summer of 1648. The regent's financial resources, her institutional powers, even her freedom to make political decisions affecting subjects, were sharply curtailed. As for the overall impact of the reforms, contemporary evaluations suggest that the whole was greater than its parts. Mazarin complained that the "best part" of the monarchy had been abolished, and Anne would not allow the reforms to be mentioned in her presence. Officiers, other privileged persons, and taxpaying subjects were naturally impressed with the new-found personal, fiscal, and institutional freedoms which the collapse of royalist power had ushered in. Members of the Parlement of Paris proudly took full credit for these windfalls of the revolt of the judges, casting themselves in the role of the Fathers of the People. Historians have perpetuated these views, conservative scholars claiming with Mazarin that the parlementary Fronde "subverted" the monarchical state,[103] and liberal writers praising the reforming judges for giving the French populace a "charter of fundamental liberties."[104]

Despite the closeness of contemporaries—or because of it—we have

---

[102] The controversy over the *chambre de justice* can be followed in Ormesson, *Journal* i; and *Journal contenant tout ce qui s'est fait*. On the bankruptcy, see above, pp. 156-157.

[103] See especially L. Madelin, *Une Révolution manquée: La Fronde*, Paris, 1931, pp. 96, 100-106; Chéruel, *Minorité de Louis XIV* iii, 5-11.

[104] See the extensive, liberal analysis by L. C. de Beaupoil, Comte de Sainte-Aulaire, *Histoire de la Fronde*, 2 vols., Paris, 1841, i, especially pp. vi, 5-37, 130-132, 148-151, 202-203; and J. Debû-Bridel, *Anne-Geneviève de Bourbon, Duchesse de Longueville*, Paris, 1938, p. 95.

reason to be skeptical; their very proximity and personal involvement undoubtedly limited the objectivity of their analysis. Mazarin's emotional reaction to the parlementary Fronde was particularly unbalanced. Unable to grasp the technical legal details of the reforms, and equating the power of government with its ability to wage foreign war, he leaped to the conclusion that fiscal reform spelled disaster for state power in general. Then, looking to the future from the assumption that the English and French crises were analogous, he feared that the reforms of the Chambre Saint Louis would lead to something similar to the civil war and virtual destruction of monarchy in England which had resulted from the parliamentary reforms of the early 1640's. (In reality, there were similar features in the reform programs in both countries, but, as we shall see, the political-institutional contexts were so different that Mazarin's predictions about the ultimate situation in France were unfounded.)[105]

If Mazarin's vision was hazy, the regent's perspective was even more restricted. As a queen mother who viewed all attacks on her son's will as treason, who had sworn to pass on royal authority to Louis XIV without the slightest loss of power, and who was proud and ill-tempered by turns, Anne was bound to exaggerate the destructiveness of the bloc of reforms forced upon her. Nor was the analysis of her opponents and their beneficiaries any more objective. The euphoria of parlementary judges and other subjects was simply the product of a spontaneous realization that they could strike back at conditions that had plagued them for four decades. Judges became imprisoned by their own rhetoric; taxpayers were overcome by their sudden good fortune.

While we must question the astuteness of these extreme, immediate views, it is unwarranted to say that they have nothing to tell us. Obviously royalist and reformist reactions to the reforms of 1648 were exaggerated, but these very reactions testify to the seriousness of the issues. Admittedly, both sides of the parlementary Fronde would seem to have concentrated far too much on pedestrian fiscal

[105] For Mazarin's attitude, see Chéruel, *Minorité de Louis XIV* III, 91-94, and 92, fn. 2; Motteville, *Mémoires*, p. 218; A. Feillet, *La Misère au temps de la Fronde et Saint Vincent de Paul*, Paris, 1862, p. 96 (letter from Mazarin to Le Tellier, Oct. 23, 1648). The excellent study by P. A. Knachel, *England and the Fronde. The Impact of the English Civil War and Revolution on France*, Ithaca, 1967, pp. 34-40, 48-49, follows Mazarin's attempts to evaluate the parlementary Fronde in the light of events in England.

matters, while basic constitutional questions such as the limits of royal authority were skirted—surely a telltale sign that no revolution or revolutionary situation was in the offing. But if the judges were not revolutionaries, and evaded those basic constitutional issues which are usually at the forefront of basic and successful revolutions, they were reformers, at least; their concentration on fiscal reforms was, itself, a sign not of superficiality but of a willingness to grapple with the immediate central problem of the day.[106] However clumsy their legal measures against *traitants* were, they constituted most of the very few early-modern devices to prevent the wartime, depression-ridden state and its subjects from being sacrificed for the economic welfare of the state's creditors. Strangely enough, the reformers' means of solution had actually been employed by the monarchy itself in the past—and were to be used with telling effect by Colbert during the early, reformist years of Louis XIV's personal reign after 1661. Indeed, the judges' savage attack on *traitants* and their insistence on tightening the treasury's borrowing procedures helped to make the Colbertian campaign possible by demonstrating the popularity and urgency of fiscal reform.

The obvious financial solution, from our vantage point, would have been to abolish the many tax exemptions of privileged provinces, officiers, nobles, and some of the bourgeoisie. But who could have suggested such an undertaking in 1648? That basic reform would have destroyed the corporative basis of the *ancien régime*; it was not to come about until a combination of many unexpected factors brought on the French Revolution of 1789. The treatment of public offices as private property was another feature of seventeenth-century government which begged for drastic alteration—it was surely not a financial solution to strengthen that practice and thereby divert taxpayers' incomes and state revenues more than ever to the pockets of the officiers. However, in protecting their investment in offices, the officials were also striking at the monarchy's equally inde-

---

[106] Kossman, *La Fronde*, especially pp. 1-2, 55-56, contends that the reforms were superficial, since they dealt primarily with finances and failed to probe into questions of political authority. Although a brilliant modification of liberal and conservative-monarchist views, his thesis explains away the very obvious mid-century crisis which both of those schools at least detected. One need not quibble over the exact date for the beginning of the Fronde, but Kossman is surely misleading when he asserts that the Fronde never "began," because it was merely an intensification of previous royal-official clashes.

fensible exploitation of the bad features of contemporary officehold-ing. The central administration had been securing income from sub-jects through the taxing of officers whose wealth ultimately came from society at large, and although this royal policy was, at best, an indirect way of financing the state's undertakings, it was, at worst, an arbitrary and inefficient operation.

Just as it is erroneous to say that the reforms were superficial because they concentrated on financial affairs, it is misleading to dis-cuss the financial reforms outside the context of contemporary politi-cal institutions and practices. Financial affairs were so closely tied to every aspect of the French government's structure that financial reform necessarily meant institutional changes as well. *Traitant,* intendant, and fusiliers were inseparable, since they cooperated in forcibly collecting revenue from subjects. Conciliar *arrêts, lettres de cachet,* and *lits de justice* were equally connected, since all were used to impose new taxes arbitrarily on the individual. Admittedly, the officers were naïve in trying to curb fiscal abuses by abolishing intendancies and shackling the councils, and their motives for under-taking administrative reforms which transferred power from a few cold-blooded servants of the state to the thousands of *trésoriers* and *élus,* hundreds of petty tribunals, and dozens of sovereign courts were partly from self-interest. We can go so far in criticizing the institu-tional reforms as to declare that they were a double disaster, because they stripped the central administration's agencies of some of its power to perform potentially useful services for the state and its inhabitants, and transferred that same power to the numerous cum-bersome and self-centered corporations of officers. Yet, at the insti-tutional as well as the purely financial level, the reforms stemmed from complex grievances which cannot be written off as being purely selfish and calculating. As an astute diarist wrote, in commenting on the underlying reasons for the reformers' destructive attack on intendancies, this onslaught sprang only in part from the sover-eign court judges' dislike of intendants who encroached "on the petty officials' functions, judging sovereignly the vast majority of cases and in so doing depriving the parlements of appellate juris-diction." It also amounted to retribution for the intendants' oppres-sion of the "people," notably for the "abuses and malversation practiced by most of them or their agents, especially by the companies of fusiliers which accompanied them under pretext of

170

providing security for their persons, [and] who committed all sorts of disorders."[107]

All in all, the reforms were a negative, but serious attempt to deal with an institutional malaise which everyone recognized but no one knew how to cure. When Louis XIV's personal administration freed itself from the stranglehold of fiscal concerns after 1661, the councils and intendancies became very efficient servants of king and subjects alike. But in the 1640's the administration's preoccupation with financial problems turned those institutions into repressive instruments of arbitrary policies, thereby making them vulnerable targets of the reformers. As a result, potentially useful vehicles of absolutism were swept under along with the outrageous abuses.

A final word needs to be said about the reforming judges' refusal to deal thoroughly and incisively with underlying constitutional issues. We must distinguish between that refusal and the incorrect inference that the officers could neither understand nor grapple with the basic question of sovereignty. For the judges knew all too well the delicate, complex makeup of the so-called absolute monarchy. Their debates in the Parlement of Paris after the *lit de justice* of January 1648 are sufficient proof of their grasp of pure theory, and their solution of working for reform within the framework of divine-right absolutism during the following summer proves that they also had practical wisdom. Thus, by avoiding an open challenge to the principle of the king's ultimate sovereignty, the officers spared themselves the stigma of being labeled revolutionaries, at the same time that carefully worded, legalistic reforms were forced on a reluctant regent, whose ministers' arguments for the king's personal will and the principle of *raison d'état* foundered on the rock of legal technicalities. Royalist arguments about state needs and expediency were met by specific references to existing French laws, promulgated by previous kings, and except in the case of arbitrary detention, the administrators had to admit that the reformers' position was unassailable.[108]

[107] Vallier, *Journal* 1, 49-50.

[108] Although based almost exclusively on the work of other historians, the brief comments in Shennan, *Parlement of Paris*, pp. 273-276, reveal an understanding of the judges' political position which is lacking in specialized studies of the Fronde. Doolin, *The Fronde*, pp. xii, 11, and 58-78, also underlines the constitutional nature of the reforms, but without understanding their complex institutional and legal framework. Moreover, Doolin's assertion that the original articles "aimed at a radi-

Thus the judges' devious treatment of sovereignty was the basic strength of the parlementary Fronde. It enabled the French reformers to steer past the regent some wide-ranging measures checking the governmental revolution of the previous decades—measures which, incidentally, were strikingly similar to the moderate reforms the Long Parliament imposed on Charles I at a comparable, early stage of the English mid-century crisis. As in England, extralegal agencies of the central administration were abolished, arbitrary imprisonment somewhat curtailed, taxes subjected to institutional approval, and the legal powers of the king's councils circumscribed. And not only was this done without a revolution, in the strict sense of the term, it was accomplished in a way which would save the Parlement of Paris from the fate which the English Parliament suffered after its reformist phase. In France, the officiers sacrificed sovereignty only to save major reforms and the leading reformist institution, the Parlement of Paris. In England, where the parliamentarians broke with royal sovereignty while in the process of achieving basic reforms, that break irreparably damaged the English Parliament's *raison d'être* as an integral element of royal authority. Hence radical revolution in England swept aside Parliament along with Crown, leaving only the Cromwellian military element to fill the vacuum.

The main reason for the weakness of the reforms of 1648 was not that they were too superficial to be taken seriously, or too radical to find their way into an absolutist structure, but that they were the product of extraordinary circumstances. True, the grievances leading to the reforms were deep-seated and widespread, but the opportunity to translate anger into action had come only when the mishandling of the renewal of the paulette by Anne's advisers had brought about the convocation of the Chambre Saint Louis. How long could rival corporations of officiers, self-contained social groups, and scattered provinces hold together as a viable opposition? Ironically, the Chambre Saint Louis actually undermined the *raison d'être* of that coalition by its very success. Since almost every element within the state had benefited in some way from the reforms of 1648, these groups tended during the later Fronde to lose their interest in maintaining the coalition, falling back into the old pattern of isolation and rivalry.

---

cal reformation of the institutions of the monarchy" makes him an unconscious supporter of "liberal" interpretations of the Fronde.

Tensions within the coalition were already evident during the parlementary Fronde, although the Parlement of Paris had done much to keep them from ruining the reform program. The parlementarians had tried to placate the rival Cour des Aides and Chambre des Comptes by including their representatives in several of the Parlement's conferences with the administration, yet the Parlement antagonized them by insisting that their registration of some taxes was invalid unless confirmed by parlementary verification.[109] The Grand Conseil had lost interest in the reforms as soon as the paulette was restored and its imprisoned members released, and only the fear that they might be isolated from the other officiers kept its judges from breaking formally with the parlementary Fronde. They congratulated the parlementary leader Broussel when he was released after the Days of Barricades, but they were extremely jealous of his tribunal's posture as the head of the reform movement. They were mollified by the Parlement's inclusion of their members in some conferences with the administration, but antagonized when the parlementarians excluded them from membership in the *chambre de justice.* And, though the Parlement's ruling was legalistically correct, the argument being that that Grand Conseil had no jurisdiction over state credit, such legalistic wrangles were precisely the issues which undermined the ephemeral *esprit de corps* of the officiers.[110]

Then there was the much more delicate problem of keeping the maîtres des requêtes united with the other officials. Their alienation from the administration in 1648 had added immeasurably to the strength of the reformist coalition, but their restoration to power as an important element of the councils could only lead to bitter rivalry with the remaining officiers. Fortunately, the maîtres remained suspicious of the administration long after their formal reinstatement— some of the maîtres who sat in the Parlement during the last months of the parlementary Fronde of 1648 rivaled the most radical parlementarians in their attacks on the regent's policies. The parlementary judges were also careful to avoid unnecessary clashes with the maîtres during those debates. Nevertheless, the maîtres and parle-

---

[109] *Journal contenant tout ce qui s'est fait,* pp. 33, 38; Dubuisson-Aubenay, *Journal* I, 81; B. N. Ms. Fr. 23319, fol. 48r.

[110] See B. N. Ms. Fr. 23319, fols. 19v, 22, 40; Ms. Fr. 18367, fol. 254r; Ormesson, *Journal* I, 540. A. N. U 336, p. 473 reveals the Parlement's admission that it had alienated the Grand Conseil.

mentarians could not reconcile their underlying differences. The abolition of the intendancies and the restrictions on the councils antagonized the maîtres, who sat in the councils and had often acted as intendants. The maîtres' legal decisions in conciliar agencies infuriated the Parlement because they were handed down as final judgments without appeal to that sovereign court. Mutual suspicions increased daily, and there was a well-founded rumor that Mazarin had seriously entertained the thought of interdicting the Parlement and placing some maîtres in charge of its members' functions. The central administration was even thinking of using the maîtres as circuit riders in the provinces, thereby reviving their old supervisory role as *maîtres des requêtes en chevauchées,* in its efforts to evade the abolition of the intendancies. Actually, the maîtres were embroiled in a vendetta with the councilors of state, who were also interested in acting as substitutes for the intendants. However, the parlementary judges and other officers could take little comfort from this petty feud within the regent's administration.[111]

Economic and social considerations also envenomed relations within the coalition. Officials began to see that the reforms were a mixed blessing, since tax rebates encouraged subjects to withhold the very taxes which were allocated for the officers' salaries. The abolition of unverified commissions also gave tax evaders and lawless elements the notion that even the judges' normal procedure of investigating crimes by commissions was illegal. The *trésoriers* became embittered when the *élus* increased tax assessments and then used the money to raise their salaries beyond the level stipulated by the reforms.[112] The Parlement of Paris, in turn, suspected the *trésoriers* of similar practices. The parlementarians had fought for the *trésoriers'* right to administer the *taille,* partially on the latter's argu-

---

[111] Ormesson's *Journal* is a fundamental source for all these developments. See also Séguier's papers, B. N. Ms. Fr. 23319, fols. 33r, 63r, 102v, 115-117. B. U. P. Ms. 64, notes the willingness of the Parlement to consider the maîtres' offer to supervise the inferior courts (dated October 8, 1648). During parlementary debate, four maîtres (Le Tiller, du Tremblay, Lallement, and Marescot) wanted all intendancies abolished without exception, contending that the maîtres could do the essential work of the intendants without violating the legal restrictions on extraordinary commissions. B. N. Ms. Fr. 23319, fol. 33r. The complicated and ambivalent role of the maîtres des requêtes certainly merits a special study as a corrective to the now orthodox view that the parlementary Fronde pitted commissaires (including the maîtres) against officiers.

[112] On these points, see Actes Royaux, F 23631, nos. 432, 436.

ment that they could add some forty million *livres* to the amount tax farmers and intendants had been able to provide for the state. However, the administration estimated that the restoration of the *trésoriers* would actually cost the treasury over nine and one-half million *livres*.[113]

Even within a single corporation, the reforms sometimes pitted one official against another. For example, the highly popular abolition of the intendancies could not have pleased parlementarians like Molé, whose own son was an intendant in Champagne.[114] The parlementary debate on state credit was particularly bitter. Some officials were deeply involved in loans with the state, either through relatives who made the actual advances or because of their habit of loaning money to persons who dealt with the state. It is impossible to tell just how many parlementarians or members of any other corporation derived excessive profits from such transactions, many officials receiving only a modest return on a legitimate investment in rentes. However, radical parlementarians indiscriminately accused all officers connected with state borrowing of being *traitants* in disguise. In order to avoid an ugly scene, Molé asked all state creditors to leave the Parlement until the debate was concluded. Many judges left to avoid a possible conflict of interest, unable to defend their incorruptibility but angered by the imputation of wrongdoing.[115]

These internal weaknesses of the reform movement were precisely the conditions which would enable Mazarin to divide and rule at the end of the Fronde. However, they were of little consolation to either the chief minister or the regent in October 1648. For the moment, Anne's administration was on the defensive and there was

---

[113] B. N. Ms. Fr. 18367, fols. 17-18, 193.

[114] That intendant, Jean-Edouard Molé de Champlâtreux, held one of the six commissions which was retained when the other intendancies were abolished. Possibly Mathieu Molé's influence with the administration and his family's friendship with Condé, who had used Champlâtreux as an intendant in his army, explains why Champagne retained its intendant.

[115] The bitter argument between the conservative de Mesmes and the radical Blancmesnil illustrates the complexity of the issue. See B. N. Ms. Fr. 23319, fols. 63-66, and also fols. 70-71, 173r. Traces of corruption among the officiers can be found in Ormesson, *Journal* I, 545-546; Vallier, *Journal* I, 56, fn. 2; Talon, *Mémoires*, p. 247. In 1651, *Procureur Général* Nicolas Fouquet said that judges who attacked profiteering were jealous because their own contracts with the treasury were not honored. B. U. P. Ms. 68, fol. 61. The most balanced and plausible view, that profiteering was not widespread, is admirably stated by Cubells, "Parlement de Paris," pp. 177-184.

a desperate shortage of money for military needs. The reform of the *taille* cost the treasury some fifty million *livres* in potential revenue, and the restrictions on tariffs swelled that amount by an additional five million *livres*. If the salaries of the officiers were fully paid, the treasury would lose another twenty-five million *livres*; the mere fulfillment of the promise to resume partial payments would be a severe blow to the administration's finances.[116] Relations with the *traitants* were strained. In September 1648, the treasury owed them one hundred twenty million *livres*, and La Meilleraye was paying them at the unusually low rate of ten million *livres* per annum.[117] The withdrawal of the intendants from the provinces threw the treasury's tax-collecting machinery into disarray. And, above all, the administration was hampered by the revived powers of the sovereign courts which were certain to oppose any new fiscal legislation or extralegal arrangements with the *traitants*. The French monarchy had evaded legal controls in the past, and the regent's regime would be sure to use every legal or illegal means to restore its administrative, financial, and judicial power. What Anne and Mazarin did not realize was that their efforts to combat the reforms of 1648 would cause still further turmoil, and ultimately turn the revolt of the judges into the Fronde of the great nobles.

[116] See A. N. U 336, pp. 265-266; Dubuisson-Aubenay, *Journal* 1, 76-77, 80. The Duke of Orléans estimated that the reform of the *taille* would deprive the treasury of 40,000,000 *livres* in overdue payments, plus the 20 per cent reduction of 10,000,000 *livres*. The reduced tariffs cost the administration some 2,000,000 *livres* from the levy in Paris and 3,000,000 *livres* from other towns.

[117] Talon, *Mémoires*, p. 281.

CHAPTER SIX

THE ROYAL SIEGE OF PARIS:
PARLEMENT, NOBILITY,
AND THE DEFENSE OF REFORM

THE DECLARATION OF October 22, 1648, was followed by a brief
period of relative calm in France. No one expected it to last, however, for there were signs of unrest in almost every region of the
kingdom. Alienated subjects who had been somewhat appeased by
the reforms of the parlementary Fronde needed little encouragement
to engage in new conflicts with Anne's administration. In outlying
provinces, the precise terms of the Declaration of October were not
yet settled, and local courts haggled with provincial governors over
amendments or *arrêts*. The situation was especially dangerous in
Normandy and Provence, because the parlements at Rouen and Aix
feared new attempts to increase their membership. The governor of
Normandy, Longueville, barely contained the restiveness of that area
by securing fiscal concessions from the regent in December. In Provence, the intendant, Alexandre de Sève (one of the six exempt from
the revocation of July), tried desperately to bring governor and parlementarians together. But Governor Alais did not want a settlement, and members of the Parlement of Aix would not have trusted
him after previous encounters, even if he had been sincere. Each
side bickered over details, while awaiting a chance to force major
concessions on its rival. Even in the remote province of Navarre, on
the Spanish border, there was sedition at Pau, although the Parlement of Pau kept it within bounds. Nowhere was there the slightest
sign that taxpayers were inclined to pay any taxes, whether confirmed by the reforms of 1648 or not.[1]

Les grands posed a peculiar threat to internal tranquility. Peace
with Austria and the seasonal lull in the Franco-Spanish campaigns
freed adventurous noble officers of wartime concerns. The state's
armies could easily become involved in the Fronde, but it was haz-

[1] See especially Mousnier, *Lettres et mémoires adressés au Chancelier Séguier* II,
873-876, 896-897; and above, chap. 5, fns. 78, 79.

ardous to predict whether their commanders would throw their support to the beleaguered regent or her internal enemies.

The Duke of Orléans and the *Grand* Condé were the greatest enigmas. While Condé was a confirmed enemy of the parlementarians, his spectacular victories against Spain in recent months made him feel that he should be richly rewarded for his services. Orléans was a well-intentioned man with a weak will. His concern for continued harmony between regent and officiers was certainly not shared by Anne and Mazarin. Their distaste for the reforms of the past summer was sharpened by fears that the princely mediator of the parlementary Fronde might side with the judges. No one could tell what these two princes might do; Mazarin viewed Condé's arrogance with suspicion and believed that Orléans was secretly negotiating with parlementary and noble friends.[2]

While those leading princes wavered, other prominent nobles plotted seriously to overthrow or weaken Mazarin. These noble "Frondeurs" were not a closely knit political party but a loose coalition of several distinguished families held together by personal connections and their common jealousy of the chief minister. The nucleus of the faction was the small group of nobles which had opposed Mazarin after the Days of Barricades, only to be thwarted by the parlementary-royal settlement of October. Paul de Gondi, one of those original intriguers, became a prominent figure in the new coalition. He had added to his personal base of power as archbishop-coadjutor of Paris, and was now supported by parish priests, some of the canons at Notre Dame Cathedral, a number of outstanding pamphleteers, and a few scions of moderately distinguished noble families. The other dominant personality was the Duchess of Longueville. She continued to overshadow her husband, charmed other persons within her family circle, and carried the additional prestige of being a sister of the *Grand* Condé. While she could not persuade that brother to side with the Frondeurs, she was successful in rallying her other brother, Armand de Conti, as well as her husband and his rival for her affections, the Prince of Marsillac (later the famous Duke of La Rochefoucauld). The Condé-Longueville family was even more powerful than Gondi's coterie, thanks to its hold on important military governorships. The Duke of Longueville held the important province of Normandy, Conti was governor of Cham-

[2] See Chéruel, *Minorité de Louis XIV* III, 85-88, 92-94, 124-127.

pagne, and Marsillac's family had personal and political roots in the southwestern provinces.[3]

Most of these noble Frondeurs also had close relations with some radical parlementarians who had flirted with the original noble *cabale* of the parlementary Fronde, including Broussel, Viole, and Blancmesnil. Although the number of parlementary Frondeurs was small and their commitment to the nobles' cause uncertain, they gave the faction a potential base of power in the Parlement of Paris. Included in the parlementary wing of the coalition were two *présidents à mortier*, de Novion and de Maisons, as well as the latter's brother, de Longueil. These judges opened their homes to meetings of the *cabale*, plotted strategy with the nobles and, if rumors were accurate, actually tried to coax Orléans and Condé into their movement.[4]

Cardinal Mazarin was fully informed of these intrigues, but his method of restricting them had mixed results. He bound Orléans more closely to his person by opening the royal councils to the duke's closest adviser, Abbé de La Rivière, and by hinting that Condé might take Orléans' place as the leading noble at court. Condé was won over by Anne's flattery, Mazarin's ingratiating manners, and the gift of several fortresses on the eastern border which the prince added to his political base as governor in Burgundy. Unfortunately, these spectacular results of his personal diplomacy reinforced Mazarin's ingrained belief that all internal problems could be solved by bribery and duplicity. And while Mazarin looked for opportunities to maneuver the rest of *les grands* into his camp, the Frondeurs became more contemptuous. His willingness to take the low political road merely increased their confidence that they could either replace him or sell their friendship at a high price.[5]

While provincial unrest and courtly intrigues laid the groundwork for new strife, the unresolved issues of the parlementary Fronde alone made a civil war possible. Without basic grievances, the Parlement of Paris could not have been induced to listen to the

---

[3] See ibid. III, 131-132; Debû-Bridel, *Anne-Geneviève de Bourbon*, pp. 73-74, 97-104; L. Batiffol, *Biographie du Cardinal de Retz*, Paris 1929, pp. 56-57.

[4] The role of the parlementary Frondeurs was noted by many contemporary writers, including Dubuisson-Aubenay, Vallier, Nemours, Montglat, Rapin, Guy Joly, Priolo, Vineuil, and La Rochefoucauld.

[5] Mazarin's personal diplomacy can be followed in Chéruel, *Minorité de Louis XIV* III.

anti-Mazarinist harangues of the handful of radical judges in the noble *cabale*. And without support from the same tribunal, no revolt by *les grands* was conceivable at this time. The great nobles had the soldiers, arms, and provincial governorships to sustain a military conflict, but they needed legal justification for taking up arms. The most implausible form of civil war on a large scale was popular uprisings in town and countryside, and, as in the first years of Anne's regency, was likely to get out of hand only if it merged with a parlementary attack on the administration.

The burden of guilt for the violence of 1649 has to be laid on the shoulders of Anne and Mazarin, for it was the administration's evasions of the reforms of 1648 which stampeded the majority in the Parlement of Paris into supporting their radical colleagues, and thereby starting a chain reaction leading to the siege of Paris. Still, one cannot help sympathizing with the plight of the regent and her first minister. They tried to meet the pressing financial needs of the state and used tactics they thought would not unduly antagonize the parlementarians. Probably most questionable was their assumption that the prosecution of the foreign war necessitated certain risks. Mazarin was convinced that foreign affairs must take precedence over internal problems. Condé's victories and the Franco-Austrian peace had been offset by internal unrest, which had stiffened the Spaniards' resolution to continue fighting. The cardinal was looking forward eagerly to the spring of 1649, hoping to launch an offensive which would bring Spain to the conference table. Only the reforms of 1648 seemed to stand in the way, robbing the military machine of funds.

The chief minister was sufficiently realistic to know that a major assault on the reforms would revive the parlementary Fronde. So, instead, he hoped to bend the recent legislation in the monarchy's favor. Revised interest rates and the security of the *taille* were used to induce *traitants* to loosen their purse strings. The *taille* was supplemented by special war taxes, euphemistically described as mere "advances" on future *tailles*, and collected by the military authorities for their use. Payments on *rentes* and salaries were also held back temporarily. These measures were designed to avoid criticism by the Parlement of Paris. There was no formal increase in taxation and hence no need to submit legislation for parlementary registration.

To provide a cloak of legality for the removal of restrictions on credit, the administration appealed to the more pliable financial courts of Paris. The Cour des Aides was asked to approve the expanded use of the *taille,* and the Chambre des Comptes was requested to raise the statutory limit on interest and remove controls on the secret *comptants.* Undoubtedly, Séguier had advised Mazarin on the legal aspects of this strategy, holding out hopes that the financial courts would fall in line. The chief minister and chancellor probably thought that their plans were foolproof; even if the Parlement objected, its members would become hopelessly involved in legalistic quarrels with the other courts over jurisdictional claims, and Mazarin could divide and rule.[6]

The scheme was so clever that it almost succeeded. The financial courts gave the revised reforms serious consideration, and parlementary attempts to interfere with the work of the other courts evoked an angry response from the Chambre des Comptes. Nevertheless, the revived hostility between the Parisian corporations failed to give Mazarin what he wanted. Even though the sovereign courts would not unite on behalf of the reforms of 1648, each was prepared to resist in its own way. Ironically, parlementary criticism of the Chambre des Comptes' docility stiffened that tribunal's determination to protect the gains of the parlementary Fronde. So instead of quickly approving the new legislation, it began to debate the legality of the administration's demands. The Cour des Aides registered the proposals, but with modifications which destroyed their usefulness. Advances on the *taille* were permitted for a minimal six-month period, and regular officiers were to administer its collection without interference from *traitants.*[7]

Predictably, the Parlement raised the strongest outcry. Although it had no legislation to debate, that sovereign court decided in mid-December 1648, to investigate all rumors of changes in the Declaration of October. When the administration charged the judges with violating an oral agreement not to hold plenary sessions, the parle-

[6] The administration's strategy has to be reconstructed from royal directives to the courts, and parlementary allegations (which Orléans and Condé were unable to refute). See especially the debates in A. N. U 336 during December; and Talon, *Mémoires,* p. 312; Ormesson, *Journal* 1, 596-597; Dubuisson-Aubenay, *Journal* 1, 89-95; Boislisle, *Chambre des Comptes,* p. 427.

[7] A. N. U 336, pp. 470-474; Ormesson, *Journal* 1, 599-601.

mentarians replied that evasions of the reforms nullified their promise. The royal declarations had clearly given the Parlement authority to enforce the reforms, and an investigation was therefore in order. After futile efforts to block a plenary session, First President Molé reversed himself and defended its legality. The sudden appearance of Orléans and Condé at the Parlement failed to subdue the judges, and, instead of persuading the parlementarians to halt their sessions, the princes found themselves listening to a wave of protests against administrative abuses. Most of the judges concentrated on violations of the Declaration of October, but the judicial radicals who had joined the emerging noble *cabale* stressed Mazarin's guilt. Without mentioning his name, these parlementary Frondeurs asked their colleagues to attack the basic cause of current disorders in the realm, namely, the administration's refusal to end the foreign war. A Frondeur president, de Novion, virtually denied royal absolutism in contending that the Parlement was the only place where such affairs of state as treaties, wars, and alliances could be authorized. A few judges went so far as to demand entirely new reforms. Condé, however, was angered by their attacks on the royal household's misuse of revenues, since he was in charge of that department; and he, as military hero, and Orléans, as titular head of the armies, were also angered by the criticism of disorders by the troops stationed around Paris.

The majority of the Parlement was probably unaware of the underlying reason for the radicals' extreme attacks on the administration. Had they known the Frondeurs' objective of overthrowing the chief minister, it is doubtful that they would have halted their own criticisms of the administration, so angry was the Parlement as a whole with the open royal evasions of past reforms. Conservatives and moderates joined the radicals in denouncing administrative abuses; but though some judges leaped to the conclusion that the Chambre Saint Louis should be reconvened, most realized that a joint assembly of that type could intensify disagreements with the financial courts, and in any case would not be supported by the Grand Conseil. The conciliatory Orléans and radical Broussel finally worked out an agreement, which seemed to placate the parlementarians without endangering royal authority or the officiers' solidarity. A parlementary committee was to examine allegations of abuses, and the Parlement could then decide on the legal means to implement its recommendations. However, this merely postponed the vital question of how the Parlement would eventually act.[8]

Orléans and Molé were naïve in assuming that the postponement would moderate the judges' opposition. The more militant members of the tribunal became impatient with the committee's slow-moving investigation. By the end of December 1648, it was clear that the Parlement would revert to its tactics of the parlementary Fronde and issue *arrêts* on its own authority. Moreover, the third *chambre des enquêtes* agreed to press for entirely new reforms, and it appeared likely that the other junior chambers would support their aims. The radicals were thus well prepared for the plenary session, and were overjoyed when Molé promised that a debate on the committee's findings would begin on January 8, 1649.[9]

The regent and her ministers were determined to stop the growing opposition before new action could be aroused against royal authority. For a while, they attempted to do so through conciliation. The superintendent of finances, La Meilleraye, was especially anxious to remove the most outstanding grievances, and as late as January 2, withdrew the unpopular requests which had been placed before the Chambre des Comptes. He also reopened bidding on some tax farms in order to secure better terms, and rejected the request of other tax farmers for a discount on their contract. All these measures used the universally hated financiers as scapegoats, and were undoubtedly aimed at finding a common bond between regent and judges in their mutual distrust of the *traitants*.[10]

The basic weakness of this conciliatory approach was that it did not solve the fiscal crisis. Revenues obtained by reauctioning tax farms would be offset by the increased unwillingness of other persons to lend money to the treasury. Hence the regent and her closest advisers began to consider the possibility of using the force of the royal troops against the sovereign courts of Paris and particularly the Parlement. Though in September, such plans had been set aside since the French armies were occupied with the foreign war, as winter set in the scheme was revived. The French forces were idle, and

[8] A. N. U 336, pp. 456-474; Goulas, *Mémoires* II, 427-433.

[9] A. N. U 336, pp. 479-480; Ormesson, *Journal* I, 604; *Journal de ce qui s'est fait ès assemblées du Parlement*, Paris, 1649, p. 3.

[10] Dubuisson-Aubenay, *Journal* I, 101; Ormesson, *Journal* I, 602; Vallier, *Journal* I, 134. Royalist circles were also aware of Gondi's efforts to secure a theological ruling in the Sorbonne against the new interest rates. A.A.E., France, Ms. 860, fols. 234-236.

Condé could now be counted on to lead the army under his command from the Low Countries to the environs of the capital.

In the end, it was fear and anger which drove the royal entourage to violence. The parlementary criticisms of Mazarin and the judges' decision to begin a full-scale debate on reform terrified the chief minister and other intimates of the queen mother. Already disturbed by the possibility of a second parlementary Fronde more radical than the first, their fears were heightened by the startling news, on December 13, that the Cromwellians were determined to abolish the monarchy of Charles I and establish a "popular" state—this news made rulers on the continent, even as far away as Sweden, shudder. In France, England's Great Rebellion had particular significance since Charles's wife, Henriette-Marie, was a French princess; and her vivid first-hand impressions of the English scene had had a strong impact when she returned to the French royal court.[11] Though Anne and Mazarin reacted in different fashions to the situation in England, their conclusions were the same: that the same fate could befall the French monarchy. The first minister, as evidenced in his personal notebook, believed that Charles I, by permitting Parliament to execute his minister, Strafford, had set the stage for his downfall. Therefore, he believed that current verbal attacks on his own person at the Palace of Justice might well bring similar death to him and the end to monarchy unless conciliation were replaced by firmness.[12] Anne, typically, was enraged and scandalized by the thought that the Parlement would dare imitate the would-be English regicides; besides, she was still determined to maintain the full power of the monarchy so that it could be passed on to her son when he came of age in 1651. Anne's uncompromising attitude was clearly revealed by her remark to Henriette-Marie: "Very soon I shall be either an absolute queen or [powerless] like you." This attitude, when civil war broke out between the administration and the Parisians in January, was further evidenced by the fact that she would not listen to an *échevin* from the *bureau de ville* who tried to convince the regent that the Parlement was the preserver of monarchy. Believing only that the judges were destroying monarchy rather than protecting it, Anne retorted: "I prefer Paris lost than disobedient."[13] Mazarin's

[11] The impact of English developments on the French administration is discussed by Knachel, *England and the Fronde*, pp. 38-41, 45-49.

[12] Chéruel, *Minorité de Louis XIV* III, 135-136 (based on Mazarin's notebooks); Goulas, *Mémoires* II, 442.

[13] B. N. Ms. Fr. 17560, fol. 12r.

trusted agent, Hugues de Lionne, writing to another agent of Mazarin after the royal family fled from Paris, underlined the preflight attitudes of Anne's group by stating that if they had remained they would have been at the mercy of a Parisian mob, incited by those who were intriguing against the regent's administration.[14]

On December 14, the very day after the alarming news from England, preparations were made to flee from Paris at the first sign of hostile actions at the Parlement,[15] and the council of state met to decide what precise measures should be taken against the parlementarians. *Surintendant* La Meilleraye, drawing on his earlier experiences as a commander, urged that the Bastille be used as the starting point for a military sweep through the capital. Others thought that the arrest of four or five ringleaders among the parlementary and noble Frondeurs would be sufficient. Mazarin, Condé, and Secretary of State Michel Le Tellier turned aside these suggestions. The chief minister recoiled from shedding blood, remembering the Days of Barricades too well to consider an attempt to arrest judges in the presence of hostile Parisians. Condé, whom many contemporaries believed to be the daredevil advocate of streetfighting, treated La Meilleraye's plans with contempt, and, in keeping with his social prejudice, military training, and sense of honor, he preferred siege warfare which would at the very most draw his troops into combat in the open countryside against any mercenary soldiers which the city might send out to break the blockade. Engaging in hand-to-hand combat with lowly city-dwellers and mere judges was certainly not, in his mind, the way to deal with rebelliousness, much as he disliked Parisians and parlementarians. Le Tellier also wanted to remove the royal entourage from Paris, but pleaded for the milder tactic of an economic blockade.

Agreement was reached finally on a plan combining the approaches of Le Tellier and Condé. Paris was to be bluffed into submission by the withdrawal of the royal entourage, an act which Parisians were meant to interpret as the prelude to a royalist siege. If the Parlement refused immediate capitulation, the city's supplies would be cut off by Condé's soldiers who could easily be deployed to prevent the entry of merchants or the exit of a military force assigned convoy duty. The inhabitants would then turn their wrath

---

[14] Lionne to Servien, January 15, 1649, in Chéruel, *Minorité de Louis XIV* III, 137.

[15] Dubuisson-Aubenay, *Journal* I, 93. (The writer was in close touch with Secretary of State de Guenégaud.)

on the judges, it was believed, and the terrified Parlement would come to terms. Men like Condé knew that his troops would soon have to return to the frontier for the spring campaign, but the council was confident that the blockade would be successful before that occurred. Within two weeks, at most, Paris and its Parlement would be firmly under royal control.[16]

The council realized that its scheme must be implemented with the utmost secrecy and speed, before the divided courts and disorganized Parisians could unite against the monarchy. The Parlement's decision to reconvene on January 8, 1649, set the royal plans in motion. On the night of January 5, while Paris was celebrating the Feast of Epiphany, the royal family slipped out of the capital in the company of courtiers and ministers. Royal quarters were established at nearby Saint-Germain-en-Laye, and Condé gathered his troops in preparation for a siege of the capital.

2

THE FLIGHT from Paris did not make civil war inevitable. Despite the incendiary work of parlementary Frondeurs, there was as yet no attempt by the Parlement as a whole to overthrow either the chief minister or the monarchy. And despite the threat of military force implicit in the royal withdrawal from Paris, there was as yet no military siege or economic blockade. The regent's irrational acts during the hours after her arrival at Saint-Germain were therefore especially tragic. In her determination to prevent the pattern of the English civil war from spreading to France, she unwittingly precipitated a civil war which might well have been avoided.

The first day after the flight, Anne sent a highly inflammatory message to the capital. That declaration accused unnamed parlementarians of negotiating with the Spaniards and conspiring to seize the king. Moreover, it was sent to the Hôtel de Ville and not directly to the Parlement. The next day, January 7, these accusations were followed by royal commands to the public authorities in Paris. The Parlement, Chambre des Comptes, Cour des Aides, and Grand Conseil were ordered to leave the city and take up residence in the towns of

---

[16] My account of the meeting follows Priolo, *Ministry of Cardinal Mazarine*, pp. 116-118. He is more trustworthy than other writers because of his close relations with the Condé family and his very precise reconstruction of the debate. See also Chéruel, *Minorité de Louis XIV* III, 136-138; B. N. Ms. Fr. 17560, fol. 16r.

Montargis, Orléans, Reims, and Mantes. Significantly, the royalist governor and *bureau de ville* of Paris were exempted from these punitive measures. Instead, they were asked to assist the administration's efforts to force compliance on the sovereign tribunals.[17] All these directives were far more provocative than any royal actions had been during the parlementary Fronde of 1648. Guilt by association made the entire Parlement appear treasonous and antimonarchical. The attempt to transfer all four courts to distant places indicated that the regent also planned to revoke the entire reform program of the previous summer, and the conciliatory attitude toward the Hôtel de Ville was a clear threat to the unity of the Parisian authorities, since it was designed to turn the civic government against the law courts.

The regent's slurs on the judges' loyalty to king, Crown, and state were the most fateful aspects of these messages. True, the attempt to divide, exile, and overturn the reforms of the sovereign courts was also provocative; but this might have drawn the Parlement toward some sort of compromise which would have sacrificed part of those reforms in return for the peaceful reentry of the royal entourage to the capital. Indeed, the confusion and utter terror which gripped Paris after the regent's flight and the arrival of her messages was so widespread that the parlementarians were on the verge of being stampeded into making major concessions. It was unfortunate for the regent that she did not simply state her major objective in the firm language which an agent of Mazarin used in a memorandum after the siege began, in February:

> We hold firm in desiring that the authority of the king be fully restored; that is, that all that has occurred in general during the past eight months [since June 1648] be suppressed from its [i.e. the Parlement's] registers, and all memory of it obliterated.[18]

But by bringing to the surface the republican issue, through the suggestion that the judges were in league with Spain against king and state, and on the verge of abolishing the monarchy in favor of a republic, Anne made the proud and self-righteous parlementarians

---

[17] *Registres de l'Hôtel de Ville de Paris pendant la Fronde*, eds. Le Roux de Lincy and Douët-d'Arcq, 3 vols., Paris, 1846-1848, II, 62-64, 70-71; Isambert, *Anciennes lois françaises* XVII, 110-114; Goulas, *Mémoires* III, 7, fn. 1.

[18] Lionne to Servien, February 6, 1649, quoted in Chéruel, *Minorité de Louis XIV* III, 200.

angry enough to resist the pressures to compromise. In short, her stinging accusations drove them to action as irrational and absurd as her own: the parlementarians finally engaged in rebellion in order to prove that they were not traitors or republicans!

The stiffening of the Parlement's resistance was apparent even during the first emergency session after the reception of the regent's letters, on January 7. Cleverly, but boldly, the parlementarians decided on a way to avoid the order for their exile without literally disobeying this express command of the king (issued, of course, in his name by the regent): they simply left the actual document unopened on the grounds that it should have been sent to the royal attorneys, not to the Parlement itself. Thus having evaded the issue of the king's personal will, the Parlement went on to attack the charges against its members. The royal attorneys were instructed to go to Saint-Germain with a profession of the Parlement's loyalty and a demand for substantiation of the accusations of treason and rebellion against the unnamed judges. If the regent, herself, could not supply legal evidence, the attorneys were to request a list of the administrators who had been responsible for leveling the false charges, so that they could be prosecuted. The parlementarians thought that Anne might use the audience with the attorneys as an opportunity to negotiate a settlement, but they made tentative plans to defend the city if the regent remained adamant.[19]

Anne's move was as cleverly legalistic as the judges' had been; she refused to see the attorneys. Unfortunately, this added insult to injury. The chancellor argued that the Parlement was without any authority until it obeyed the orders to go to Montargis. Obviously, the regent could not meet representatives of a body which did not legally exist; the attorneys were now mere subjects. Without paying any attention to the issue of the royal slanders of January 6, which were the most important concern of the Parlement, the chancellor merely demanded total obedience, and made it clear that unless the Parlement went to Montargis, the administration would lay siege to the capital.[20]

This highhanded response ended all possibility of compromise.

---

[19] A. N. U 336, pp. 482-490.

[20] Talon, *Mémoires*, pp. 319-320. The *avocat général*'s report of the chancellor's words is confirmed by other writers, including Orléans' friend, Goulas, and Anne's lady-in-waiting, Madame de Motteville.

When the Parlement reconvened on January 8, it firmly refused to capitulate. The most astonishing aspect of the parlementary response was that it was virtually unanimous. Even the normally outspoken apologist of royal authority, President de Mesmes, told his colleagues that they must remain united, and that no judge should be allowed to desert to Saint-Germain. In their private negotiations with Anne's intermediaries, First President Molé and presidents de Nesmond and de Bellièvre of the conservative *grand chambre* made their own positions equally clear. Molé told an agent of Mazarin that the authors of the slander against the Parlement should be severely punished. The other presidents notified Secretary of State Brienne that though the Parlement wanted to be reasonable, its members would defend themselves with "a legitimate defense against an unprecedented oppression." Hence conservatives joined radicals in voting on January 8 to find ways to raise an army of defense against the expected siege by Condé.[21]

The Parlement was not alone in its emotional reaction to the regent's position; the Chambre des Comptes and Cour des Aides of Paris also rejected the requests for their transfer. Furthermore, they resisted the regent's efforts to turn them against the Parlement. Despite their jealousy of the Parlement's prestige and bitterness over the parlementarians' arrogance toward them in December, the two financial courts categorically rejected royal charges against the Parlement. Only the normally proroyalist Grand Conseil sided with Anne, but its opposition to its sister courts was ineffectual. Grand councilors were halted by parlementary order when they tried to obey royal commands for the transfer of their tribunal, and, trapped in Paris, they could only make the futile gesture of suspending all their functions to show their loyalty to the regent.[22]

In organizing resistance to the royal siege, the parlementarians fell back on measures traditionally used when Paris was in danger from foreign invasion. But nothing could alter the fact that they were engaging now in a civil war. The formation of a grand coalition of

<hr/>

[21] See A. N. U 336, pp. 490-496 for the debate and voting. The belligerent attitude of the conservative judges is noted in ibid., p. 490; Molé, *Mémoires* III, 314-315; H. A. de Loménie de Brienne, *Mémoires*, Michaud and Poujoulat collection (ser. III, vol. III), Paris, 1838, p. 103.

[22] B. N. Ms. Fr. 25025, fol. 8v; F. de P. de Clermont, Marquis de Montglat, *Mémoires*, Michaud and Poujoulat collection (ser. III, vol. v), Paris, 1838, p. 203; Ormesson, *Journal* I, 617; Retz, *Oeuvres* III, 139-140, 143-144.

all the public authorities of Paris (except the Grand Conseil) was in actuality the establishment in Paris of a wartime government in opposition to the royal administration. Committees were formed for war, finance, dispatches, information, and passports. Money was borrowed, with the Parlement's prestige as collateral; royal funds still in the capital were appropriated, and taxes were levied on the inhabitants. The financial tribunals, military governor of the city, major merchant guilds, and a civic government which was terrified into rebellion by a proparlementary mob, all played their part. Dominating the coalition was the Parlement of Paris, whose debates decided what would happen in the committees, and whose first president worked behind the scenes to keep his own tribunal united and rivalries with other public authorities from destroying the outward display of solidarity.[23]

Along with the resort to arms by Saint-Germain and Paris came the entry of the great nobles to the civil war. The moment *les grands* learned of the Parlement's decision to defend Paris, they flocked to the Parlement and offered their personal prestige, wealth, military leadership, and authority as provincial governors, to the Parisians. Condé and Orléans, alone among the princes and great nobles, remained loyal to the regent. Condé's friends and relatives, including Conti, the Duke and Duchess of Longueville, and the Prince of Marsillac, pledged their allegiance to the Parlement of Paris. They were joined by the handsome and popular Duke of Beaufort, the dukes of Bouillon and Elbeuf, Marshal La Mothe-Houdancourt, Archbishop-Coadjutor de Gondi, and many lesser dignitaries.

It is amusing to read the insulting comments contemporaries made about the military pretensions of these noble Frondeurs. However, despite the ineptitude of *les grands* as generals, and despite their petty squabbling for the best positions in the rebel army, their prestige and presence in Paris at the outset of the siege, when many still thought of capitulating to the regent, gave a sorely needed boost in morale. While they made few sorties against Condé's royal army—and then almost always with disastrous results—they gave the rebellion something which neither judges nor merchants and artisans could provide.

This rallying of noble Frondeurs to the side of the Parlement of

---

[23] The organization of the city's defense can be followed in the accounts by Talon, Ormesson, Molé, and the *Journal de ce qui s'est fait*. Molé's role is stressed by Goulas, *Mémoires* III, 6-7.

Paris also helped to expand the civil war beyond the area immediately surrounding the capital. Since many of *les grands* held military governorships in distant provinces, and the Parlement also had an indirect influence over the independent provincial tribunals, the rebels of the capital could expect to influence the political climate in virtually every part of the kingdom. Even though the provincial Frondes which erupted in Normandy, Provence, Anjou, Maine, Poitou, and elsewhere at this time had indigenous origins, local revolts were encouraged, and in part caused, by the news and support that came from Paris. The parlementary judges in Paris sent circular letters to the provincial parlements, informing them of the major decisions made by their tribunal against the regent,[24] and the noble Frondeurs who held governorships either fomented popular uprisings in town and countryside or raised their own armies to fight against the monarchy at the local level.[25]

The relations between the local Frondes in Normandy and Provence and the Parisian uprising were particularly close. The Parlement and inhabitants of Rouen needed little encouragement to oppose an administration which had evaded implementing reforms for the Norman populace. Their movement was greatly strengthened with the arrival from Paris of the noble Frondeur and governor of Normandy, Longueville. Royalist forces under the Count of Harcourt were kept out of Rouen by order of the local parlement, and Longueville was able to enter the city in triumph late in January. Meanwhile, the circular letter from the Parlement of Paris arrived, giving its sister court at Rouen the opportunity to collaborate with the Parisians. The Rouen judges asked the parlementarians in Paris to support their opposition to the imposition of new offices on their tribunal. The Parlement of Paris responded with a letter of sympathy and promises to remonstrate with the regent. In Provence, the royalist proclivities of the provincial governor complicated matters but did not prevent cooperation between Aix and Paris. The Count of Alais tried to use his authority as governor to resume an old feud with the

[24] See, inter alia, Actes Royaux, F 23668, nos. 772, 774, 778, 796, 805, 816 (parlementary orders and instructions to various authorities), 829 (account of the Fronde at Reims); *Courier François*, Paris, 1649, II, 4 (circular letter to provincial parlements).

[25] See, inter alia, Actes Royaux, F 23668, no. 829 (the role of Conti in the Fronde at Reims as governor of Champagne); B. N. Ms. Fr. 25025, fol. 20r (the seizure of Meaux by the Marquis de Vitry, Frondeur governor of the town); Kossman, *La Fronde*, p. 137 (the Fronde in Anjou under the governor, Duke of La Trémouille).

provincial parlement. With the aid of two thousand troops, he revived the half-forgotten scheme of previous years to create new judgeships. Alais could not have chosen a less suitable time for his offensive. Infuriated by his demands and encouraged by news from Paris, the inhabitants of Aix reacted immediately. Townspeople ousted the royalist civic government while the Parlement of Aix forbade the creation of new positions. Then an agent of the Frondeur prince, Conti, arrived on the scene, and a letter of sympathy from the Parlement of Paris. By March, Provence was torn by civil war between the governor and many nobles on one side, and most of the inhabitants and judges at Aix on the other. The intendant, de Sève, must have been grief-stricken by these developments, since he had been pleading with Séguier, Mazarin, and Alais to accept the local parlement's demands, realizing that this was the only way to prevent a provincial war and the fusion of the movements in Paris and Provence.[26]

3

ALTHOUGH the siege of Paris was fraught with danger for the besiegers as well as the besieged, the parlementary rebels were placed in the most difficult position. Despite the strength coming from the expansion of the civil war to other districts outside Paris, time was a factor on the regent's side. The economic blockade against the rebels in Paris was almost complete, supplies became scarce, and the price of necessities soared. The regent refrained from pressing militarily, partly because of Mazarin's desire to avoid shedding blood, but more because of her conviction that economic warfare would be successful.

Paris' only hope was the slim chance that it could hold out until the provincial Frondes diverted substantial numbers of royal troops from their role of preventing food suppliers from entering the capital, or the end of winter brought relief in the form of a Spanish invasion. Both possibilities had implications just as abhorrent to the judges as a victory by royalist forces. If the regent could prove that the defense of Paris was no mere continuation of the legalistic parlementary Fronde, but part of a military venture which pitted Parisians, provincials, and foreigners against the king and monarchy itself, the parlementarians' greatest weapon of self-defense would be

[26] *Courier François* IV, 4-5; Mousnier, *Lettres et mémoires adressés au Chancelier Séguier* II, 997-1003; Kossman, *La Fronde*, pp. 121, 142-143.

blunted. No longer could they invoke that legalistic *via media* of 1648, which had combined outward deference to royal absolutism with specific attacks on royalist institutions. Indeed, once that complex ideological stand was undermined, the reforms of 1648 as well as the Parlement's very existence, would be in jeopardy. So the Parlement could not unsheathe the conventional weapons of war which alone made military victory possible, nor could it afford to surrender without a fight to the besieging royalist forces. Anne's advisers must have felt that they had these meddlesome judges at their mercy at last. How could the parlementarians refurbish their old sophistries of the legalistic revolt of the judges, and adapt them to military defense of the reforms of 1648?

The historian who looks at the siege of Paris from this perspective cannot help being impressed by the way in which the Parlement met the dilemma. It was so successful that the tribunal continued to shape the course of the Fronde. Between January 8, when civil war began, and April 1, when a royal-parlementary treaty ended the siege, the judges realized two major objectives: First, they withstood every ideological attack made against them by the regent's administration, and second, they kept their restive noble allies under parlementary control. A third achievement was closely connected with the first two, but it was neither as complete nor as impressive. Specifically, the parlementarians in Paris were able to rally some support of their *via media* from the other public authorities of the realm.

Like the opposition in many rebellions, the parlementarians in 1649 made the distinction between loyalty to the Crown and obedience to the orders of the king's agents, contending that they were fighting against Mazarin, not Louis XIV or Anne of Austria. In January, a solemn parlementary declaration charged the cardinal-minister with usurping royal authority and using it against the interests of both the monarch and his subjects. As a high court of law, the Parlement proceeded to try Mazarin for crimes against the state. The verdict was no surprise, since the Parlement was both plaintiff and judge. Mazarin was denounced as the "disturber of public peace, enemy of the king and the state." The Parlement sentenced him to expulsion from the royal councils and the kingdom.[27]

Even though Mazarin ignored the judges' verdict and continued to act as chief minister, the trial was a very dangerous act on the

[27] Isambert, *Anciennes lois françaises* XVII, 115; Talon, *Mémoires*, pp. 323-328.

part of the judges, for it was precisely the move the recently formed *cabale* of parlementary and noble Frondeurs had been seeking. As a political measure, it bound the Parlement far more closely to the "nobles of the sword" than was healthy for "nobles of the robe" wishing to spread the myth that they were engaged in a purely legal struggle against maladministration. From the perspective of law, the decision against Mazarin was far more questionable than any parlementary action during 1648. Only the king or regent had the right to choose and dismiss ministers. Even if one interpreted the functions of the Parlement broadly to include the right to punish ministerial wrongdoing, it was obvious that the proceedings in this case were highly irregular. Mazarin was not given a hearing, and some judges admitted that his sentence was just as arbitrary as any handed down by the regent in the recent past.[28]

Nevertheless, the trial and verdict accomplished what the Parlement as a whole wanted at this time. The judges made Mazarin the scapegoat of the current troubles in France by leveling a charge of treason which looked like a legal decision. To many subjects who had come to distrust and hate both Anne and Mazarin in 1648, the parlementary trial of the cardinal-minister gave legal sanction to their personal conviction that the regent's administrators were evil and their judicial opponents good. Anne could not even successfully employ the counterargument that Mazarin's appointment and conduct were approved by the king, for the young Louis XIV was still a minor, and it was evident that both legally and in fact Mazarin was the creature of a mere regent whose own political wisdom was in question.

The execution of Charles I in February provided the Parlement of Paris with another opportunity to make its rebellion appear legitimate. This time the judges were able to answer the charge of republicanism, which had come to the surface on the eve of the siege and continued to be voiced in royalist circles after January 8.[29] Henriette-Marie had remained in the capital when the rest of the French royal family moved to Saint-Germain. The parlementarians quickly drafted a public letter of condolence to Charles's widow. Their message bitterly denounced the English regicides as evil men who, "violating every human, natural and positive law, dipped their murder-

[28] A. N. U 336, p. 495.
[29] See Madame de Motteville's views in her *Mémoires*, p. 234.

ous hands in the blood of that most just king." The parlementarians piously exclaimed that "this cruel deed [is] so unprecedented that it will be abhorred by all people forever."[30] The emotional language of that proroyalist "tract" does indicate that the Parisian judges fully believed what they said. However, their very sincerity in upholding monarchical government served to strengthen their position as rebels against the French king's ministers, and it would seem that the parlementarians were more interested in proclaiming their devotion to the institution of monarchy than in acting on it. They agreed to provide Henriette-Marie with a pension, and then delayed payments because all available revenue had to be used for the defense of Paris against the widow's nephew, Louis XIV! Henriette-Marie obtained money from the judges only by threatening to leave Paris and take up residence at Saint-Germain.[31]

As the siege continued, the regent's administration tried to test the parlementarians' professed royalism by confronting them with a series of orders, issued in the king's name. As in the case of the *lit de justice* of January 15, 1648, the regent sought to place the parlementarians in an untenable position: either they would have to honor the commands and capitulate, or be exposed as the rebels that they were. But the parlementary response was not as Anne and her advisers would have had it. The resourceful judges found an appropriate excuse for refusing to open one royal letter after another. On February 12, they objected that a royal message was delivered by a herald, and sent royal attorneys from the Parlement to Saint-Germain with the reply that heralds were sent only to foreign rulers or the state's enemies, and that since the Parlement was neither, it had no right to receive the herald.[32] Bewildered by such brazen manipulation, the regent's ministers could find no way to force their opponents into facing the issue of royal authority. The contents of royal letters were public knowledge, since identical messages were sent to the royal attorneys, other public authorities, and even to individual parlementary judges. Yet the Parlement had not officially seen them, and hence could not be charged with failing to obey the king's will.

[30] *Courier François* VI, 7-8.
[31] B. N. Ms. Fr. 25025, fol. 16v. (This reliable journal conflicts with other accounts which claim that Henriette-Marie refused the pension.)
[32] A. N. U 336, pp. 540-545; B. I. Ms. Godefroy 274, fol. 7r.

The actual conduct of the war was a much more difficult undertaking for the parlementarians than their legal battles with the regent. The tribunal which refused to acknowledge that it was harboring traitors and republicans cringed at the thought of admitting that it was raising arms against the monarchy. The parlementarians were especially uncomfortable with comparisons between their "legitimate" defense of Paris and the illegally constituted dictatorship of the ultra-Catholic "Leaguers," who had held the capital against royalist forces during the late sixteenth-century religious wars. On the conclusion of parlementary debates which bristled with references to the "League," they decided to organize the city's defense through the existing courts and other public authorities in the capital. No judge wished to have the Parlement assume dictatorial powers, and none desired to create any totally new institution even as a temporary expedient.[33] Therefore, they saw to it that though the Parlement directed the war effort—and everyone in Paris and Saint-Germain knew it—in principle, a coalition of the duly constituted public corporations, representing the Crown, was in charge.

The Parlement's efforts to obscure the fact that it was at war with the monarch were complicated by the very different pressures from its noble allies. *Les grands* were "nobles of the sword," who could not easily be reconciled to a purely defensive campaign. Their threat to the parlementarians' *via media* was great because they not only commanded the rebel army, but sat in the committee of war which determined military strategy. In the Parlement, where many of them also participated in debates, they had their associates in that band of radical parlementarians who had caballed with them ever since the Days of Barricades. Those who were dukes and peers now exercised their seldom-used privilege of attending plenary sessions, while Gondi sat as the representative of the Archbishop of Paris, who delegated his privilege to the coadjutor.

It is virtually impossible to determine the ultimate aims of these proud, powerful, and alienated men. At first, they had come to Paris in search of adventure and to escape the frustration of being left out of the regent's inner council. They had grasped at the unexpected opportunity to win honor on the battlefield, to disrupt the realm so much that Anne would have to take them seriously, and perhaps to overthrow Mazarin. As the siege wore on, they began to reveal more

[33] See the debate in A. N. U 336, pp. 491-497.

specific intentions, namely to blackmail the regent into giving them important governmental positions, honorary titles, and pensions.[34] But whatever their ultimate aims, it soon became clear that their methods, contrary to those of the Parlement, stressed violence, disruption, and, by implication, anarchy. So, apart from the obvious bonds of hatred for Mazarin and opposition to the siege of Paris, there was little that judges and nobles had in common. The Parlement as a whole was trying desperately to hold on to the gains of 1648, and had taken up arms only because its members had no alternative. They still represented the Crown, and wanted to make the defense of Paris look like a mere extension of their legalistic squabbles with the opposing part of the Crown, led by the regent. By contrast, the princes and great nobles seemed intent on expanding the purely defensive conflict into an offensive campaign, to seek out and destroy Condé's army. Nor did they scruple to ally with Spanish forces in the Low Countries. *Les grands* saw nothing wrong with such connections, considering themselves to be both subjects of the king and quasi-independent lords. But to the parlementary judges, with few exceptions, the great nobles were engaged in treason.

From the beginning of the siege, the Parlement took every precaution to keep the nobles in a subordinate position. Fortunately, its members had the advantage of being the initial body which had resisted the siege, and the nobles recognized this fact. When they arrived in Paris, they swore to defend the judges and to take orders from them. The parlementarians made full use of that declaration: by accepting it, they put the nobles on record as having no interests of their own; and, by placing the document in the first president's hands rather than entering it in the court's register, the wily judges avoided the implication that the alliance committed the Parlement in any way to its allies.[35]

The parlementarians also established guidelines for the military campaign. When civil war became inevitable, they ordered the royalist forces under Condé to stay at least twenty leagues from the capital.[36] This pronouncement also clearly implied that the function of the Parisian troops was to stay within that zone to hold it against

---

[34] Their demands were revealed during the negotiations at the end of the siege. Molé, *Mémoires* iii, 453-470.

[35] See ibid. iii, 337-338; Retz, *Oeuvres* i, 625-629.

[36] A. N. U 336, pp. 483, 505-506.

any royalist sorties. To be sure, the Parlement placed nobles in positions of responsibility as members of the war council, as commanders, and even as commander in chief in the case of Conti. However, this must be seen as a diplomatic gesture rather than an abdication of power. It played on the vanity of the nobles and let them engage in the military activities which the judges and inhabitants of Paris were far less competent to pursue, while leaving the Parlement with ultimate control over political and military policy.

Before long *les grands* became frustrated. They disliked acting as an escort for the convoys of supplies to the blockaded capital and they won little glory during their brief skirmishes with Condé's seasoned troops. Early in February, the Prince of Conti tried a different strategy. He secretly invited the Spanish army under Archduke Leopold to enter France from the Low Countries. Then the noble Frondeurs and a few judges in their cabal tried to bring the Parlement into this Frondeur-Spanish alliance. A letter which had been signed by Leopold, but actually composed by the Frondeurs, was sent to the Parlement on February 19.[37] On the surface, the Spanish offer was very tempting, for the persons who had drafted it knew how to appeal to the parlementary way of thinking. First, Mazarin was accused of offering peace to Spain in return for help in crushing the Parisian rebellion. After playing on the fears of the judges, the letter went on to say that the archduke had no intention of engaging in such an ignoble alliance but did seek a genuine Franco-Spanish settlement. Then the letter broached the crucial issue: the Parlement was asked to act as mediator between France and Spain. No phrase was left unturned by the cabal in its effort to beguile the parlementarians. They were addressed in flattering terms as the "natural tutors" of French kings; their role as mediator was made to appear perfectly legal; it was contended that the parlementary decree against Mazarin left their tribunal as the sole legitimate authority in the realm.[38] Of course, the cleverly written document was a trap. What it did not say was that in accepting the Spanish offer, the judges would in reality be joining forces with the Frondeurs and the Spaniards. Formally, there would be no union; yet in fact, the parlementarians

[37] G. Joly, *Mémoires*, Michaud and Poujoulat collection (ser. III, vol. II), Paris, 1838, p. 21 (including fn. 2); L. A. de Vineuil, *Mémoires*, in F. de La Rochefoucauld, *Oeuvres* II, eds. D. L. Gilbert and J. Gourdault, 4 vols., Paris, 1868-1912, pp. 536-537; Retz, *Oeuvres* II, 232-246. Conti's request for the Spanish invasion is in Vallier, *Journal* I, 21, fn. I.

[38] See Talon, *Mémoires*, pp. 335-338.

would be acknowledging that the Parlement and the kingdom of Spain had the same common enemy—the French administration headed by Louis XIV, Anne, and Mazarin.

The parlementarians were, indeed, tempted through the appeal to their pride and through their desire for international peace. Many judges feared that if they rejected the offer, they would be giving up a good opportunity to bring an end to the foreign war, an acknowledged underlying cause of France's internal troubles. The few judges who were members of the cabal of Frondeurs also supported the proposal, with the hope of escalating the conflict with the royal administration. Nevertheless, the majority of the Parlement was unwilling to engage in any unilateral negotiations with the Spaniards, arguing that this was the domain of their monarch. The final decision was a compromise, but it dashed the hopes of *les grands*. The parlementary conservatives could not prevent their tribunal from opening and reading the letter, but the parlementary Frondeurs could not persuade it to send even a formal reply to the archduke. The letter was sent directly to the administration at Saint-Germain for royal perusal.[39]

Pressures to expand the defensive war into an offensive campaign were more difficult to overcome than the temptation to engage in treason. The convoy duty of the rebel forces was ineffective even as protection for merchants bringing necessities to the capital. Moreover, the nobles argued that the distinction between defensive and offensive war was mere sophistry. War was war, and any means should be used to attain the objective of defeating the royalist troops. Rebel generals like the Duke of Elbeuf repeatedly raised the issue of an offensive campaign, and the well-liked Duke of Beaufort even suggested that nobles who held governorships of provinces or fortified towns be given commissions to raise troops against the regent. Each time these suggestions were made, the discussion at the Parlement was heated and thorough, indicating that the judges themselves were wavering in their commitment to a limited war, but at every debate the Parlement decided to postpone any escalation of the war, hoping that the regent would decide to negotiate a settlement.[40]

The delicate task of keeping the other public authorities of the realm firmly committed to the parlementary *via media* was more complex. The parlementarians were restricted by their own legalism,

[39] A. N. U 336, pp. 547-554; Ormesson, *Journal* 1, 672-677.
[40] A. N. U 336, pp. 555-559; Ormesson, *Journal* 1, 680-681, 688.

which prevented them from giving orders to corporations outside their jurisdiction. They were trapped by their pride, which would not allow them to treat any tribunal as their equal even though this hampered cooperative ventures. And they were terrified by the prospect of unleashing a massive civil war throughout the realm, which would undermine their moderate posture as a respectable opposition to royal policies. Unlike the situation in 1648, there was no common issue like the paulette to bring the officers of the realm together in aims if not action. Even the emotional issue of Mazarin's right to govern evoked varying responses. The political stand taken by a local governor was frequently more important to provincials than the alleged crimes of a chief minister, whose role in administrative wrongdoing was unclear to them. And it was difficult to convince those who lived far from Paris that the fall of the capital would adversely affect their local affairs.

Unquestionably, the Parlement of Paris was more successful in surmounting difficulties within Paris than in dealing with the hundreds of corporations and communities outside the city's gates. The formation of the governmental coalition of Parisian authorities under the leadership of the Parlement to withstand the siege was a spectacular achievement. Of course, the Chambre des Comptes and Cour des Aides did not accept that tutelage gracefully. Indeed, they joined the coalition with far less enthusiasm than they had demonstrated in refusing to side with the administration; undoubtedly fear of physical beatings by proparlementary workers and the petty bourgeoisie played a role in their combining with the Parlement. However, that factor has to be placed in proper perspective, for the parlementarians had made their own decision to resist the blockade within earshot of a howling mob, and few historians would argue that the mob was responsible for the Parlement's stand. Why, then, should the motive of fear seem to be important in the case of the other courts? Their members *were* afraid, but they knew that with the reforms of 1648 at stake, their only choice was to side with their rival tribunal, the Parlement.[41] Their decision was made easier by the parlementarians' decree against Mazarin which, more than anything else, forced them to support the cause they knew they had to uphold. The case of the Grand Conseil was very different, however. The issue of

[41] The role of the "mob" was stressed by royalist accounts. See B. N. Ms. Fr. 17560, fols. 11-12.

the paulette, which had been the major reason for its alienation from the regent in 1648, was no longer a factor. Hence no pressure from the Parlement or any mob could compel that tribunal to join the coalition of Parisian authorities. The Grand Conseil's position was similar to that of the maîtres des requêtes. As conciliar agents, the maîtres tried to obey royal orders to leave the city, but the Parlement refused to give them passports. With a few notable exceptions, the maîtres refused to support the parlementary cause, playing out their role as ineffectual neutralists within an alien camp.[42]

As the siege progressed, the Parlement's relations with the Chambre des Comptes and Cour des Aides also deteriorated. This was largely the fault of the parlementarians, who were more interested in coordinating the efforts of individual courts than in respecting the sensibilities of rival officials. In the long run, this insensitivity harmed the cause of the reforms of 1648 by poisoning relations between the sovereign courts at Paris. Yet in the short run, parlementary leadership saved the reforms and all the sovereign courts which had benefited from them. While the Chambre des Comptes and Cour des Aides complained of the Parlement's making both preliminary and final decisions on war policy, they did accept their nebulous function of being consulted. They paid their contributions to the war effort grudgingly and offered less than the parlementary judges, but they were still listed as voluntary contributors, in contrast to those *traitants* trapped within the city's walls and upon whom were placed forced levies. The financial courts also participated in the preliminary royal-parlementary conferences, in early March, which brought an end to the royal siege. And although they boycotted the final session because of parlementary insistence on having the largest delegation, the Chambre des Comptes and Cour des Aides did not desert the cause of reform. The regent's advisers knew that the settlement ending the siege would have to satisfy the financial courts as well as the Parlement, and the agreement was registered in all three tribunals.[43]

---

[42] Proparlementary speeches at the Parlement by the notorious royalist maître Foullé look like an attempt to cover up his past activities. But the inclusion of one maître des requêtes at the peace conferences in March surely indicates that the maîtres were trying to gain concessions from the monarchy despite their profession of royalism. See A. N. U 336, pp. 487-488.

[43] Relations between the Parlement and the financial courts can be followed in B. N. Ms. Fr. 17560, fol. 12; Ms. Fr. 25025, fols. 19r, 21r; Ms. Baluze 291, fol. 74

The *bureau de ville,* and the bourgeois elements which it theoretically represented, also played a major role during the siege.
Recent studies of the civic government's bitter feud with the Parlement have stressed the negative aspects of the complex bourgeois-
judicial relationships, and historians have failed to recognize the very
real support the Parlement was able to solicit. They do not explain,
for example, why the Hôtel de Ville sabotaged the Parisians' efforts
to defend their city or question whether this was a significant obstacle to the parlementarians.[44] The fact is that the civic officials, led by
the *prévôt des marchands* and *échevins,* did not truly represent the
city, or even its bourgeois elements. When the Hôtel de Ville tried
to side with the regent right after the royal family's departure, it
certainly did not represent the Parisian bourgeoisie. And when the
bureau de ville did all it could to hamper the city's defense after
being forced to side with the Parlement, it represented no one except
its members. *Prévôt* Le Féron, for example, was a notorious political
trimmer who had been virtually appointed by the regent in 1648.
Everyone knew that he was a tool of the administration and that he
was betraying the interests of his own social group. Had he followed the stand of his peers, he would have been a firm opponent
of the siege, since he was a member of the Parlement and a relative of the radical President de Novion. The same was true of most
of the *échevins,* who found it easier to accept their role as royalist
appointees than to defend the judicial or merchant elements from
which they had risen to civic positions. However, more surprising
than this predictable Mazarinist attitude was the fact that at least one
of the *échevins* managed to break from the royalist influence over
his office. Fournier repudiated the rest of the *bureau* when the civic
officials paid their respects to Anne at the outset of the siege. While
the others pledged their support for the regent, he infuriated her
by defending the Parlement's position.[45]

Many merchants, supposedly represented by the Hôtel de Ville,
were just as opposed to the administration as Fournier, despite the
fact that few of them were eager to engage in a civil war which they
knew would interrupt commerce and cut off supplies to the city.

(list of voluntary and involuntary contributions to the city's defense); Vallier, *Journal* I, 144-148; Boislisle, *Chambre des Comptes,* p. 433.

[44] See especially Kossman, *La Fronde,* pp. 80-88.

[45] B. N. Ms. Fr. 17560, fol. 12r (the conference at Saint-Germain); A. N. U 336,
p. 497 (the favorably received report of the *échevin* Fournier at the Parlement).

This meant that when the *bons* and *petits bourgeois* were forced to choose between Saint-Germain and Paris, many sided with the rebels, just as they had lobbied and rioted against fiscal impositions since the beginning of the regency. In December 1648, the major guild of mercers lodged a new complaint at the Parlement against the administration's evasions of the reforms of 1648, and after the blockade started, special bourgeois companies of militiamen were formed to risk their lives in defense of the city. While we do not know whether the wealthiest of the bourgeoisie were included in the ranks of this emergency militia, we do know that the six major guilds were committed to the parlementary cause. Even the regent's ministers at Saint-Germain knew this. So when a royal herald was sent to Paris with threatening messages for the Parlement, he was secretly instructed to avoid contact with the Mazarinist Hôtel de Ville and to spend his time with the parlementarians *and* the guildsmen. The secret memorandum specified that if the herald was forced to visit the civic government, he should insist that the *bureau de ville* call the six major guilds to the conference. The administration wanted to drive the *bons bourgeois* into its camp, but also knew that it could not obtain from them the automatic support which the Hôtel de Ville wished to give. It was a waste of the herald's time to talk with the city fathers; it was all-important to consult the guildsmen.[46]

The many conciliar *arrêts*, which sought to disrupt Parisian business during the siege, also attest to the proparlementary position of the *bons bourgeois*. If the administration had taken that element of the Parisian population for granted, it certainly would not have issued decrees nullifying all commercial contracts within the capital, nor would it have taxed the country estates of Parisians or diverted revenues destined for the rentiers' pockets. The regent's advisers had proclaimed economic war, to be sure, but these measures were so pointedly directed against the wealthy bourgeoisie of the capital that they cannot be described as designed to subdue the Parlement of Paris alone.[47]

The way the Parlement responded to the would-be "treason" from the unrepresentative *bureau de ville* is also very illuminating. The

---

[46] A. N. U 336, pp. 444-445; B. N. Ms. Fr. 17560, fol. 12r; and ibid., fols. 64-67, "Instruction générale du herault allant à Paris pour le Parlement, le corps de ville et M. le prince de Conty 12e Feb. 1649."

[47] See, inter alia, A. N. U 28, fols. 333v-334r; Actes Royaux, F 23668, nos. 804, 816; F 23631, no. 443 (list of Parisians taxed). For a very different view of the *bons bourgeois* during the siege, see Kossman, *La Fronde*, pp. 88-94.

judges could have written off the Hôtel de Ville as an incorrigible body of Mazarinists, or they might have allowed the poor workers and almost as poor *petits bourgeois* to mob the city hall and massacre the *prévôt*. But they decided to do neither. Instead, they followed a strategy worked out largely by First President Molé, through which they stumbled on a solution far more helpful to the judges' cause than either of the alternatives.

When it became apparent on January 9 that the Hôtel de Ville would side with the regent against the Parlement, a crowd of undetermined composition (probably petty bourgeois and artisans) thronged before the Palace of Justice, shouting "To arms! all is lost, we are betrayed." The merchants with shops in the courtyard of the Palais de Justice immediately closed their doors, fearing damage to their property. Crowds also gathered at the nearby Hôtel de Ville and threatened the life of the *prévôt des marchands*. Le Féron's close relative, the Frondeur president de Novion, blurted out that the *prévôt* should resign in order to calm the mob. However, on January 10, Molé restored a semblance of order to the Parlement with a brilliant speech, declaring that the Parlement should not "satisfy the people's appetite," and thereby "violate public safety," and insisting that Le Féron be retained and protected. Parlementary radicals had to go along with this conservative stand, upholding the Parlement's collective aim to preserve control over the capital and the potentially lawless populace. As a result, the Mazarinist civic government was propped up by the Parlement against the mob's desire for "natural justice."[48]

This decision had two distinct advantages. First, it reassured the proparlementary *bons bourgeois* that they could continue to support the cause of the Parlement without running the risk of damage to their property by lawless supporters of the rebellion. Second, it preserved the fiction that the rebellion was a legitimate undertaking: the duly constituted civic government officially headed the coalition at Paris, and the special wartime committees met at the Hôtel de Ville. The fact that the Mazarinist *bureau de ville* agreed to assume its role in the coalition only out of fear of mob violence is not very significant when weighed against these parlementary accomplishments. It was far better for the parlementarians to control an unwilling partner than to tamper with the *bureau de ville*'s structure or

[48] B. N. Ms. Fr. 25025, fol. 13r; Ms. Fr. 17560, fol. 12; A. N. U 336, especially pp. 501-502.

allow others to wreak vengeance on its members. Even a revolutionary civic government, purged of royalists and packed with parlementary supporters, would have been far less satisfactory than the compromise the judges worked out, since the Parlement would have been betraying its own position as a law-abiding and legitimate opposition to the regent's administration.

The Parlement's relationship with corporations within its jurisdictional area but outside the capital was determined in part by the situation within Paris. The judges were naturally fearful that as the economic blockade tightened, the lower social orders and *bons bourgeois* would become impatient with the Parlement's *via media*. Starvation might well drive the poorest inhabitants into frenzied reprisals against the judges; and the more wealthy elements might easily drift toward reconciliation with the administration, the loss of profits and disruption of their business outweighing any long-term benefits to be derived from a successful defense of Paris and the reforms of 1648. As already noted, the administration did all it could to drive those parlementary allies from the coalition, one conciliar *arrêt* after another being issued with that objective in mind. Financial officials in the countryside were to send tax revenue directly to Saint-Germain, not to the capital for conversion into judges' salaries and payments to well-to-do rentiers. Peasants and villagers were threatened with strangling or hanging if they took food and merchandise to Paris. Town councils were told to forward to Saint-Germain all royal revenues in their possession in order to aid the movement of royalist forces, and in some cases, royalist agents actually purged these *bureaux de ville* in order to further the economic war against Paris. The Parlement of Paris, itself, was singled out for punishment by conciliar decrees, authorizing the lesser criminal courts in its *ressort* to take over its appellate jurisdiction.

The parlementarians could not hope to cope with all these problems, although they countermanded almost every conciliar *arrêt* with decrees ordering local authorities and inhabitants to resist this economic pressure.[49] In many cases, parlementary *arrêts* were not enough; the parlementarians had to hope that outside groups would be both willing and able to support their cause. One suspects that many communities merely defended themselves against marauding

---

[49] Royal decrees and parlementary counterdecrees are numerous. See, inter alia, Actes Royaux, F 23611, no. 956; F 23668, nos. 789, 790, 792, 796, 802, 807, 825; and fn. 47.

royalist forces. We know, for example, that in January, royalist soldiers stormed into the neighborhood of Meudon, forcing the inhabitants of nearby villages to flee with their livestock into the town. Villagers and townspeople then fended off an attack by the troops, who vanished after seizing a few animals. In some cases, towns were more helpful to the cause. At Reims, the duly constituted civic government was able to thwart a *coup d'état* by a rival, royalist group, thanks to the legal support of parlementary *arrêts*, firmness by the townspeople, and the timely intervention by agents of the Frondeur governor, Conti. Somehow, supplies and tax revenues continued to trickle into the capital, although scarcity and rising prices began to turn the poorest Parisians to rioting, and some merchants toward a reluctant royalism. Even a few conservative members of the Parlement threw their support to the regent, acting as spies and relaying messages to Saint-Germain. There was also much confusion among the officers in the courts and bureaus of central France. A typical situation occurred at Orléans where the civic government defended the Parlement's cause by repulsing a royalist army, while the town's *présidial* court took orders from the chancellor. On the other hand, many other courts must have followed the example of the *présidial* officials at Troyes, who refused to betray the Parlement by taking over its appellate functions.[50]

Obviously the siege of Paris was devastating for central France as well as for the capital; town and countryside were ruined, and in the process the loose coalition of the parlementary Fronde was weakened even more than had been the case during the autumn of 1648. Nevertheless, the coalition did still exist, and to the very end of the siege it included corporations and communities many miles from the center of the civil war. Moreover, the parlementarians held to their objective of maintaining a legal, as well as a broadly based, opposition. Repeatedly, they refused to issue orders beyond their authority, and brushed aside all requests to authorize an offensive war against the regent. When the *trésoriers*, *élus*, and *présidial* judges in Poitou offered to take up arms on behalf of the Parlement, that tribunal politely thanked them and suggested that they confine their activities to legal channels.[51]

[50] On these local conflicts, see B. N. Ms. Fr. 25025, fols. 19-20; Actes Royaux, F 23668, no. 829; Dubuisson-Aubenay, *Journal* I, 150, 163-164.

[51] Chéruel, *Minorité de Louis XIV* III, 239-240.

The Parlement of Paris expected far less of the sovereign courts outside its *ressort* than from the lesser officials at Poitou and elsewhere in central France. But although physical separation and jurisdictional boundaries made close cooperation between Paris and distant provincial capitals virtually impossible, it was nonetheless a tactical mistake in the long run for the Parlement of Paris to be so aloof since this deterred the Parisian and provincial Frondes after 1649 from breaking down barriers to cooperation. The Parisian Parlement's circular letters to its provincial counterparts during the siege did not even request formal union, but rather politely and vaguely suggested that some support would be welcome. By being overly legalistic and cautious, the Parisian judges led the provincial parlements to underplay the importance of events in the capital and therefore gave them an excuse to avoid making the decision to unite with the Parlement of Paris which the Chambre des Comptes and Cour des Aides of Paris were forced to take. Those financial tribunals without a doubt were more vulnerable to pressures from the Parlement of Paris, but they had been given a clearcut choice, while the distant parlements were not given a comparable demand. Nor did the Parisian court give the type of support sought by parlements with the greatest grievances. Instead of issuing *arrêts* countermanding the creation of judgeships in the parlements of Aix and Rouen, for example, the parlementarians at Paris merely stated that they were opposed to the creations and would remonstrate to the regent. As has been noted, the Parlement of Paris did not wish to take action which was clearly illegal or outside its jurisdiction. However, it failed to see the two sides to this kind of legalism. When the Parlement of Rouen delayed responding to the Parisians' circular letter suggesting support, the Parlement of Paris was angry; its members thought that the Norman judges should have issued an *arrêt* similar to their declaration exiling Mazarin! It was a comedy of errors and mutual misunderstandings, each tribunal denouncing the legalism which its own members courted so assiduously. To add to the confusion, the Parisian court accused the Norman judges of sabotaging parlementary-royal conferences in March by refusing to lower their demands.[52]

It is difficult to determine the precise response of all the provincial courts, but the sparse evidence suggests that most gave only what

[52] On the relations between the parlements at Paris, Rouen, and Aix, see A. N. U 28, fols. 336ff.; *Journal de ce qui s'est fait*, pp. 19ff.

the Parlement officially requested. We do not find *arrêts* denouncing Mazarin and banishing him from the realm, merely innocuous letters of sympathy. In some cases, the towering influence of a provincial governor, like Condé in Burgundy, may have prevented a parlement from giving even a polite reply. In the case of Toulouse, the local *gens du roi* quietly sent the circular letter to Saint-Germain, and the Parlement of Toulouse sent a letter of support to Paris only after the Parisian judges relayed a second message.[53] However, these evasions were less significant obstacles to cooperation than geographic separation, traditional rivalries, and the obstinate legalism so prominently displayed at the Palace of Justice in Paris. The Parisian judges did try to make amends by vigorously supporting the cause of the parlements of Aix and Rouen at the peace conferences in March. However, their success in gaining concessions for their provincial counterparts could not offset the damage which had already been done. The Parlement of Paris maintained its treasured *via media*, and in so doing lost the slight chance it had to bind all the officiers together. Ironically, in adhering so exclusively to its own interests, the Parlement did not recognize the fact that sister courts in places like Grenoble and Aix were deeply involved in similar quarrels with Anne's administration. (The Parlement of Aix was in such need of outside assistance that its members, in appealing to the Parlement of Paris, swallowed their pride and called that high court "the most august body in the realm.")[54]

4

THE parlementarians' *via media* was relatively successful in at least keeping the civil war of 1649 under control; but it did not give the judges what they most desired—peace. Ironically, the anarchic tendencies which the Parlement most dreaded were precisely the factors which terrified Mazarin into seeking a settlement. The provincial Frondes in Provence and Normandy tied down royalist forces which might have been used to make the economic blockade of Paris completely effective. The noble Frondeurs' relentless demand for an

---

[53] Mousnier, *Lettres et mémoires adressés au Chancelier Séguier* II, 910. The administration was so sure of the Parlement of Dijon in Burgundy that it transferred suits involving the intendant of Provence, de Sève, from the Parlement of Aix to that rival court. Actes Royaux, F 23611, no. 973.

[54] See Mousnier, *Lettres et mémoires adressés au Chancelier Séguier* II, pp. 1008-1009 (Parlement of Grenoble); A. N. U 28, fols. 337-338.

aggressive campaign by the Parisians added further worries to the
military strategists at Saint-Germain. Above all, the threat of an early
spring offensive by Spanish forces from the Low Countries altered
the chief minister's strategy, and canceled out all the royalists' successes elsewhere. Mazarin knew of Conti's written request for Spanish aid in February, and the invasion of French soil by Archduke
Leopold in March confirmed his worst fears. The Franco-Spanish
conflict overshadowed the cardinal-minister's successful maneuver to
keep Marshal Turenne's Rhenish army loyal when that French
nobleman defected to the Frondeurs' cause. The foreign war also offset royalist victories in Normandy, which had prevented the Frondeur Duke of Longueville from bringing military relief to Paris.
Mazarin knew that the siege of Paris had failed in spite of the highly
effective economic blockade, and he persuaded Anne to come to
terms with the Parlement of Paris before the foreign and civil wars
could merge. The initial threat of a Spanish invasion in February
brought the administration to the conference table; the actual Spanish entry in March compelled the regent to accept first a preliminary
agreement and then a final treaty with the parlementarians.[55]

Once the regent and her chief minister decided to negotiate, there
was no difficulty in breaking the formal barrier created by parlementary evasions of royal directives and the regent's refusal to consider the Parlement a legitimate tribunal. During the most bitter
days of the siege, many parlementary moderates had maintained personal contact with Mazarin. Anne had no trouble in leaking word
to the Parlement early in February that "provided she could conserve
her son's authority, she would prefer mildness to violence."[56] Parlementary moderates and even Frondeur judges, such as Broussel,
immediately sensed that this was a concession, in tone if not in sub-
stance. Coming from the extremely proud and imperious regent, it
implied a willingness to compromise. The judges made formal contact a few days later, when the royal attorneys in the Parlement presented Anne with their colleagues' reasons for refusing to receive the
royal herald on February 12.[57] The regent could not help chiding

---

[55] Mazarin's reaction to the military situation can be followed in his *Lettres*, especially III, 308, 315.

[56] Ormesson, *Journal* I, 652.

[57] On the Parlement's legalistic decision to deny admission to the herald, see
above, p. 195. This was the work of Broussel, who had conferred with his conserva-

the *gens du roi* for their tribunal's affront to the herald, but she did treat them with civility. Then, the noble Frondeurs' use of the propagandist letter from the Spanish governor of the Netherlands gave the Parlement a chance to probe the regent's intentions. The first president, who knew how to handle the delicate situation, headed a parlementary delegation which presented the unanswered letter to Anne. Molé met secretly with Anne's ministers, and arranged for formal conferences. He also demanded that the regent guarantee the entry of supplies to Paris during negotiations, knowing that such a promise would ensure parlementary ratification of his private agreement to negotiate.[58]

The formal conferences between the regent's representatives and a delegation from the public authorities of Paris took place at Rueil, near Saint-Germain.[59] After a week of haggling, on March 12, the delegates signed a preliminary settlement. Another round of parleys resulted in modifications which were registered by the Parlement on April 1, 1649, and then by the other Parisian courts and the parlements of Aix and Rouen.[60] This treaty of Rueil was an astonishing achievement, since the rebels' desire to expand the reforms of 1648 and the regent's wish to revoke them seemed irreconcilable. Fortunately, the two delegations were led by superb diplomats.

On the rebel side, Molé stood out as the key figure. He had proved his loyalty to the Parlement by staying in Paris and defending its

---

tive colleagues in advance and agreed to propose a response to the visit which might lead to negotiations with the regent. The Frondeur Gondi claimed that Broussel's proposal followed his own, very different scheme to prevent any reconciliation, but this is an obvious fabrication. In fact Broussel's motion was in sharp disagreement with suggestions which Frondeurs like Conti made on the floor of the Parlement. See Ormesson, *Journal* I, 661-665; A. N. U 336, pp. 540-545; and the spurious account by Gondi in Retz, *Oeuvres* II, 255-257.

[58] Molé, *Mémoires* III, 349-356.

[59] The excellent accounts of the negotiations are in complete agreement, and are the basis of the following paragraphs. See *Procès-verbal de la conférence à Ruel*, in M. Petitot, ed., *Collection des memoires relatives à l'histoire de France*, XLVI (1825), pp. 389-428; *Suitte du journal de ce qui s'est passé au Parlement* (Paris, 1649), pp. 344-425; *Registres de l'Hôtel de Ville* I, 338-370; the royalist account of preliminary demands by both sides, written by Lionne, in Chéruel *Minorité de Louis XIV* III, 201-208; and Vallier, *Journal* I, 266-280, 285-288.

[60] The treaties of March 12 and April 1 are in *Suitte du journal de ce qui s'est passé*, pp. 378-381, 422-425. The verified versions registered in the Chambre des Comptes and Cour des Aides of Paris, and the parlements of Rouen and Aix, are in Actes Royaux, F 23611, nos. 976, 990, and 992.

cause, much to the displeasure of royal courtiers who thought that he should have defected to Saint-Germain. On the other hand, he had debated vigorously against the proposals of *les grands* and apparently did not treat seriously the Parlement's official stand that Mazarin must be removed from office as required by that court's sentence of banishment. Molé also regarded the Parlement's assumption of royal powers as a temporary tactic rather than a permanent right. During negotiations, he told Orléans that "the power of kings was limited by the ordinances and laws of the kingdom," but there was no question in his mind concerning the regent's right to govern. The Parlement was for him a guardian of the law, but it was not superior to either the monarchy or existing laws.[61]

Cardinal Mazarin, Molé's royalist counterpart, was the first president's equal as a negotiator, though much his inferior in trustworthiness. Quite in keeping with his character, the chief minister graciously accepted the rebel negotiators' refusal to confer in his presence. With his approval, royalist agents worked out a clever arrangement with Molé and de Mesmes: the two delegations met in separate rooms, conferring by means of messengers. Mazarin's position in Anne's administration was thus tacitly acknowledged, but the fact that he had charge of the royalist delegation was conveniently obscured.[62]

It was to Mazarin's credit that he was able to keep Anne's temper from ruining the negotiations, just as it was an indication of Molé's influence that he could keep in check the tensions within the rebel delegation, which, though dominated by parlementarians, included both conservatives and radicals as well as delegates from the jealous financial courts and the Mazarinist Hôtel de Ville. Fortunately, the noble Frondeurs let the judges act on their behalf although, as we shall see, they attempted to influence and even disrupt the conferences from the distance of Paris.

The demands laid down by the regent's side included modifications of the reforms of 1648. Specifically, the royalist delegation requested that a parlementary *arrêt* of July 20, 1648, be revoked, along with amendments which the Chambre des Comptes and Cour des Aides had added to the royal declaration of October 22, 1648. If

---

[61] Molé's position can be followed in *Suitte du journal de ce qui s'est passé*, especially p. 375; and the praise of the usually hostile author of A. N. U 336, pp. 576-577.

[62] See, inter alia, Martin, *Histoire de France* XII, 326-327.

accepted, these demands would have seriously weakened the judiciary's control over royal fiscal policies, for the Parlement's decree had forbidden taxation without its approval; and the amendments not only guaranteed the functions and salaries of financial court judges, but protected subordinate fiscal officials against the possible revival of their archenemies, the intendants. The regent's immediate intentions were clear: her ministers asked for authorization to float a loan of twelve million *livres* as an advance on the *taille*, bearing an interest rate of 10 per cent, and that interest to be paid through *comptants*.

Anne's negotiators also argued for restrictions on general parlementary sessions, recalling the number of times assemblies had been called into being to defend the reforms of the Chambre Saint Louis. The Parlement's chambers were not to meet jointly for three years; thereafter, plenary assemblies could be held only on approval by the conservative *grand chambre*, and under restrictions which barred participation by most radical *enquêtes* and *requêtes* judges. Underlying these provisions was the implication that the Parlement had acted illegally and rebelliously during the siege. To dramatize that interpretation and further undermine the Parlement's power within the government, the administration intended to add punitive measures. The leading Frondeurs in the Parlement were to suffer an indefinite exile and the court itself was to be transferred *sine die* to the quiet town of Saint-Germain. Through these measures, Anne sought to realize the objective that had eluded her throughout the siege: the admission by the Parlement, through its acceptance of punishment, that its members had engaged in rebellion. Indeed, the projected exilings and transfer were a mortal blow to the assumption that the Parlement was an integral and loyal part of the Crown, which in turn was the very foundation of the parlementary resistance since 1643.

The rebel delegates not only parried these diplomatic thrusts, but forced the other side onto the defensive by demands of their own. They wished to preserve the reforms of 1648 and argued for concessions to the parlements of Aix and Rouen, as well as a further rebate on the *taille* in the area around the capital.

The agreement at Rueil gave slight concessions to the regent in fiscal matters, but these were couched in language which made further royal evasion of the reforms of 1648 exceedingly difficult. The royal treasury was authorized to secure advances on the *taille* at 8.33 per cent interest (a compromise between the desired 10 per cent and the statutory 5.5 per cent) but only until the end of 1650. Moreover, the regular financial officials, rather than *traitants*, were to administer the actual collection of the *taille*. Finally, the repayment of the loan was to be made through regular channels and under the scrutiny of the Chambre des Comptes, rather than through the secret *comptants*.

The honor and indivisibility of the Parlement were also upheld by the settlement. The regent conceded a general amnesty to all supporters of the Parisian rebellion, including the parlementary radicals who had been singled out for punishment. In the preliminary treaty, the rebels agreed that the Parlement should admit guilt by going to Saint-Germain for a *lit de justice* before resuming functions in Paris. But even that slight humiliation was waived by the final treaty, which authorized the continuation of the Parlement at its regular place of assembly in the capital. The preliminary agreement also reduced royal control over future plenary sessions to the written stipulation that none should take place during the rest of 1649. That provision, however, was virtually nullified by the final treaty. The parlementarians made only an oral agreement, while obtaining the regent's written authorization to protect the reforms of 1648. If the regent tampered with those reforms during the rest of 1649, the Parlement could then convoke a plenary session despite the oral prohibition. And beginning in 1650, such assemblies could take place regardless of the circumstances.

In general, the preliminary and final settlements of Rueil preserved the *status quo*. The regent received only slight financial support for the costly war against Spain, the reforms of 1648 were left virtually intact as far as the sovereign tribunals of Paris were concerned, and the honor of the parlementarians was upheld. While the rebels received only vague promises of a reduction of the *taille* in the area surrounding the capital, the parlementary delegates obtained relief for the parlements at Aix and Rouen. All the new judgeships in the former tribunal were revoked, and many of the recent creations affecting the latter court were rescinded. One can only conclude that the settlement was a victory for the rebels, and particularly for the Parlement of Paris, since the reversion to the prewar situation left the monarchy in the desperate financial position which had resulted from the parlementary Fronde. To be sure, Cardinal Mazarin remained in office, and it was widely assumed that as long as he continued to advise Anne there could be no assurance that the reforms of 1648 would be honored. However, the rebel delegates had discovered that Mazarin was the one issue on which the regent refused to yield, and so they were compelled to permit his retention and even to let him sign the peace treaty, in order to obtain temporary confirmation of the reforms of 1648. The Parlement's decree banishing Mazarin was revoked, along with all other hostile *arrêts* issued by that court during the siege. In return, the regent withdrew all punitive measures enacted against Paris and the Parlement during the blockade.

In the long run, the settlement's most glaring weakness was its failure to accommodate the interests of *les grands*. The actions of the noble Frondeurs during the royal-official conferences in March should have warned Anne's advisers and the judges that they could not ignore these adventurers. Instead, the regent treated them with contempt, and the judges neglected their interests. By avoiding the nobles' demands for governorships, sinecures, and pensions, the administration helped drive them toward a noble Fronde. By deserting its allies of January and February, the Parlement of Paris seriously undermined its moderating influence over *les grands* and virtually ensured that the Fronde of the nobility would be far less restrained than the revolt of the judges had been. It is true that the judges and ministers had reason to make a separate agreement, and both sides knew that if the royal-parlementary conflict was patched up, *les grands* could not continue the conflict by themselves and certainly could not join forces with the Spaniards. However, that short-term advantage should have been weighed against the long-term prospect of an independent noble Fronde.

The decision by their parlementary allies to negotiate a settlement came as a shock to the noble Frondeurs. Hotheads like the dukes of Beaufort and Elbeuf wanted to incite the Parisian poor to riot against this betrayal of the rebel cause. There was even a suggestion that the Parlement be purged through a noble *coup d'état*. However, more cautious Frondeurs like Gondi argued that it was better to sanction the conferences officially, while trying to hinder their progress. This task proved more difficult than the noble Frondeurs had contemplated. The rebel delegates at Saint-Germain were deter-

214

mined to secure a treaty, and even at the parlementary sessions which continued during the negotiations there was growing hostility to *les grands* by some of the Frondeur judges.[63] While the noble Frondeurs tried to play on the hopes and fears of the Parlement, they were also bedeviled by divisions within their own ranks. Beaufort and Elbeuf kept insisting that the anti-Mazarinist elements of the Parisian populace be incited to seek revenge against the Parlement for negotiating with Mazarin. Gondi and Bouillon had other plans, which the archbishop-coadjutor thought safer than unleashing an unpredictable mob on the Palace of Justice. He hoped that the Duke of Longueville would be able to march to the relief of Paris, and he knew that Bouillon's brother, Marshal Turenne, was on the verge of taking his Rhenish army over to the rebel side. Unfortunately, Gondi was unable to divulge the details to Beaufort, who could not keep secrets and would surely have talked prematurely. And while Gondi waited for relief and Beaufort became irritated by the coadjutor's unexplained refusal to incite a Parisian riot against the parlementarians, Mazarin was busy uncovering the Frondeurs' plots. As we have already seen, he kept Longueville contained in Normandy, and frustrated Turenne's scheme. The marshal defected, but money advanced by Condé kept his soldiers loyal and the would-be Frondeur fled to the Spanish Netherlands.[64]

Meanwhile, Condé's Frondeur brother, Conti, continued to flirt with the Spanish enemies of the French monarchy. It is not clear whether that rebel prince would have been willing to fight with the Spaniards against his own king at this stage of the Fronde but, in any case, his failure to let these foreign allies know where the Frondeurs stood on internal issues undermined Spanish-Frondeur cooperation. Archduke Leopold suspected that Conti was using the threat of a Spanish invasion to frighten Anne into a settlement with the Frondeurs, and Conti's official endorsement of the parlementary-royal conferences at Rueil confirmed his suspicions. As a result, Leopold kept delaying his entry to French soil. When he finally invaded northeastern France, he advanced slowly and remained ready to pull

---

[63] This is clearly shown in the debates recorded in A. N. U 336. The supposedly solid position of the radical *chambres des enquêtes* had already collapsed by mid-February. The entire fourth chamber was apparently at that time opposed to *les grands*.

[64] There is a good account of the Frondeurs' maneuvering in P. G. Lorris, *La Fronde*, Paris, 1961, pp. 93-98.

back if a settlement between the regent and his Frondeur allies should occur. Ironically, too, the Spanish invasion cut short a royal filibuster against the parlementary delegates' demands, and caused Mazarin to sign the preliminary treaty of March 12, thus frustrating the designs of both the Spaniards and the noble Frondeurs.[65]

For a few short days prior to this preliminary settlement, the nobles had a slight chance of turning defeat into victory. Turenne had defected to the Frondeurs, but news of his army's desertion to the royalist side had not yet reached Paris, and it was still confidently expected that Longueville would also come to the relief of Paris with troops raised in Normandy. The noble Frondeurs played on the parlementarians' fears that Mazarin had no intention of making compromises at Rueil, and tantalizingly suggested that because of the imminent arrival of Turenne and Longueville they could afford to stop the conferences. Already infuriated by a temporary halt of supplies from Saint-Germain, which also suggested a breach of promise by the regent, the Parlement angrily quashed a royal decree charging Turenne with treason, and ordered Molé to stop negotiations until new supplies reached the capital. Then, to the amazement of the Parlement, word was received that Molé had disregarded orders and signed a preliminary treaty at Rueil.[66]

The noble Frondeurs' efforts to block parlementary ratification of that treaty, in mid-March, added further strains to the shaky noble-parlementary alliance. *Les grands* made the tactical error of blaming Molé for settling the war without consulting the generals. This placed the nobles in the awkward position of pleading for parlementary support for their own interests, while admitting that they had been fighting under false pretenses. Letters from the regent, Condé, and Orléans increased the parlementarians' disillusionment by divulging the Frondeurs' intrigues with the Spaniards. The nobles completed the debacle by inciting a crowd outside the Palace of Justice to demonstrate against the treaty. The judges were stunned by the shouts of "No peace! No Mazarin" and "Republic." Precisely those Frondeur judges who had begun the debate on peace with intemperate criticism of Mazarin's retention now joined their con-

---

[65] See ibid., pp. 96-97, 105, which quotes from Conti's unpublished letters to the Archduke Leopold; Mazarin to Servien, March 13, in Mazarin, *Lettres* III, 318-319; and a memorandum addressed to Chancellor Séguier, B. N. Ms. Fr. 17560, fol. 108r.

[66] These developments can be followed in A. N. U 336 and *Journal de ce qui s'est fait*.

servative colleagues in supporting the treaty. Once again, many radical parlementarians had adopted a conservative stance in the face of a wave of violence against their own institution, just as they had during the mob scenes against the *prévôt des marchands* in January.[67] Using a formula worked out by Molé and Le Tellier, the Parlement ratified the preliminary settlement and sent its delegates back to Rueil to gain concessions for the nobles.[68] This was a crushing defeat for the nobles, disguised as victory. Because of their recent obstructionist tactics against peace they had no confidence that the delegates would seriously press their case for indemnities. Ironically, the parlementary-noble alliance served the parlementarians at the very moment when it was falling apart. For the Parlement was able to take advantage of the new conference by forcing the regent to modify the clauses in the preliminary treaty that rankled its members.

During the final conferences of late March, the nobles tried once more to influence the parlementary sessions at Paris. And once again, bad luck and mismanagement spoiled their chances. The Parlement rejected a spurious letter from the archduke, which had been drafted by Gondi, Bouillon, and a Spanish envoy. As in February, the Spaniards' promise to protect the Parlement and negotiate a settlement with France through the high court was sent to the regent for her consideration. The Spanish issue came to an inglorious end when the archduke learned that the Parlement was negotiating with the regent on behalf of the nobles. He informed Conti that "he no longer had any desire to waste time," and withdrew his forces from French soil.[69] Nor were the judges seduced by clever noble declarations which played on their guilty consciences. *Les grands* claimed to have fought loyally on the Parlement's behalf to oust Mazarin. Since the parlementarians had allowed the chief minister to remain in power, the nobles disingenuously asked for support in gaining military governorships and other forms of protection against revenge by the cardinal. Untouched by this type of appeal, the judges merely registered the declarations outlining the nobles' new position, and halfheartedly asked their delegates to raise the issue of Mazarin's ouster

[67] Proof of the nobles' provocation of the demonstrations can be found in Estrées, *Mémoires*, pp. 268-269; Talon, *Mémoires*, p. 347; Vineuil, *Mémoires*, p. 540; Molé, *Mémoires* III, pp. 378-379; Motteville, *Mémoires*, pp. 262-263.

[68] The Molé-Le Tellier correspondence is in Molé, *Mémoires* III, 386-387.

[69] Quoted in Lorris, *La Fronde*, p. 106.

to placate *les grands*. The desperate nobles sent their own delegation
to bargain secretly with the cardinal, but he refused to make any
major concessions. Molé also brushed aside Conti's last-minute
request for suspension of the final treaty until the nobles were satisfied. The first president replied angrily that the nobles had no reason
to complain, since they had negotiated secretly on their own behalf.[70]

Parlementary debate on the final treaty lasted for two days, but
the outcome was never in doubt. The Parlement protected itself
against a noble-incited mob by having the Hôtel de Ville's militia
clear the Palace of Justice of some fifty demonstrators. Molé and
other conservatives convinced their fellow judges that the nobles'
demands for compensation were impossible and that their intransigence alone stood in the way of the peace which most Parisians
desired. Even the confirmed Frondeur judge, Blancmesnil, was
satisfied. He still wished to see Mazarin removed from office, but he
told the Parlement that it should reserve further action until circumstances permitted a more convincing appeal to the regent. The Treaty
of Rueil was accepted unconditionally with few dissenting votes, and
registered by the Parlement on April 1.[71]

The Peace of Rueil left the Parlement satisfied, but marked a serious and almost irreparable breach between parlementarians and
nobles. The judges now viewed *les grands* as unreasonable men who
would not scruple to place their selfish interest above internal peace.
Les grands looked on their parlementary allies as traitors to the common cause. The siege of Paris had given them the opportunity to
revolt—officially in the name of the chief Parlement and the capital
of the realm, but in fact for their own interests as well. Having
experienced a relatively mild civil war, they were unlikely to return
to peaceful ways. And their experience with the Parlement of Paris
made it still less likely that they would let the judges control them
in any future conflict with the regent. While they retained a grudging respect for parlementary ingenuity, and were fully aware that
they could not realize their ambitions without some assistance from
the judiciary, they did not intend to repeat the mistakes of 1649.
Future wars with the regent would be initiated and sustained largely

[70] The maneuvering by nobles and parlementarians can be followed in A. N. U
336, pp. 580-589; and Molé, *Mémoires* III, 476-479.
[71] A. N. U 336, pp. 591-599; Talon, *Mémoires*, pp. 350-352.

by *les grands*. The parlementary Fronde had finally become the noble Fronde.

While the siege of Paris preserved the reforms of 1648 and brought *les grands* openly into the revolt of the judges, it had not borne out Mazarin's fears that the Fronde would become an English-style revolution if left unchecked. In France as in England, a moderate, reformist movement had given way to a clash of arms, but there the resemblance ended. The Fronde had remained a moderate movement, avoiding the polarization of the Great Rebellion which had culminated in the abolition of monarchy. The major reason for France's not following the English path is, beyond question, attributable to the ability of the Parlement of Paris to retain its *via media* of 1648. The timorous judges paid for their moderation by antagonizing their noble allies. However, the price of a full-fledged coalition between the *noblesse de robe* and the *noblesse d'épée* would have been much higher. A union of robe and sword would have placed the latter in control of the reformist movement, destroyed the judges' carefully constructed, legalistic opposition which had saved the reforms of 1648, and left nothing but anarchy in its place—for *les grands* had even less understanding than the officials of ways to cope with the realm's fiscal-institutional malaise. We need to bury once and for all the historical myth that the Fronde failed because of a split between its parlementary and noble wings. We need especially to avoid forced, misleading comparisons between the Great Rebellion and the Fronde. The ability of the military and parlementary wings of the English Revolution to remain united until they had toppled Charles I from his throne had only a negative lesson for the Parlement of Paris. Such a combination was to be avoided, since it had undermined the position of the moderate parliamentary wing as part of the Crown, leading to Parliament's abdication of effective power in the postrevolutionary English state. The division of the Fronde into rival parliamentary and noble movements was to usher in equally tragic developments: the degeneration of the Fronde into widespread civil wars, and the ultimate collapse of the forces opposed to Anne's administration. But the estrangement between robe and sword also helped to keep the Fronde's reformist movement alive, just as a union of the opposition forces in England ensured the temporary defeat of the royalist cause.

PART III

THE NOBLE FRONDE

1649-1652

CHAPTER SEVEN

FRONDEURS, CONDÉANS, AND MAZARINISTS: A CONFUSION OF INTERESTS

AFTER THE Peace of Rueil, France became the victim of such a chain of events that the revolt of the judges in 1648 and the siege of Paris in 1649 looked like minor disturbances by comparison. Contemporaries were bewildered by the anarchy of this so-called "noble Fronde," and even the greatest historians of the subject have failed to make sense of the confusion. Scarcely a province escaped the ravages of civil war. The capital of the realm was plagued with noble feuds and finally torn apart by royalist demonstrations, anti-Mazarinist rioting, and the tyrannical actions of *les grands*. What began as isolated provincial revolts and noble intrigues in mid-1649 escalated into a major civil war the following year. By 1651, rebellion had given way to a grand coalition of Mazarin's judicial and noble enemies, which forced the chief minister to flee from the realm. Then, late in 1651, a second and much more extensive civil war broke out between Mazarinists and anti-Mazarinists. War-weariness of the French public and victories by the administration's armies finally brought an end to that holocaust and the Fronde itself a year later.

Much of the confusion surrounding the noble Fronde was due to the aims of its major protagonists, the great nobles of the realm and their adversary, Mazarin. *Les grands* divided into two distinct factions during the summer of 1649, and to the very end of the Fronde, three years later, those groups seemed as interested in destroying each other as in pursuing their common mission of opposing Mazarin. Historians have been struck by the pettiness of the nobles' quarrels, and usually leap to the conclusion that no basic issues separated the two groups. Indeed, it has become a truism to say that *les grands* of the noble Fronde were merely expressing the urge of seventeenth-century nobility to emulate their lawless feudal ancestors. A brief look at the composition and motivations of the noble parties shows that this is an oversimplification. Both drew membership from the old Frondeur faction of 1648-1649, but the group led by the Frondeur Gondi was very different from the one which rallied to the support of the ex-royalist general Condé.

Although Gondi's party inherited the Frondeur label which had been borne by the noble defenders of Paris in 1649, it never intended to oppose the Mazarinist administration with armed rebellion. This was understandable since the leading generals and military governors of the old Fronde had deserted to Condé's rival camp. The Frondeur leaders after the siege of 1649 were Gondi and Châteauneuf, and their most distinguished followers were Beaufort and Broussel. All were interested in purging the regent's administration, but, with the exception of Broussel who remained to the end of his life a selfless reformer, their ultimate goal was really to capture high offices in the administration. Archbishop-Coadjutor Gondi and ex-minister Châteauneuf coveted Cardinal Mazarin's position. Both hoped that their chances of becoming chief minister would be enhanced if Anne could be persuaded to nominate them and the Pope to elect them to the College of Cardinals. The Vendôme family wished to regain control of the admiralty for the Duke of Vendôme and bring about its ultimate reversion to his son, Beaufort. Such ambitions could most easily be realized by intriguing rather than by rebelling.[1]

Despite their basic disinterest in military revolts, these Frondeurs were a threat to internal peace. They constantly tried to embarrass Mazarin by bringing the grievances of provincial parlements to the floor of the Parlement of Paris, though they lacked a base of power in the provinces, since they had no military governorships. At the capital, where they had their greatest influence, they were capable of far more violent action. Beaufort, who had become the idol of Parisian workers and the petty bourgeoisie during the siege, and was known as *"le roi des Halles,"* would not hesitate to use mob violence as a weapon to wring concessions from the regent, even if Gondi had some scruples about such tactics. Selective bloodletting appealed to both men, and, perhaps, to Châteauneuf as well. Beaufort had

---

[1] The emergence of the new Frondeur party is examined in Lorris' and Batiffol's biographies of Gondi (Retz). Both are too partial to the coadjutor. See the critique of Batiffol by Kossman, *La Fronde*, p. 146, fn. 4; and the very sound assessments of Gondi's aims and character by Talon, *Mémoires*, p. 418; and Priolo, *Ministry of Cardinal Mazarine*, p. 160.

already been arrested for plotting Mazarin's assassination in 1643-1644. Gondi suggested in his memoirs that he was above such tactics, but he nevertheless appears to have advocated the assassination of Condé in 1651, and one wonders whether he would have held back if an opportunity to kill Mazarin had presented itself. Châteauneuf had been imprisoned by Richelieu in the 1630's for uncertain loyalty, and by Mazarin in 1648 for suspicious activities. In their drive for power, it was quite possible that these Frondeurs might create havoc within the body politic and threaten the monarchy and the Parlement of Paris with destruction.

By contrast, the Condéans' strength lay in the provinces. Until Condé's pride and Mazarin's duplicity led to the former's complete rupture with the royalist cause in 1650, the Condéans refrained from raising military revolts. But when the break came, they were well-equipped for a bloody civil war. Condé was governor of Burgundy, and he was supported by his brother Conti and brother-in-law Longueville, who brought their provinces of Champagne and Normandy into his camp when they defected from the old Frondeur party after the siege of Paris. In the *Grand* Condé and the ex-Frondeur Marshal Turenne, the Condéans also had the two most celebrated French generals of the age. Moreover, Condé had strong interests elsewhere, as a relative of the Provençal governor, Count of Alais, and the personal enemy of the Mazarinist governor of Guienne, Duke of Epernon. For a while in 1649, he confused the situation in Provence by backing Alais against both Mazarin and the local parlement. In Guienne, he consistently opposed both Mazarin and the Mazarinist governor, and in 1651 added to his power there by exchanging his governorship of Burgundy for that of Guienne.

On the surface, then, the activities of the Condéan "party" were more open than the cloak-and-dagger maneuvering of the Frondeurs. However, Condé's unpredictable nature made their ultimate goals an enigma to contemporaries and an unsolved riddle for historians. Condé had the qualities of leadership, bravery, and decisiveness which all the Frondeurs lacked; what he did not have was a clearly defined objective. He was happiest in the midst of a battle, whether against the Spaniards before the Fronde, in pursuit of the parlementarians' forces during the siege of Paris, or surrounded by Mazarinist generals in 1651-1652. Securing the prize deprived him of an adversary and compelled him to bridle his restlessness, and the frequent attempts to negotiate settlements with the rival Frondeurs or the hated and despised Mazarin always ended in an abrupt severance of ties, marked by a dramatic confrontation and a studied insult which seemed calculated to cause not just a rupture but civil war. This pattern was already apparent during the summer of 1649, when Condé made inordinate demands on Mazarin as a reward for besieging Paris. For months, the two viewed each other with suspicion; but when the chief minister tried, in September 1649, to blunt the prince's opposition by giving him dictatorial control over the administration, Condé continued to press for further concessions. The violent break of 1650 was a logical result.[2]

The turmoil that the Frondeurs caused by their intrigues, conspiracies, and demagoguery paled beside the destructive rebellions which were the Condéans' trademark. While a man of Mazarin's talents for intrigue should have been able to outwit or outmaneuver the Frondeurs, not even he could decipher Condé's ambitions, let alone reconcile them with his own interests. Individual Condéans could be enticed into the royalist camp: the ex-minister Chavigny temporarily in 1651, the ex-general of the French army of Germany, Turenne, permanently in 1652. But until his final settlement with Mazarin in 1659, long after the Fronde, Condé could never be induced to compromise his independence.

His relations with the Parlement of Paris were equally shadowy. Like the Frondeurs, he had his supporters in that tribunal, as well as in the other sovereign courts of the capital. The parlementary judge Deslandes-Payen was an eloquent leader of the Condéans, and President de Nesmond looked after the prince's estates and wealth while he was in prison in 1650. President Viole was a constant ally, and councilor Laisné a close adviser during the campaign of 1650 in Guienne. For a while Condé had close relations with First President Molé, whose son, Champlâtreux, had served before the Fronde as intendant for Condé's royal army. In 1652, Broussel added his prestige to the Condéans' cause by deserting the Frondeurs and becom-

---

[2] On the development of Condé's party, see especially Priolo, *Ministry of Cardinal Mazarine*, pp. 144-181. The biographical material in Duc d'Aumale, *Histoire des princes de Condé*, 8 vols., Paris, 1885-1896, vols. v and vi, fails to penetrate Condé's character. Lorris, *La Fronde*, p. 123, comes closer to the truth in analyzing the prince's internal struggle as one between ambition and duty. In view of Condé's inability to define his own goals, it would be even more accurate to say that he was torn between personal pride and devotion to the monarchy.

ing *prévôt des marchands* at a time when Condé held virtually dictatorial control over Paris.[3] Yet the Condéans were as much a threat to the parlementarians as to the regent. They demanded that the Parlement of Paris sanction their offensive warfare against the regent, despite the parlementary opposition in 1649 to similar aggression. And despite Condé's personal distaste for the Parlement's debates and his contempt for its *arrêts*, he was far more willing than the Frondeurs to use terrorism to influence its members. His relations with the parlementary judges never recovered from the mutual distrust spawned by the role of prince and parlementarians as bitter antagonists during the siege of Paris in 1649. Indeed, Parisians of every background never fully forgave Condé for besieging their city, and the prince was on his guard whenever his political interests compelled him to visit the capital.

The Duke of Orléans, a major personage in the noble Fronde, played a unique role, being reluctant to side completely with either of the two noble factions. He had conspired against Richelieu and then acted as mediator between Parlement and regent during the revolt of the judges. During the siege of Paris he remained loyal to the regent and Mazarin, yet kept the respect of the parlementarians by refusing to take an active role in the siege. After the Treaty of Rueil, he continued his quest for a lasting peace within the realm, while the Frondeurs intrigued and Condé broke with Mazarin. As the uncle of Louis XIV, member of the *conseil d'état*, and *lieutenant général* of the realm until the king came of age late in 1651, Orléans was a person whom no political faction or body of officiers could ignore, and his support was eagerly sought by Anne and Mazarin, Gondi, Condé, and the Parlement of Paris.

In general, however, Orléans remained a staunch monarchist, though he became implacably hostile to Mazarin and therefore sympathetic with both Frondeurs and Condéans. This satisfied no one. Orléans' encouragement intensified the opposition of Frondeurs and Condéans to the regent's administration, while his royalism and

[3] A good guide to Condé's clientage in the Parlement of Paris is B. N. Ms. Fr. 25025 and 25026, which has many detailed references. For an individual example see S. Vernes, "Un Frondeur: Le Président Viole," *Revue d'Histoire Diplomatique* (1951), pp. 16-38. In the absence of a systematic study of voting patterns, family connections, personal loyalties, and numerous other considerations, see also Cubells, "Le Parlement de Paris," pp. 184-190, which lists the most important members of the Condéan faction as well as the parlementary Frondeurs and Mazarinists.

compromising nature acted as a brake on their ambitions. He was too much of a rebel to satisfy Anne, and his hatred for Mazarin made his royalism of no service to the regent. His attitudes paralleled the attitudes of most judges in the Parlement of Paris, who also combined royalism with hostility to Mazarin, yet the prince and the parlementarians could not understand each other. Perhaps this was because the noble Fronde made Orléans a typical nobleman-rebel in spite of himself, while the same events forced the judges to temper their opposition for the sake of internal peace. During the last years of the Fronde, Orléans frequently took part in parlementary sessions, exchanged compliments, appeals, and commands with the judges, and on occasion actually determined the outcome of parlementary debates. But the parlementarians watched Orléans as closely as they watched Gondi, Condé, and Mazarin.[4]

The role of the Mazarinist faction during the noble Fronde was equally complicated, since Mazarin continued his well-established policy of solving problems by duplicity and intrigue. The chief minister was admittedly placed in a very awkward position by the emergence of two hostile noble factions—and it was tempting to play them against each other rather than to forge a broad governmental coalition of all parties based on mutual trust. It was also very difficult to coordinate internal and external policies, since the very men (Turenne and Condé) who alone could have made his campaigns against Spain a success could not be trusted with military commands; they might use them against the regent's regime instead of leading their soldiers into battle in the Low Countries and Catalonia. Nevertheless, by intensifying party rivalries, the cardinal caused unnecessary suspicion on the part of the Frondeurs, along with the fact that agreements with them were always temporary and questionable. He also hardened the lines between Mazarinists and Condéans by ignoring Condé's desire to remain loyal to the throne and by inferring from the prince's haughty attitude toward his person that no real accord was possible on any issue. Hence Mazarin's strategy of dividing and ruling failed, and accelerated the trend toward political factionalism, anarchy, and civil war.

The politics of duplicity, and the civil strife which was its byproduct, also caused confusion within the Mazarinist camp itself. Although it has been presumed that Mazarin was in complete con-

[4] Dethan's biography of Orléans is the fundamental secondary account.

trol of the royal administration during the noble Fronde—even when he was forced into exile twice in 1651-1652—the regent's regime was actually far less united than it had been during its first years. In 1650, Mazarin decided to direct the military campaign against the rebel nobles in person, and hence he split the *conseil d'état* into two parts. He and Anne tried to coordinate the military and civilian policies as an itinerant team, but Mazarin could not fully appreciate the much more moderate military position of the Duke of Orléans and Secretary of State Le Tellier, who viewed issues from the very different perspective of their Parisian residence. Then, too, Mazarin's attempts to divide and rule forced him to reshuffle the administration constantly in an effort to bribe one noble faction or keep its rival out of power. Hence devoted Mazarinist servants had to contend with Frondeurs and Condéans within the administration, itself. Some of these arrangements could have been successful if Mazarin had worked harder on the side of the noble partisans. Instead, he made the Frondeur-Mazarinist ministry of 1650 into a house divided. Frondeurs like Châteauneuf and President de Maisons tried to placate the officers of the realm, while Mazarin's military campaigns against *les grands* necessitated evasions of the fiscal reforms of 1648. Also, brief Condéan-Mazarinist ministries in late 1649 and mid-1651 were extremely fragile coalitions. The administration during the last civil war of 1651-1652 was almost as divided, since ministers like La Vieuville and Molé (still first president of the Parlement) were chosen largely because of their hostility to Condé, and were never fully trusted by Mazarin.

Finally, the constant administrative shifts and the ever-increasing hostility of all factions toward the chief minister forced some Mazarinists out of the inner circle of the administration. Chancellor Séguier was sacrificed in 1650 to make room for the Frondeur keeper of the seals Châteauneuf. Le Tellier's banishment under pressure from a parlementary-Condéan alliance in 1651 removed the one secretary of state who, having coordinated the work of all the secretaries in 1649 and 1650, could possibly moderate the administration's internal policies. Mazarin's banishment earlier in 1651 added to the administrative chaos; his attempts to dictate to Anne from his seat of exile in the Rhineland confused the regent, who was constantly torn between following his advice from a distance, and pursuing an independent policy dictated by the fast-moving events which escaped the ex-minister's attention. During his second exile in 1652, however, things were better; Anne usually obeyed Mazarin's written commands, and Le Tellier's restoration brought a sense of political unity to the regent's inner circle.[5]

The instability within the administration made royal-official relations particularly difficult, too. It was the key positions of minister of justice (held by the chancellor, or his substitute, the keeper of the seals) and finance (the superintendency) which changed hands most frequently, and they were most closely related to the affairs which concerned the Parlement of Paris and other corporations. So contradictory were conciliar *arrêts*, Mazarin's directives, and the commands of local Mazarinist governors that at times it was not clear who controlled royal-official relations.

In spite of all this confusion, however, there was some continuity in the broad attitude of the Mazarinists toward the officers. Though the administration as a whole tried to accelerate its previous program of evading the reforms of 1648, it proceeded with far greater caution than it had on the eve of the siege of Paris. Despite the state's financial plight, Mazarin knew that the officers were more useful as a potential ally, or even as a neutral force, than as an implacable foe of the administration, and that now the greatest internal threat to royal power was no longer the reformist officials, but the princes and great nobles. Even the decision by the Parlement to place a price on his head during the final months of the Fronde did not alter that view. Mazarin wrote to an agent in Paris in 1652: "There is no need to negotiate with the Parlement which has shown no hostility to the king and with whom [we have no quarrel]; and it appears that we have only to deal with the princes, since they alone have armed against His Majesty."[6]

Mazarinist efforts to keep the officers in tow took different forms. In May 1649, Chancellor Séguier suggested to Le Tellier that it would be helpful to portray the siege of Paris as a royalist victory.[7]

---

[5] One must treat Chéruel's treatment of Mazarin's role during the noble Fronde with the utmost caution, since it virtually equates the administration with Mazarin, sees all rival nobles and noble factions as outsiders and traitors, and in general follows Mazarin's opinion. Much of my reconstruction of Mazarin is based on B. N. Mss. Fr. 25025 and 25026. See also the critique of Chéruel by Kossman, *La Fronde*, passim.

[6] Mazarin to Abbé Fouquet, May 12, 1652, Mazarin, *Lettres* v, 109.

[7] The letter is quoted in Porchnev, *Les Soulèvements populaires*, pp. 529-530.

Between the lines, it can clearly be inferred that Séguier was trying to discourage *les grands* and other malcontents from siding with the judges and inhabitants of the capital; if the defense of Paris had been as inept as the chancellor tried to show, it would obviously be a waste of the nobles' time to woo the officiers in the future. It was characteristic of Séguier to twist the truth, but this particular distortion marked a subtle change in his attitude toward the parlementarians since it showed that he was beginning to respect them enough to lie about their power. About this time, the Duke of Orléans received a memorandum emphasizing a more positive aspect of the Mazarinists' new stress on royal-official relations, and listing the potential sources of trouble and groups to be placated in the capital: rentiers must be paid their interest, officiers their salaries, commerce protected against disorders by troops quartered in the neighborhood, and various urban elements given other concessions.[8] Anne's regime was unable (and partially unwilling) to execute this program continuously during the noble Fronde, but the attempt by some ministers to try reveals the dramatic reversal of the earlier tactics used by d'Emery which had provoked the parlementary Fronde.

There was also a concerted effort to influence parlementary opinion and decisions on matters relating to *les grands*. Toward the end of 1649 and during the first months of 1650, the regent's regime went so far as to entrust the Parlement of Paris with state trials of leading Frondeurs. Thereafter, that tribunal was informed of seditious or rebellious conduct by nobles. Royal negotiations with provincial parlements which threatened to join the Condéans' rebellions were also divulged to the Parisian judges. Sometimes, the Mazarinists' objective was merely to prevent any parlementary intervention, sometimes to secure registration of declarations condemning rebel nobles, and occasionally (but clandestinely) to seek parlementary mediation in provincial conflicts. At the same time, Mazarin redoubled his efforts, by bribery, to weaken parlementary independence. Ultimately, this tactic was aimed at making the Parlement docile on all matters, including the issue of state reform. However, the sharp increase in bribery after the Peace of Rueil was primarily directed at destroying the power of *les grands*. Thus friends of Condé, like Molé and his son Champlâtreux, associates such as de Novion, and the Frondeur sympathizer and later Condéan supporter Broussel were especially

[8] B. N. Ms. Fr. 17560, fols. 111-112.

courted by Mazarin's agents. Beginning in 1650, the chief minister's personal agent, Jean-Baptiste Colbert, sought to determine the influence of the noble factions within the Parlement of Paris. While the success of these efforts varied, their very existence underlines the chief minister's interest in isolating the Parlement from *les grands*.[9]

It is interesting to note that during the period of the noble Fronde only one *lit de justice* was held and no *lettres de jussion* were issued to the Parlement of Paris. Even the royal ceremony on September 7, 1651, held to announce the end of the king's minority and his assumption of full royal authority, contained no direct attack on the Parlement. Theoretically, to be sure, the central administration was thereafter in a much better position to impose the so-called "personal will" of the king on the parlementarians: a monarch who was legally of age was a more effective exerciser of his power than a regent, who merely acted in his name and was considered by many contemporaries to be shorn of the king's right to hold *lits de justice* or issue *lettres de jussion*. And, indeed, the regent—who actually continued to head the administration because of the king's youth—drew on the argument that the king was now ruling in order to undermine the parlementarians' stand that they were acting on his behalf in opposing Mazarin. Nevertheless, the *lit de justice* was not used as a device to rescind any of the reforms of 1648. Only after the military collapse of the last noble revolt, in the autumn of 1652, was the administration to employ the king's personal will against the reform measures of the parlementary Fronde.

The Parlement of Paris could not isolate itself from the outside influences of the noble Fronde, or the disparity of interests displayed by Frondeurs, Condéans, and Mazarinists. Most parlementary judges tried to remain independent of all these factions, and the majority succeeded. Nevertheless, all members of that tribunal were swayed by pressures from the three sides, and they were constantly subjected to eloquent appeals by the small but committed cadre of parlementary supporters which each of the outside parties had in the Parlement.[10] As the increasingly debased motives of the outside factions gradually pushed the more elevated principles of the parlementary Fronde into

---

[9] There are copious references to attempted bribery in the published collections of Mazarin's letters and Colbert's correspondence. One suspects that in many cases Mazarin's agents gave an exaggerated account of their success in influencing judges.

[10] See Cubells, "Le Parlement de Paris," pp. 186-190.

the background, the judges became less certain about the proper stand to be taken. The task of opposing unfettered Mazarinist absolutism without falling into the trap of condoning the results of the nobles' anarchical activities became almost impossible. And while the parlementarians sought desperately to curb the excesses committed by all three factions, they were faced with two additional problems which were almost as insoluble. The first was the issue of reform, which continued to cast its shadow over the Palace of Justice, as Anne tried to evade the reforms of 1648 and the Parlement sought to protect them. The second was the fact that Mazarin's furtive attempt to overturn the reforms of 1648 ran into stiff opposition in the provinces, just as it did in the capital, and the provincial Frondes became more involved and widespread after the siege of 1649. The role of *les grands* as provincial governors compounded the problem, since the nobles tried to make officiers their allies in the provinces just as they did in Paris. In effect, the line between the old revolt of the judges and the new rebellions by *les grands* became blurred in one province after another. The parlementarians in Paris could no more ignore these troubles than they could evade their responsibility to protect the reforms of 1648, or their duty to find a peaceful solution to the conflicts between the administration and the noble factions.

In one sense, the Parlement of Paris had an envious role during the noble Fronde since provincial corporations, noble factions, and the regent's administration all courted its support. Indeed, the parlementarians were the recipients of far more requests from all sides than they had been during the revolt of the judges which had centered on their tribunal. Paradoxically, as law and order gave way increasingly to anarchy and civil war, the immense prestige of the Parlement as the leading body of law enforcement in the realm made support from the tribunal all the more desirable for all outside parties. Mazarin, Condé, Gondi, and the provincial parlements at Aix, Bordeaux, Toulouse, and elsewhere all wished to give their lawlessness the sanction of legalism which the judges in the Palace of Justice alone could bestow. Yet in seeking to play the role of mediator on an almost national scale, the judges were courting disaster. Their quest for internal peace, order, and reform could easily lead them toward a partisan position which would destroy their *via media* of 1649 and undermine the very legalism which had made the reforms of 1648 possible. It was even possible that the Parlement of

Paris would mirror the divisions of the realm so completely that its members would destroy each other and their corporation.

2

THE FIRST civil war of the noble Fronde did not begin until Mazarin impulsively arrested the Condéan leaders early in 1650, thus inciting Condé's followers to take up arms in the provinces. However, the events of the previous nine months set the stage for that uprising. From the moment the Parlement of Paris ratified the Peace of Rueil, on April 1, 1649, the ambiguous legacy of the siege of Paris cast its shadow over the capital and the rest of the realm. From the perspective of the parlementarians in Paris, the most important responsibility was to restore calm to the capital and the surrounding area. The task was more burdensome than most studies of the Fronde indicate.[11] Royalist forces continued to roam the countryside, requisitioning supplies, clashing with peasants and villagers, and occasionally looting. The ex-soldiers who had been recruited to defend Paris were even more troublesome. The peace treaty stipulated that the parlementary army should be disbanded, but it was exceedingly difficult to force its men to return to civilian life. For weeks after the official settlement, bands of rebel troops plundered, killed, and robbed the hapless inhabitants of the area around the capital. Under the circumstances, it was difficult to persuade even the thousands of civilians who had been uprooted by the siege to return to peaceful activities. In Paris alone, there were fifteen thousand refugees from the war.[12]

The problem of demobilization could not be separated from the regrouping of noble factions during the first months after the siege. Many of the old Frondeurs were instrumental in keeping the freelance bands in being, whether these restive nobles rallied around the new Frondeur party or joined Condé's group. Frequently there were clashes between royalist troops and their former enemies. As late as July, for example, the old Frondeur judge and future leader of the Condéan faction in the Parlement, Deslandes-Payen, was involved in such an altercation. As prior in the town of La Charité-sur-Loire,

[11] But see J. Jacquart, "La Fronde des princes dans la région parisienne et ses conséquences materielles," *Revue d'Histoire Moderne et Contemporaine* VII (1960), 257-290.
[12] See the memorandum to Orléans, cited in fn. 8.

he organized resistance to a band of Mazarinist soldiers who tried to enter that center. The Fronde in Poitou, which had coincided with the siege of Paris, also showed signs of reviving. The old Frondeur governor of Poitiers, Duke of La Trémouille, complained of disorders by royalist soldiers and asked the Parlement of Paris to let him assemble the nobles of the province and attack the forces.[13]

The streets of Paris were no more immune to disturbances than the farmlands and villages surrounding the capital. Mazarin's decision to delay the royal family's return to the city did not help. It angered merchants who suffered from the loss of sales to the royal entourage. It gave *les grands* who lingered in the capital virtual license to display their contempt for the chief minister. It encouraged the few radical parlementarians who remained deeply suspicious of the administration's good will to complain of illegal tariffs on the city and the baneful influence of Italians (i.e., Mazarin and his relations).[14] Despite frequent disputes between Mazarin and Condé, it was the Frondeur faction that caused most of the disturbances in Paris during the summer of 1649. Embittered by the Treaty of Rueil and fearful that Condé would manage to dominate Mazarin, they could only release their frustrations in street fights and other displays of noble "honor." While Gondi paid a visit to Anne's itinerant court and deliberately neglected to pay his respects to Mazarin, Beaufort clashed with Mazarinist nobles in Parisian street cafés. Angered by insulting remarks about his inept generalship during the recent siege, the duke snatched the tablecloth from his tormenters' table and spilled the dishes and food on the floor. In the ensuing scuffle, Beaufort and his companions drew their swords and routed their adversaries. An almost endless list of similar altercations could be cited, many of which involved parlementary friends of both Frondeur and Mazarinist nobles.[15]

Mazarin tried to rally Parisians and other Frenchmen to the administration's support by launching a new offensive against the Spanish Netherlands. But this turned out to be another setback for the Mazarinist faction in the realm. Unable to come to terms with either Condé or Turenne, the chief minister entrusted the campaign to the less competent Count of Harcourt. Harcourt could perform

---

[13] B. N. Ms. Fr. 25025, fols. 29v, 57v.   [14] Ibid., especially fols. 25r, 36v.
[15] Most contemporary *mémoire* writers give detailed accounts. See especially the *Mémoires* of Vallier and Estrées, and B. N. Ms. Fr. 25025.

no miracles with his makeshift army, put together from the remnants of the royalist and rebel forces which had fought each other during the siege of Paris. After failing to capture the main objective, Cambrai, the Mazarinist general resorted to the tactic of roaming the enemy's countryside in search of the elusive Spaniards. During the rest of 1649, though French armies held their own in the Low Countries, northern Italy, and the rebel Spanish province of Catalonia, this was not enough to save Mazarin from criticism by war-weary subjects. The imperious demands of war compelled the administration to tax subjects arbitrarily wherever it had the backing of troops; but throughout the rest of the realm, tax resistance became even more marked than during the parlementary Fronde. Throughout the Loire basin, bands of salt smugglers, numbering into the thousands, defied every effort to collect *gabelles*, shouting "*nous allons au sel.*" Tax collectors dared not enter many regions. Conciliar *arrêts*, parlementary decrees, and the journals of impartial observers all testify to the rampant breakdown of royal finances and the almost universal hatred of Mazarinist troops, royal taxation, and the symbol of this royal "tyranny."[16]

Nowhere was the anti-Mazarinist lawlessness more apparent than in the capital itself. The *Mazarinade* pamphlets which had been unleashed during the parlementary Fronde and continued to flood the capital during the siege became still more vitriolic and numerous during the summer of 1649. Harcourt's failure to take Courtrai was followed immediately by a dramatic increase in pamphleteering. Undoubtedly the Frondeurs had control over much of this clandestine press, for even Condé was slandered by pamphlets like *Discours sur la depputation du Parlement à M. le Prince*. The most offensive language and scathing innuendos were of course reserved for Mazarin and Anne. One pamphlet left little to the imagination, indelicately hinting at intimate relations between the regent and minister with its suggestive title: *Le Custode du lit de la reine, qui dit tout.*[17]

So long as the royal entourage wandered, almost aimlessly, in an effort to stay away from the troubled capital, the Parlement of Paris

---

[16] See especially Actes Royaux, F 23612, no. 19 (conciliar account); F 23668, no. 870 (parlementary account); Mousnier, *Lettres et mémoires adressés au Chancelier Séguier* ii, 1030 (reports to the chancellor); Talon, *Mémoires*, pp. 358-360.

[17] See especially Retz, *Oeuvres* ii, appen. xi, "Une page de l'histoire de la presse en 1649," pp. 660-674; Goulas, *Mémoires* iii, 86; Talon, *Mémoires*, p. 360; Vallier, *Journal* i, 353.

shouldered most of the responsibility for keeping Paris calm. The *surintendant des finances*, Marshal La Meilleraye, tried to set aside funds for payment of rentes and salaries; tax evasion and refusal by near-bankrupt tax farmers to advance revenues made each conciliar *arrêt* which came from his pen a dead letter.[18] Chancellor Séguier was of little help. His unpublished memoranda reveal his obsession with flagrant violations of the settlement of Rueil by rebel soldiers, Parisians, and peasant taxpayers, while scarcely noting the lawlessness on the Mazarinist side. Orléans and Le Tellier probably did what they could to placate Parisians and restore good will between subjects and the administration, but it was not enough. The memorandum to Orléans, noted earlier, placed the need to "reestablish good faith" at the top of the list of measures required to make the Peace of Rueil a lasting one. But how could Orléans accomplish this when the proposal for the royal family's return to Paris, which rounded out the list, was spurned by Mazarin? Molé's letters to Le Tellier harped on similar themes, but the monotonous repetition of his suggestions in letter after letter indicates that the secretary of state could not impress on the chief minister the importance of his demands.[19] There were even rumors that Mazarin was paying secret agents to stir up trouble in Paris so that he would have an excuse to stay away from the capital. However, it is doubtful whether the wily chief minister was that Machiavellian—or stupid. His hesitation to return, though an error in judgment, was based on very real fears.[20]

As a body, the Parlement of Paris was relatively successful in restoring order on its own authority. Plenary sessions, which would have touched off debates on royalist evasions of the peace and the reforms of 1648, were not held during these turbulent times. The criminal *chambre de la tournelle* handed down sentences against pamphleteers, vendors, and disturbers of the peace, and cases involving noble friends of judges in that chamber were frequently prosecuted by the more impartial *grand chambre*. Anne and her ministers thought the parlementarians should have been more severe in their

[18] See, inter alia, Actes Royaux, F 23631, nos. 446, 449, 453.

[19] B. N. Ms. Fr. 17560, fol. 108r, "Mémoire pour Monsieur le Chancellier touchant l'infraction de traité de paix"; Molé, *Mémoires* IV, 4-54 (letters between Molé and Le Tellier).

[20] See the accusations in B. N. Ms. Fr. 25025, fol. 63; and the critical view of Mazarin by Kossman, *La Fronde*, p. 147. Information in the governmental correspondence is scattered and sketchy. See B. I. Ms. Godefroy 274, fols. 91-92, 97, 104.

sentences, but in reality they had little reason to complain. While the administration upbraided a few Frondeur judges for refusing to vote the death penalty, it failed to note that they were overruled by their colleagues. Moreover, some Parisians thought that the parlementary campaign against lawlessness was too severe. Occasionally, parlementary *arrêts* and judgments were so unpopular that they provoked riots which were more serious than the original crimes. The *huissiers* who tried to proclaim one parlementary decree were stoned by a mob, while an angry crowd spirited away the condemned printer of the pamphlet *Le Custode* before the hangman could carry out the sentence.[21]

When the conservative members of the *grand chambre* wisely refused to handle explosive political suits, they were attacked from all sides. Nevertheless, they held firm, which helped keep the city quiet. The most famous example was the regent's attempt to prosecute the Duke of Beaufort for his attacks on her noble friends. The Frondeurs wished to use the trial as an opportunity to embarrass the regent; Anne wanted stern justice meted out to the man who had humiliated Mazarinists. Had the trial taken place, it might have caused a major disturbance in Paris. Since Beaufort was a duke and peer, the case would have gone before the full Parlement. The danger of allowing a plenary session at that time was obvious to men like Molé. Moreover, Beaufort had such a popular following in the capital that the Palace of Justice would have been surrounded constantly by an uncontrollable and unpredictable crowd. Molé, Talon, and Chancellor Séguier all used their influence with the regent, and dissuaded her from pursuing her vendetta against the popular Frondeur nobleman. The decision was, to be sure, tainted somewhat by the self-seeking motives of the judges; and Talon feared that if the Parlement had been compelled to indict Beaufort, even the bourgeoisie of Paris would have turned against that tribunal.[22] In some other cases, the Parlement evaded or delayed judgments simply because its own members were joint defendants with young noble-

[21] See especially Aumale, *Histoire des princes de Condé* v, 695 (the administration's attitude); B. N. Ms. Fr. 25025, fol. 63 (criticism of the Parlement's severity); and ibid., 42r; Talon, *Mémoires*, p. 361; Grand-Mesnil, *Mazarin, la Fronde et la presse*, pp. 239-252 (for parlementary action).

[22] Letter by Lenet to Condé, June 24, 1649, quoted in Aumale, *Histoire des princes de Condé* v, 670; Talon, *Mémoires*, p. 360.

men-Frondeurs. How could the parlementarians render an impartial decision in the case involving Frondeur judges and noblemen who had attacked two royal valets, shouting "that is for the king, that for Mazarin and that for *la Mazarine*," with every blow?[23] It was easier to do nothing and hope that these hotheads would grow tired of such pranks.

The parlementarians accompanied these fitful attacks on Parisian disorders with measures against lawlessness in the surrounding area. Here again, the judges were faced with a dilemma; if they attacked the Mazarinist soldiers and *traitants*, the very revenues which were destined for payments to rentiers and officers would not be forthcoming. If they condoned such activities and concentrated their ire on tax evaders and former rebel troops, they would undermine the reforms of 1648 and their own popularity. A close reading of the Parlement's *arrêts* reveals that the bewildered judges tried to attack both evils, hoping that law and order would be reestablished, while legitimate tax collection would continue. The Frondeur Duke of La Trémouille was refused permission to arm the noblemen of Poitou, taxpayers were ordered to pay their *gabelles* and *aides*, and parlementary *arrêts* and loans floated on Molé's personal credit were used to pay off and disband rebel armies. These procedures were balanced by equally stringent decrees against plundering and illegal taxation by royalist forces, and by criminal action against *traitants* who had collected taxes beyond the levels stipulated by the reforms of 1648 and conciliar *arrêts*. The Cour des Aides of Paris was less active than the Parlement, but its judges also performed a delicate balancing act by trying to reconcile the regent's requests for increased taxation, complaints by well-to-do merchants against these levies, and their own interest in securing payment of salaries and interest on rentes.[24]

The Parlement's actions did not restore total order to the Parisian area, but they kept the capital peaceful enough to lure the royal family back in August 1649. Paradoxically, fears of new troubles in Paris clinched the regent's decision: knowing full well that the Parlement of Paris might become involved, through appeals from provincial

---

[23] B. N. Ms. Fr. 25025, fol. 58.

[24] Actes Royaux, F 23668, nos. 846, 858, 863, 866, 870, 878, 882 (parlementary *arrêts*); F 23611, no. 997, and B. N. Ms. Fr. 25025, fol. 44v (action by the Cour des Aides). See also Kossman, *La Fronde*, p. 91.

judges, in disputes just then erupting between governors and parlements in some provinces, she and her ministers wished to be in closer touch with the capital and its leading tribunal.

The conciliar *arrêts* and private newsletters of this time indicate clearly the seriousness of the provincial upheavals.[25] Even the sovereign courts of Normandy, which had been mollified by the Treaty of Rueil, were launching new attacks on royalist taxes and tax farmers, despite repeated *lettres de jussion* by the council of state. The entire southern band of provinces was aflame with revolts by peasants, poor townspeople, and the lesser nobility, quarrels between parlements and Mazarinist governors, and even resistance to taxation by provincial Estates. In Guienne, actual fighting broke out between the local inhabitants and judges on one side and the troops of Governor Epernon on the other. By July, the war in Guienne came to resemble the siege of Paris after the Parlement of Bordeaux was deprived of its functions. In neighboring Limousin, the petty nobility protested that the reduction in the *taille* promised by the reforms of 1648 had not been honored. In Provence, Governor Alais' demands of money, supplies, and lodging for his troops plunged that province into civil war, cutting across social lines and pitting supporters of the Parlement of Aix against followers of the governor. All these disturbances affected the province of Languedoc, which lay between troubled Provence and Guienne. The Parlement of Toulouse threatened to support its sister courts against Alais and Epernon, and flooded the countryside with *arrêts* against royalist troops, illegal intendancies, and arbitrary increases in the *taille*. While the local parlementarians ordered inhabitants to refuse food and lodging to Mazarinist agents, and appealed to the regent to honor the reforms of 1648, the local Estates of Languedoc quashed conciliar *arrêts* which imposed taxes without parlementary registration. Even in Dauphiné, which was one of the most loyal provinces during the Fronde, the Parlement of Grenoble forced royalist troops out of the area and expelled the Mazarinist *procureur général*, who had hampered his tribunal's cooperation with the Parlement of Paris during the recent siege. While the local parlementarians ordered a point-by-point enforcement of the reforms of 1648, the Estates of Dauphiné reasserted its ancient claim to approve royal taxation.[26] The central

---

[25] For a very different appraisal, see Kossman, *La Fronde*, pp. 123-126, 130-135, 143.
[26] See especially Actes Royaux, F 23611, nos. 911, 955, 1003; F 23631, no. 467; and

administration's plight was increased by the refusal of Mazarinist governors to obey any orders from the regent and its own vacillation between conciliation and repression of the provincial malcontents. When Mazarin did consider using force, it was almost impossible to rush fresh troops to trouble spots. A regiment from Flanders had to be sent by sea to Guienne, since a cross-country trek would have incited further rebellions.[27]

Of the many provincial revolts, only two came to the attention of the Palace of Justice in Paris. That was enough to cause consternation within royalist circles and confusion in the Parlement. Early in August 1649, First President Molé was desperately trying to postpone a plenary session which the parlements of Aix and Bordeaux desired. On August 14, Condé was informed by a parlementary acquaintance that if the regent came back, parlementary intervention in the provincial disputes might be avoided. The vacillating, but still royalist, Condé became convinced that the royal family must return to the capital before the Parlement met in plenary session. Four days later, the ministers, courtiers, and royal family entered the capital.[28]

The calming effect—for the moment—of the royal family's return exceeded the expectations of the most rabid Mazarinists. Crowds cheered, and even the *bête noire* of Parisians, Cardinal Mazarin, was treated with respect. In an unusually astute display of courage, Anne took quarters in the easily accessible Palais Royal, rather than the defensible Louvre or the virtually impregnable Arsenal. Soon Mazarin, too, became bolder, walking the streets with a bodyguard and visiting the city's churches.[29]

The Parlement fell in line—with a little prodding from the royal administration. Despite the agitations of a few Frondeur judges, most of the tribunal's members were hesitant to intervene in provincial affairs for fear that they would only cause trouble in Paris and a prolongation of civil strife in southern France. The normally radical

---

the newsletters from the provinces in B. N. Ms. Fr. 25025, especially fols. 30, 34, 44, 59, 60, 62, 90, 98.

[27] B. N. Ms. Fr. 25025, fol. 117v. Mousnier, *Lettres et mémoires adressés au Chancelier Séguier* II, 1023-1024, reveals the hostility of the governor of Guienne, Epernon, to the administration's vacillation.

[28] See the letter from Machault to Condé, Aug. 14, 1649, quoted in Aumale, *Histoire des princes de Condé* V, 702.

[29] See Martin, *Histoire de France* XII, 339.

judges in the *enquêtes* chambers were almost equally divided over the desirability of a plenary parlementary session. Many of them respected their tribunal's promise at the Treaty of Rueil not to assemble for the remainder of 1649, and they knew that the regent hoped for a quick settlement in both southern provinces. Anne ended their indecision by calling a deputation of some twenty-five judges to her residence on September 2. To ensure nonintervention by the Parlement of Paris, a royal agent had already forced the Count of Alais to sign a treaty renouncing his attacks on the judges and inhabitants of Aix. This settlement had been published at Aix on August 25. The regent informed the Parisian judges of the agreement and promised that a settlement in Guienne, mediated by Orléans and Condé, was imminent. Under the circumstances, the deputation did not need to be warned that parlementary assemblies would only increase domestic troubles. Two days later, the *grand chambre* and *chambres des enquêtes* discovered a way to extricate their tribunal from the provincial problems without offending the southern parlements, the regent, or each other. The senior chamber drafted a polite reply to the judges at Aix and Bordeaux, which professed support without openly proclaiming union with their cause. The *enquêtes* read and modified the letters through deputies who met with the senior judges, thus avoiding a plenary session. And the *enquêtes* judges salved their own consciences by declaring that their acquiescence should not be considered a precedent for unilateral action by the senior chambers on the issue of plenary sessions.[30]

3

IT WAS fortunate that the Parlement of Paris retained some sense of unity and moderation. These qualities were desperately needed during the last four months of 1649, when the malaise of the French state became more and more serious. One after another, the responsible authorities in the realm lost control of fast-moving events, leaving a power vacuum which the parlementary judges in the capital alone had any possibility of filling. For all its internal tensions, and its contradictory hopes for order and reform, the chief law court of the kingdom was the only sure stabilizing element during those months.

The most alarming development now was the intensification of

[30] B. N. Ms. Fr. 25025, fols. 75v, 87-92; Talon, *Mémoires*, pp. 362-363.

feuds between the Mazarinist, Frondeur, and Condéan factions. They had intrigued with each other and jockeyed for position during the summer of 1649. By autumn, the lines were becoming drawn much more sharply. In September, the Condéans and Frondeurs almost joined forces against Mazarin after a particularly violent dispute between the chief minister and Condé. Mazarin had been holding out hopes of governorships, offices, and honorary titles to both noble groups, and alienating one as much as the other. When Condé stalked away from a conference with Mazarin after criticizing the administration's handling of the war against Spain, he became a hero even for the Frondeurs. Gondi, Turenne, Bouillon, and La Boulaye all toasted his health. There was speculation that the young prince would go to the Parlement of Paris and demand the enforcement of a parlementary *arrêt* of 1617 which had forbidden foreigners to hold administrative posts. Obviously, such a move would be directed against the ex-Italian, Mazarin. Mazarin managed to prevent such an attack by patching up his quarrel with Condé, but only at the price of infuriating the Frondeurs and giving the prince a position which Mazarin could not tolerate for long. Condé was given a virtual veto over all major appointments in the royal armies, the diplomatic corps, provincial governorships, and the royal household. All dispatches were to be handled by the formal *conseil d'état*, which was under Condé's influence, rather than through Mazarin's personal agents. The chief minister also relinquished control over financial decisions to the prince, and this crushing blow to the cardinal's influence was followed in November by the restoration of the once-hated and now Condéan supporter, d'Emery, to the superintendency of finances.[31]

While Mazarin watched for an opportunity to strike back at Condé, and the prince tried to settle down to his ill-suited role of supervising the administration, the Frondeurs began to wage a relentless campaign to embarrass Mazarin and unseat Condé. The Parlement and inhabitants of Paris were to be the unwitting instruments of their grand scheme. The smouldering grievances of the Parlement of Aix, the still unresolved conflict between the Parlement of Bordeaux and the governor of Guienne, and the poorly paid rentes held by judges and merchants in Paris were all inflammatory issues, tailor-

---

[31] For the intrigues and subsequent agreement between Condé and Mazarin, see B. N. Ms. Fr. 25025, fols. 101-103; Chéruel, *Minorité de Louis XIV* III, 292-300.

made to the Frondeurs' design of causing an uproar on the floor of the Palace of Justice and the streets of Paris. To be sure, the issues were not as clearly drawn as the Frondeurs believed. Condé also supported the Bordeaux judges, while opposing their Provençal counterparts. However, the involved and seemingly inconsistent interests of the prince actually played into the hands of the Frondeurs. His desire to build a base of power in Guienne by favoring the Parlement of Bordeaux added to the confusion in that southwestern province. And his persistence in opposing the Parlement of Aix just because it was fighting against his relative, Governor Alais, threatened to shatter the shaky Provençal settlement of August. At meetings of the council of state, Condé confused everybody. He denounced the Provençal judges as "republicans" and chased their representatives from conciliar deliberations. When some council members took a similar stand against the Bordelais rebels, the prince sarcastically suggested that they try to copy his military victories by marching in person against the southern judges. Condé's outbursts and the Frondeurs' opportunism certainly did not help Mazarin. He could not take sides in the Provençal affair without playing into the hands of either the Frondeurs or Condéans. Even in Guienne, where he was pitted against both noble factions, he had to tread warily for fear of rousing the ire of the interested parlementarians in Paris.[32]

While the political factions squabbled, a sudden change in southern conditions forced the Parlement of Paris to retreat from its quasi-neutral position of August. By a strange coincidence, both southern parlements trotted out new grievances directly related to the reform program of 1648. At Aix, the local judges complained that the royal council had transferred all suits involving the Count of Alais' supporters. The Parlement of Aix pointed out to the Parisian tribunal that such evocations from its jurisdiction were contrary to the royal declaration of October 1648, and bluntly warned that all of France's parlements were thereby threatened with the loss of their judicial functions. From the Parlement of Bordeaux came a clever appeal

---

[32] The account of Condé's actions in B. N. Ms. Fr. 25025 is followed closely by Lorris, La Fronde, pp. 127-129. Evidence of the Frondeurs' plans can be found in Talon, Mémoires, pp. 362, 368-369; B. N. Ms. Fr. 25025, fol. 119r; Priolo, Ministry of Cardinal Mazarine, p. 160. There is absolutely no doubt of the Frondeurs' plans, since their strongest supporters in the Parlement always led the agitation for support of the provincial courts and rentiers.

against the royal interdiction of July against its members. The Parlement of Paris had hesitated to condemn that particular violation of the reforms of 1648 while hopes of a settlement between the regent and the Bordelais judges remained strong. Now that war had resumed and the council of state was intent on implementing the interdiction, the southern tribunal had every reason to expect action rather than condolences from its northern counterpart.[33]

The belated intervention by the Parlement of Paris was moderate but determined. Since the southern appeals came when the Parlement was in fall recess, the skeleton Parlement known as the *"chambre des vacations"* was able to avoid pleas by its Frondeur members for a plenary session. However, it proceeded to apply pressure on the regent both directly and indirectly. Replies to the southern tribunals' appeals were written to show that the Parlement of Paris strongly supported their demands for justice, but had no intention of taking unilateral action. At the same time, a deputation from the skeleton Parlement went to the regent to remonstrate against her administration's injustices.

At the conference of October 25, the Frondeur judges were well represented. They virtually demanded an end to the interdiction of the Parlement of Bordeaux and the withdrawal of evocations from the Parlement of Aix. To underline their position, the judges attacked recent Mazarinist pamphlets, which said that the regent need not observe the Declaration of 1648 because it had been forced on Anne against her will. One distinguished parlementarian, President de Novion, courageously told Anne that all France's troubles were caused by breaches of faith. In answering for Anne, Chancellor Séguier employed the legalistic argumentation which had so often emerged in past confrontations with the Parlement of Paris, that the Parlement of Bordeaux was itself violating the reforms of 1648 by demanding the arbitrary removal of Governor Epernon. Séguier also used those reforms with telling effect against the Parlement of Aix, contending that some types of evocation had been retained by the reform declarations; the Provençal judges were therefore wrong in criticizing the removal of suits from its control. Having placed the law on the administration's side, he declared that the Provençal allegations were "lies," since Anne had not exercised her legal rights

[33] B. U. P. Ms. 65, fols. 41-43, 93-95, 103-108; B. N. Ms. Fr. 25025, fols. 107-108.

in Provence. As was his habit, he covered all eventualities by concluding that the pretended grievances of both courts were being thoroughly investigated.[34]

The vigorous parlementary protest had a sobering effect on Mazarinist circles. Séguier probably had the best of the argument as far as legal issues were concerned, but even he must have sensed the administration's vulnerability on the moral question of its recent promises to the southern parlements. As a practical matter, the Parisian judges' determination to secure a genuine settlement in southern France could not be ignored. The Mazarinist ministers were understandably unhappy with de Novion's speech. They knew that the southern parlements must be accommodated in order to keep Paris and its Parlement from turning against the regent. In the succeeding weeks, the Provençal judges were apparently placated, and serious efforts were made to satisfy the tribunal at Bordeaux.[35]

The royal-parlementary conference had a very different impact on the Frondeurs. They, too, sensed that it made a royal-provincial accommodation inevitable, thereby robbing them of a major issue. This made them all the more desperate to find ways of embarrassing the regent. In part, they clung to the hope that the royal-provincial troubles could be used as propaganda before a settlement came. In December, Frondeurs in the *chambres des enquêtes* repeatedly demanded a plenary parlementary session on the basis of rumors that the regent did not intend to satisfy the Parlement of Bordeaux.[36] However, the Frondeur party concentrated its attention on the far more explosive issue of the municipal rentes, which Gondi had begun to exploit in September.

For a faction with the resourcefulness, imagination, and desperation which the Frondeurs displayed at this time, the rentes presented a splendid opportunity. Superficially, the only issue at stake was nonpayment of interest on those municipal bonds. But every public authority, private individual, and political faction in Paris was deeply involved. The royal administration was committed by the Declaration of October 22, 1648, to resume part payment of the interest,

---

[34] B. U. P. Ms. 65, fols. 104-119; B. N. Ms. Fr. 25025, fols. 119-120. See also the accounts by Vallier, Talon, Molé, and Motteville.

[35] On the administration's attitudes and action, see Goulas, *Mémoires* III, 139; B. N. Ms. Fr. 25025, fol. 148v; B. U. P. Ms. 65, fol. 132.

[36] B. U. P. Ms. 65, fols. 132, 161-163; B. N. Ms. Fr. 25025, fols. 148v, 157v.

which had been withheld prior to the parlementary Fronde. Anne had to weigh the advantages of keeping Paris quiet by paying the rentiers, against the competing financial demands of the Franco-Spanish war. The municipal government at the Hôtel de Ville and the sovereign courts at the Palace of Justice were placed in an equally difficult situation. All these institutions wanted to maintain order in the capital, but the regent, and not they, had the money which alone could satisfy the demands of the rentiers. As guarantors of the agreement of 1648, they were more likely to become the victims of rentier frustration than to be thanked for trying to place pressure on the royal treasury. Moreover, each of these bodies had individuals whose personal interest in the matter placed them on opposite political sides. There were rentier judges and *échevins* who were secretly paid their interest because of connections within the regent's administration, and others who were as luckless as the mass of rentiers.

The Frondeurs were fortunate enough to have leaders who were popular in Paris, followers who belonged to the cosmopolitan group of rentiers, and a number of sympathizers who were both rentiers and parlementarians. The party took advantage of the administration's solemn promise to pay the rentiers a substantial sum, starting in September. When the tax farmers forced the regent to withdraw her promise by defaulting on payments earmarked for the rentes, the Frondeurs incited mass demonstrations at the Hôtel de Ville. Although the municipal government was legally entrusted with the administration of the rentes, it had no money, and in any case the *prévôt des marchands* was anathema to the crowd because of his Mazarinist connections. A hastily assembled body of civic officials and members of the Parlement, Chambre des Comptes, and Cour des Aides tried to placate the angry rentiers by agreeing to arrest the tax farmers. However, this was simply a means to save the *traitants* and the *prévôt des marchands* from being torn to pieces by the mob. The controversy was now a legal matter, and it was obvious that the Parlement alone could deal with the interconnected issues of public order, state reform, and the rentes. Rentiers laid their claims before the *chambre des vacations*, and the *traitants* presented counterclaims.

The *chambre des vacations* handled the delicate situation with amazing skill. In October, the skeleton Parlement heard appeals from both sides, and started proceedings against the tax farmers. This frightened the contractors, and they agreed to pay some of the interest charges on the rentes in return for their freedom. The special chamber also forbade all demonstrations by rentiers and rejected a request by the second *chambre des enquêtes* to call back the entire Parlement for a full investigation.

When the regular Parlement returned from its autumn recess in November, the situation was vastly improved, but the Frondeurs refused to let the issue die. The new *surintendant*, d'Emery, tried to increase payments, only to be greeted with skepticism by the rentiers and anger by the Frondeurs. Frondeur leaders, such as Gondi and Beaufort, now intended to use the issue of the rentes to intimidate the regent and destroy Condé's power by attacking his friend d'Emery. Led by the rentier Guy Joly, who was Gondi's personal secretary, the Frondeurs met with the rentiers at the Hôtel de Ville and reorganized a syndicate of rentier representatives which had been formed earlier. Ostensibly, the syndics were to supervise payment of the rentes. However, the syndicate was an illegal body, and one which made no pretense of impartiality in dealing with the *traitants* or the *surintendant*. More ominous was the fact that the syndics included several of the most radical members of the Parlement, including President Charton, who had barely escaped arrest by the royal administration during the Days of Barricades in August 1648. Moreover, the Frondeur leaders, Gondi and Beaufort, publicly supported the rentiers' action, and many radical parlementarians demanded a plenary session of their tribunal to legalize and work with the syndicate. Not all these radical judges were Frondeurs, however, and those who were probably had no idea that the leading Frondeurs were simply manipulating events to their advantage. Joly himself noted that the judge-syndic Loisel knew nothing of his plotting.[37] But the Parlement was badly divided between those who sympathized with the rentiers and those who thought that the situation was again getting out of hand.[38]

The person who dominated the intricate negotiations that followed was the Parlement's first president, Molé. He had no intention of allowing the illegal syndicate to dominate the Parisian scene,

---

[37] G. Joly, *Mémoires*, p. 27.

[38] B. N. Ms. Fr. 25025, fols. 102-135 has an excellent account of all aspects of the rentier issue. See also Actes Royaux, F 23668, no. 889; B. U. P. Ms. 65, fols. 35-36, 119-124; *Registres de l'Hôtel de Ville* II, appen., note D, "Sur les rentes de l'Hôtel de Ville"; and extracts from Mazarin's notebooks in Retz, *Oeuvres* II, 548-553, fns.

and was equally opposed to his radical colleagues' plan to have the Parlement, as a whole, intervene. He therefore moved quickly to crush the syndicate and evade a parlementary assembly. Under his direction, the conservative *grand chambre* declared the syndicate illegal. To mollify the *chambres des enquêtes*, which claimed that only a full Parlement could take such action, he agreed to a special assembly of the *prévôt des marchands*, rentiers, and delegates from all parlementary chambers.

This tactic almost backfired since the meeting at Molé's house on December 4 was attended by some five hundred rentiers, armed with pistols and knives. The first president held his ground, conceding some measures to guarantee payment of the rentes, while evading demands for removal of the ban on the rentier syndicate. This placed the rentiers in an untenable position. They could not complain of ill-treatment, yet they suspected that Molé's words meant nothing so long as the conservative *grand chambre* and the Mazarinist Hôtel de Ville, rather than their syndicate, remained in charge of the rentes. The Frondeurs in the rentier group were even more disheartened by Molé's maneuver, for it deprived them of their chief instrument of disorder, the syndicate. In the mob scene that ensued, the Frondeurs harmed their cause still further. Joly shouted that Molé and other conservative judges were Mazarinists. President Le Coigneux was accused of opposing the rentiers because he had secretly been paid full interest on his rentes, and was punched in the back. The *prévôt des marchands* had to flee from the meeting to save himself from almost certain death at the hands of those who suspected him of being an agent of Mazarin. Molé's son, Champlâtreux, quickly seized the opportunity to pin the label of "rebels" on the Frondeurs, accusing them of trying to incite sedition in order to advance their cause. That night, the Frondeurs were further shaken when one of their party barely escaped arrest for his role in the meeting. Molé administered the *coup de grâce*, on December 10, by declaring that the illegal syndicate would be replaced by a committee, carefully chosen by conservative members of the sovereign courts, civic government, and guilds of Paris.[39]

These events set the stage for the most bizarre occurrence of the entire Fronde: the double-assassination plot of December 11. Historians will probably never be able to piece together all the conflicting

[39] The best account is B. U. P. Ms. 65, fols. 124-136.

reports. However, it is certain that the Frondeurs were the chief villains, the Parlement of Paris the one element which kept the plots from plunging the city into total confusion, and Mazarin, opportunist, who ultimately turned the episode into another civil war.

The day began with a simulated attempt to kill the Frondeur-syndic Guy Joly, staged by some of the Frondeur party. Evidently they sought to gain sympathy for the dying rentier cause by making Joly look like a martyr. Whether the secondary figures in this dream were privy to the scheme cannot be determined. In any case, sympathizers of the rentiers and Frondeurs did their best to invoke the assistance of the Parlement and Parisians. A parlementary president, Charton, rushed to the Parlement, claiming that the "assassins" had meant to kill him and not Joly, and demanding full debate by the entire Parlement. The Marquis of La Boulaye ran through the streets of the central city, exhorting the inhabitants to take up arms and erect barricades as they had in August of 1648. Pierre Broussel demanded that the Parlement order the city's gates closed to prevent the royal family from leaving and laying siege to the capital as in January.[40] Still another incident occurred during the evening of the same day. As Condé's unoccupied carriage sped through the streets of Paris, shots were fired at it. According to the most persistent rumors, it was the Frondeur La Boulaye who intercepted the carriage and had his bodyguards shoot with the intention of assassinating Condé. It is impossible to tell whether La Boulaye was actually the culprit and, if so, whether he acted as a Frondeur, Mazarinist double-agent, or on his own initiative. The most plausible reconstruction is Guy Joly's suggestion that La Boulaye was desperately trying to curry favor with the chief minister by attacking Mazarin's archrival, Condé. After his abortive attempt to incite a riot earlier in the day, La Boulaye knew that he was a prime target for prosecution by the administration, though by taking action which would sow seeds of suspicion between Condéans and Frondeurs, he may have hoped to be rewarded, and not punished, by Mazarin, whether Condé were killed or not.[41]

[40] The guilt of the leading Frondeurs and notably Gondi is unquestionable. See especially Chéruel, *Minorité de Louis XIV* III, 318-333. La Boulaye's motives are difficult to determine. Broussel seems to have been unaware of the Frondeurs' plans; his action was caused by fear of a new royalist siege.

[41] G. Joly, *Mémoires*, p. 30. Charges by La Rochefoucauld and Gondi that Mazarin had masterminded the attempt on Condé's life are far-fetched. See La Rochefou-

In any case, the important consideration is not the actual guilt of the Frondeurs, La Boulaye, or Mazarin, but the cumulative effect of the events of December 11 on Paris and France. The chief minister was suspected in some quarters of having plotted to destroy both the Frondeurs and Condéans, but the Frondeur party bore the brunt of hostile public opinion for inciting a riot.[42] If Mazarin had allowed events to run their course, he might well have emerged as victor. Paris was tense for days after the double-assassination affair, and Mazarinist circles were terrified lest Paris should erupt in violence; but nothing happened.[43] This was partly due to the Parisians' refusal to take the Frondeurs' charges of a plot against Joly seriously. More important was the role of the Parlement of Paris and its leaders. In the first place, *Avocat Général* Talon persuaded Le Tellier to have Orléans patrol Paris with the civic militia, rather than letting the still-hated Condé march through the streets with troops.[44] Then, too, the Parlement as a whole remained calm, and scrupulously impartial. Plenary sessions were held, but without the usual confusion— the judges merely voting to investigate the events of December 11, including the Frondeurs' charge of an alleged plot against Joly.

When the investigation showed that Joly's wound was self-inflicted, the parlementarians dropped their pretense of impartiality and began to hear testimony against the most obvious guilty members of the Frondeur party. They needed little prodding from Condé and the regent to mete out punishment to those who had allegedly plotted sedition against the state and the assassination of Condé. In fact, the majority of the Parlement was at this point so convinced of the Frondeurs' guilt that a quick trial would have gone against Joly, La Boulaye, and a few minor figures—enough to destroy the Frondeurs' popularity and power.[45]

---

cauld, *Oeuvres* II, 154; Retz, *Oeuvres* II, 559-562. Mazarin had infiltrated the rentier-Frondeur movement with spies and took advantage of the confusion and rumors of a plot against Condé by suggesting that the prince send his carriage through the city to test the rumors. However, royalist fear of a massive uprising after the Joly affair was too strong to suggest that Mazarin was as coolheaded and machiavellian as his detractors believed. While taking advantage of the Frondeur-Condéan rivalry, he probably did not direct La Boulaye's madcap adventure against Condé.

[42] See the commentary in B. N. Ms. Fr. 25025, fol. 151r.

[43] Ibid., fols. 151-155.   [44] Ibid., fol. 155r; Talon, *Mémoires*, p. 371.

[45] This belief was held by persons of every political persuasion. See, inter alia, Ormesson, *Journal* I, 785-786; G. Joly, *Mémoires*, p. 30.

While the Frondeurs' fortunes were sinking, parlementary conservatives quietly assumed the task of meeting the remaining grievances of the rentiers of Paris and the judges of Bordeaux. First President Molé, President de Mesmes, and *Avocat Général* Talon worked
behind the scenes to impress on the royal administration the need to
end the civil war in the south. New demands by their radical fellow
judges for a parlementary debate on that issue helped them convince
the regent's ministers. On December 22, Orléans and Molé were able
to announce the arrangement of terms between the regent and representatives from Bordeaux.[46] The conditions were onerous for the
monarchy, but they made a definitive peace possible—if only Mazarin and Anne respected them. The Parlement of Bordeaux was to be
freed from the interdiction, illegal impositions and military harassment were to cease, and the hated Governor Epernon was to be
quietly removed from the province on the understanding that he
would never be restored to power.[47] The Bordelais settlement was
all the more encouraging since tensions in other provinces seemed to
be lessening, and even in Languedoc the regent had sharply reduced
the opposition of Estates and tribunals by withdrawing some taxes
and reducing others.[48] A settlement of the question of the rentes was
more difficult to effect. However, Molé worked continuously on the
problem. On December 29, the Parlement decreed that a syndicate
of eighteen rentiers, chosen every six months by an assembly of the
city's courts, civic officials, and notable bourgeoisie, would supervise
the administration of the rentes. Every three months, a committee
drawn from all of the Parlement's chambers would hear complaints
from the rentiers.[49] Though the question of the rentes was to re-
emerge several times during the rest of the Fronde, the danger of its
becoming a popular issue had passed. The Palace of Justice, and not
the streets of Paris, would henceforth be the place where grievances
over nonpayment would be settled.

Unfortunately, parlementary action on the rentes, provincial strife,
and the sedition of December 11 did not end the Fronde. Yet, while
the Parlement of Paris had not fully reconciled the diverse, rival ele-

[46] See Talon, *Mémoires*, p. 371-372; B. N. Ms. Fr. 25025, fols. 152-157; B. U. P.
Ms. 65, fols. 161-165, 171-172.

[47] B N. Ms. Fr. 25025, fols. 157-158.

[48] Ibid., fol. 132.

[49] There were adjustments of the settlement in January and February of 1650.
See B. U. P. Ms. 65, fols. 157-161, 231-233; Actes Royaux, F 23668, no. 897.

ments involved in current troubles, its members were not to blame for the succeeding intensification of the Fronde. True, they were still torn by old divisions between the conservative *grand chambre* and the radical *enquêtes*, and the developments of the last months of 1649 had made cooperation between the two groups even more difficult than during the parlementary Fronde. There was also latent parlementary hostility to Mazarin and continued suspicion that the regent wanted to overthrow all the reforms of 1648. But the judges, with few exceptions, were too wary of another siege to provoke a new conflict. The only development which could bring about another wave of violence was a deterioration of relations among the three factions of Mazarinists, Frondeurs, and Condéans. And of the leaders of those groups, Mazarin, as chief minister, bore the greatest responsibility. He had an especially good opportunity to bind up wounds, for the Frondeurs were temporarily too eclipsed after December 11 to wreak vengeance on any rival party, while Condé had not yet attempted to cause sedition or rebellion despite his unpredictable nature and his uncertain relations with Mazarin. It was therefore tragic that Mazarin not only failed to build on the foundations laid by recent events and the actions of the Parlement of Paris, but, by fanning the flames of partisan politics, prepared the way for a conflagration far more serious than the siege of Paris.

CHAPTER EIGHT

COALITION AND THE
PARLEMENTARY MEDIATION

No ONE KNEW better than Cardinal Mazarin that the Frondeur party's decline in influence after the Joly affair gave him an excellent opportunity to restore order to France. However, that master politician realized that he had to contend with two rival factions; it would be folly to complete the destruction of the Frondeurs and thereby make himself all the more dependent on Condé. The chief minister was left with two options: he could forsake partisan politics altogether and try to draw both noble parties into a ministry of all talents, or he could exploit party animosities so that the Frondeurs and Condéans would destroy each other. The first approach, given the bitter feuds which had divided Mazarinists, Frondeurs, and Condéans, was questionable; in any case, Mazarin rejected it, and opted for the continuation of his strategy of dividing and ruling. He lulled Condé into a false sense of security by encouraging him to press his suit against the Frondeurs, at the same time eluding the overconfident Condéans' demands for new governorships and pensions. Meanwhile, he urged prosecution of the Frondeurs in the Parlement, while secretly courting their support. Mazarin intended to weaken the Frondeurs to the point where they would be helpless as a party but useful as allies against Condé. By pressing the trial against Gondi's faction, he could frighten them into begging for mercy, and they would become the secondary partner in a Mazarinist-Frondeur coalition powerful enough to free Mazarin from Condé's domination. When they had served that purpose, the Frondeurs could be detached from the alliance and allowed to go their own harmless way.

This was a daring scheme, requiring full, if unwitting, cooperation from the Parlement of Paris. Since the parlementary judges were the central figures in the trial of the Frondeurs, any shift in Mazarin's treatment of that faction would have to be accompanied by a corresponding adjustment by the parlementarians. However, it was by no means certain that the divided and unpredictable tribunal would become such a compliant vehicle of the cardinal's partisan politics. Even if he succeeded in duping the judges, he still had to face the possibility that either the Frondeurs or the Condéans might not play the role assigned to them. The policy of divide and rule might very well degenerate into a long, three-sided civil war leaving everyone, including Mazarin, its victims.[1]

The first setback for the chief minister came when he overplayed his hand. In his eagerness to place the Frondeurs at his mercy, Mazarin tried to drag the leading members into the trial of their followers. On December 22, the *procureur général*, acting on orders from the royal administration, asked the Parlement to try Gondi, Beaufort, and their parlementary sympathizer, Broussel. The reaction at the Parlement by both friends and enemies of the Frondeurs was shock at this vindictive and partisan tactic. There was not a shred of evidence against the three men which would stand up in a court of law. Preliminary hearings against La Boulaye, Joly, and the other lesser defendants had turned up only hearsay that Beaufort and Gondi had talked of killing Condé and inciting the Parisians to riot. Evidence against the venerable Broussel rested on the fact that he had talked privately with La Boulaye during the day of the Joly affair. The case against the three major defendants was further weakened by the refusal of the two *avocats généraux* to sign their names to the *procureur général*'s deposition, despite pressures from the royal administration. Talon and Bignon objected that the three prestigious defendants could not be proved guilty and that a trial of such prominent Parisians at this time would only endanger the uneasy peace of the capital.[2]

In the confusion that followed, the Frondeurs' fortunes revived. They were able to regain much of the sympathy they had lost by the events of December 11, drag out the proceedings against the three major defendants, and prevent the Parlement from taking measures against the lesser defendants whose fate had been all but sealed before the *procureur général*'s action. Particularly damaging was Gondi's ability to show that the state's key witnesses were common

[1] Mazarin's tactics and strategy are discussed in detail by Chéruel, *Minorité de Louis XIV* III, 335-364.

[2] See especially Talon, *Mémoires*, pp. 371-373; and B. U. P. Ms. 66, fol. 174.

criminals, paid by Mazarin to infiltrate the rentier and Frondeur meetings, and whose testimony was a tissue of lies.[3] On the streets of Paris, the Frondeurs received the plaudits of the very persons who had refused to support them on December 11, and there were shouts of *"vive Monsieur Beaufort."* Mazarin may have wondered how the Parisian situation could change so completely overnight. If so he had only himself to blame. He had been warned by Molé and other par-lementary conservatives that the Parlement's antagonism toward the Frondeurs would disappear, unless the original trials were concluded quickly.[4]

In attempting to repair the damage caused by his partisan attack on the Frondeurs, Mazarin committed a second and far more serious blunder. The chief minister altered his political position by allying secretly with his Frondeur enemies. Then, backed by Frondeur sup-port and Orléans' approval, he seized the leading Condéans on Janu-ary 18, 1650. What looked at first like a brilliant display of power politics turned out to be a Pyrrhic victory for Mazarin. He no longer had to worry about Condé, who was arbitrarily imprisoned in the chateau-fortress of Vincennes along with the prince's brother, Conti, his brother-in-law, Longueville, and a personal friend in the Cham-bre des Comptes, President Perrault. But the means used to achieve this *coup d'état* made the Condéan party more dangerous than ever. The arrests, based on vague charges of treasonous intentions, gave Condé's noble followers a cause they had previously lacked,[5] and they were able to slip away from the capital to their provincial strongholds to raise local rebellions on behalf of their leader.

The Frondeurs had no reason to rebel, but their role in the *coup d'état* made these new allies almost as dangerous as Mazarin's Con-déan enemies. Mazarin's failure to crush them in December had

---

[3] Lorris, *La Fronde*, p. 143, contains instructions from the administration to these agents. There is an interesting account of how the *procureur général* was to use his witnesses: "Memoire pour advertir M. Le proc. gl. touchant Lescot et autres témoins," B. N. Ms. Fr. 17560, fol. 120r.

[4] See Mazarin, *Lettres* III, 445-446; Chéruel, *Minorité de Louis XIV* III, 335.

[5] Kossman, *La Fronde*, p. 150, rightly argues that Condé's activities did not merit imprisonment. His most heinous crime was an attempt to wrest the key fortress of Le Havre in Normandy from Mazarinist control. This threatened to place all of that province under his party's control, but many individuals (including Mazarin) were guilty of similar conduct. Whatever Condé was at this time, he was no rebel, merely a practitioner of contemporary political arts. For a different view, see Chéruel, *Minorité de Louis XIV* III, pp. 338, 360-361.

compelled him to make extravagant promises in January, as the price for their support against Condé. Despite the secrecy of his pact and his ambiguously phrased promises, it is clear that he virtually agreed to share control of the administration with the Frondeurs. He held out the hope that Gondi would receive a cardinal's hat, Châteauneuf the chancellor's seals, and parlementary president de Maisons the superintendency of finances.[6] His indebtedness was increased by events that followed the *coup d'état*. Beaufort and Gondi marched through the city's streets with armed bands and kept Paris quiet by demonstrating their support of the arrests. It was an astonishing display of the Frondeurs' revived popularity with Parisians. The inhabitants, remembering that Condé had been their enemy and the Frondeurs their defenders during the siege of 1649, cheered the Frondeur leaders and lit bonfires to celebrate the fall of the prince.[7]

Mazarin's relations with the Frondeurs became all the more uncertain after the regent's administration started to launch a military offensive against the provincial Condéan rebels. The chief minister was compelled to join the royalist armies, thereby leaving Paris in the hands of a skeleton government headed by Orléans. While the cardinal was happy to be at the regent's side, and in charge of the anti-Condéan campaign, he knew only too well that political conditions in the volatile capital city might worsen during his absence. His only hope was that the weak-willed Orléans could keep the caretaker government from falling into Frondeur hands while the Mazarinist forces were tracking down the Condéans. His treatment of the Frondeurs themselves was calculated to keep them loyal through promises and occasional rewards, while refusing Frondeur demands which would give them a dominant position in Orléans' government. In view of his previous commitments to them, this was a difficult task, even for a master politician like Mazarin.

By contrast with the threats posed by the two noble factions, Mazarin's prospects of good relations with the Parlement of Paris after Condé's arrest in January 1650 were very promising. Still, the parlementarians were an unpredictable lot and had to be watched as closely as the Frondeurs and Condéans. The chief minister knew that the Parisian judges' acceptance of the princely arrests was based

<hr />

[6] See Chéruel, *Minorité de Louis XIV* iii, pp. 365-367.
[7] Priolo, *Ministry of Cardinal Mazarine*, pp. 193-195.

on anything but devotion to his person. Frondeur supporters in the Parlement had acted purely out of partisan interests, while many judges had acquiesced out of lingering hatred for the prince who had fought against them during the siege. Still others hoped that Condé's detention would somehow end the political factionalism that had plagued France in recent months. Such a combination of self-interest and altruism was tenuous at best. The prolongation of the new civil war, a rupture in the Frondeur-Mazarinist alliance, or a backlash of sympathy for the imprisoned princes could break the loose bond between minister and judges.

The very fact that the *coup d'état* was accomplished by an act of executive justice was bound to prove troublesome. Most parlementarians thought the arrests violated a reform article of 1648 which guaranteed private subjects against arbitrary punishment, *Avocat Général* Talon being virtually alone in justifying the detentions as a state affair! He argued that the princes were arrested not for ordinary crimes but for suspected acts against the state. Nevertheless, even Talon had his reservations, feeling that the regent had either said too much or not enough in trying to explain her motives to the Parlement. A ruler, he wrote in his journal, "should never engage in so personal a revelation to his subjects in matters which concern *arcanum imperii*." By taking the parlementarians into her confidence, Anne invited some form of intervention by the judges. By being unable to reveal anything more damaging than mere suspicion of treasonous intent, she made a verdict of "not guilty" inevitable when and if the Parlement did demand a parlementary trial.[8] The uneasiness which the *avocat général* confined to his personal diary First President Molé expressed publicly in the regent's presence. On hearing of the arrests, that friend of Condé and opponent of arbitrary detention exclaimed: "Ah Madame, what have you done? These are children of the royal house."[9]

For the moment, the Parlement bowed to state necessity and accepted the detentions with scarcely a murmur; and in response to a partisan royal request that the trials of the anti-Condéan Frondeurs be terminated in accordance with the judges' "honor" and "consciences," the parlementarians acquitted Broussel, Gondi, Beaufort,

[8] Talon, *Mémoires*, p. 380.
[9] Claude Joly, *Mémoires*, Michaud and Poujoulat collection (ser. iii, vol. ii), Paris, 1838, p. 161.

and Charton before the end of January. The following month the always-dangerous plenary sessions came to an end, as the criminal chamber, the *chambre de la tournelle*, was entrusted with proceedings against the lesser defendants in the Joly affair. One by one, these men were released with the mild punishment of temporary exile from the capital.[10] It remained to be seen whether the Parlement could continue to support Mazarin as the civil war became more intense and the chief minister more and more partisan. Also, lurking in the background was the still-inflammatory issue of the reforms of 1648, which could cause new opposition to erupt in the Palace of Justice. The inexorable military and financial demands on a state faced with both civil and foreign war made new violations of the reforms inevitable. In January 1650, the regent asked the Cour des Aides of Paris to employ its members as supervisors of tax collectors in the central provinces. This clever substitute for the old intendants was approved by the financial tribunal, though with severe restrictions.[11] In the months that followed, Anne's ministers supplemented these quasi-legal judge-intendants with maîtres des requêtes and other conciliar agents. It was an open secret that these new intendants would usurp the role of the local officiers, levying taxes without proper registration and collecting them without deference to legal forms or the officiers' machinery.[12] At the end of 1649, rumors that parlementary judges might be asked to perform similar duties had angered the parlementary radicals so much that Anne's ministers had quietly yielded.[13] Now that maîtres des requêtes, councilors of state, *intendants des finances*, and councilors in the Paris Cour des Aides were assuming the role which the parlementarians had refused, the issue of state reform threatened to complicate the civil war of 1650 even more. By the middle of the year, *trésoriers de France* were lodging appeals against the intendants before the

[10] See Talon, *Mémoires*, pp. 381-382; Dubuisson-Aubenay, *Journal* i, 215-216, 247; *Journal du procès du Marquis de la Boulaye* (in Marquis de Beauvais-Nangis, *Mémoires*, M. Monmerqué and A. H. Taillandier, Paris, 1862), pp. 345-349.

[11] See especially Actes Royaux, F 23612, no. 4 (registered commissions of several members of the Cour des Aides), no. 19 (detailed account of the work of these agents); B. N. Ms. Fr. 25025, fol. 161r.

[12] There is a wealth of information in the Actes Royaux, F 23612, 23631, and 23669 series. See also the many articles by Esmonin, especially "La Suppression des intendants pendant la Fronde et leur rétablissement," *Bulletin de la Société d'Histoire Moderne* (1935), pp. 114-119.

[13] There is an excellent account in B. N. Ms. Fr. 25025, fols. 131r, 142r, 147-148r.

Cour des Aides, Parlement, and their own syndicate at the capital.[14] The situation was even more disturbing in the outlying provinces of the realm, where local officers often had to contend with new intendants, Mazarinist governors who supported them, and rampaging royalist troops who were battling with equally undisciplined Condéan armies.

2

MAZARIN must have believed that he would achieve a decisive victory over the Condéan rebels, which would allow him to turn quickly to the task of subduing the troublesome provincial officers and his grasping Frondeur allies. Instead, from February to August, 1650, the Condéan upheaval pursued an erratic course. *Les grands* never inflicted serious defeats on the royalist armies but they always managed to escape disaster themselves. The chief minister had friends in key military governorships, and he also replaced the imprisoned Condéan leaders with Mazarinist governors in Normandy, Champagne, and Burgundy. But the Condéan followers, holding many lesser governorships, were able to rally support even in the areas which were officially claimed by Mazarin's supporters. What is often described as a single rebellion was in fact several, loosely connected uprisings, each of which had some Condéan leadership, armies composed of petty nobles and their peasants, and at least tacit support from some judges, civic officials, and townspeople. Madame de Longueville tried to hold Normandy for her imprisoned husband, while the former Frondeur general Turenne established his headquarters at Stenay in the northeast. Several of Condé's friends acted on his behalf in Burgundy, and in the provinces southwest of Paris, one native nobleman after another rallied to the princes' cause. Except for Guienne, none of these uprisings constituted a major problem for the monarchy, but collectively, they did pose a very real threat. There were not enough royalist forces and generals to crush each revolt simultaneously. Mazarin was forced to rush from one trouble spot to another, pacifying a province only to discover that its elusive troublemakers had slipped away to adjoining provinces. In February, Normandy fell easily, thanks largely to the government's favorable treatment of the local parlement and tax-weary population. Then the royal entourage rushed across France to Burgundy,

---

[14] Charmeil, *Les Trésoriers de France*, pp. 394-395.

where the Parlement of Dijon's first president was defending Condé against verbal criticisms by the newly installed royalist governor, Vendôme. Resistance by the local parlement and Condéan nobles collapsed as soon as the royal family appeared on the scene with troops. In the meantime, Madame de Longueville had fled from Normandy to Stenay, where she and Turenne made a pact with Spanish forces in the nearby Low Countries. Mazarin arrived in time to hold back the invading Condéan-Spanish armies in June, but before the enemy could be annihilated the main force of the royalist army had to be withdrawn to southwestern France. Most of the Condéan leaders had gathered there and were in the process of securing support from Spain itself. By August, the royal administration's military position was as difficult as it had been at the beginning of the Condéan revolt, even though it had gained control of most rebel provinces. The chief minister, royal family, and main royalist army were bogged down in a war of attrition against the province of Guienne, while Spanish forces under Turenne were reentering France from the northeast and threatening Paris.[15]

Provincial officers were often as bewildered as Mazarinist ministers by the strange course of this Condéan uprising. However, royal efforts to aid the war effort by arbitrary recruitment, taxation, and justice caused many sovereign courts and lesser corporations to raise their own rebellions. Mazarin and his fellow ministers tried to keep these officers from sabotaging the royalist cause, but the military campaigns constantly diverted their attention. Moreover, the same administrative confusion which had plagued the central government's relations with provincial corporations in 1649 reappeared in 1650. Without intensive regional study of the administration's handling of the officers' opposition, it is impossible to tell precisely what was happening. However, one general point emerges from the mass of conciliar arrêts in Paris, directives by the itinerant royal administration, and independent actions of local intendants and Mazarinist governors. Royalist authorities were demanding obedience from the officers and receiving little satisfaction. Even in relatively quiet Normandy, where the officers had been virtually bribed to remain on the royalist side of the civil war, the sovereign courts continued to modify royal tax legislation.[16] In Burgundy, Dauphiné, Provence,

---

[15] See the accounts by Chéruel, Kossman, Bazin, and Martin.
[16] Actes Royaux, F 23611, no. 1011.

Languedoc, Guienne, and Brittany, the local parlements were particularly obstinate. They countermanded orders from Mazarinist governors, investigated the illegal activities of the few intendants who were allowed to continue after the parlementary Fronde, chased illegal intendants away from other provinces, and tried civilian agents of Mazarinist governors, intendants, and generals. On the few occasions when royalist authorities dared to take the local parlementarians into their confidence, the latter curtly refused to register either the intendants' commissions or fiscal legislation.[17]

In Burgundy, where the Parlement of Dijon had earlier accepted the Mazarinist victory over the Condéan rebels, there was new trouble. Governor Vendôme tried to placate the parlementarians on his entry to their city by saying that the Parlement would henceforth be his only intendant. However, the Mazarinist governor soon forgot his promise. When he secured the services of a maître des requêtes, who had already aroused the hostility of Norman provincials in February, the parlement and other corporations in Burgundy turned against both the governor and his "intendant." The fate of the maître is not clear, but we know that the parlementarians succeeded in vetoing new fiscal measures, and obstructed the governor's efforts to secure supplies for his troops.[18]

There was equal unrest in Provence. Although that province had been one of the major centers of rebellion in 1649, it seemed pacified as a result of major royal concessions late that year. But appearances were deceiving. In March 1650, a deputation from the Parlement of Aix went to Paris with a grievance list. During their conference at the council of state, the parlementarians heaped verbal abuse on Governor Alais, declaring that he was the chief cause of Provençal unrest. According to them, the governor had not only disregarded his promise to withdraw the soldiers from the province, but was now making local subjects pay for their maintenance. In August, the Parlement of Aix joined townspeople at Marseilles, Arles, and Aix in demanding Alais' removal from the governorship.[19]

Lesser corporations and near-impotent subjects were probably less

---

[17] B. N. Ms. Fr. 25025, fols. 169-313 has detailed information which conflicts with Kossman's interpretation of the officiers' opposition as being mild.

[18] See especially B. N. Ms. Fr. 25025, fol. 265r; and Charmeil, *Les Trésoriers de France*, p. 392.

[19] B. N. Ms. Fr. 25025, fols. 178v, 285r.

vocal or successful in their opposition, but on occasion they could be as troublesome as sovereign courts. At Bourges, Limoges, Rodez, Chalons, and Amiens, the local *trésoriers* clashed with royalist intendants.[20] In Limousin, peasants and petty noblemen became so enraged by the forced collection of the *taille* that they organized massive demonstrations.

The troubles in Limousin were connected with the most serious uprising of 1650, a regional revolt drawing support from sovereign courts, lesser officiers, and taxpayers in western Languedoc and Guienne, and centered in the capital of Guienne and the seat of the provincial parlement, Bordeaux. The regent could not keep that upheaval from crossing provincial borders, for the governor of Guienne's jurisdiction overlapped the boundaries of the Parlement of Toulouse, in Languedoc; also, local intendants and royalist armies roamed at will. The trouble started with Governor Epernon's refusal to honor the Bordelais-royal settlement of December 1649. Instead of leaving the province of Guienne as agreed, Epernon laid an indemnity on a huge area for its part in the earlier civil war, terrorizing the countryside with armed marches and acting in concert with two maîtres des requêtes, Thomas de Morant at Montaubon, and Etienne Foullé at Limoges. The activities of Foullé caused a storm of protest in Limousin and Guienne. On one occasion four thousand peasants besiged the intendant in the town of Tulle, south of Limoges, and left only when he freed a well-known local *gentilhomme* who had organized resistance to the forced collection of the *taille*. A local *présidial* court was frightened into assisting Foullé, but the region's *trésoriers* refused to cooperate. About the same time, the Parlement of Bordeaux took the initiative, separately. After sending a deputation to the regent in protest against the governor's overall policies, the sovereign court forbade Epernon to collect taxes for his troops, and commanded Foullé to come to its chambers for interrogation. The Parlement of Toulouse unleashed yet another attack on the beleaguered governor of Guienne. Epernon had interfered with their *ressort* by asking local *sénéchal* officials to collect his indemnity in Languedoc as well as in Guienne. The Languedocian high court quashed Epernon's *ordonnances*, and went on to attack the governor's intendant, Morant. Local *trésoriers* who resisted that intendant-maître were supported by parlementary *arrêts*, and agents

[20] Charmeil, *Les Trésoriers de France*, pp. 385-396.

of the Parlement of Toulouse were given commissions to obstruct Morant's work.[21]

During the summer of 1650, this opposition in southwestern France began to merge with the Condéan rebellion in the same region. At the end of June, the Parlement of Toulouse respectfully registered a royal declaration outlawing the main Condéan generals—including Bouillon, Turenne, and La Rochefoucauld. However, the debate which preceded that decision was highly partisan. Mazarinist judges clashed verbally with colleagues who attacked the chief minister for arresting "great" princes, and some Condéan judges declared that Mazarin was capable of wishing to dethrone the king. By July, the Parlement of Toulouse was raising an army of two thousand infantrymen to attack the forces gathered by intendant Morant for the governor of nearby Guienne, and the following month, the parlementarians combined support of the Condéan movement with this attack. Remonstrances against all violations of the reform program of 1648 were drafted, including a pointed reference to the arbitrary detention of the royal princes. At the same time, the regent was asked to replace Governor Epernon, who had tyrannized over the local officers and helped organize the Mazarinist offensive against the southwestern Condéan forces. Appeals were also sent to the Parlement of Paris and other parlements to support the southern judges' defense of the reforms of 1648.[22]

Developments in Guienne were even more dramatic. Condé had supported the Parlement of Bordeaux against Epernon in 1649, and that tribunal was anxious to repay its debt. While the Toulousan parlementarians were still wavering in June, the Bordelais judges refused to register a royal declaration against the Condéan rebels, and by the end of that month, Bordeaux was crowded with the most distinguished followers of Condé, who had fled to the southwest in order to escape from the Mazarinist armies. An emotional appeal by Condé's wife, and demonstrations by a local mob incited by the Condéan leaders, ended all pretenses of neutrality at the Parlement of Bordeaux, and the parlementarians formally united with the Condéans. Anticipating later action by their counterparts at Toulouse, the Bordelais judges demanded that the regent remove Gover-

---

[21] B. N. Ms. Fr. 25025, fols. 173v, 175r, 184v, 192-193, 197; and Charmeil, *Les Trésoriers de France*, pp. 381-382.

[22] B. N. Ms. Fr. 25025, fols. 233r, 253, 256v, 261r, 270-271, 282v.

nor Epernon, punish intendant Foullé for his alleged crimes, and give the princes at Vincennes a fair trial. For the second time during the Fronde, the Parlement of Bordeaux also requested support from the Parlement of Paris, sending agents to the capital with copies of its remonstrances to the regent.[23]

Paris remained outwardly tranquil during the spring of 1650; yet Mazarin feared the Frondeurs' influence within the capital more than the open rebellion of the Condéans in the provinces.[24] It has been argued that the chief minister left Paris in 1650, not because of the gravity of the Condéan rebellion, but to flee from a situation he could not control to one he thought he could. This interpretation probably exaggerates Mazarin's plight with the Frondeurs in the capital and certainly underestimates the provincial threat; but it does recognize the minister's difficulties.[25] He submerged himself in the military campaign while avoiding a personal confrontation with his Frondeur allies, only to discover that neither approach was successful. Between his forays to individual provinces, Mazarin was compelled to return briefly to Paris in an effort to keep the fragile Mazarinist-Frondeur alliance from breaking apart. However, each visit to the capital (February 21-March 5, May 2-June 2, and June 29-July 4) resulted in further strains in the coalition. The vague promise of rewards made in letters to individual Frondeurs had to be turned into specific concessions when they met in person. But these concessions satisfied neither party. Mazarin, of course, always feared that he had given away too much power. The Frondeurs, on the other hand, were frustrated because, no matter how many offices and favors they received, it was clear that Mazarin held the reins of power. He was in constant contact with the regent, while they had influence only on the caretaker government in Paris headed by the Duke of Orléans.

The Frondeurs were all the more exasperated since Mazarin often converted Frondeur appointees into Mazarinists, instead of building a genuine Frondeur-Mazarinist coalition. For example, though the Frondeurs forced the cardinal to appoint the parlementary Frondeur Antoine Lefèbvre as *prévôt des marchands*, it turned out that the new head of the municipal government was as Mazarinist in his

---

[23] Ibid., fols. 234r, 237r, 244r; Lorris, *La Fronde*, pp. 171-176.
[24] Priolo, *Ministry of Cardinal Mazarine*, pp. 207-208.
[25] Kossman, *La Fronde*, especially p. 162.

policies as his predecessor.[26] Then, when the Vendôme family was lavished with positions and honors, the duke employed his new position as head of the admiralty and governor of Burgundy to support every Mazarinist policy. Vendôme's son, Mercoeur, was just as compliant when he replaced a Condéan supporter as viceroy of French-occupied Catalonia. Within that family, only Beaufort, the other son, remained a true Frondeur—and not without reason since all he secured was the promise of inheriting the admiralty. The inveterate Frondeur, Gondi, also was insulted by Mazarin's offer of a poor-paying ecclesiastical sinecure (which he declined), and injured by Anne's refusal to ask the Pope to make him a cardinal.[27]

The only real hope the Frondeurs had of influencing major government decisions was through their friendship with the Duke of Orléans. But Mazarin had anticipated that possibility, and had had his friend and secretary of state, Le Tellier, remain in the capital to watch Orléans closely. As much as Le Tellier disapproved of Mazarin's harsh handling of the Condéan rebellion, he was still a faithful servant of the chief minister and a dedicated opponent of the Frondeurs. Through his role as the dominant secretary of state and his friendship with Orléans, stemming from years of cooperation on military matters, Le Tellier was able to keep the duke from Frondeur influence.[28]

Although the maze of conflicting evidence is bewildering, it would seem that the Frondeurs were less inclined than Mazarin to break their pact of the previous January. They were placed in a very difficult position: they could not stir up trouble in Paris without helping the cause of their Condéan rivals, nor could they side completely with Mazarin without losing their popularity. Given the situation, they played a cautious role in agitations by Parisian rentiers for further concessions from the Parlement, at the same time hoping to capitalize on the fact that the important Parisian fortress of the Bastille was in the hands of Broussel's son.[29] Several of their clan-

---

[26] B. N. Ms. Fr. 25025, fols. 238r, 245v, 253r; Priolo, *Ministry of Cardinal Mazarine*, p. 216.

[27] Chéruel, *Minorité de Louis XIV* III, 386-387; IV, 55, 89-90, 95-96; Kossman, *La Fronde*, pp. 160-161.

[28] Dethan, *Gaston d'Orléans*, pp. 376-378; Priolo, *Ministry of Cardinal Mazarine*, pp. 217-218; Chéruel, *Minorité de Louis XIV* IV, 9, 41-43.

[29] The Bastille had fallen into his hands during the siege of Paris in 1649. Although Mazarin had failed to persuade Broussel that the fortress should be

destine activities may well have been aimed merely at frightening Mazarin into making further concessions to their party. Certainly the role of the few Frondeurs whom the chief minister brought into the administration at Paris cannot be criticized. The new keeper of the seals, Châteauneuf, for example, proved far more conciliatory toward the Parlement of Paris than Chancellor Séguier (who retained his office but lost the chancellery's seals and all power) had been. Châteauneuf suppressed many of the chancellery fees that had violated the reforms of 1648, and seriously considered the possibility of prosecuting *traitants* who had made excessive profits. Also, when d'Emery died and was succeeded, as *surintendant*, by President de Maisons of the Parlement, another voice of reason was added to the administration. Although Mazarin later complained that de Maisons had no credit with the *traitants*, the new *surintendant* did manage to pay some interest on the municipal rentes. If the chief minister was angry with these men, it was largely because their conciliatory attitude toward judges and other subjects undermined his attempts to evade the reforms of 1648 and to bring in necessary revenue for his anti-Condéan armies. Despite Mazarin's view, their actions actually helped the regent by keeping Parisians relatively quiet at a time when an uprising in the capital would have made any settlement of the provincial troubles impossible.[30]

3

THE MODEST role of the Parlement of Paris during the initial stages of these internal troubles continued until the summer of 1650. Instead of holding plenary sessions to discuss violations of the reforms of 1648, as a few members requested, the senior chambers just quietly intervened when isolated grievances came to their attention. Parlementary *arrêts* supported the merchants of the city and the wine growers of Champagne and Brie against forced collection of unverified taxes, and both the Parlement and the Chambre des Comptes of Paris sided with local *trésoriers* against intendants, sometimes

---

returned to royalist control, it had played no role in the noble Fronde. See Chéruel, *Minorité de Louis XIV* IV, 7-8, 53-54.

[30] B. N. Ms. Fr. 25025, fols. 182-183, 192r, 320v, brings out these unknown facts. The role of the noble Frondeurs both as individuals and a group during the Condéan rebellions is still unclear, and scholars have had to choose between the diametrically opposed and equally distorted opinions of Gondi and Mazarin.

overruling conciliar *arrêts* which backed the latter.[31] However, the conciliatory attitude of the Frondeur ministers de Maisons and Châteauneuf helped to keep friction in the capital to a minimum, and Orléans and Anne contained the few pathetic attempts by the Condéan party to rally the Parlement to their cause, the duke keeping the judges informed of the Condéans' connections with the Spaniards and other acts against the state. On the few occasions when Anne and Mazarin visited the capital, the regent stressed the need for parlementary loyalty against the noble rebels. When the dowager-princess of Condé appealed in person on behalf of her imprisoned sons in April, the Parlement was momentarily confused, but finally decided to respect the regent's request that she leave the capital. The Chambre des Comptes turned aside similar pleas for justice on behalf of the princes and their supporter, President Perrault of that tribunal. The Parlement also cooperated with Orléans and Châteauneuf in breaking up mass meetings by Condéan nobles who had flocked to the capital. The danger was probably not acute, but the parlementarians took no chances; they knew that the Condéans were circulating petitions for the release of the princes and were using that emotional issue to lobby for an Estates General. Over feeble protests by the *chambres des enquêtes*, the *grand chambre* unilaterally prohibited "all assemblies, treaties, leagues, and associations which may be prejudicial to the king's service and the tranquility of the state." With equal equanimity, the Parlement promptly registered a royal declaration which outlawed the chief Condéan rebels.[32]

The Parlement's otherwise relative complacency could not continue indefinitely, however. By mid-summer, the gravity of the civil strife and the growing disenchantment of the Frondeur party with Mazarin forced the parlementarians in the capital to take a closer look at their futile position. Instead of helping the cause of peace and order, they had condoned a militaristic Mazarinist policy which caused endless havoc to the countryside. Instead of restoring the rule of law, their relative silence had encouraged precisely those administrative practices which had supposedly been prohibited by the reform leg-

---

[31] B. N. Ms. Fr. 25025, fols. 175v, 209r; B. U. P. Ms. 66, fols. 76-77, 123-124, 127; Actes Royaux, F 23669, no. 13; Charmeil, *Les Trésoriers de France*, especially pp. 394-395.

[32] On these developments, see especially Talon, *Mémoires*, pp. 382-390.

islation of the parlementary Fronde. And instead of meting out revenge to Condé for his part in the siege of Paris, they had unwittingly helped to bring other parlements into the Condéan movement, hopelessly confusing the issue of the princes' freedom with the grievances of their sister tribunals in southern France.

As the Parlement of Paris began to waver, events conspired to make the Palace of Justice the center of national attention once more. At the end of June 1650, the appeal from the Parlement of Bordeaux reached Paris. The Parisian judges could not ignore the request, since it cut across partisan lines and touched on every major political problem of the day: the Condéan rebellion, the arbitrary actions of the governor of Guienne which were condoned by Mazarin, the reappearance of intendants, arbitrary taxation, and, finally, attempts to pass off military repression as law enforcement.

Early in July, the Parlement of Paris began to debate the appeal from Bordeaux. But the issues dividing provincials were not so simple for the judges in Paris. The divisions within their tribunal, kept in check during recent months, became sharper as the basic political issues were brought into focus, causing the singularly nonpartisan *avocat général*, Talon, to leap to the conclusion that voting in the Palace of Justice took place purely along party lines.[33] Though this was not completely so, he was right to a degree. A few Condéan judges, led by Deslandes-Payen, let their commitment to the princes blind them to all other considerations. Some Frondeur judges advanced proposals for parlementary mediation in the southern conflict, hoping to embarrass Mazarin without helping the rival party of Condéans. Mazarin, himself, was more active than ever trying to gain the support of Molé and other friends of Condé, and, although his bribery failed to influence most judges, it added to the confusion.[34] Most judges were torn between distaste for a rebellion which was ruining the countryside and aiding the Spaniards, and their hatred for a Mazarinist administration which was constantly undoing the work of the parlementary Fronde. The situation in the Parlement

---

[33] Ibid., p. 391.

[34] The maneuvering by Mazarinist, Frondeur, and Condéan factions, and Mazarin's attempts to build a party in the Parlement, are revealed in the chief minister's *Lettres*, especially III, 465-466, 631-639; J.-B. Colbert, *Lettres, instructions, et mémoires* I, 31.

was certainly complicated when the pro-Frondeur Broussel could spend as much time denouncing the actions of the intendant Foullé as in dealing with the issues dividing the nation's political factions, and when First President Molé could vacillate between personal sympathy for his friend Condé and almost Mazarinist opposition to any parlementary action in the prince's favor.

The complex relationships between Mazarin and Orléans, and between Orléans and Gondi, added more to the confusion. Mazarin still hoped for a military solution of the war in Guienne, while Orléans was working with Le Tellier to convince the chief minister that a diplomatic settlement should be attempted. The duke was unalterably opposed to any parlementary interference, fearing that this would only hamper his delicate negotiations with Mazarin. Gondi at first opposed parlementary action—but for different reasons. If the judges took any clear stand on the civil war, the Frondeur party would be hard-pressed to avoid siding with either Mazarin or the Condéans. When the Parlement decided to discuss the appeal from Bordeaux, Orléans tried to convince the judges that they should simply authorize him to continue his mediating efforts, while the Frondeur leaders echoed his words without conviction.[35]

Despite the unbelievable complexity of competing interests and desires which surrounded their debates in July and early August, the parlementary judges managed to keep sight of the needs of the moment. The majority realized that the most immediate and pressing issue was neither the freedom of the princes nor the rigid enforcement of the reforms of 1648, but rather, whether France would continue to suffer civil war. Internal strife was, of course, intimately connected with royal contraventions of the reforms, and particularly the arbitrary imprisonments of January 18; but so long as any fighting continued, no resolution of the problems, themselves, which had caused the civil war, was possible. Indeed, parlementary debates on the civil war brought out the widespread conviction that any strong move on behalf of state reform or justice for the princes would only prolong and intensify the conflict. Orléans made the point as eloquently and passionately as any one, saying that no one desired the princes' freedom more than he, but that their immediate release would encourage more provinces to unite with the Condéan

---

[35] The best account is Lorris, *La Fronde*, pp. 178-181.

rebels. President de Mesmes made the same point: that the Parlement had assembled to pacify the realm, and that intervention on the princes' behalf would defeat this purpose.[36]

The partisan supporters of Condé could not refute these arguments. When Condéan judges tried to raise the issue of the princes' freedom, Orléans stopped them by threatening to leave the debate if they persisted, and the Condéans could only water down their propositions to the point where they were innocuous. On one occasion they proposed remonstrances for the regent to consider the princes' plight when the "state of affairs" in the realm permitted. Later, they were still more diplomatic, asking Orléans to intercede informally with Anne after the Condéan rebels laid down their arms. Even with these qualifications, the Condéan propositions were defeated on both occasions by a comfortable margin.[37]

Equally important was the Parlement's rejection of demands by Broussel and other radicals for an investigation of all evasions of the reforms of 1648. It was a significant decision because there was apparently an extensive enough parlementary file and information on illegal royal actions—in addition to the Parlement of Bordeaux's charges against the intendant Foullé—to launch an investigation comparable to the Chambre Saint Louis' work in 1648 or the Parlement of Paris' short-lived debates prior to the siege of 1649. But the majority of the tribunal did not want to repeat its actions of 1648 or 1649—the noble Fronde created enough trouble without adding a new parlementary Fronde.[38]

The role the parlementarians tried to play in the civil war, itself, was as important as their decisions to avoid subsidiary issues. They were not convinced that Orléans could persuade the regent to work out a compromise with the chief rebels in Guienne, knowing that Orléans spoke only for himself when he guaranteed the dismissal of the governor of Guienne and an amnesty for all rebels save those who had engaged in treasonable relations with Spain. They were equally unimpressed with *Avocat Général* Talon's legal opinion that

[36] See Goulas, *Mémoires* III, 238; B. N. Ms. Fr. 25025, fol. 250r; Vallier, *Journal* II, 165-174; Chéruel, *Minorité de Louis XIV* IV, 109-112.

[37] B. U. P. Ms. 66, fols. 166, 260-261. The vote on July 7 was 115-67 or 110-71, according to the figures most favorable to the Condéans. Observers never agreed on any tally during the Fronde.

[38] See B. U. P. Ms. 66, fols. 177-178, 195-196.

the outstanding differences between rebels and regent were "public affairs" which the regent alone had the authority to resolve.[39] Half by luck and half by legalistic cunning, the Parlement accepted a resolution by Broussel. This ratified Orléans' terms, but added an extremely important provision: a parlementary delegation, as well as one from the duke, would urge Anne to accept Orléans' terms and also consider the other grievances of the Parlement of Bordeaux. The legalistic nature of this decision (July 7) was evident in its wording. The Parlement did not explicitly go beyond Orléans' terms, or even suggest that its delegation would act as a mediator independently of the duke's envoys to the regent. But the vague reference to the Bordelais judges' conditions left more latitude for negotiations than Orléans' rather precise terms; and the intrusion of parlementary deputies clearly provided mediators if the regent and Mazarin discovered that they could not negotiate directly with the rebels in Guienne. Thus the parlementarians placed their prestigious tribunal behind the movement for a settlement without encroaching on royal authority. This legalistic maneuver was as brilliant as the Parlement's actions during the parlementary Fronde and the siege of Paris. As in the past, it was also the result of some frantic shifting of positions by various parlementary groups. Some parlementary conservatives were opposed to any intervention by the Parlement, but knew they would be outvoted. They rallied to the mild form of intervention suggested by Broussel in order to defeat a much stronger resolution by the Condéans which implied support for the imprisoned princes.[40]

Broussel's proposal involved the Parlement in the task of ending a war which was more easily condemned than halted, since the internal divisions the parlementarians had been able to overcome were mild by comparison with the situation outside the Palace of Justice. War atrocities by Mazarinist troops stiffened resistance in the Parlement of Bordeaux, which had been on the verge of negotiating with Mazarin. The southern judges countered with their own atrocities

<hr />

[39] Talon, *Mémoires*, p. 391; Goulas, *Mémoires* III, 237; Motteville, *Mémoires*, p. 348.

[40] A complete analysis of the maneuvering would require a needlessly extended footnote. Broussel was befuddled when asked by the Condéans to clarify his proposal, and actually gave three different versions during the course of the debate. Even the noble Frondeurs were slightly bewildered. See B. U. P. Ms. 66, fols. 158-168; Dubuisson-Aubenay, *Journal* I, 288; Talon, *Mémoires*, p. 391; B. N. Ms. Fr. 25025, fol. 250.

against Mazarinist agents, added the banishment of the chief minister to their list of demands, and sent requests for support to the other
parlements of the kingdom.[41] Mazarin was intractable. He would
not consider amnesty for the noble allies of the Bordelais judges, a
condition which was essential if any settlement was to be reached.
Moreover, the cardinal bitterly resented the veiled offer of mediation
by the Parlement of Paris, and in his letters he criticized even the
scrupulously conservative *avocat général*, Talon.[42] As a result, the
southern war became more bitter in August, and a Condéan-Spanish
army under Turenne invaded France from the northeast.

The new offensive by Turenne was the most serious challenge to
the Parisian judges' plan for peace. Turenne, actually, was less interested in fighting against Mazarinist forces than in freeing the
imprisoned princes at Paris. However, his madcap scheme threatened
to unhinge the tenuous coalition of moderates in the capital. Some
observers, including Mazarin, believed that Turenne might be able
to join forces with his supporters in the Parlement of Paris and seize
the capital as well as the princes. The Frondeurs (supposedly allied
with Mazarin) had their own, independent plans. Taking advantage
of Turenne's threat, these nobles tried to persuade Orléans to remove
the princes from Vincennes to the Bastille. Since that fortress was
commanded by the son of their supporter, Broussel, this would place
the Condéan leaders in their hands. Who could tell at this juncture
what would happen to the Condéan rebellion if the ambitious Frondeurs held such power over the rival factions of Condéans and
Mazarinists?[43]

Somehow, the badly divided skeleton government under Orléans
and the very confused parlementarians in the Palace of Justice made
the right decisions. The duke sent Mazarin a new proposal of peace
which became the basis of the eventual settlement. The question of
the princes' freedom was to be set aside, but a comprehensive amnesty
would be offered to the southern rebels. The Parlement played its
part by refusing to commit itself to the specific demands of the Bordelais judges and by sending a polite but vague reply to a similar
appeal from the Parlement of Toulouse. Indeed, the Parisian judges
were becoming so disillusioned by the intransigence of the southern

---

[41] Lenet, *Mémoires*, p. 347; Martin, *Histoire de France* xii, 358.
[42] Mazarin, *Lettres* iii, 691, 699-700; Chéruel, *Minorité de Louis XIV* iv, 124-125.
[43] See Dethan, *Gaston d'Orléans*, pp. 379-381; Lorris, *La Fronde*, pp. 188-189.

tribunals that they were ready to withdraw their plenipotentiaries unless some concessions were made to the Mazarinist side.[44] The thorny problems created by Turenne's advance toward Paris were also resolved. The defense of the capital was organized by Orléans and representatives from the Parisian corporations. With the Parlement taking the lead, the sovereign courts provided the necessary funds by advancing their paulette fees for the following three years and taxing all *traitants* who were in Paris.[45] In a stormy council meeting, Orléans persuaded all factions of the skeleton government to agree on a residence for the princes which could offend no one. The prisoners were transferred to Marcousis, a site safe from attack by Turenne, and controlled by the Frondeur minister, Châteauneuf, but legally part of Orléans' princely domains.[46]

These decisions calmed Paris and paved the way for an end to the civil war. Turenne had no reason to besiege Paris after the princes' departure, and withdrew his Condéan-Spanish forces to the eastern provinces of the realm. The Frondeurs were mollified by the choice of the new prison for the Condéan leaders, and Turenne's near-seizure of Paris made them believe that they must vigorously support a settlement of the war; as long as it continued there was a possibility that Condéan elements might wrest Paris from their control. (Already, Condéan placards accused them of being outright Mazarinists and undermined their popularity in the capital.) Mazarin, too, was disturbed by the volatile situation in Paris, and wished to end the southern conflict, as well, so that he could concentrate his attention on the Spaniards and their French commander, Turenne.[47]

Once the chief minister decided to negotiate in good faith with the Bordelais rebels, he left nothing to chance. Mazarin sent Orléans' daughter to Paris with news of his change in tactics. The Parisian

---

[44] B. U. P. Ms. 66, fols. 226-230, 322-327; Vallier, *Journal* II, 165-174; Dubuisson-Aubenay, *Journal* I, 300-303.

[45] See Actes Royaux, F 23612, no. 27; B. N. Ms. Fr. 25025, fol. 286; Boislisle, *Chambre des Comptes*, pp. 441-442; Talon, *Mémoires*, p. 395.

[46] Aumale, *Histoire des princes de Condé* VI, pp. 35-38; Priolo, *Ministry of Cardinal Mazarine*, pp. 222-229; Chéruel, *Minorité de Louis XIV* IV, 138-142; B. N. Ms. Fr. 25025, fols. 290-291.

[47] This reconstruction is based mainly on Chéruel, *Minorité de Louis XIV* IV, 152-160. The Frondeurs' attitude is very difficult to document, and Mazarin's hostile interpretation of their attitude must be balanced with Gondi's much more favorable view. See Retz, *Oeuvres* III, 116-117.

delegation of parlementary judges and Orléans' personal representative also returned from the south with official word of the regent's willingness to seek a settlement. The Duke of Orléans, for once in accord with Mazarin, played his part by consulting with the most conservative parlementarians before the Parlement debated on the peace feelers.[48] When that tribunal finally discussed the matter, its members had only two reservations: they had to be convinced that their good offices would be accepted by the Parlement of Bordeaux, whose representatives in Paris seemed more interested in condemning royalist atrocities, and they wanted to be sure that their mediation would not be viewed by Anne as an usurpation of royal authority. On September 5, the Parlement decided to send a new deputation to the south with an offer to mediate if the regent gave official authorization and the Parlement of Bordeaux was willing to compromise.[49] When regent and Bordelais judges made the proper concessions, the Parisian delegation was able to negotiate a treaty. The peace was formally celebrated on October 1, 1650, and its terms were solemnly verified at the parlements of Paris, Bordeaux, and Toulouse.[50]

The settlement brought honor to the Parisian judges, general satisfaction for the southern courts, and some important concessions to the Condéan nobles.[51] However, Mazarin was furious with the Parisian judges for conceding too much.[52] It is true that the noble followers of Condé in southern France did escape without imprisonments or losses of property, but they had to endure banishment from Bordeaux and renounce their alliance with the Spaniards. Both anti-Condéan conditions went beyond what the Parlement of Paris and Orléans had originally authorized, and the duke was actually angry at his personal plenipotentiary for exceeding his instructions. Mazarin should have been pleased that the plenipotentiaries had not taken the southern judges' request for his own removal seriously, and that he was equally well served on the issue of the princes' detention. (Only one delegate from the Parlement of Paris had insisted on their freedom, and he was promptly silenced by his colleagues during the

[48] A.M.L. d'Orléans, Duchesse de Montpensier, *Mémoires*, Michaud and Poujoulat collection (ser. III, vol. IV), Paris, 1838, pp. 65-66; Talon, *Mémoires*, p. 394.
[49] B. U. P. Ms. 66, fols. 303-319; Talon, *Mémoires*, pp. 394-396.
[50] B. N. Ms. Fr. 25025, fol. 306r.
[51] For the terms of the treaty, see Bazin, *Histoire de France* IV, 146-147.
[52] Mazarin, *Lettres* III, 803; Chéruel, *Minorité de Louis XIV* IV, 161, 177-178.

negotiations.)[53] Finally, the Parisian mediators' requirement that a replacement be found for the Mazarinist Epernon as governor of Guienne was a realistic measure, which even Mazarin had approved prior to the settlement; peace with the southern tribunals could not have been secured on any other terms.

For all its weaknesses, the settlement of October 1650 gave France an opportunity to resolve the remaining problems which had caused, and then prolonged, the Fronde. Except for Turenne, who remained in eastern France with the Spanish forces, the treaty brought an end to fighting within the realm. It came too late to free royalist troops for a major offensive against Spain before the French and Spanish armies went into winter quarters, but it provided an opportunity for Mazarin to negotiate with Spain before new internal troubles turned the foreigners away from the conference table. It left the officers of the realm uncertain of the administration's attitude toward the reforms of 1648, but it halted the civil war which had been the major cause of official-royal clashes. Despite the chaotic condition of the monarchy's finances and administrative machinery in the provinces, there was a real chance that agreement with *les grands*, the parlements, and Spain might bring nonprivileged subjects back to their long-forgotten habit of paying taxes and respecting royal authority.

The greatest responsibility was Mazarin's, since he and Anne held the ultimate authority to pacify all the dissident elements. His most urgent task was to undo the harm caused by the imprisonment of Condé, Conti, Longueville, and President Perrault. To keep them in prison after their followers had laid down their arms would only look like vindictiveness and encourage new Condéan rebellions. It would also leave the Frondeurs an opportunity to dabble in new intrigues. They had gained nothing but ingratitude from Mazarin and growing hostility from Parisians for playing the role of reluctant Mazarinists during the Condéan revolt. A prolongation of the princes' detention would surely encourage them to ally with the Condéans against the chief minister.

There was one additional factor which dictated a reconciliation with the princes, and it was the most important one. The Parlement of Paris could not be expected to play the mediating role it had

[53] The negotiations can be followed in Lenet, *Mémoires*, pp. 388-403; Vallier, *Journal* II, 198-203.

played so well during the troubles of 1650 forever. Its internal divisions, which had been barely contained during the Condéan revolt, were liable to come to the open at any moment, and the arbitrary imprisonment of the princes was the most likely issue to bring on a new crisis. There was, of course, no way of predicting how the parlementarians might react to the prolongation of the princes' detention, since debates during the crucial months of July, August, and September had revealed how divided the outwardly calm tribunal was on the subject of reform and justice. Many judges were leaning toward order and peace at any price, while others were exceedingly unhappy with even a temporary shelving of the issue of the princes' freedom and the general problem of maintaining all the reforms of 1648. A few presidents declared that politically motivated imprisonments by the regent, without clear evidence of wrongdoing, were necessary, and they openly stated that if men like Turenne and Bouillon had been added to those already in jail, the Condéan revolt could not have taken place. Others argued that preventive detention was acceptable if exercised by men of "good will," but that so long as Mazarin remained in power, such a practice was unacceptable.[54] The polarization between advocates of order and supporters of reform was demonstrated once again when the intendant Foullé came to the Parlement of Paris to defend himself against charges by the Bordelais judges. He made a brilliant defense, and must have convinced many parlementarians that he was correct in using force to subdue subjects who rebelled even against impositions registered in the parlements. But he also horrified men like Broussel who knew that he lied when he said that he had used legitimate methods, acting through local officers and without extreme cruelty.[55]

If the Parlement raised such issues again—a distinct possibility while the princes remained in prison and the fate of the reforms of 1648 remained in doubt—the result could take one of three forms: the judges might shift sharply toward peace and order, out of desperation; they might become so divided that new civil turmoil would run its course without the parlementary intervention which had saved France so recently; or, most likely, the shift would be toward a more violent break with royal authority than France had witnessed

[54] B. U. P. Ms. 66, fols. 333-336.
[55] See ibid., fols. 174-177. The interrogation of Foullé continued, with interruptions, until January 1651.

during the parlementary Fronde of 1648 or the siege of Paris in 1649. That the Parlement of Paris would unite closely with the other sovereign courts was unlikely. The moderate cooperation of 1648 had been followed by fragile and limited unity during the siege of 1649, and then the refusal of the parlementarians in Paris to support fully either the Parlement of Bordeaux or Parlement of Toulouse in 1650. But differences in interests between geographically separated tribunals did not preclude the possibility that if the Parlement of Paris took the lead, instead of acting as a mediator, other parlements might be encouraged to begin new parlementary Frondes, each with its peculiar motives. The estrangement between the judges in Paris and *les grands*, which had begun during the siege of 1649 and increased after the assassination plots and arrest of the princes in the winter of 1649-1650, did not rule out the possibility that the Parlement of Paris might unwittingly encourage a new noble Fronde simply by opposing arbitrary imprisonment.

There was also the latent hostility to Mazarin, which had been kept alive by Mazarin's inept foreign policy, arbitrary acts against officials, and almost willful instigation of the Condéan rebellion. In July, a few parlementarians in Paris had returned to the opinion of 1648 and 1649 that the cardinal was the cause of all France's ills, and more had made the same charge in August, demanding his removal —along with requests for the princes' freedom. In September, still more had assailed the chief minister, in violent and provocative language, one judge calling him *charlatan, coquin, infâme.*[56] They had been shouted down, or ignored, only because their colleagues hoped that by restoring peace Mazarin could be brought to his senses. But a court of law composed of unhappy men of good will, a few supporters of the restless Condéan and Frondeur parties, and a first president who remained a close friend of Condé despite his leanings toward royalism, was at best a very uncertain element in a very unsettled country.

[56] See especially ibid., fols. 237-239; Dubuisson-Aubenay, *Journal* 1, 322.

CHAPTER NINE

THE ANTI-MAZARINIST
COALITION AND THE
FALL OF MAZARIN

CARDINAL MAZARIN did not capitalize on the opportunities presented by the Peace of Bordeaux. Instead, his inept handling of the delicate internal affairs of France occasioned a new wave of protests which led to his fall from power five months later, in February 1651. The Frondeur and Condéan factions of *les grands* formed a temporary alliance against the chief minister. Even the poorest nobles and the usually docile Catholic clergy began to protest against his leadership. New provincial movements by officers and taxpayers sapped the financial, administrative, and military strength of the Mazarinist regime. And, as so often before, the Parlement of Paris was confronted with all the current troubles. This time, however, it became the leader of the anti-Mazarinist forces rather than mediator between rebels and royalists. That shift, alone, made the current turmoil more dangerous than the Condéan revolts of 1650.

The chief minister's troubles during the winter of 1650-1651 were caused not by what he did, but, in the final analysis, what he did not attempt—to strike out boldly at the kingdom's unresolved problems. Most astonishing was the fact that he did not follow the tactic of dividing and ruling which he had tried so often in the past. Admittedly, that strategy would not have solved the underlying issues, but it would at least have prevented the potential and actual anti-Mazarinist elements from uniting against him.

One cannot help concluding that the cardinal lost his nerve. The politics of duplicity had given way to politics of indecision. While he willed another temporary alliance with either the Frondeurs or Condéans, he hesitated to employ the means to achieve it, fearing as he did any closer association with the intrigue-prone Frondeurs, or a new partnership with the Condéan faction which had just gained his respect by eluding military disaster despite the imprisonment of its leaders. Having convinced himself that any hasty realignment of parties would only place him at the mercy of his new ally, he played for time in the expectation that, sooner or later, both noble groups would lose their support among subjects, thus allowing him to destroy them.[1]

Mazarin's distrust of Gondi and the other Frondeur leaders bordered on hysteria. He was convinced not only that they still sought to oust him from power, but that they would stop at nothing to achieve that end. The unnerving example of the English monarchy's collapse in 1648 had frightened the cardinal into the impetuous siege of Paris in 1649. Since that time, he had never quite forgotten the English experience. Unfortunately, he linked republicanism across the English Channel with Frondeur intrigues in the French capital. A chance remark made by Gondi to Le Tellier during the Condéan rebellions of 1650 seems to have greatly influenced Mazarin's opinion about the Frondeurs. The archbishop-coadjutor had casually stated that cries of "*République*" had been heard in Paris during the siege of 1649, and added that it would have been easy to proclaim a republic at that time by merely removing a few monarchists. Though Gondi was not a republican, his remark was intended to strengthen his party's position within the monarchical structure.[2] Forced to choose between loyalty to an unpopular minister and an alliance with a rebellious, rival faction, he seems to have been letting Le Tellier know that his support against republicanism was sincere, but that it had to be bought. Le Tellier and another Mazarinist agent, Jean-Baptiste Colbert, placed a different interpretation on Gondi's curious remarks. They reported the conversation to Mazarin, adding the comment that Gondi was surely a republican.[3] After the civil war, Mazarin's suspicion of Gondi and the Frondeurs increased. His personal notebooks, letters, and conversation were crammed with allusions to Gondi's plans to "abolish the monarchy" and to play the role of a Cromwell. The cardinal even claimed that Gondi was the cause of all of France's troubles.[4]

His views of the Condéan threat were equally perverse. Arguing from the fact that the Condéan general, Turenne, was still fighting

[1] See especially Mazarin's analysis in his letters, in Chéruel, *Minorité de Louis XIV* IV, 225-228; and the excellent criticism of this indecisiveness by Martin, *Histoire de France* XII, 361-362.

[2] See the convincing arguments by Batiffol, *Biographie du Cardinal de Retz*, p. 79.

[3] See ibid., p. 78, including fn. 7; Knachel, *England and the Fronde*, pp. 42-43.

[4] Chéruel, *Minorité de Louis XIV* IV, especially pp. 178, fn. 1, 225, 232-233.

on the Spanish side, Mazarin concluded that it would be folly to strengthen the Condéans by freeing Condé.[5] There were two flaws in this seemingly logical argument. First, Turenne was by no means the puppet of Condé that Mazarin pictured. To persecute the prince because his free-lance supporter was an unrepentant rebel was a peculiar form of revenge. In the second place, Mazarin seemed to overlook the fact that the Condéan rebellions had been caused by his confinement of Condé. The most obvious way to reconcile the prince's followers to complete obedience was to remove their original grievance.

Mazarin was forced into a position of stalling for time. He encouraged each faction to believe that he was on its side, while refusing to make any firm commitment until one or both blundered and lost popular support. This fatal indecision had two effects: it led both Frondeurs and Condéans to believe that they could never count on any genuine rapprochement with the chief minister, and it encouraged them to seek security by subordinating their own rivalries to the need for cooperation against their mutual enemy and tormentor. Despite constant negotiations with Mazarin, the Frondeurs were rebuffed every time a renewal of the old Mazarinist-Frondeur alliance seemed in sight. Neither Orléans nor Mazarin's faithful agent, Servien, could convince the cardinal that he must shore up the tottering alliance if he wished to avoid his downfall.[6] His most critical mistake was in evading Gondi's request for nomination to the College of Cardinals. Also, afraid to commit himself to the Frondeurs, Mazarin kept prolonging the royal family's absence from the capital. This made the Frondeur leaders all the more suspicious of the chief minister's intentions, and caused unrest among bourgeois Parisians who disliked being deprived of lucrative sales to the royal entourage. The chief minister did not return with Anne to Paris until November, following Orléans' warning of an incipient tax revolt by merchants, and Le Tellier's desperate plea that Mazarin's presence alone could contain noble factionalism.[7]

Meanwhile, the chief minister squandered several opportunities to mend fences with the Condéans. They were eager to secure the release of the princes and, in their desperation, suggested that Condé might go into voluntary exile in return for his freedom. Mazarin

[5] Ibid. IV, 158-159, 184-186, 225.   [6] Ibid. IV, 209-212, 229-230.
[7] Ibid. IV, 169-171; Kossman, *La Fronde*, pp. 180-181.

remained suspicious, refusing to consummate an agreement. Indeed, he made any negotiation over the key issue of the princes' detention virtually impossible by persuading Orléans to send them from Marcoussis to Le Havre in Normandy. That was the fortress which Condé had tried to seize a year before; now it was a Mazarinist possession. Perhaps the cardinal thought that the transfer would place him in a better position to bargain. However, it signaled to the Condéans his deep-seated suspicion and lack of good will.[8]

So the frantic three-sided negotiations among Frondeurs, Condéans, and Mazarinists continued, poisoning relations between Mazarin and his rivals, and giving *les grands* full opportunity to explore mutual interests. While all three parties were negotiating with each other and the outcome still remained in doubt, Mazarin tried to strengthen his position with his internal enemies by a military attack on the Spaniards and Turenne in the Low Countries, and though it was too late in the year to mount a major offensive, the cardinal went to the eastern front in December and led the French armies to victory. The impact on the internal factions of his military success was precisely the opposite of what he had expected. The Condéans, probably remembering that the attempted seizure of parlementary opponents during the Days of Barricades in 1648 had come immediately after Condé's victory at Lens, were convinced that the chief minister would try to follow his external triumph with a *coup d'état* in the capital. So Condé's followers immediately withdrew their offer of Condé's banishment, and sought an alliance with the Frondeurs as insurance against a Mazarinist attack. A definitive Frondeur-Condéan agreement was not reached until some time in January 1651, but by the end of 1650 the two noble parties were cooperating closely. Their aims were clear: freedom for the princes, a cardinal's hat for Gondi, and the replacement of the Mazarinist ministry by an administration headed by the Frondeur Châteauneuf.[9]

The intensification of party factionalism and the Mazarinist defeat of Spanish forces under Turenne were accompanied by growing

[8] See Martin, *Histoire de France* XII, 362-363; Chéruel, *Minorité de Louis XIV* IV, 192-194, 220-224; and the letter from Condé's wife to the Parlement of Paris, ibid. IV, 202-203.

[9] Chéruel, *Minorité de Louis XIV* IV, especially 225-226, 251-253; Goulas, *Mémoires* III, 276, 290-292; Retz, *Oeuvres* III, 131-199, 219-227.

unrest throughout France. The victories over Spain in the east did not offset losses to the Spaniards in Catalonia and the Mediterranean. Subjects despaired of an international settlement, and they resented the new fiscal demands and billeting of soldiers necessitated by the continuation of the seemingly futile war. Whether or not they knew of the Spaniards' willingness to negotiate a settlement with France because of their own rebellions in Catalonia and elsewhere, they blamed Mazarin for not trying. Thus resistance to the administration's fiscal and military policies became all the more closely linked with hatred of the chief minister.[10]

Some of this unrest might have been tempered if key provinces had been placed under moderate governors who knew how to cooperate with local officers, rather than under those who constantly clashed over financial and administrative issues. As it was, the chief minister was bedeviled by these frictions and his own partisanship. Orléans could not keep Languedoc under control because of his presence in Paris, and his inability to supervise the new intendants, military commanders, and other Mazarinist agents in that province. In Guienne and Provence, dangerous power vacuums developed as a result of the agreement to remove Epernon and growing opposition to Alais. The chief minister hesitated to appoint a successor to Épernon until he could be certain of party alignments within the state. He might choose someone only to discover that the noble faction to which that individual belonged was his sworn enemy. Rumors persisted that Mazarin might even reinstate Epernon. The cardinal's position in Provence was equally complicated. In August, he had asked Alais to leave, but the count took advantage of the fact that he was not formally deprived of his governorship and lingered in his province. No one knew what would happen to the governorship. An air of uncertainty also hung over the provinces of Normandy, Champagne, and Burgundy. Condéan governors were in jail, but their Mazarinist successors were merely holding temporary commissions until the fate of Longueville, Conti, and Condé could be decided. Finally, the province of Brittany was in danger of becoming anti-Mazarinist, even though Anne, who was titular governor, had been too busy elsewhere to cause trouble in that distant area, and the act-

[10] Significantly, the Parlement of Bordeaux had refused to greet Mazarin when its members had thanked Anne for securing the peace treaty of October.

ing governor, Marshal La Meilleraye, was so preoccupied with financial affairs and then with military matters that he postponed a clash with the local parlementarians at Rennes. During the last two years of the Fronde, the presence of troops and his attempts to wring financial concessions from his province gradually undermined the good will which had been created by benevolent absentee rule.[11]

Led by provincial parlements, the officiers and inhabitants of several areas demanded sympathetic governors and a reduction of fiscal abuses. The Parlement of Grenoble clashed with a new intendant, Barthélemy Hervart, just as it had resisted his predecessor, Jacques Le Tillier, earlier in the year. Despite the recent royalist withdrawal of indirect taxes and assurances that regular judicial procedures would be respected, the Parlement of Bordeaux was unhappy with the delay in the announcement of a new governor. The Count of Alais' failure to leave Provence increased tensions in that province, and the Parlement of Aix began to agitate for a new governor favorable to its interests. Still more ominous was the general deterioration of royalist influence in Languedoc. Under the leadership of the Parlement of Toulouse, several sovereign courts throughout southern France became locked in a bitter dispute with the tax farmers of Anjou, Provence, and Languedoc. The administration's decision to have the royal councils handle all appeals against these *traitants* made a bad situation worse. And the return of intendant Morant to the south, after earlier clashes with the parlementarians at Toulouse, added to Mazarin's troubles. By the end of 1650 the Parlement of Toulouse was fighting the administration with every legal weapon in its arsenal—reversing conciliar decisions, issuing *arrêts* against the intendant, and appealing to the regent against her administration's approval of Morant's activities. Most disturbing of all was an attempt by three provincial parlements to take their grievances to the Parlement of Paris. The judges at Aix actually sent a delegation to the capital in an effort to secure their sister tribunal's support for a new governor. From Toulouse came a written appeal for "union" against all royal violations of the reforms of 1648, and the Bordelais judges seem to have been engaged in a clandestine effort to interest individ-

---

[11] There is no comprehensive study of the provincial governors. The foregoing analysis is drawn from scattered information in secondary accounts, notably Kossman, Chéruel, and Bazin; and B. N. Ms. Fr. 25025.

ual Parisian judges in their quest for a favorable replacement for Epernon.[12]

The appeals from these courts were all the more disturbing since other groups within the kingdom were also beginning to take their grievances to the prestigious court. In November 1650, a large group of nobles in Paris began to organize a movement on behalf of the imprisoned Condéan leaders. Their plan was to combine an appeal for justice at the Parlement of Paris with a demand that the regent convoke the Estates General. Some merchants and clerics were also interested in this program. Even the national assembly of the French clergy, which had been the most docile group in the realm since the beginning of the regency, showed signs of resistance. It was too much to expect that the clergy as a body could unite formally with the Parlement of Paris, which had a long tradition of encroaching on clerical immunity from the secular courts. Nevertheless, the General Assembly of the Clergy was now setting goals that could conceivably place it on the side of the Parlement of Paris. The clerical assembly was convoked to approve the *don gratuit*, or "free gift," and other subsidies which the First Estate voted periodically in lieu of regular taxation. Some clerics raised the issue of Conti's imprisonment, arguing that the clergy had a right to protest since Conti was the *abbé général* of the Order of Cluny and hence a member of their Estate. In October 1650, Mazarin and Anne curtly rejected the appeal when it was delivered by a clerical delegation to their temporary residence at Mantes. Offended by the administration's refusal to listen to these remonstrances, the General Assembly of the Clergy at Paris refused to renew the *don gratuit* in November and December, and persisted in its support for the imprisoned younger brother of Condé.[13]

Mazarin had reason to be fearful of the pressures for reform and justice which provincial courts and privileged estates were beginning to place before the Parlement of Paris. The Parisian tribunal was already so involved in both controversies that the appeals might easily touch off a combined parlementary and noble Fronde. During the

[12] See B. N. Ms. Fr. 25025, fols. 310v, 313r, 327, 348v, 354v; B. U. P. Ms. 67, fol. 24; Actes Royaux, F 23611, no. 1014; F 23631, no. 511; Charmeil, *Les Trésoriers de France*, pp. 387-388.

[13] B. N. Ms. Fr. 25025, fol. 327; Kossman, *La Fronde*, pp. 189-190; Blet, *Le Clergé de France et la monarchie* II, 61-64.

last months of 1650, the Parlement of Paris had begun once more to investigate evasions of the reforms of 1648, forcing the administration to abolish a special Parisian commission of maîtres des requêtes and councilors of state which was summarily judging persons who forged government letters. Commissions in the countryside were subjected to similar opposition. For example, the parlementarians sided with merchants on the Loire River against unregistered taxes and attempts to prosecute tax evaders without appeal to the regular courts.[14] It was easy for the judges to link these attacks on the reforms of 1648 with the prolonged detention of the princes, since that was the most glaring example of arbitrary administrative action. On several occasions during the last months of 1650, individual parlementarians demanded a full-scale debate of all administrative irregularities, citing illegal impositions on goods entering the city, forced payment of the *taille* in rural communities, soldiers' attacks on merchants, and secret arrangements between the treasury and *traitants*. Every time these issues were raised, the question of the princes' detention was brought into the discussion. Frequently, individual judges combined the issue of arbitrary detention with Mazarin's failure to end the Franco-Spanish war, suggesting that he was incapable of governing in the interests of subjects.

As time passed, however, it became evident to parlementarians, nobles, and Mazarin, himself, that the judges would concentrate their attention on the question of the princes' arbitrary imprisonment. To be sure, the Parlement dealt with other evasions of the reforms, but quietly and without resorting to a plenary session: when individual administrative malpractices were noted, specific *arrêts* were issued; parlementary committees were authorized to look into rumors of other contraventions, which succeeded in keeping radical judges busy; and, apparently, appeals from provincial parlements were not considered serious enough to merit any official support, although the Parisian judges may have acknowledged their letters.[15] Meanwhile, the Condéan nobles placed enormous pressure on the Parlement to intercede on behalf of their leaders. Appeal after appeal was sent by the relatives of Condé, Conti, and Longueville for justice.[16] Mazarin

---

[14] B. U. P. Ms. 66, fols. 345-348; B. N. Ms. Fr. 25025, fols. 307, 357-361; Actes Royaux, F 23669, nos. 70, 87.

[15] B. U. P. Ms. 66, fols. 348-349, 359-360, 392-396; Ms. 67, fols. 3-5, 12-13.

[16] Talon, *Mémoires*, p. 400; Motteville, *Mémoires*, p. 359.

was incapable of seeing that the parlementarians were sincerely interested in the princes' plight, but he was certainly aware that *les grands* were using that controversy to turn the judges against him, and viewed every incident in the Palace of Justice as a result of noble intrigues. He also had warnings from Servien, who told him that if the Condéan and Frondeur factions managed to unite with the Parlement of Paris on the question of the princes' detention, they could unseat Mazarin and even cause new uprisings by the "people" and the provincial parlements.[17]

2

ALTHOUGH the role of the Parlement of Paris was the key to the internal situation, Mazarin proved as incapable of controlling the Palace of Justice as he was inept in dealing with the latent opposition from *les grands*. Thinking that he could manipulate the court of law by controlling a few judges, he concentrated on the offices of *procureur général* and first president. He succeeded in naming Nicolas Fouquet as successor to the retiring royal attorney, Blaise Meliand, only to discover that the change did not help his cause. Both men were devoted servants, but Fouquet had to overcome inexperience and strong animosities before he could function effectively. In 1652, Fouquet was to serve his master well; but during the winter of 1650-1651 he was a liability. He was disliked by the noble Frondeurs who had wanted one of their supporters installed in the office of *procureur général*. Fellow judges disapproved of his former activities as a special commissioner of the administration, and Orléans was unhappy with his appointment. Poor Fouquet did not even know how to handle the intricate legal problems his office thrust upon him. During the first months he constantly went to the keeper of the seals, Châteauneuf, for advice on legalities. This was particularly damaging to Mazarin's cause, since the complicated problem of the princes' appeals for justice demanded quick and decisive intervention by the *procureur général* before anti-Mazarinist judges could work out their own strategy.[18]

Mazarin's overtures to First President Molé caused an even worse situation. The chief minister had been trying for months to bribe Molé, or at least weaken his friendship with Condé, by offering to

[17] Chéruel, *Minorité de Louis XIV* IV, 209-212, 235.
[18] See especially B. N. Ms. Fr. 25025, fols. 310v, 314r, 327v, 329.

appoint Molé's son secretary of state. But he needlessly antagonized the first president by delaying the appointment because he was uncertain of the family's commitment to himself.[19] Molé was too much of a monarchist to break completely with the administration, and too much of an opportunist to turn against Mazarin while the chief minister's fate was still in the balance. Nevertheless, Mazarin's evasion led the first president to intensify his commitment to secure the release of the princes, and he went so far as to flirt with the Condéan-Frondeur coalition. He probably thought that by allying himself with *les grands* he could limit their aims and moderate their methods, at the same time seeing in the coalition a means to secure the release of the princes. But he gave no indication of supporting their plan to oust Mazarin—although he later opposed the cardinal's restoration—and he strongly objected to their tendency toward violence, and feared that they would either assassinate Mazarin or incite a Parisian uprising. Allying himself with such unpredictable persons was a dangerous move, but with his influence in the Parlement and his role as a tacit member of the nobles' coalition, there was hope that his friend Condé could be freed and order restored to France, without an upheaval in the administration.[20]

Unable to count on Molé or to use Fouquet's position effectively, Mazarin grew more and more desperate as he saw his enemies uniting against his policies. When the Parlement began to review the appeals for justice from the princes' relatives in December 1650, the chief minister conceived of two countermoves. The first scheme was to draft a royal declaration reinterpreting the reform clause of 1648 regarding personal freedom, stating that crimes against the state were not immune to executive punishment, and that the regent had not intended to imply such a concession in the declaration of October 22, 1648. The projected declaration was rejected, however, since it was obvious that the Parlement would ignore it. Mazarin also suggested to his fellow ministers that the regent present the same clarification of the article on arbitrary imprisonment to a grand assembly of all Parisian authorities, including the civic government and the major guilds. However, it was again pointed out to Mazarin that, because the noble factions were so influential in Paris, the appeal

[19] Ibid., fol. 354v.
[20] See G. Joly, *Mémoires*, p. 40; Mazarin, *Lettres* iii, 924; Retz, *Oeuvres* iii, 131-199.

would fall on deaf ears.[21] As a last resort, the chief minister had the regent notify the Parlement that she wanted to review the case herself, but was prevented by illness. She asked the judges to suspend their investigation until she recovered. The regent *had* been ill in recent months, but the parlementarians knew that she was well enough to act if she so desired. They gave her four days to recover, and when the period of grace expired, resumed their debate.[22]

The parlementary debate was as stormy and confused as any deliberation in the Palace of Justice during the Fronde. Most judges tried to be moderate, but they were strongly sympathetic toward the princes, and some were openly hostile to Mazarin. A few members denounced the chief minister for disregarding the Declaration of October 1648, insisting that royal authority was subordinate to the laws of the land, and particularly that piece of legislation, and concluded that the Parlement should implement the declaration's clause on arbitrary punishment by freeing the princes, without even asking the regent's permission. There were also those who suggested that the regent be asked to dismiss her chief minister for his flagrant violation of French laws and his mishandling of internal and foreign affairs. Others wished to evade the issue of Mazarin's right to govern and merely remonstrate for the princes' release. Some judges were so committed to Mazarin, through bribery or fear of a new civil war, that they opposed all forms of protest. It was Molé, assisted by President Le Coigneux, who led his colleagues to a compromise. Both judges courted the favor of their most radical colleagues in eloquent speeches attacking Mazarin's disregard for law, and obliquely suggesting that he was the cause of the unending strife which had plagued France in recent years. But then, moderating their tone, they argued merely for remonstrances on behalf of the princes. By the time they had concluded, even the leading Condéan judge, Deslandes-Payen, was resigned to the legalistic tactic of issuing a remonstrance to the regent, knowing that the regent would have difficulty avoiding the wishes of the most prestigious corporation in the realm.[23]

The carefully constructed legalism implicit in this parlementary

[21] B. N. Ms. Fr. 25025, fol. 329r; Chéruel, *Minorité de Louis XIV* IV, 228-229.
[22] Talon, *Mémoires*, pp. 401-403; Motteville, *Mémoires*, p. 361.
[23] B. U. P. Ms. 66, fols. 390-469; B. N. Ms. Fr. 25025, fols. 343-344.

decision of December 30, 1650, strongly resembled the Parlement's negotiation of the treaties of Rueil, in 1649, and Bordeaux, in 1650. However, the parlementarians' intervention at the end of 1650 helped to deepen the crisis instead of easing tensions. Beneath the correct, absolutist language of the parlementary *arrêt* lay the irreducible fact that the judges had thrown their moral support behind a major point of the Frondeur-Condéan coalition's demands. In 1649, the parlementarians had spurned their noble allies' quest for pensions and offices. In 1650, they had supported amnesty for *les grands*, but tempered this with their acquiescence in the banishment of the Condéan generals from Bordeaux. Now they asked the regent to free the Condéan leaders, while ignoring the military activities of the Condéan general, Turenne. The irony was that if Mazarin had previously granted on his own what the parlementarians now asked him to do, peace and order might have been achieved. But by taking the initiative, which the chief minister refused to assume, the judges placed their corporation in a partisan position. Their partisanship was not explicit, but it encouraged the anti-Mazarinist parties to hold out for further concessions and, more tragically, stiffened Anne's and Mazarin's resistance to any concession.

Parlementary legalism simply could not withstand the partisan pressures of succeeding weeks. The regent made a mockery of the judges' plea for benevolent absolutism, first by delaying an answer to the remonstrances on the flimsy excuse of illness, and then by giving a reply that amounted to an incisive criticism of the judges' own position. She promised to free the princes *if* their supporters laid down their arms and broke with Spain; and she reminded the parlementarians of their duty to keep subjects obedient to the Crown, particularly at a time when Spanish troops remained at France's borders, ready to strike if internal turmoil persisted. Molé tried to answer Anne by saying that misgovernment was the real cause of internal and external problems, and he warned her that the provincial parlements were ready to unite with his own tribunal on behalf of the princes. His reply left the regent unmoved.[24]

Anne's intransigence unwittingly forced the parlementarians to take an openly partisan position in favor of the Condéan-Frondeur coalition. Orléans' sudden rupture with the royal administration, at

[24] B. N. Ms. Fr. 25025, fol. 357; B. U. P. Ms. 67, fols. 37-39; Vallier, *Journal* II, 265-267.

the beginning of February 1651, made the judges' partisanship more extreme than it would otherwise have been. The duke had wavered for months between loyalty to Mazarin and sympathy for the princes, but in January 1651, he became convinced that Mazarin's policies were making a reconciliation of political factions impossible, and endangered the monarchy itself. So, on January 30, Orléans signed a treaty with the Frondeur-Condéan coalition, committing himself to the princes' freedom and the establishment of an anti-Mazarinist administration.[25] Two days later, he had a violent argument with Mazarin. The chief minister declared that his enemies were acting like Cromwell, Fairfax, and the English Parliament, clearly implying that French troublemakers sought to unseat him, and ultimately, to remove Orléans and Louis XIV, himself, from power. Such a vivid comparison of English regicides and Mazarin's political foes enraged Orléans; he abruptly ended the conference, calling Mazarin a "madman," and vowing never to return to the *conseil d'état* until the chief minister was removed from Anne's administration. This dramatic break between prince and minister was precisely what the Condéan and Frondeur factions needed to achieve a total victory over Mazarin. Gondi went in triumph to the Parlement and gave a detailed account—which, by his own admission, was embellished to inflame the parlementarians.[26] Orléans, himself, sought out several judges and talked with each for fifteen minutes. By the end of these interviews, it was clear that the duke was firmly committed to the unconditional release of the princes and the banishment of Mazarin from the kingdom.[27]

The news of Orléans' clash with Mazarin drove the Parlement into an almost irrational verbal attack on the chief minister. The very fact that the king's uncle had joined the anti-Mazarinists was enough to throw the judges into the arms of the Frondeur-Condéan leaders, but Mazarin's inference that the Parlement was anti-monarchist was far more inflammatory. If there was one charge that the legalistically minded judges would not tolerate it was the suggestion that they were republicans. The majority of the Parlement had the sense to vote down suggestions that Mazarin be tried and

[25] See Dethan, *Gaston d'Orléans*, pp. 385ff.

[26] Accounts vary. See Orléans' reconstruction, B. U. P. Ms. 67, fols. 69-71; and Knachel, *England and the Fronde*, pp. 83-84.

[27] B. N. Ms. Fr. 25025, fol. 265r.

the princes freed by the Parlement on its own authority. But by a two-thirds majority, the court decided to remonstrate to the regent for the banishment of the chief minister from the realm, the release of the princes, and to make a declaration absolving them of all guilt for their allegedly treasonous activities in 1649.[28]

The Parlement's decision of February 3-4, 1651, ultimately created confusion within the regent's administration and utter chaos within the realm. Its immediate results, however, were far less alarming. The parlementarians could congratulate themselves on their ability to achieve by legal means what the grand coalition of *les grands* had been unable to realize. Anne did not dare to resist the demands of her most august body of legists, knowing that the legalism of the judges had given all the anti-Mazarinist forces of the realm a sanction which even the personal will of a monarch or his regent could not overcome. So after hesitating briefly, Anne and Mazarin agreed that the cardinal should leave Paris, and, on the night of February 6, he left the city and took up residence—temporarily—at Saint-Germain.

The grand coalition of Parlement, Orléans, Condéans, and Frondeurs still had some unfinished business. The princes were not yet freed, and Mazarin's presence outside the city's gates made his opponents fear that he might try to return to power. Their fears were well founded; Mazarin had carefully drawn up plans to outwit his persecutors. The wily chief minister had instructed the regent to stay in Paris if Orléans and the Parlement became conciliatory to her authority. If there was no chance for her to revive her authority—and recall Mazarin—then the royal family should slip out of Paris within a few days, and join him outside the city. The seemingly unperturbed ex-minister believed that this would place both the regent and himself out of danger. First President Molé would, because of his hatred of the Frondeurs, oppose their faction, and if they tried to instigate disorders in the capital, he could use his control over the Parlement to stifle the *émeute*. Mazarin also hoped to split the Condéan-Frondeur coalition by dangling the prospect of the princes' freedom before the Condéans, and playing on Orléans' fear of an anti-Orléanist alliance of Mazarinists and Condéans. The cardinal even thought that the royal family and he could establish a

---

[28] B. U. P. Ms. 67, fols. 49-95.

secure base of operations in Normandy, counting on the Parlement of Rouen to support his cause.[29]

The plan probably could not have succeeded even if Anne had escaped. Molé was in control of neither the Parlement nor Paris, although he was in close touch with both Anne and Mazarin, and was trying to find a just settlement which would restore Mazarin and at the same time free the princes. Orléans was certainly emotionally incapable of patching up his quarrel with Anne and Mazarin, and neither the imprisoned Condé nor his followers in Paris were ready at this time to forgive Mazarin for his prolonged persecutions.[30] Besides, Anne could not escape. Just before Mazarin's flight, Orléans had ordered the Hôtel de Ville, military commanders, and all other authorities in Paris to obey him instead of the regent, and the Parlement of Paris, after some hesitation, had voted orally to acknowledge this temporary dictatorship. Because of rumors on the night of February 9-10 that Anne was going to leave the capital, the duke ordered the civic militia to guard the Palais Royal while Parisians milled around and shouted *"aux armes."* The next day the Parlement legalized this action, and the Hôtel de Ville and Anne herself consented to Orléans' questionable use of public authority. The civic guards were placed at the gates of Paris, and remained there until March 30.[31]

Anne was a captive in her own palace, unable to resist further demands from the parlementarians. On February 7, the judges thanked her for removing Mazarin from power, though Orléans' impassioned plea led them to insist, at the same time, on the unconditional freedom and pardoning of the princes. They also requested a royal declaration excluding from the royal councils all foreigners, including naturalized Frenchmen, and those with oaths of allegiance to foreign princes. Since "foreign princes" referred to the Pope as well as to secular rulers, it was clear that the judges meant to purge the central administration of all cardinals, archbishops, bishops, and other holders of ecclesiastical offices under papal suzerainty, as well

---

[29] Chéruel, *Minorité de Louis XIV* iv, 263-265.

[30] See B. N. Ms. Fr. 25025, fol. 371; Motteville, *Mémoires*, p. 373; and the letter by the Count of Maure to the Condéan agent Lenet, Feb. 5, 1651, in Aumale, *Histoire des princes de Condé* vi, 478-479.

[31] *Registres de l'Hôtel de Ville* ii, 169-183; B. U. P. Ms. 67, fols. 108-112, 134; B. N. Ms. Fr. 25025, fols. 368-369; Martin, *Histoire de France* xii, 367-369.

as persons who were foreigners in the stricter sense. But it was just as clear that the projected anticlerical and antiforeign declaration was primarily designed to make permanent the recent flight of Mazarin—a naturalized Frenchman, and a cardinal with an oath to the Pope. Indeed, in their determination to prevent his return, the parlementarians demanded that Anne banish the ex-chief minister from the entire realm as well as from her councils. When she replied in general terms that she would comply with the judges' wishes, they added an *arrêt*, on February 9, that if Mazarin did not leave France in two weeks he could be attacked by subjects, and criminal proceedings would begin in the Parlement.[32] The regent finally gave orders for the princes' release on February 10, after her aborted attempt to flee. Mazarin decided to go to Le Havre and negotiate their release on his own authority, thinking that he could save himself by an eleventh-hour agreement. However, this failed. Condé could not be influenced, and the princes and President Perrault were freed, returning in triumph to Paris on February 16. On February 28, a royal declaration of their innocence was registered by the Parlement of Paris,[33] and early in April, after slowly crossing France, the cardinal took up exile in the archbishopric of Cologne.

3

THE CRUSHING defeat of the Mazarinist faction, in February 1650, proved to be a disaster for all French subjects. As popular as the princes' release and Mazarin's exile were in the short run, these events merely added to France's internal turmoil. Parlementarians were as much to blame as their political allies or Mazarin himself. The Parisian judges may have congratulated themselves on their ability to force fundamental changes on the regent by legalistic, nonviolent means, but, clearly, their *via media*, which had so often curbed the political extremes of the Fronde, was fast becoming a purely destructive force. The weaknesses of parlementary legalism were brought into focus by the Parlement's efforts to make the ex-chief minister's banishment permanent by means of the projected anticlerical declaration which the judges sought to impose on the regent. That declaration became the center of a divisive political controversy, as the Parlement of Paris stood for it, the clergy and nobil-

[32] Talon, *Mémoires*, pp. 412-413; Motteville, *Mémoires*, pp. 376-377.
[33] It is in Vallier, *Journal* II, 297-298.

ity opposed it, and Frondeur-Condéan cooperation broke down over its implementation. Thus the loose, grand alliance of anti-Mazarinist groups was shattered, leaving a political vacuum more disturbing than either Mazarinist "tyranny" or anti-Mazarinist dictatorship.

As soon as the Parlement asked Anne to draft a law excluding clerics from high state offices, the clergy objected violently. The General Assembly of the Clergy ignored the fact that the Parlement had obtained the clergy's own goal of releasing the prince-cleric Conti, and, instead of thanking the judges, they accused them of maligning the First Estate. The clergy quickly united with the lesser nobility, who had flocked to Paris on behalf of the princes and were now holding a special assembly of their own. It mattered not that most basic interests of the nobles differed sharply from the concerns of the high ecclesiastical dignitaries, the nobles, for example, being much more critical of the foreign war which was killing their youth. On one crucial issue the Second Estate could agree with the First: both hated the judicial officials who tried to encroach on clerical immunity from secular courts, opposed the entry of clerics to the royal councils, and kept impoverished noblemen from venal offices. The clergy bypassed the nobles' separate grievances and concentrated on the Second Estate's broader request for an Estates General. Whether the clerics knew of noble plans to create a royal council representing all social orders or not, they could certainly use the national meeting to advance their own claims to high offices. On March 15, the General Assembly of the Clergy voted to unite with the noble assembly in calling for the convocation of the Estates General. The Parlement replied with vicious attacks on the two assemblies and thinly veiled opposition to the Estates General. The parlementarians had no intention of permitting a national assembly which would be dominated by the first two estates. Such a body could only undermine established authorities, including the monarchy and the judges of the Third Estate.[34]

The Frondeur and Condéan leaders were placed in an awkward position by the feud between the Parlement and the clerical-noble front. Gondi and Châteauneuf coveted the title of cardinal, and hence supported the noble and clerical opposition to the Parlement

[34] See especially Blet, *Le Clergé de France et la monarchie* II, 66-81; Talon, *Mémoires*, pp. 415-432; and the highly informative *Journal de l'Assemblée de la Noblesse tenue à Paris en l'année mil six cens cinquante-un*, Paris, 1651.

over the anticlerical declaration. But they also dared not openly antagonize the Parlement which they had finally brought under their influence after months of intrigue. Condé had to balance his support of the noble assembly with his thinly veiled opposition to Gondi's ambitions. Orléans was hopelessly bewildered by his desire to accommodate his parlementary allies, Frondeur friends, and fellow nobles. All these men were interested in the Estates General, which was opposed by the Parlement![35]

To all appearances, the coalition which had toppled Mazarin continued to operate during the furor over the anticlerical royal declaration and projected Estates General: Orléans and Châteauneuf acted on behalf of *les grands* in the *conseil d'état* after plotting strategy with Condé, Gondi, and Beaufort. But Anne was able to form an inner council of Mazarin's trusted servants, Le Tellier, Lionne, and Servien, and, together, by encouraging the feud between the parlementarians and their clerical-noble adversaries, they worked to undermine the unity of Parlement, Condéans, and Frondeurs. Orléans, Gondi, and Condé simply could not smooth over that controversy, even though they tried to mediate by taking part in parlementary debates and conferring with the noble and clerical assemblies.[36]

When the coalition was on the point of falling apart, the regent intervened in a manner which reflected Mazarin's tactics more than her own brand of politics. Knowing that she had gained all that she could from the dispute between the judges and their adversaries, Anne worked quickly to prevent the controversy from destroying her own authority. The assembly of nobles had to be dissolved before it could force an Estates General on the monarchy. On March 24, the regent made the hollow concession that an Estates General would be called one day after the king's assumption of his full regal powers, on September 8, 1651. The nobles could no longer argue that they had a reason for continuing their sessions, even though it was obvious that as soon as Louis XIV came of age he would use his regal powers to prohibit that national assembly. Confronted by Anne's

---

[35] Chéruel, *Minorité de Louis XIV* IV, 294-303, has an excellent account but his unflattering portraits should be compared with the detached views of Martin, *Histoire de France* XII, 371-373; Dethan, *Gaston d'Orléans*, pp. 392-394; and Lorris *La Fronde*, pp. 216-219.

[36] See Chéruel, *Minorité de Louis XIV* IV, 293, 296, 302.

"offer," parlementary insistence that they halt their meetings, and a similar request from the mediating Orléans, the assembled nobles dissolved their gathering.[37]

The regent had less opportunity to maneuver over the issue of the anticlerical declaration, but she succeeded in placating the Parlement without antagonizing the clergy. The General Assembly of the Clergy knew that a royal declaration was inevitable, given the current anti-Mazarinist climate of opinion in the realm, and they were flattered by Anne's effort to exclude cardinals from the ban. They could only side with the regent, hoping against hope that some day she might be able to rescind the offensive ban on cardinal-ministers, forced on her by the Parlement. To underline their loyalty, the clergy dissolved their assembly after voting a modest financial gift. To make their royalism unmistakably clear, the clerics' spokesman told the king: "Sire, your minority, very wisely conducted until now by the admirable care of the queen, although unable to avoid the occurrence of some agitations within the state, has seen our body [remain] steadfast in the fidelity which we have sworn to it."[38]

The parlementarians were, of course, much happier than the clergy with the outcome of the controversy. On April 19, they registered a royal declaration which met most of their demands. All foreigners, including naturalized Frenchmen, were to be excluded in future from the royal councils. On the insistence of the Parlement, French and foreign cardinals were included in the ban. The regent gained only one concession, more important for the future than the present. The declaration was drafted to look like a concession extorted by the Parlement rather than a grace freely given by the regent. When the king came of age in September, there was a possibility that he could overrule the anticlerical declaration and recall Mazarin.[39]

The furor over the Estates General and anticlerical declaration was the first major blow to the anti-Mazarinist forces, since it made future cooperation between the Parlement of Paris and the First and Second Estates virtually impossible. However, the Parlement was less disturbed by that breach with traditional rivals than by the feuds which erupted among the great nobles and princes over the same issues. After all, the Parlement had managed to determine who

---

[37] See Doolin, *The Fronde*, pp. 45-46.
[38] Blet, *Le Clergé de France et la monarchie* ii, 81.
[39] The declaration is in B. U. P. Ms. 67, fol. 300.

would be excluded from the royal councils, and without formally usurping the regent's right to choose her ministers. The quarrels of *les grands* over the question of who would actually fill Mazarin's vacant position could not be smoothed over by such legalistic measures as a royal declaration officially granted by the regent. The judges did not intend to play a formal role in that fight over the spoils of victory, and their self-styled position as preservers of royal absolutism would not permit them to name ministers, even if they had been inclined to take such a fateful step. So they clung to the legalistic position which had saved them so often in the past but now prevented them from making the reorganization of the post-Mazarinist administration an orderly process.

The ban on cleric-ministers brought into the open the ambitions of Gondi and Châteauneuf, as well as Condé's concealed opposition to both men and Orléans' inability to play his self-proclaimed role of mediator. The royal declaration was as much of a blow to the two Frondeurs as it had been to Mazarin. The archbishop-coadjutor and the *garde des sceaux* could still hope to become cardinals, but they could not use that clerical office as a steppingstone toward the position of chief minister in France. Châteauneuf had been so opposed to the declaration that he had refused to attach the royal seals to it. Now his only hope was to ingratiate himself with Anne, convince her that Mazarin should never be recalled, and gradually show himself capable of assuming the cardinal's role as her chief adviser. Indeed, that is precisely what he had been attempting to do since Mazarin's precipitous flight from Paris in February. Gondi did not have Châteauneuf's advantage of being a member of the administration, and he had to take a different position. He sought to block the anticlerical declaration by lying about his influence over the Parlement, unabashedly telling Anne that she did not have to give in to the judges, and that if he were made a cardinal, he could ruin the Parlement's power within six months.[40] Neither of these ambitious men succeeded in their ambitions, for Anne was quick to take advantage of Condé's jealousy and Orléans' inept neutrality. In April 1651, she suddenly reorganized the post-Mazarinist administration. The changes were a crushing blow to the Frondeurs and an insult to Orléans who was not consulted. The new men were either friends of Condé or enemies of the Frondeurs. The anti-Frondeur Molé was

[40] See B. N. Ms. Fr. 25025, fol. 370v; Chéruel, *Minorité de Louis XIV* iv, 302, for the roles of Châteauneuf and Gondi.

made keeper of the seals in place of Châteauneuf. The devoted servant of Mazarin, Chancellor Séguier, was allowed to resume his old position. Condé's friend Chavigny was appointed minister and given a seat in the council of state.

Orléans' attempt to revive the moribund Frondeur-Condéan coalition only succeeded in making the breach irreparable. At a secret conference called by the duke, Condé rejected the Frondeurs' demands for a more equitable distribution of administrative positions; the only change he would tolerate was the removal of Molé, and that was due to Orléans' personal hostility toward the first president. Condé treated the Frondeurs with disdain, especially their fantastic suggestion that *les grands* incite an uprising in Paris against the regent. So the Frondeurs left the meeting feeling betrayed by Condé. Orléans was placed in the awkward position of owing more to Condé than to the Frondeurs, and began to drift toward friendship with his fellow prince.[41] And Condé's stand against the Frondeurs made his support all the more desirable to the regent. Anne retained Séguier and Chavigny, while dismissing Molé and giving Condé some of the positions he desired. Condé relinquished the governorship of Burgundy for a similar position in the wealthy province of Guienne and control over a few places within his old Burgundian province and elsewhere. It has been estimated that the *Grand* Condé now controlled one-fourth of France as a result of his new possessions, the retention of old ones, and the scattered governorships of his relatives and friends.[42]

Unfortunately, Anne's concessions to the prince were both too little and too great. She had not given him everything he had desired, notably the governorship of Provence for his brother Conti. The exiled Mazarin, on the other hand, in his letters to the regent, accused Servien and Lionne of giving the prince too much. Anne, in obvious confusion, immediately began to intrigue with the Frondeurs against Condé! The plot looked almost like a carbon copy of the Mazarinist-Frondeur conspiracy which had placed Condé in jail the previous year, but this time the objectives were more unrealistic. There were suggestions that Condé be assassinated; and there was a tacit agreement that, whatever the means might be, the objective was to end Condé's political career, bring the Frondeurs into the administra-

[41] See, inter alia, Chéruel, *Minorité de Louis XIV* IV, 311-322.
[42] See the list of Condéan possessions in Cosnac, *Souvenirs du règne de Louis XIV* I, 277-292.

tion, and recall Mazarin. However, probably none of the conspirators actually expected any of these events to take place before Louis XIV came of age in September. There were also lingering suspicions between Mazarinists and Frondeurs that each side was not sincere in its promises. But public knowledge of the plotting placed the prince on his guard. In July 1651, Condé fled from Paris, not knowing what he would do, but convinced that if he escaped to his provincial strongholds he would at least avoid an assassin's dagger.[43]

4

THIS LATEST, open breach between Anne and Condé, in July 1651, shattered some illusions the judges in the Parlement of Paris had clung to during the previous six months. No longer could the parlementarians go on believing that the mere exiling of Mazarin and the release from prison of the princes would solve France's internal problems. Instead, they were faced with the growing likelihood that the quarrel within the royal family resulting from both actions would degenerate into a new civil war. Between July and September, the parlementary judges tried desperately to fend off such an unwelcome turn of events, but they failed to achieve their basic aim of peace. Though some of their countermoves were successful, they were victimized by the same dilemmas which were to plague the Parlement when a second Condéan rebellion ushered in the final phase of the Fronde during the fall of 1651. Throughout the summer of that year, the parlementarians were caught between two equally undesirable forces. They could not support Condé's side of the new princely controversy without encouraging rebellion. They could not support Anne without running the risk that if she prevailed over Condé, her next move would be to recall Mazarin. Meanwhile, both the regent and the prince placed relentless pressure on the Palace of Justice to back their respective causes, for, despite the Parlement's inability to control recent events, its prestige was still great. Anne and Condé were well aware that parlementary support for one of them might be enough to tip the delicate balance of power within the state.

Condé's appeals to the Parlement played on its fear of Mazarin's restoration and the judges' unhappiness with the continuation of the

---

[43] On these intrigues, see Chéruel, *Minorité de Louis XIV* IV, especially 338, 340, 353-361.

cardinal's influence, despite his exile. It was common knowledge that the ex-minister was exchanging messages with Anne by letter and personal agents. Even though changing conditions within France frequently compelled the regent to employ strategy that violated Mazarin's instructions, she shared his aims: to defeat Spain, crush the noble factions, and chip away at the foundations of the reforms of 1648. Despite the relatively moderate composition of the formal council of state, Anne tried to continue those policies with the assistance of her inner council of three Mazarinist agents, Secretary of State Le Tellier, the minister Servien, and the regent's *secrétaire des commandements*, Lionne. Orléans was a frustrated father-figure in the formal council, unable to decide whether to throw his full support to Condé or hope that Anne might free herself from the ex-minister's lingering influences. He tried to mediate between regent and prince, but without success. Séguier seems to have plunged into the details of judicial work as an escape from the real problems of the administration. President de Maisons was a forlorn figure as *surintendant des finances*, disliked by the Mazarinists because of his cooperation with the Parlement on fiscal matters and too weak to speak out against Mazarin's policies.[44] Whenever Condé sent warnings to the Parlement of Mazarin's imminent return, divulged news of his communications with Anne, or called for the dismissal of the remaining Mazarinist administrators, he struck a responsive chord in the Parlement. And when he declared that he could not feel safe from a personal attack on his person, as long as any Mazarinist influences remained within the administration, he half-convinced the parlementarians that his opposition to the regent was justified. His appeals were frequent, and they were delivered in the most attractive way. He sent one letter after another to the Parlement, then had his brother Conti appear on his behalf, and finally made daring visits to Paris, during which he attacked Mazarinists and Frondeurs from the floor of the high court while studiously avoiding the regent, except for brief, formal encounters.

Anne countered Condé's appeals with her own propaganda, answering his charges with countercharges. She blandly promised never to recall Mazarin and instructed First President Molé to repeat her vow every time Condéan judges or Condé accused her of work-

[44] Again, there is no adequate study of the administration. This reconstruction is based on information in Chéruel, Dethan, and B. N. Ms. Fr. 25025.

ing toward the cardinal's restoration. Against Condé's insistence that Mazarin's servants be ousted from the administration, the regent unveiled the telling argument that she alone had the right to choose ministers. Indeed, she dusted off the old royal Declaration of October 22, and read to the judges the famous clause against arbitrary punishment—Lionne, Servien, and Le Tellier could not be removed against her will without violating that reform. Repeatedly, she informed the Parlement of Condé's military preparations and intrigues with Spain.[45]

While Anne was taking the high road against Condé, Mazarin and his agents followed the low road. More and more money, and office after office, was offered to parlementarians as an inducement to vote against Condéan demands. The self-congratulatory reports written by Mazarin's agents exaggerated their success, but reveal some of the tensions within the Parlement which this bribery brought to the surface. More judges succumbed to the lure of Mazarinist bribes than in previous years. Even Broussel was tempted, although he refused to sell his integrity. However, it was First President Molé and his son, Champlâtreux, who typified the complex response of the Parlement as a whole. Those two conservative judges were unalterably opposed to the Frondeurs' penchant for violence, and disenchanted with Condé's self-righteousness, which was bringing the kingdom to the brink of civil war. At the same time, they knew that the issue of Mazarin's influence within the administration was just as responsible for the unsettled conditions in France. Indeed, they tried to preserve royal power by arguing that Mazarinist influences should be removed from the regent's entourage. Mazarin was therefore naïve in equating Molé's proroyalist position with loyalty to his own person. The cardinal was still more unrealistic in trying to guarantee that judge's royalism and Mazarinism by promises of a high governmental position. Molé did not spurn such offers, but obviously intended to use his current position as first president and future post of keeper of the seals to shore up the monarchy at the expense of both Mazarin and Condé.[46]

[45] See B. U. P. Ms. 67, fols. 347-361, 382-383; *Le Journal ou histoire du temps présent*, Paris, 1652 (a volume of the *Journal du Parlement de Paris*), pp. 9-18, 22-23.

[46] Mazarin's intrigues can be followed in his *Lettres* iv; his *Lettres à la reine, à la Princesse Palatine* . . . ed. J. Ravenal, Paris, 1836, especially p. 56 (an extremely naïve appraisal of Molé's support, dated May 12); B. N. Ms. Fr. 25025, fol. 434. Chéruel's acceptance of Mazarin's position that the cardinal was building a national-

The plight of the parlementarians becomes clearer when we turn from these outside pressures and internal tensions to an examination of the Parlement's formal responses. Mazarin's lingering influence within the regent's administration was a particularly vexing problem. Long before Anne's open quarrel with Condé, Mazarinism proved to be virtually impossible to eradicate. As the ex-minister wended his way slowly to Le Havre and then the Germanies, the parlementarians established machinery designed to watch his movements and hasten his retreat. Once he took up residence in exile, that machinery was used to investigate the constant rumors of his imminent return as well as to intercept his clandestine correspondence with Anne. However, the Parisian judges were frustrated each time by lack of accurate information and uncertainty about their right to take legal action. Committees of judges, entrusted with the task of gathering incriminating evidence for prosecution, simply added more data. Parlementary commissioners traveled through eastern France to spy on the preparations of Mazarinist governors and commanders for the cardinal's return, but returned with little concrete proof. The Duke of Mercoeur was threatened with criminal reprisals for his willingness to ally with Mazarin by becoming engaged to his niece. This did not stop the duke from marrying the lady, and the Parlement's demand to see the marriage contract accomplished nothing. Some parlementary judges suggested that Mazarin be hanged in effigy at all entrances to the capital; their less imaginative but more practical colleagues voted down that proposal. Admittedly, parlementary vigilance dampened Anne's enthusiasm to restore her former adviser prematurely; but it did not stop her from planning for the future or continuing her contacts with him.[47]

The Condéans' assault on the remaining Mazarinists in the administration added to the parlementarians' difficulties. The judges had to ask themselves whether they had any right to interfere with the regent's employment of Le Tellier, Lionne, and Servien. And they had to grapple with Anne's attempt to divert their attention from

---

bourgeois party has to be balanced with Molé's actions and speeches which implied that the ex-minister was still narrowly partisan in his interests. See Chéruel, *Minorité de Louis XIV* IV, 425-426.

[47] The parlementary actions are recorded in B. U. P. Ms. 67, fols. 188-202, 307, 406; *Le Journal ou histoire du temps présent*, pp. 11, 32-33, 41-42; Dubuisson-Aubenay, *Journal* II, 97-99.

that question with the charge that Condé was engaging in treasonous negotiations with Spain and rebel-prone French noblemen. On July 14, with the aim of providing a general framework for reconciliation, while avoiding direct references to the most controversial charges by either party, the Parlement voted three—futile—measures: Condé was asked simply to let Orléans mediate his quarrel with the regent; Anne was requested to promise in writing never to recall Mazarin, and to make any concessions which might avoid civil war (a vague allusion to the possible dismissal of the remaining Mazarinist ministers).[48]

Royal-parlementary negotiations over the formal declaration against Mazarin's restoration immediately bogged down. The document was not presented by Anne to the Parlement until the very eve of Louis XIV's majority in September. Meanwhile, the timid parlementary allusion to the Mazarinists in Anne's administration became a source of embarrassment to judges and regent alike. First President Molé finally resolved his fellow judges' legal scruples by securing the Mazarinists' dismissal without infringing on royal prerogative. His tribunal refused to demand a conciliar purge, but Molé made it clear in a personal audience with Anne that the three men must be dismissed. Anne consented, after seriously thinking of retiring to a cloister rather than accept such a humiliation.[49] The result was chaos within the administration. The removal of Le Tellier was the most serious loss. He had dominated the other secretaries of state, and the remaining three could not coordinate their activities after his departure. Anne sought advice from various obscure figures, but the most prominent were Italians and hence blocked from formal appointments by the anticlerical and antiforeign royal declaration of April 19. Much of her advice, about which we know virtually nothing,[50] however, actually came from Molé, who was also outside the administration.

While Anne floundered, Condé became more arrogant than ever

[48] *Le Journal ou histoire du temps présent*, pp. 26-33; B. U. P. Ms. 67, fols. 378-406; Ms. 68, fols. 149-154.

[49] Talon, *Mémoires*, pp. 437-438; Dubuisson-Aubenay, *Journal* II, 89; Motteville, *Mémoires*, pp. 403-404.

[50] See B. N. Ms. Fr. 25025, fols. 390v, 452v; Priolo, *Ministry of Cardinal Mazarine*, pp. 280-281; Chéruel, *Minorité de Louis XIV* IV, 377-378.

instead of taking advantage of Orléans' mediation. The young prince was irritated by the regent's spiteful decision to dismiss his friend Chavigny at the same time that Le Tellier and the other Mazarinists were removed, and he was suspicious of every overture Anne made with the Frondeurs. By August, Condé's friends were distributing throughout Paris an inflammatory pamphlet whose message was revealed by its title: *Articles Agreed upon by M. the Cardinal Mazarin and M. Châteauneuf . . . the Coadjutor of Paris and Mme. the Duchess of Chevreuse.* Anne countered by sending a formal charge of treason against Condé to the Parlement and Hôtel de Ville. The most dramatic episode resulting from this war of words came on August 21, when both Condé and Gondi appeared with armed retainers in the Palace of Justice. Gondi was pinned between the doors of the assembly hall, and only quick assistance by Molé's son saved him from being killed in the melee following the hurling of insults.[51]

The Parlement refused to continue its efforts to mediate until the rival factions came unarmed to court sessions. Then the judges assumed a superior attitude toward both Condé and Anne. The prince could not secure a formal parlementary censure against the regent, despite her undocumented charges of treason. The regent, herself, was unhappy because of the informal tongue-lashing she received in which Molé asked her—discreetly—not to inflame passions by loose, inflammatory language, and chided her for departing from the monarchy's accustomed impartiality. Molé insisted that an apology to Condé was necessary for the sake of internal peace, even if the prince was guilty of treason. Once again, the Parlement's efforts to take a middle-of-the-road stand proved futile. Though Anne did make the grudging concession of sending the Parlement a declaration exonerating Condé,[52] her apology came too late; Condé had fled once more to his provincial strongholds and did not hear the declaration when it was registered at the *lit de justice* of September 7. Had he been present, however, he would have been skeptical of the queen mother's sincerity, for the September ceremony also proclaimed Louis XIV's assumption of full regal powers. This, of course, virtually nullified the regent's declaration on Condé's behalf, and at

[51] See Vallier, *Journal* ii, 395-423; *Registres de l'Hôtel de Ville* ii, 204-210.
[52] *Le Journal ou histoire du temps présent*, pp. 65-68, 83-85; Vallier, *Journal* ii, 425-426.

the same time released her from the need to continue the hypocrisy she had displayed toward prince and Parlement in recent months.

5

THE POLITICAL squabbles of 1651 created a climate which was no more conducive to state reform than to the preservation of internal peace. It is possible that Mazarin's exile caused a slackening of royalist attacks on the Declaration of October 1648,[53] but, indirectly at least, the achievements of the parlementary Fronde were threatened more than ever; and parlementary interests had to be diverted to more pressing issues. Civil war was imminent, with both sides making military and financial preparations for that conflict, and this, in turn, promoted new confusion within the central administration's military, financial, and judicial branches. Far more than the preservation of past reform, the judges' task became one of simply protecting life, liberty, and property against the lawlessness of all political factions.

Military disorders by troops loyal to Anne, Mazarin, Orléans, and Condé elicited more parlementary *arrêts* between February and September of 1651 than any other issue. Appeals came to the Palace of Justice from all quarters. Destitute *gentilshommes* at Meaux and the wealthy bourgeoisie of Senlis complained of the same things: soldiers not only killed and looted, but were subsequently released from prison by the orders of their commanders.[54] Judges of all political views, from the conservative Talon to the radicals Blancmesnil and Broussel, reminded their tribunal that soldiers' disorders often were caused by poor pay, which in turn was the result of tax evasions.[55] To halt such military misconduct, the parlementarians often had to forget their opposition to illegal taxes, and to tone down the criticisms of tax farmers made during the parlementary Fronde. To be sure, the judges continued to uphold appeals by the Loire River merchants against *traitants*, and even overruled conciliar *arrêts* favorable to royal tax farmers. On the other hand, the judges intervened decisively in favor of other *traitants* in the Parisian *faubourg* of Saint-Germain-des-Prés, ordering merchants to bring their wine and wood

---

[53] This assumption by Mousnier, "Recherches sur les syndicats d'officiers," p. 98, runs counter to evidence in the Actes Royaux and B. N. Ms. Fr. 25025.

[54] B. N. Ms. Fr. 25025, fol. 422v.

[55] B. U. P. Ms. 67, fols. 317-320; *Le Journal ou histoire du temps présent*, pp. 8, 13.

for inspection at the toll gates. One *arrêt* went so far as to threaten the local bourgeois with seizure and arbitrary sale of their goods if they continued to evade legal impositions.[56]

So desperate was the Parlement that it began to send its own commissioners to the provinces in an effort to settle disputes between soldiers and civilians. First the criminal *chambre de la tournelle*, and then the Parlement as a body, established this parlementary version of the royal intendancy, and by May there was a provision for sending *commissaires* to every province within the Parlement's *ressort*. Parlementary commissioners were empowered to judge without appeal all fiscal disputes arising from the soldiers' efforts to requisition supplies and collect special military taxes. These agents did differ from the royalist intendants in that they were controlled by the Parlement, worked through the local petty courts, and respected the individual civilian's rights more than the needs of the state. It is difficult to determine how successful they were, but the formation of additional parlementary commissions in June, July, and August makes it clear that the obstacles to law enforcement were formidable. The *surintendant*'s lack of money for the commissioners' expenses delayed their departure, and when they finally arrived in their districts, they sent back pessimistic reports. One judge-commissioner stated that when he reached the scene of recent disorders, he was either threatened with death by the soldiers or unable to find evidence of wrongdoing because the local commander had been forewarned of his arrival.[57]

Sometimes circumstances allowed the parlementarians to combine zeal for reform with a concern for order. For example, treasury rebates to *traitants* were not only illegal, but fostered the breakdown of discipline in the royalist armies by diverting soldiers' salaries. The Parlement, in this case, could attack the hated *traitants* and at the same time secure income to pay the troops and hence keep them under discipline. But even here, the Parlement ran into difficulties. On one occasion, an attempt to punish *traitants* was opposed by the *surintendant*, who came to the Parlement and defended his arrangements with tax farmers. De Maisons argued that he had drawn up a new contract, which brought the treasury a special advance of

[56] Actes Royaux, F 23669, nos. 141, 184, 185, 186.
[57] See *Le Journal ou histoire du temps présent*, pp. 6-13, 47, 68; B. U. P. Ms. 67, fols. 318, 366; Ms. 68, fol. 110.

800,000 *livres* in return for a long-term reimbursement to the *traitants*. The Parlement, though convinced that in actuality the *surintendant* was returning some 7,400,000 *livres* to the farmers, hesitated to take unilateral action in the face of the minister's explanation, and merely established a commission to investigate the contracts. The outcome of the controversy is not known, but the judges' confusion over their right to press legal action on their own reveals their bewilderment. Frequently during the extended debate over that issue, the quarrel between Anne and Condé distracted the Parlement's attention. At one point, the most radical judges in the *chambres des enquêtes* decided to suspend all investigations until Condé's quarrel with the regent was resolved. Obviously, this was no time to argue with the superintendent of finances over petty violations of the Declaration of October 1648.[58]

When the Parlement managed to win decisive victories against administrative malpractices, it did so only after a long and involved struggle. The most interesting case involved appeals from nobles in Poitou against the illegal imposition of the *gabelle* on the tax-exempt Second Estate of their province. The administration tried to placate the nobles and halt parlementary investigation by issuing a simple *arrêt* restoring the exemption. The Parlement objected that a formal royal declaration was the only acceptable way to guarantee such a basic right of the nobility; a mere conciliar *arrêt* could easily be rescinded. After Molé argued the Parlement's case with the administration, a declaration was drafted, was then held up by Séguier's refusal to sign it, and was finally approved by other administrators. This apparently satisfied the nobles, and the Parlement registered the declaration in September.[59]

The Parlement's disputes with royalist intendants were equally bitter, since the latter were undoing the very work which parlementary commissioners were undertaking. Two examples illustrate the situation. At Bourges, the *bête noire* of the officiers was a maître des requêtes who had orders to assist a nearby royalist army. As early as the end of 1650, the *trésoriers*, much like special parlementary com-

---

[58] B. U. P. Ms. 67, fol. 366; Ms. 68, fols. 58-62, 64-66, 73-76, 90; *Le Journal ou histoire du temps présent*, pp. 10, 47; Dubuisson-Aubenay, *Journal* II, 81.

[59] Actes Royaux, F 23612, no. 78; B. U. P. Ms. 68, fols. 128, 168-170, 190-191; B. N. Ms. Fr. 25025, fol. 469. Broussel complained in October that the declaration was being violated, but his colleagues did not take his allegations seriously.

missioners of the time, began to investigate the soldiers' disorders, but every time they intervened, the maître secured *arrêts* from the royal councils which quashed the *trésoriers'* ordinances. The controversy dragged on into September 1651. Then a royal council issued a particularly obnoxious decree, overruling the *trésoriers'* selection of a colleague as a special commissioner in charge of restoring military discipline. But all the local officers could do was appeal to the permanent syndicate of *trésoriers* in Paris. The plight of the *trésoriers* and *élus* at Soissons was comparable, with the exception that they had to combat royalist accusations of maladministration as well as opposition by a royal intendant and the central councils. The royalist commissaire led the challenge, asserting that the financial officials were altering tax rates to suit their own interests and, in general, conspiring "to make themselves indispensable for the collection of royal taxes." The *trésoriers* countered with orders for the local inhabitants to oppose with force all efforts by the royal commissioner and troops to collect taxes on their own authority.[60]

Neither royalist charges against these petty officers nor fears of undermining the royal armies' financial support could halt the inevitable clash between parlementarians and intendants. In 1651 as in 1648, the Parlement of Paris seized the opportunity to attack those archenemies who threatened the security of subjects and the functions of officials, high and low. Parlementary intervention was graphically illustrated by a dispute with Henri Gamin, maître-intendant at Amiens. The dispute had originally involved the royal councils and Gamin, as well as taxpayers, local *trésoriers*, and the Chambre des Comptes of Paris. When Gamin obtained a conciliar *arrêt* overruling the Chambre des Comptes' support of the *trésoriers* and tax resisters, the *trésoriers* appealed directly to the Parlement of Paris, in mid-1650. By 1651, the controversy had become inflamed by *arrêts* issued at the Parlement and counterdecrees in the councils. Gamin's death failed to restore calm; it merely gave the parlementarians a chance to issue a comprehensive *arrêt*, in September 1651. Picardy was one of the six provinces exempt from the ban of 1648 on intendants, but the parlementarians were determined to limit royalist commissioners to the military functions which the reforms specified. The judges insisted that Gamin's successor submit his commission for parlementary verification before starting his duties, and forbade

[60] Charmeil, *Les Trésoriers de France*, pp. 95, 161, 389, 391.

individual *trésoriers* to assist him unless authorized by an assembly of their bureau at Amiens.[61]

The parlementarians' problems, in 1651, were compounded by their uncertain relations with provincial parlements, lesser officials, taxpayers, and that most vacillating of all Frenchmen, Orléans. While the Parlement and the prince could agree on their common objective of reconciling Anne and Condé, they viewed each other's intervention in military matters with suspicion. Orléans, still titular head of the royal armies as *lieutenant général* until the king's majority, had no patience with the judges' lectures and criticism of the rampages of the armies, fearing further confusion. Also, with the backing of Marshal Villeroy, the duke attacked the Parlement's use of commissioners to investigate civilians' complaints about army activities, asserting that commanders must have exclusive control over discipline. The Parlement tried to mollify Orléans by promising that the judge-commissioners would operate "in conformity with royal ordinances." But the duke continued to grumble that parlementary intervention encouraged local officials and subjects to disrespect all military authorities.[62]

If the parlementarians at Paris could not reach agreement with the royal prince who had inspired their attacks on Mazarin in February, they had even less success uniting with provincial parlements. Though the latter were just as opposed as the Parisian tribunal to royalist evasions of reforms, and had as much reason to be hostile to lingering Mazarinist influences in the regent's administration, these issues never provided the bond some radical parlementarians in Paris wished to forge. The Parlement of Paris dutifully informed its sister tribunals throughout France of every *arrêt* against Mazarin and publicized its continuing efforts to purge the state of Mazarinist influences and military-administrative disorders. But the response of provincial parlements depended on a variety of local circumstances. Above all, each high court had to weigh the advantages of involvement in the latest royal-official disputes against the risk of stirring up new provincial troubles and the possibility of making the regent indifferent to local grievances. In each province, parlementary deci-

---

[61] See Actes Royaux, F 23669, no. 157. The early stages of the controversy have been recounted in Charmeil, *Les Trésoriers de France*, pp. 395-396.

[62] B. N. Ms. Fr. 25025, fols. 345-347; B. U. P. Ms. 67, fols. 319, 342-344; *Le Journal ou histoire du temps présent*, p. 13.

sions on that vexing question often depended on the peculiar relations among regent, governor, and parlement, or the degree of local hatred for Mazarin, or even the memory of half-hearted Parisian support for provincials in the past.

In general, those parlements that had been the least militant during the Fronde's earlier phases tended to remain neutral. The parlementarians at Rennes, Dijon, and Metz, in particular, refused to be stampeded by Parisian appeals into precipitous decrees against the cardinal, in February and March. The Parlement of Metz, which had played virtually no role during the Fronde, remonstrated against Mazarin only when its members discovered that his place of exile in Cologne was uncomfortably close to their *ressort*. At Dijon, the parlementarians seemed most interested in securing freedom for Condé, who had been a popular governor of their province; when they decided to issue an *arrêt* confirming Mazarin's banishment, they hastened to send word of their decision to the prince, and they informed the Parlement of Paris of their pleasure when Condé was freed. The judges at Rennes had no such personal attachment to the anti-Mazarinists, and not even letters from Condé and Orléans or the pleadings of an Orléanist agent convinced them that "all the sovereign courts should unite to oust Mazarin." Finally, they condescended to thank the regent for exiling the cardinal and freeing the princes, adding remonstrances for a royal ban on foreigners in the councils. Even the Parlement of Grenoble delayed action against the chief minister, despite its recent tendency to stray from the neutral position it had held at the outset of the Fronde. According to one informant, the local judges hesitated to become openly anti-Mazarinist for fear of antagonizing their former *avocat général*, Servien. Since he was one of the key Mazarinists in the administration after Mazarin's fall, any resentment by him would inevitably turn the regent against the officials in Dauphiné. However, they changed their attitude when rumors arose that the cardinal might establish residence in the province! Despite pressures from local agents of Servien and Lionne, the Parlement of Grenoble quickly issued an *arrêt* against Mazarin.[63]

The provincial parlements which had quarreled continually with Mazarin and Mazarinist governors were quicker to unite with the

[63] B N. Ms. Fr. 25025, fols. 379, 383-384, 387r, 390, 402r; Ms. Baluze 291, fols. 61-62; B. U. P. Ms. 67, fols. 202, 234, 259-260.

Parlement of Paris. Barely a week after the Parlement of Paris launched the anti-Mazarinist campaign of February 1651, its counterpart at Bordeaux issued similar *arrêts* against Mazarin and on behalf of the imprisoned princes. Moreover, the Bordelais judges quickly notified the Parisian high court of their prompt action. That immediate response from the province of Guienne was clearly the product of deep-rooted grievances. The local parlementarians wanted to put an end to years of harassment by the Mazarinist governor Epernon; by joining the attack on Mazarin, they hoped to remove a chief minister who stood in the way of their governor's removal from office. Then, too, the Parlement of Bordeaux owed a political debt to Condé for his support against Epernon in 1649; the judges could not afford to antagonize their princely benefactor. Their only hesitation was whether to work toward securing Condé as their new governor. After initial qualms about his suitability as a neighbor, the judges at Bordeaux threw their full support behind his candidacy in the spring of 1651. At Toulouse, the parlementarians acted almost as quickly, taking their lead from the anti-Mazarinist governor of Languedoc, Orléans. The parlementarians in nearby Provence were somewhat more cautious. Delicate negotiations were underway to secure an acceptable successor to Governor Alais, and the Parlement of Aix wanted Anne's support for their lobby. However, there was no doubt about that court's underlying anti-Mazarinism, as its subsequent firm decree against Mazarin and letter of union with the Parlement of Paris showed. The Parlement of Rouen remonstrated against Mazarin as promptly as the judges at Bordeaux, despite a recent cooling of relations with Governor Longueville, who was Condé's brother-in-law and one of the imprisoned princes. Vivid memories of their quarrel with Mazarin in 1647-1649 overshadowed the Norman judges' fear of playing into the hands of a potentially dangerous governor.[64]

Finally, all France's parlements took some form of action against Mazarin during the first months of 1651. Then the explosive quarrel between Condé and Anne threatened the realm with a new civil war, tempering the officials' opposition to the central administration. To be sure, the disorderly conduct of royalist troops angered many provincials. But though the Parlement of Paris apprised provincial courts

[64] B. N. Ms. Fr. 25025, fols. 379v, 387r, 414v, 420; B. U. P. Ms. 67, fols. 157-159, 186, 266-267; Dubuisson-Aubenay, *Journal* II, 31.

of its measures against rampaging soldiers, and at least two high courts, at Rouen and Grenoble, sent word to the chief Parlement that they had issued similar *arrêts*, the *Grand* Condé's appeals to the parlements to fuse that opposition with support of his own far more militant stand against the regent brought forth a very negative response. For example, the parlements at Rouen and Dijon refused to discuss the appeals, replying with cautiously worded, complimentary letters. The parlementarians at Rennes were initially inclined to be more sympathetic, since the regent had sent Marshal Grammont to Brittany with heavy-handed demands of military and financial support for the royalist armies. Thinking that Condé's influence in royalist circles would curb the administration's demands, the Breton judges adopted the prince's program. In July, they forbade Mazarin's restoration and asked Anne to dismiss the ex-minister's three agents. The following month, the Parlement of Rennes discovered to its regret that Condé's quarrel with Anne had destroyed his influence in the administration. The local judges abruptly changed their tactics, refusing to debate Condé's request for further aid. The Parlement of Toulouse was distracted by its own feud with the provincial Estates of Languedoc. Hopeful that Governor Orléans would force the tax-voting Languedocian assembly to rescind a special levy opposed by the parlementarians, it refused to become involved in Condé's troubles. Several of its councilors bluntly told an agent of Condé that they wished to serve only the king and would not take the prince's side. The regent helped her cause by sending three agents to negotiate with the southern court. Meanwhile at Aix, the Provençal court was still lobbying with the regent for an acceptable governor. Its members were, if anything, embarrassed by Condé's quarrel since they were hoping to have his brother, Conti, made governor. The regent deterred them from uniting with the Parlement of Paris by promising satisfaction if they remained quiet. When they did intervene in the celebrated courtly dispute, they limited themselves to the vague suggestion that Anne assure Condé of his personal security. The parlementarians at Grenoble, out of remorse for slighting Servien earlier in the year, remained neutral in Condé's dispute.[65]

There can be no doubt that each parlement still wished to preserve the reforms of 1648. The Parlement of Toulouse was, at this very

[65] B. N. Ms. Fr. 25025, fols. 402, 404, 409, 421-425, 434, 442-444, 453r, 472r; B. U. P. Ms. 67, fol. 325.

time, supporting the *trésoriers de France* at Montaubon against a royalist commissioner. If that tribunal's success in blocking the weak provincial Estates' compliance with royal demands for extraordinary taxes is any indication of the power of provincial parlements, the central government still had much to fear from the officers. Nevertheless, there was a distinct change in the mood of provincial parlementarians in the summer of 1651. They had lost their second great opportunity of the Fronde to unite unequivocally with the Parlement of Paris. They might continue to oppose arbitrary royal policies, but the form and vigor of their particular responses was now very uncertain. Significantly, the parlements of Bordeaux, Toulouse, and Aix ceased to write to the Parlement of Paris for assistance in their local struggles against royalist exactions, despite their strong appeals during the previous winter. The Parlement of Paris was also ominously silent, as it had been during the winter of 1650-1651 when those provincials had appealed without success for Parisian support. The estrangement between provincial and Parisian parlements became all too clear when the parlements of Aix and Bordeaux sent delegations to the capital during the summer of 1651. Those high courts not only directed their appeals to Anne, Orléans, and Condé, but had their delegates in the capital avoid all contacts with the Parlement of Paris.[66]

In turn, lesser officers and ordinary subjects became increasingly weary of the conflicts between parlements and regent as France slipped into near anarchy during 1651. Chancellor Séguier received one vivid account of the tragedy that was casting its shadow across France from an informant who declared that entire villages were renouncing their allegiance to their lords and engaging in servile contracts with any local *gentilhomme* or *seigneur* who promised protection from the roving bands of troops which plagued so many communities.[67] This attitude was similar to that of the Parlement of Toulouse and the petty *lieutenant criminal* under the supervision of

---

[66] In the spring of 1651, a few members of the Parlement of Paris pleaded with the Mazarinist Epernon not to resign his governorship, which had not been formally revoked after the Treaty of Bordeaux in 1650! The duke's reply that parlementary pressure had already forced him to resign may refer to informal lobbying by anti-Mazarinist judges in the Parlement of Paris. However, his formal removal may well have been the result of parlementary opposition during 1650, not in 1651. See B. N. Ms. Fr. 25025, fol. 414v.

[67] Charmeil, *Les Trésoriers de France*, p. 392.

the Parlement of Paris. At Toulouse, as in Paris, the authorities were stunned by news that an apology of the English Revolution, written by the English republican John Milton, had appeared in France in a Latin edition. In both cities the book was burned in a public ceremony, and a Frondeur pamphlet also denounced the volume.[68] During the siege of Paris in 1649, the Parlement of Paris had recoiled in horror at the news of Charles I's death, and the parlementarians had been whipped into a frenzy early in 1651 by Mazarin's inference that they were republicans. However, the tone of the antirepublican reaction within the judiciary later in 1651 differed in degree from earlier responses. The anger of French subjects had previously been directed at the central administration for causing France's internal troubles; now they were becoming frightened and bewildered by the seemingly endless and senseless Fronde. The question for many officiers and other subjects was whether the price they were paying to curb the excesses of a rapacious administration and to keep Mazarin out of France was becoming too high.

[68] Knachel, *England and the Fronde*, pp. 59-60.

CHAPTER TEN

CONDÉAN REBELLION,
UNIVERSAL ANARCHY,
AND ROYALIST REVIVAL

ON SEPTEMBER 7, 1651, following his thirteenth birthday two days earlier, Louis XIV entered the Parlement of Paris to assert his right to exercise full regal powers. The pomp of the occasion belied the political situation of a realm about to be engulfed in the most horrifying and anarchical rebellion of the entire Fronde. At the ceremony, the declaration of Condé's innocence was read, and Anne exchanged her legally weak position as regent for the theoretically strong one as agent of a king who was of age. This alteration in her position gave Anne license to persecute Condé, and his refusal to attend the ceremony gave her reason enough to pursue her quarrel with him, despite the solemnly proclaimed pardon.

The king's assumption of regal status and Condé's flight placed the Parlement of Paris in precisely the position it had been trying to avoid since the beginning of the Fronde, and particularly since its ill-fated decrees which had led to Mazarin's exile. Having attempted to reconcile reform and order, royal authority and the interests of officers and ordinary subjects, it was now caught between two irreconcilable forces which combined to offer nothing but anarchy for France.

With the backing of the king's full authority, Anne could—and soon would—claim that she had the right to recall Mazarin. Whatever the legality of parlementary *arrêts* or the limitations of royal declarations during a royal minority, the parlementarians could not easily deny that a king who had attained his majority could override all other authorities in the realm. Neither the parlementary *arrêts* against Mazarin nor past royal declarations which had first banished the cardinal and then proclaimed his permanent exile would hold up, in the long run, against new royal orders expressing Louis XIV's support of his mother's former chief minister.

Recent noble feuding and the subsequent Condéan rebellion also gave Anne all the justification she needed for her contention that *les grands* were destroying the country. Jurists with an eye to legal niceties could not see in the second Condéan uprising the justification which had buttressed the first one in 1650. This time, the rebels were not fighting against the arbitrary imprisonment of their leader; for Condé, himself, was the commander of their forces. In terms of logic, there was but one conclusion: the young king and his mother were the sole persons who could save their subjects.

However, logic and regal authority were not the only considerations of the moment, and so the parlementarians at Paris were far from convinced of the rightness of the royalist position. The judges knew, above all, that absolute monarchy would be most readily accepted by subjects if a ruler upheld the laws he proclaimed—in the present instance, those banishing Mazarin from council and kingdom. Legally, it was questionable whether Anne could override the Declaration of October, 1648, without at least presenting just as formal a declaration before the Parlement of Paris and the other sovereign courts of the capital and the provinces. Morally, too, it was debatable whether she could recall Mazarin after giving her word in writing that he would never be restored, and after the accusations of maladministration and state crimes which she had included in those declarations. Since Anne could not be trusted to abide by such legal-moral scruples, it was possible to rationalize this second Condéan revolt. Theoretically the prince was fighting to uphold the legal banishment of Mazarin, to protect his person against possible assassination by Anne and her Frondeur accomplices, and implicitly to preserve the rights of all subjects guaranteed by the reforms of 1648.

The dilemma of the judges was increased as the second Condéan rebellion degenerated into something far worse than a legal-moral conflict between Condé and Anne. As the year 1652 progressed, the noble Fronde spread from the provinces to Paris, so to speak, drawing the siege of Paris in 1649 and the first noble-provincial uprisings in 1650 into one. Moreover, the question of the fate of the reforms which dated back to the original parlementary Fronde in 1648 was constantly injected into the second noble Fronde. Hence it is clear that the last phase of the Fronde of 1648-1652 was actually all phases combined in a single, climactic struggle to decide all the complex and interconnected issues of the immediate past. The parlementarians in Paris had been able to employ legalistic tactics to preserve order and secure redress of grievances during the parlementary Fronde. They had, with greater difficulty but equal ingenuity, defended both aims during the siege of Paris. And they had been able to mediate an end of the first Condéan revolts. They had yet to test their legalism in the face of all those Frondes combined, and under the stress of a polarization of forces going far beyond the deep divisions of previous years.

Anne took little time to press the advantages given her by the proclamation of Louis XIV's majority. The day after that event, the central administration was altered drastically. Molé was made keeper of the seals, the Marquis of La Vieuville superintendent of finances, and Châteauneuf the chief minister. This administration was ostensibly a Mazarinist-Frondeur coalition; but the eminent Frondeur Châteauneuf was intended to be no more than an interim head of councils. The regent's aim was to buy the Frondeurs' loyalty with offices that could be withdrawn when conditions permitted Mazarin's return. Molé was more hostile than ever to the Frondeur faction and an invaluable, immediate counter to that party's influence within the administration. La Vieuville was touted by Mazarin as being wealthy, influential with the Parlement and Chambre des Comptes of Paris, capable of restoring fiscal solvency without alienating anyone, and above all willing to follow Anne's orders without question. With the informal return of Le Tellier to the royal councils, in October, and his reinstatement as secretary of state, in December, another important anti-Frondeur was added to the list. These men also gave the reshuffled administration an emphatic anti-Condéan bias. Molé had broken completely with Condé because of the prince's sullen resistance to peaceful overtures by Orléans; La Vieuville's most striking trait was his antipathy to the Condéans; and the Frondeurs in the administration were eager to wreak vengeance on Condé for allowing them to fall from power in mid-1651.[1]

The one thing that the reconstituted administration lacked was total commitment to Mazarin. The Mazarinist Colbert completely misjudged Molé—contemptuously stating that he could be counted on if given enough meat to satisfy his stomach.[2] Both Molé and Le Tellier were to oppose the cardinal's restoration when Anne made that move. Châteauneuf had no intention of inviting Mazarin to

[1] See Chéruel, *Minorité de Louis XIV* iv, 337, 421-422, 440; *Histoire de France sous le ministère de Mazarin*, 3 vols., Paris, 1882, i, 77; Priolo, *Ministry of Cardinal Mazarine*, p. 287.

[2] Colbert, *Lettres* i, 161.

return, much less of yielding his leading position to the ex-minister. Then there was the awkward presence of Orléans, deprived by the king's majority of his position as *lieutenant général* and yet still formally a member of the *conseil d'état*. His past friendship with Gondi, his fast-growing attachment to Condé, and his fear that Mazarin's return would unleash a wave of popular attacks on the monarchy itself, made him anathema to the cardinal. It was difficult to know what to do with that member of the royal family since he came to council meetings frequently enough to play a role and yet was emotionally detached from the council.[3]

Thus the new regime had serious internal weaknesses, not to be resolved until the end of the Fronde, a year later. Had Mazarin stayed out of the picture, the coalition might have been welded into a genuine team. And if Anne and Mazarin had fully exploited the talents of men like Molé, Le Tellier, and La Vieuville, an accommodation with the Parlement of Paris and other officiers might have been realized. Molé's dual role as keeper of the seals and parlementary first president gave the administration an important bridge with the officiers. He tried to conciliate suspicious colleagues by refusing to seal any document before determining whether its dispatch would offend them.[4] Le Tellier's talents as a mediator had already been fully revealed. And, as we shall see, La Vieuville was capable of trying to conciliate bourgeois rentiers and Parisian judges. Anne and Mazarin also wished to gain the invaluable support of both groups, but they never rose above the view that Parisians were instruments of royal and Mazarinist power, hence being prevented from fully exploiting the human resources within the coalition.

While the central administration was being reorganized, Anne and her exiled minister worked hard to strengthen their position within the military branch of the government. Mazarin persistently wooed the chief Condéan generals of the first noble uprising in 1650, Turenne and Bouillon. They were to be on the cardinal's side in 1652. He was also drawing several lesser commanders into his sphere of influence and raising a mercenary army in the German territories

---

[3] See especially, Chéruel, *Ministère de Mazarin* I, 70-78; Dethan, *Gaston d'Orléans*, pp. 398-401.

[4] This practice was inaugurated during Molé's brief tenure as keeper of the seals in April 1651. It was resumed in September and continued during 1652. See B. N. Ms. Fr. 25025, fol. 409r; 25026, fol. 110.

near his place of exile. As in the past, Mazarin was in constant touch with the military governors of the provinces, and this time he was more successful. The Mazarinist Duke of Mercoeur was being groomed as successor to Alais in the ever-dangerous province of Provence, a position which Conti had coveted. The one-time Condéan stronghold of Normandy was a question mark, but Governor Longueville was becoming estranged from his wife and her brother, Condé, and this, in time, would result in his becoming a full-fledged Mazarinist. Marshal La Meilleraye was counted on to hold Brittany. Epernon's assumption of the governorship in Condé's former province of Burgundy placed another Mazarinist in a key position. There was some hope that Orléans would keep his province of Languedoc relatively calm.[5]

The changes in the central administration and provincial governorships were closely connected with Anne's and Mazarin's attempt to control the Parlement of Paris and other sovereign courts of the realm. Molé was expected to use his dual role as parlementary first president and *garde des sceaux* to turn the Parlement of Paris against Condé and to secure parlementary acquiescence for the cardinal's imminent restoration. Indeed, it has even been claimed that Molé was the head of a "monarchist party" in the Parlement of Paris during the second Condéan revolt.[6] Several parlementary presidents were also considered sure allies by Mazarin, and he counted more than ever on the man he had chosen as *procureur général* a year before, Nicolas Fouquet.[7] Attempted bribery and influence in other tribunals is more difficult to detect, but it is known that La Vieuville was appointed in part for his influence in the Chambre des Comptes of Paris. In faraway Provence, the administration had managed to purge the Parlement of Aix of several leading anti-Mazarinists by the end of 1651.[8] Bribery in the Parlement of Toulouse would come later.

It is clear that Mazarin intended to combine a triumphant restoration on the king's orders with a military campaign which would

---

[5] This information is drawn from scattered references in Chéruel and Kossman.

[6] Chéruel, *Minorité de Louis XIV* IV, 426.

[7] Mazarinist attempts to influence Molé and other parlementarians can be followed in Mazarin, *Lettres* IV, 537, 544-545; Ormesson, *Journal* II, intro., pp. vii-xi (correspondence between the Fouquet brothers and Mazarin).

[8] Letter from Gallifet to Broussel, Aix, January 23, 1652, B. N. Ms. Baluze 291, fols. 33, 35.

leave Condé crushed and the Frondeurs unable to dominate the administration. It is equally clear that he planned to make the Parlement of Paris a major instrument of his reinstatement. Although he had mistrusted that Parlement sufficiently to consider proclaiming Louis XIV's majority at the Parlement of Rouen,[9] he realized more than ever that he could not afford implacable hostility within the chief court of the realm. Undoubtedly he approved of *Surintendant* La Vieuville's concerted drive to court the favor of Parisian officiers and rentiers by ensuring payment on salaries and rentes.[10] The cardinal could not possibly have viewed those conciliatory acts as a means toward a genuine rapprochement with the Parlement of Paris, but he certainly accepted them as a way to bribe reluctant Mazarinists.

For a while, Mazarin's plans succeeded. It has been argued that the cardinal deliberately provoked Condé into rebellion during the autumn of 1651.[11] We need not accept that hypothesis in order to grasp the advantages the new civil war gave Mazarin. The Condéans were almost as militarily weak as Mazarin had expected, and the ex-minister's personal diplomacy had laid the groundwork for his opponents' defeat. Instead of joining his southern forces with the northeastern armies of Turenne and Spain in a giant pincers movement against the central royalist forces, Condé saw his military coalition reduced to a tattered remnant in Guienne. In the northern theater, Turenne defected to the Mazarinists and the Spaniards decided to attack French fortresses in the Low Countries rather than risk a march into the heart of France. South of Paris, Mazarinist commanders captured one place after another from the Condéans, allowing the royal family and a few ministers led by Châteauneuf to take up residence in Poitiers. Further south, Condé was able to establish headquarters in Bordeaux, but could not hold the countryside of Guienne and western Languedoc.[12]

His only notable achievement in the southwest was to secure some half-hearted support from the Parlement of Bordeaux. That high court needed little prompting to side with its old princely ally when the issue was Mazarinism; parlementary Mazarinists were forced to flee to their country estates, leaving a supposed Condéan majority.

---

[9] Chéruel, *Minorité de Louis XIV* IV, 407.

[10] For Mazarin's stand, see ibid. IV, 425; Chéruel, *Ministère de Mazarin* I, 17.

[11] Kossman, *La Fronde*, pp. 198, 205-206.

[12] See the accounts by Chéruel, Martin, and Kossman.

Immediately, the remaining Bordelais judges balked at Condé's efforts to secure military-financial support from France's archenemy, Spain, and when the parlementarians voted their own war taxes, they promptly told the prince that he could use the money for purely defensive purposes. Still, Condé's support in the province of Guienne far outstripped the resources at his disposal in neighboring Languedoc. The Parlement of Toulouse adopted a position which was openly hostile to Condé and, in effect, quasi-royalist. The Languedocian judges' loyalty was to Orléans, not Condé. Not only was the Duke of Orléans their governor; he was still trying to mediate a settlement between Anne and Condé. In sharp contrast, a Condéan general, Marsin, was making a mockery of the duke's efforts by using the province of Languedoc as a recruiting ground and paymaster of Condéan forces. Predictably, the Parlement of Toulouse circumvented pro-Condéan maneuvers by a few members, dispatched parlementary commissioners throughout western Languedoc to rally the populace against the rampaging Condéan soldiers, and ordered all local officiers and inhabitants to destroy bridges in the path of the invaders.

Other parlements, whether previously docile or rebellious, fell in line. At Dijon, the Burgundian judges who had once sympathized with their imprisoned governor, Condé, now remained loyal to the new Mazarinist gubernatorial leadership, and engaged in a war of words with the Condéan governor of an isolated fortress. The Parlement of Aix was too divided by Mazarinist, Condéan, and neutral factions to do anything. In Brittany, the judges at Rennes were too busy feuding with the provincial Estates and Governor-Marshal La Meilleraye to worry about Condé's fate. Inexperienced in the art of dealing with the administration, the Parlement of Rennes timidly sent a delegation to protest before the regent. Anne greeted their entreaties with derisive laughter.[13]

Military disasters and the absence of widespread outside support forced the Condéan rebels to use tactics which added to their troubles. Subjects were antagonized whenever they seized royal funds, commissioned rebel "intendants," or turned royal regiments into Condéan forces. No matter how legal such measures were considered by the anti-Mazarinist side, they appeared arbitrary to subjects who suffered. This was true, whether the offender was the Parlement of

---

[13] B. N. Ms. Fr. 25025, fols. 489, 493-497, 500v, 504v, 508-510, 526r.

Bordeaux, a petty court or bureau which happened to side with the Condéans, or the *Grand* Condé himself. Anne's administration exploited these popular feelings by playing on the illegality of Condéan activities and by using them as an excuse for continuing its own illegal practices. Thus, a conciliar *arrêt* of October 1651 solemnly denounced Condé for forcing minor financial officials to pay his troops, and thereby rationalized the illegal acts of a royalist intendant in southern France, Denis Marin. The royal decree even called upon the *trésoriers* of Montauban and Bordeaux to expedite any payments authorized by that intendant. In December, another conciliar *arrêt* condemned arbitrary actions by the Parlement of Bordeaux. The decree cited such abuses as the employment of parlementary "intendants" and the collection of war taxes. Inserted in the *arrêt* was a clever appeal to the rival Parlement of Paris, for the document noted that some of the funds for the war chest were drawn from taxes approved for royal use by the Parlement of Paris and collected within that tribunal's *ressort*.[14]

This royalist propaganda and close supervision by members of the administration helped to keep the Parlement and inhabitants of the capital docile during the first months of the civil war. When Anne left Paris to wage war against Condé, she left behind the *surintendant, garde des sceaux*, and a lone secretary of state, de Guénégaud.[15] They had little trouble keeping Orléans loyal and Gondi under control. The Frondeur archbishop-coadjutor never had a chance to build a third party of judges, nobles, and bourgeoisie to counter the twin evils of Mazarinist tyranny and Condéan rebellion. Orléans refused to head Gondi's movement, and the scheming coadjutor's personal problems forced the Frondeur to take an ambivalent position within the Parlement. Gondi dared not break with the administration since Anne had finally presented his name to the Pope but might withdraw his nomination to the College of Cardinals. On the other hand, he had to free himself from his recent image as a Mazarinist if he hoped to build a neutralist party. Hence he tried to pose in public as Mazarin's enemy, while leading his parlementary friends in constant verbal attacks on Condé.[16]

Gondi's peculiar strategy and the Parisian Parlement's antipathy

[14] Actes Royaux, F 23631, no. 545; F 23612, no. 84.
[15] B. N. Ms. Fr. 25025, fol. 489r.
[16] See especially Batiffol, *Biographie du Cardinal de Retz*, pp. 93-95.

to the Condéan rebellion played into Mazarin's hands. Condéan judges undermined Gondi's neutralist position by shouting that his intrigues with Mazarinists were the basic cause of the civil war. Frondeur judges replied with the equally damaging charge that it was the Condéan rebellion that was destroying the state.[17] The Parlement as a whole opted for a moderate royalist position. In October, it forbade the levying of taxes or conscription of soldiers without explicit authority from the king—a deliberate blow at the Condéan revolt. The parlementarians also urged Orléans to continue his efforts to mediate between Condé and Anne, while rejecting Condé's demand that the king's exclusive authority to sign a treaty of peace be transferred to the duke. The Parlement had no intention of legalizing such a dangerous usurpation of the Crown's treaty-making powers, and sensed that Condé was trying to find excuses to continue his revolt. When Condé refused to seek peace with Anne, and even spurned the mediation of an Orléanist-parlementary delegation authorized by the queen mother, the Parlement was drawn into a quasi-Mazarinist position in spite of itself.[18]

After hesitating for weeks to verify a royal declaration which condemned Condé as an "enemy of the state," the Parlement registered that all-important document on December 4 with only forty dissenting votes. Fitful attempts to balance this severe blow to the Condéans with anti-Mazarinist pronouncements could not obscure the importance of the decision. In vain, the judges met fresh rumors of Mazarin's imminent return to France with orders for border officials and subjects to resist his invasion. Their entreaties with the queen mother to repudiate her former confidant were even more pathetic. Parlementary investigation of Mazarin's activities turned up no incriminating evidence, and Talon's decision to send parlementary commissioners to Picardy and Champagne was useless since these "intendants" had no military forces to employ against Mazarin.[19]

The Parlement's condemnation of Condé on December 4 was precisely what Mazarin had been impatiently waiting for. He had desperately wanted some legal justification for his return to France, refusing to cross the border while the outcome of the parlementary debate was in doubt, even though the queen mother had privately

---

[17] See, inter alia, B. N. Ms. Fr. 25025, fol. 522v.
[18] See B. U. P. Ms. 68, fols. 193-215, 220; Talon, *Mémoires*, p. 447.
[19] Talon, *Mémoires*, pp. 448-455.

asked him to join her early in November. Momentarily, Mazarin considered bypassing the Parisian judges and asking the nearby Parlement of Metz to legalize his reentry; that plan had to be discarded when Anne refused to publicize his recall by sending the necessary official letter of reinstatement which the judges at Metz were to register.[20] Then news of the vote in the Palace of Justice against Condé reached the ex-minister. He promptly crossed the Franco-German border and began his journey across France to Poitiers.[21]

2

Mazarin's return to France may have pleased Anne as much as it did the cardinal, but it was most impolitic. Just when the Parlement of Paris and provincial tribunals were rallying to the side of the monarchy and the rebellion was on the verge of collapsing, Mazarin set back his cause by injecting his personality into the delicate political-military situation. Within Anne's administration, there was virtually no support for his ill-timed restoration. Molé, Châteauneuf, Le Tellier, and Brienne urged Anne to reconsider. Apart from Châteauneuf, who knew Mazarin's return marked the end of his career as chief minister, their motives cannot be questioned. Both Molé and Le Tellier knew that Mazarin's premature restoration would only incite new opposition to the administration and harm the war effort.[22] It has also been argued, convincingly, that Châteauneuf's firm direction of military policy made Mazarin's presence totally unnecessary. Châteauneuf had persuaded his fellow ministers that the correct military strategy was to attack Condé's main forces in the southwest rather than concentrate on the Condéan-Spanish forces in the east at Stenai. Of course, the chief minister had additional, personal reasons for suggesting that move; it would keep the regent from the eastern borders and hence delay Mazarin's reunion with her. Nevertheless, Châteauneuf managed to convince Anne, herself, that his was the correct strategy, and it appears that Mazarin, too, was working out a similar military plan.[23]

Mazarin's blunder was followed by an equally disastrous decision

[20] B. N. Ms. Fr. 25025, fol. 492r.

[21] See Kossman, *La Fronde*, pp. 206-207 (based on Mazarin's correspondence with Anne).

[22] Dethan, *Gaston d'Orléans*, p. 402; Chéruel, *Ministère de Mazarin* I, 70-71; Colbert, *Lettres* I, 169-170.

[23] See Lorris, *La Fronde*, pp. 280-281.

on the part of the queen mother. In December, she insisted that Molé and La Vieuville leave Paris and join her administration at Poitiers immediately. It was a strange request, since the *surintendant* and *garde des sceaux* were the only persons in the capital who seemed capable of controlling the sudden wave of violence sweeping across the city as the Condéan-Mazarinist feud intensified, and Molé tried to dissuade the queen mother.[24] He knew from recent observation and personal experience how susceptible the city was of still further changes in its political climate. As recently as November, Paris had virtually ignored Condéan efforts to incite demonstrations by workers against the loss of income caused by the royal family's withdrawal from the city and the consequent drop in employment and sales for Parisians. Then, in December, Mazarin's plans to return and Orléans' increasingly anti-Mazarinist stand had sparked one protest after another against Mazarinism, some Parisians clamoring for tax relief and threatening La Vieuville's life, and others going to Molé's house to voice their hatred of Mazarin. It is understandable why those two men were the targets of the mob. La Vieuville alone could promise the Parisians the 50 per cent tax reduction they demanded, and Molé had thwarted Orléans' efforts to block the anti-Condéan declaration which the first president had skillfully brought to a vote on December 4. The *surintendant* could not, of course, give Parisians all they wanted, so his immediate response to the mob was to flee for his life. But Molé was as coolheaded as during his many previous confrontations with mobs. This time, he stood in his doorway, thrust his long beard in his tormentors' faces and chased them away with the threat of having them hanged.[25]

Why did Anne want to remove the moderating influence of these men? To charge either her or Mazarin with willfully throwing Paris into confusion is probably a misrepresentation of the Mazarinist position.[26] To be sure, La Vieuville's departure, late in December 1651, caused the disruption of some payments to Parisian creditors; and the confusion was increased by the fact that the entire financial

---

[24] Talon, *Mémoires*, pp. 455-459, is a good factual account of Molé's stand. See also Chéruel, *Ministère de Mazarin* I, 87; B. N. Ms. Fr. 25025, fols. 528-529.

[25] On these disturbances, see B. N. Ms. Fr. 25025, fol. 510; Lorris, *La Fronde*, pp. 278-279; Chéruel, *Ministère de Mazarin* I, 79-81.

[26] See the hostile views of Lorris, *La Fronde*, p. 282; and Kossman, *La Fronde*, p. 211.

ministry's personnel, except for *intendants des finances* Morangis and d'Aligre, went to Poitiers with the *surintendant*. But it is important to note that money continued to be set aside for payments of salaries and rentes. A veritable flood of conciliar *arrêts* not only provided for the needs of Parisian judges and rentiers, but threatened tax officials and *traitants* with punishment unless they forwarded revenues destined for those restive groups.[27] And while Molé's departure, at the same time, left the Parlement of Paris without an experienced and respected supporter of law and order, there is every indication that the regent's advisers had not lost their determination to make the Parlement a vehicle of their policy of reviving royal authority. The most plausible interpretation is that Molé and La Vieuville were considered to be too valuable to be left in Paris, where sheer distance had hindered their attempts to coordinate royal policies on justice and finance. At Poitiers, Molé was able to advise the regent on how she should stem the new wave of anti-Mazarinist feeling in the Parlement of Paris and the other sovereign courts of the realm,[28] and La Vieuville, also being in Poitiers, could place pressure on the numerous *partisans* who resided in the capital to join the royal administration and increase their loans.[29] Theoretically, the *surintendant*'s move to Poitiers made it possible to secure more money for both the war chest and Parisians—although it proved impossible to satisfy both needs, and Parisians eventually suffered. If Anne really intended to destroy the fiscal and judicial resources of the capital, she certainly went about it in a most circuitous way.

Whatever Anne's intentions may have been, the withdrawal of the moderate ministers and Mazarin's restoration erased all the political gains the royalist-Mazarinist forces had made since September. The most immediate consequence was Orléans' complete rupture with Anne and Mazarin, and the end of his attempts to reconcile the queen mother and Condé. Previously, Molé's presence had acted as a

---

[27] See, e.g., Actes Royaux, F 23631, nos. 562, 563, 567; and Mazarin's position, noted in Chéruel, *Ministère de Mazarin* I, 118-119.

[28] Molé had been a constant adviser of Anne following Le Tellier's dismissal in July 1651. B. N. Ms. Fr. 25025, fol. 452v.

[29] B. N. Ms. Fr. 25026, fol. 16r; Actes Royaux, F 23631, no. 555; and the apology made in the Parlement by *Intendant des Finances* d'Aligre, in H. Courteault, ed., "Journal inédit du Parlement de Paris pendant la Fronde" (Dec. 1, 1651-Apr. 12, 1652), *Annuaire-Bulletin de la Société de l'Histoire de France*, Paris, 1911, p. 108.

moderating influence on the duke; and the *garde des sceaux*'s own private campaign to bring Anne and Condé together somehow encouraged Orléans to do the same (even though Orléans and Molé had been suspicious of the motives of each other's peacemaking). With Molé gone and Mazarin returning, Orléans charted a new course: in January, he signed a treaty with Condé committing both to fight against the administration's armies until the cardinal was forced into banishment once more. The army which Orléans officially commanded in central France was turned over to a Condéan general, and the duke himself agreed to act as Condé's lieutenant in the capital.[30]

Orléans' defection hastened the collapse of the Frondeur party, but this strange turn of events was of little consolation to the Mazarinists. In the first place, it brought more ex-Frondeurs into the Condéan camp: Orléans was followed by Beaufort, and Beaufort by Broussel— notable additions to the long list of prestigious Condéan names. Nor could Anne really believe that the Frondeurs were totally destroyed as a political force; after all, they had recuperated from equally shattering defeats in 1650 and 1651. To be sure, Mazarin's arrival at Poitiers, at the end of January 1652, led to the Frondeur Châteauneuf's abrupt resignation, when his military plans were outvoted by Mazarinist councilors. On the other hand, the Pope thwarted Mazarin's attempt to prevent Gondi from becoming a cardinal. In February, the Papacy honored Anne's original nomination—which she now regretted—and Gondi became Cardinal de Retz. With this prestigious position making him the ecclesiastical equal of Mazarin, Gondi-Retz could continue to dream of supplanting his old rival. He had a few followers in the Parlement, and he continued to intrigue with Condé, Orléans, and Mazarin. Despised by the prince, mistrusted by the duke, feared by Mazarin, and hated by most members of the anticlerical Parlement, Gondi-Retz remained an uncertain figure during the last months of the Fronde.[31]

The most significant result of the political upheaval during the winter of 1651-1652 took place within the Palace of Justice. Without losing their devotion to monarchical principles, the parlementarians resumed their old feud with Mazarin. Molé's departure left the Par-

---

[30] Lorris, *La Fronde*, p. 286; Chéruel, *Ministère de Mazarin* 1, 105-106.

[31] Chéruel's extremely critical treatment of Cardinal de Retz should be compared with the sympathetic account in Batiffol, *Biographie du Cardinal de Retz*, pp. 97-107.

lement in the hands of less prestigious presidents, an *avocat général* who did not know how to cope with the Mazarinist-Condéan polarization, and a Mazarinist *procureur général* who could buy a few votes but not win the minds of the wavering majority. The flood of anti-Mazarinist *arrêts* which followed the first president's withdrawal did not provide the Condéan rebels with any positive material assistance, but these negative attacks on Mazarin did harm the Mazarinist cause by focusing on the most unpopular royal act, the ex-chief minister's restoration. On December 29, 1651, when irrefutable proof of Mazarin's reentry to French soil reached the Palace of Justice, the Parlement erupted in anger. Mazarin was condemned for *lèse-majesté*, and a price was placed on his head. It was the most partisan and intemperate *arrêt* of the entire Fronde. Yet the judges clung to the fiction that they were not attacking or usurping royal authority: their decree was meant to enforce the king's will as clearly enunciated in the previous declaration of Mazarin's permanent banishment. The parlementarians added the diplomatic amendment that a delegation of their members should travel to the temporary royal residence and remonstrate with Anne, for the sake of internal peace, to remove Mazarin.[32]

The parlementary attempt to convince subjects that Mazarin's restoration was illegal caught the royal entourage by surprise. The blow to the chief minister's position was severe enough that he contemplated taking criminal action against the leading proponents of the *arrêt*. *Avocat Général* Talon convinced Mazarin that it would be better to employ a more moderate defense.[33] When the parlementary delegation reached Anne on January 18, 1652, it was informed that the king had personally asked the cardinal to rejoin his councils. The delegates listened in astonishment as the keeper of the seals, Molé, defended the Mazarinist position. Molé coyly "presumed" that their court had condemned Mazarin without knowing of the king's orders, and asked them to correct their mistake by revoking the anti-Mazarinist declaration of December 29. Five days later a royal decree

---

[32] Talon, *Mémoires*, pp. 459-460.

[33] This is Mazarin's version. Chéruel, *Ministère de Mazarin* 1, 99. Talon's vacillation between an anti-Mazarinist and promonarchical position at this time is puzzling, to say the least. In view of his consistent policy of advocating a benevolent but strong monarchy, it would seem more logical to believe that he was still trying to maintain that aim than to imply base motives of courting first the support of the Condéans and then Mazarin (as many self-righteous contemporaries charged).

quashed that parlementary *arrêt*.[34] However, the attempt to combine Molé's diplomatic language with a written decree enunciating the king's express will failed to halt the Parlement's attack on Mazarin; on the contrary, it led it to draw up an elaborate apology for the decision of December 29. That apology, published in March, was almost a carbon copy of the anti-Mazarinist decrees drafted during the siege of Paris in 1649. This time, the impact of the judges' legalistic arguments was blunted by the fact that they ran counter to the will of a fully empowered king rather than a mere regent. Nevertheless, the Parlement circumvented that constitutional issue by asserting that Mazarin had seized possession of Louis XIV, and that all orders being issued in the king's name were actually acts of tyranny by his chief minister against his own person as well as against his subjects. Thus the parlementarians interpreted their noncompliance with royal commands to be a most helpful type of support for royal authority and public welfare against the alleged usurper, Mazarin.[35]

The parlementary war of words against Mazarin was fairly effective in destroying the constitutional basis of his restoration, and it helped to undermine the moral basis of the royalist war against Condéan rebels. What it could not accomplish was a decisive military defeat of the Mazarinist cause. In contrast to the situation during the siege of 1649, the parlementarians in 1652 were hampered by the fact that they were not being attacked by royalist forces. There was no excuse for taking up arms against the administration, and few judges suggested that this be done. The only practical way to fight was by financing the campaigns of the anti-Mazarinist Condéan armies. But this, too, was impossible, given the situation at the beginning of 1652. The Parlement as a whole simply did not want civil war or the physical devastation which accompanied it. And, as so often in the past, the specter of the sixteenth-century League came back to haunt the Palace of Justice. Orléans and other Condéan nobles at parlementary debates pleaded in vain that union with the princes against Mazarin was very different from an antimonarchical, dictatorial league. It made no difference to moderate anti-Mazarinist judges that the brilliant arguments against Orléans came from a few colleagues

[34] Talon, *Mémoires*, pp. 462-463; *Le Journal ou histoire du temps présent*, pp. 172-177. Molé's position seems similar to Talon's. See fn. 33.
[35] *Le Journal ou histoire du temps présent*, pp. 238-251.

who were bribed with Mazarinist money or enticed by royal offices offered by the Mazarinist *procureur général* and other agents of the cardinal in Paris. The majority of judges agreed with their arguments, though they questioned their motives.[36]

Orléans and Condé were almost as irritated as Mazarin by parlementary legalism. The *Grand* Condé was delighted when Molé left Paris in December, believing that the first president had been the sole obstacle to parlementary union with his cause. And though the Parlement continued to evade making a commitment even after Molé's departure, the prince thought Mazarin's restoration would soon convince the Parisian judges that his cause was just.[37] Neither he nor Orléans could understand their distinction between legal and military opposition to the hated cardinal-minister. Orléans was incredulous when the Parlement combined its original anti-Mazarinist decree of December 29, 1651, with a bland request for the duke to use the king's authority and his own against Mazarin. Its position was made clearer during succeeding debates when some judges told Orléans he could do whatever he wished, but the Parlement could not officially condone or authorize any military-financial attacks on the Crown.[38] Time and again, parlementary *arrêts* actually denounced the raising of arms and collection of taxes without express royal consent, thereby contradicting the court's own suggestions that Orléans do precisely those things on his own authority. As late as May 1652, the *grand chambre* burned a Condéan pamphlet which claimed that the Parlement had authorized Orléans to act as viceroy of the realm.[39] The only parlementary concession to the Condéans was to suspend the royal declaration against Condé. But this was of little help to the prince, for the *arrêt* of January 12, 1652, which removed the charges, stated explicitly that this was a temporary act,

[36] See the almost verbatim notes of speeches by Menardeau, de Mesmes (brother of the more famous Henri, who had died), de Novion, Le Coigneux, etc., during January 1652 in Courteault, "Journal inédit."

[37] Letters from Condé to Machault and Orléans, January 4, 1652, quoted by Aumale, *Histoire des princes de Condé* vi, 504-505.

[38] One judge summarized with an economy of words his tribunal's dilemma; the triumph of the Condéan armies would bring "the decline of the monarchy"; royalist success on the battlefield would ensure "tyranny." B. U. P. Ms. 69, fols. 194-195.

[39] V. Conrart, *Mémoires*, Michaud and Poujoulat collection (ser. III, vol. IV), Paris, 1838, pp. 549-553.

dictated by the need to press prior charges against Mazarin. As soon as the cardinal should leave the state again, the Parlement promised to enforce the royal declaration against Condé.[40]

As the war dragged on with no solution in sight, the parlementarians' legalism became more anachronistic and their motives less and less elevated. They talked glibly of Orléans' ability to fight Mazarin with forces under his command, but betrayed their selfishness by becoming self-righteous as soon as the issue of money was raised by the duke. When troops from either side approached the capital, they solemnly issued *arrêts* ordering the combatants to stay out of their neutral zone. There was one particularly long and inconsequential debate concerning a march by Condéan-Spanish forces under Nemours from eastern to south-central France. The judges clearly did not know what to do. Royal orders commanded them to condemn the marchers as Spaniards. Orléans retorted that the soldiers were merely mercenaries in the pay of the Condéans. Most parlementarians did not want to condone a Spanish invasion and yet they knew that if the northern and southern forces of the anti-Mazarinists were able to unite, this would greatly enhance the prospect of forcing Mazarin out of power. Not only were moderate judges unable to make up their minds, their few Condéan and Mazarinist colleagues were afraid to bring the issue to a vote for fear that the other side would win. As a result, Nemours was able to take his troops unmolested across central France, devastating the countryside as they marched. If the Condéans derived any satisfaction from the Parlement's failure to act in this case, they were stupefied by other judicial decisions. While Nemours was marching toward Angers, the conservative *chambre de la tournelle* condemned the rebel Duke of Rohan for seizing the Mazarinist head of the *présidial* court at Angers.[41]

Fears of anarchy and narrow corporate concerns became an obsession with the parlementarians. They were outraged when it was rumored that parlementary members, sent to prevent Mazarin's return, had been killed or wounded. When they discovered that the only Mazarinist atrocity against their tribunal was the arrest of a

---

[40] Talon, *Mémoires*, pp. 461-462; *Le Journal ou histoire du temps présent*, pp. 169-171.

[41] See, inter alia, Talon, *Mémoires*, pp. 464-469; Vallier, *Journal* III, 154-162; Dubuisson-Aubenay, *Journal* II, 161-173.

single judge, they still persisted in their anger. The Parlement's most radical and conservative members were appalled by the narrow vision of their tribunal, as a whole. During debates, the majority of judges neglected the raging, costly civil war, spending hours, instead, criticizing the treasury's misuse of funds that should have been set aside for Parisian officers and rentiers. The parlementary majority was understandably terrified lest the ill-paid rentiers engage in riots, but it overlooked the fact that the far more violent war it was allowing to continue robbed taxpayers of profits normally converted into taxes for the same rentiers. The stormy issue of *gages* and rentes only served to weaken already shaky relations with other corporations, and it became apparent that the *trésoriers* in some regions had cooperated with the Mazarinist regime, sending local tax money to the royal treasury at Poitiers rather than to the Parisian *bureau de ville* for payment on the municipal rentes. Parlementary reaction was at best confused, and at worst, extremely hostile: some judges accused the *trésoriers* of being ungrateful after parlementary protection in 1648; other judges retorted that the Parlement was itself to blame for the current betrayal, arguing that the high court had not done enough during the parlementary Fronde to ensure the *trésoriers'* loyalty now. The ill-fated reconvocation of the Chambre Saint Louis, in March 1652, marked the *reductio ad absurdum* of this internecine warfare. Called to discuss royalist attacks on the reforms of 1648 which protected officials' salaries and rentiers' interest payments, the joint sessions broke down in squabbles between Parlement and Chambre des Comptes. Some Mazarinist parlementarians deliberately widened the breach by speaking of their tribunal's "superiority" over the other sovereign courts of the capital. However, the divisions would have come into the open even without such provocations.[42]

These disputes with the other sovereign courts and *trésoriers* were self-defeating displays of narrow corporate interests, detracting from the common grievances of all the officials. For example, *trésoriers'* salaries had been reduced below the level stipulated by the reforms of 1648, giving them a common cause with sovereign court judges.[43] And apart from the Grand Conseil, which had drifted from the

---

[42] On the rentes and *gages*, see especially Courteault, "Journal inédit," pp. 100-101, 108-109; B. U. P. Ms. 69, fols. 177-178; B. N. Ms. Fr. 25026, fol. 46r; Boislisle, *Chambre des Comptes*, p. 447.

[43] B. N. Ms. Fr. 25025, fol. 527r.

reformist camp at the end of 1648, all the Parisian courts were still both reformist in interest and at least mildly anti-Mazarinist by conviction. If the Chambre des Comptes and Cour des Aides had not yet issued *arrêts* against Mazarin, it was because they were not criminal courts and hence lacked the authority to act. The Cour des Aides came very close to mirroring the ambivalent position of the Parlement, forbidding Orléans' aides to seize the royal *tailles* while insisting that royal revenues be forwarded to Paris for *gages* and rentes. This was in stark contrast to the Grand Conseil which used its ecclesiastical jurisdiction to condemn parlementary decrees against Cardinal Mazarin.[44]

Relations between the Parlement of Paris and its provincial counterparts were as uncertain, despite the nearly universal hostility to Mazarin and support for the reforms of 1648. When the Parisian court issued its anti-Mazarinist decree of December 29, 1651, it merely notified the provincial parlements. Only when Orléans objected a few days later did the parlementarians add an appeal for the provincial courts to pass similar decrees.[45] The response to this and later appeals from Paris varied according to local conditions—even in the province of Normandy where superficial similarities with Parisian conditions caused the Parlement of Rouen to emulate its Parisian counterpart's decrees against local intendants.[46]

The position of the Parlement of Rouen was complicated by divisions in Normandy's main princely family. Madame de Longueville backed her brother Condé, urging the Norman parlementarians to support his cause. But her estranged husband was working just as hard to place the judges in the Mazarinist camp. The Norman high court's solution was to issue several anti-Mazarinist *arrêts* which were milder than the anti-Mazarinist resolutions of the parlements at Paris, Toulouse, and Bordeaux. Couched in the language of remonstrances, qualified by the phrase "subject to the king's good pleasure," and watered down by the omission of any reference to a price on Mazarin's head, these decrees revealed the uncertainty of a provincial court which did not know how the leading noble family of the area stood on the civil war undertaken by their most distinguished

[44] B. N. Ms. Fr. 25026, fols. 36r, 48.
[45] Courteault, "Journal inédit," pp. 56-57.
[46] B. N. Ms. Fr. 25026, fol. 21v; Charmeil, *Les Trésoriers de France*, p. 384.

relative. The Parlement of Aix, too, was badly divided by factions which supported Mazarin, Condé, and Alais. Its members could agree on nothing more than a letter to the Parlement of Paris telling of their decision to ask the king whether he wished to maintain Mazarin! Equally pathetic was the stand of the Parlement of Grenoble. After hesitating to discuss the requests from Paris, the judges in Dauphiné finally wrote to the king, asking him to restore peace by any measures he considered "necessary." Most astonishing of all the responses was the one which came from Brittany. The Parlement of Rennes was locked in a bitter conflict with the Mazarinist marshal La Meilleraye, who was pillaging the judges' country houses and raising special war taxes. Hence it simply asked the Parlement of Paris to support its provincial cause. Even after the Parisian court responded by withholding the title of "duke and peer" from the marshal, the Breton judges replied with a face-saving apology for their delay in remonstrating against Mazarin. They finally became bold enough to ask the king to free the member of the Parlement of Paris who had been arrested while trying to prevent Mazarin's reentry to France, and remonstrated against Mazarin's return. Perhaps sensing that they had become overly partisan, the local parlementarians qualified their position by forbidding the recruitment of soldiers without express orders from the king. Only in Toulouse, Bordeaux, and Dijon did the local parlementarians conform to the pattern established by the Parlement of Paris. The strong anti-Mazarinist position at Dijon can be rationalized as a gesture of good will toward its former governor, Condé. The Bordelais judges were understandably drawn even more closely to Condé since he was their present governor; and as the civil war progressed their commitment was strengthened by the queen mother's threat to punish them by transferring their court to another town. The abrupt shift of the Parlement of Toulouse from earlier hostility toward Condéan troops to a violent anti-Mazarinist position is not so easily explained. Undoubtedly the decision by Governor Orléans to join Condé, in January 1652, made the judges' transition an easy one. However, they issued anti-Mazarinist resolutions several weeks before Orléans' formal volteface, and prior to the anti-Mazarinist *arrêt* of December 29 by the Parlement of Paris. Then, on receiving word of that decree, the judges at Toulouse followed suit by placing a price on Mazarin's head and working closely with Orléans against the Mazarinist cause.[47]

By spring of 1652, the anarchy-producing acts of administrators, soldiers, and officers had profoundly disturbed the majority of subjects, who were the civil war's greatest victims. If enthusiasm for either the Mazarinist or Condéan cause had ever existed, it was not evident after six months of fighting; nor did vacillation by the corporations of officials suggest to subjects any solution for the kingdom's internal problems. Subjects could not understand the mentality of sovereign court judges who would flood the realm with anti-Mazarinist decrees and at the same time offer nothing more than lukewarm support for the anti-Mazarinist Condéan rebels. The officiers' propaganda had two, equally negative, effects: it gave subjects all the information they needed to produce hatred for both Mazarinists and Condéans, and it tarnished the Parlement of Paris and other corporations as stabilizing elements in the Fronde. Consequently, individuals, social groups, and entire communities reacted by either groping desperately for a neutralist position in the civil war or by lashing out at all combatants for failing to bring peace. Thus a rebel captain who resisted Mazarin's reentry to France, in January 1652, complained to the Parlement of Paris that the local populace was unsympathetic, popular dislike of the chief minister being overshadowed by the local inhabitants' more personal anger at the captain for failing to keep his troops disciplined. In Paris, at the same time, some well-to-do burghers were willing to lend money to Orléans, though a close observer, on the other hand, said that the number who refused to pay was just as great. By early March, the number of Parisian merchants who refused to finance campaigns against Mazarin had greatly increased, while the remaining anti-Mazarinist bourgeois were becoming desperate. The latter pleaded with Orléans to chase Mazarinist troops from the environs of the capital, obviously suffering from the loss of trade. When Orléans suggested that they go to the Hôtel de Ville to seek action, they replied that the civic government was Mazarinist; when he suggested they go to the Parlement, they exclaimed that the parlementarians were "even worse." Nearby, at Orléans, the inhabitants split

---

[47] The actions of all these Parlements are described succinctly by B. N. Ms. Fr. 25026, fols. 5-8, 13-14, 17, 25-26; Courteault, "Journal inédit," pp. 49, 78-79, 90, 102-103, 110; B. U. P. Ms. 69, fols. 105-107. See also fn. 8.

into hostile factions as armies from both sides of the war approached. When a few prominent noblemen and some artisans forced an emergency town meeting on the Mazarinist civic leaders, that gathering could only agree on a neutralist stand: provided the rebels stayed away, the town would prevent the entry of royalist forces. Toward the end of the month, the bourgeois of Agen barricaded the streets to prevent Condé's entry to their city, though eventually the civic government was forced to billet the prince's garrison and raise a regiment of infantry with its own revenues. In April, the towns of Nevers and Molens welcomed the news that the royal family was coming, but petitioned the king to leave Mazarin behind. There were towns, such as Corbeil, which sought consistently to keep both sides out, and a few which offered money to both sides for neutrality.[48]

3

By April 1652, the prospect of any solution to the anarchical civil war looked dimmer than at any time since its beginning the previous autumn. Civilian inertia, legalism in the law courts, and military weaknesses turned the internal conflict into a war of attrition. Both Condé and Mazarin grasped the fact that Paris and its Parlement might hold the key to victory which eluded them on the battlefield.

Unhappy with the progress of the war in his area of greatest strength, southwestern France, Condé broke camp and marched toward the capital. He defeated one royalist army at Bléneau, then avoided the army of the greatest Mazarinist commander, Marshal Turenne, and entered Paris in mid-April. His arrival was a dramatic move to preserve his alliance with Orléans and to intimidate the vacillating parlementarians, and he was just in time to prevent a rumored coalition between the king's uncle and the old Frondeur leader, Gondi-Retz. While Cardinal de Retz was too discredited to have profited from such an important defection to his sagging party, the loss of Orléans would have dealt a staggering blow to the Condéan faction's prestige. Just as important for Condé was the potential support from the Palace of Justice. Hence, one of his first public acts after arriving in the capital was a visit to the Parlement, followed by similar ceremonies at the other sovereign courts. What the prince wanted, and urgently requested, was unequivocal backing of his

[48] All these incidents are recorded in B. N. Ms. Fr. 25026, fols. 8r, 48v, 50v, 54, 60v, 68r.

rebellion, in place of the quasi-neutralist position which had condemned Mazarin while withholding authorization to tax and recruit for the Condéan cause.

Condé's entry to Paris heightened Mazarin's interest in the capital. The cardinal-minister did not know what the prince could achieve, but he was obviously alarmed by his archenemy's presence in that key center and the encampment of Condéan troops on the city's outskirts. At the end of April, Mazarin and Anne again established royal headquarters at Saint-Germain. For Parisians, it was a frightening picture, for Condéan and Mazarinist troops laid waste to the surrounding towns and countryside, occasionally clashed with each other, and gave every appearance of wishing to invade the capital itself.

Mazarin's relations with Parisians were more complicated than Condé's since he, unlike the prince, did not have access to the city. In fact, the public authorities had reluctantly agreed to let Condé, though not his troops, in the capital, while keeping the gates closed against the queen mother and her hated minister. However, the resourceful Mazarin believed that his diplomatic skills could eventually turn the capital into a royalist stronghold. The small circle of committed Mazarinists in the capital, headed by *Procureur Général* Nicolas Fouquet and his brother, worked harder than ever to bribe parlementarians, merchants, and other prominent Parisians.[49]

It is not entirely clear what the chief minister expected from the Parlement. He told an agent at one time that the princes and not the judges had taken up arms against the king, and hence the administration did not need to negotiate with the parlementarians. On the other hand, he vaguely hoped that the Parlement would authorize the entry of the royal family to Paris, and he expressed that hope in his letters. He eagerly awaited delegations from all Parisian corporations, but appeared most anxious to court the parlementary delegates. In fact, Mazarin constantly wrote to the *procureur général* and other agents for advice on the proper answer to the successive visits of parlementarians. By June, he was not only preparing conciliatory responses, but actually hoping for some sort of royal-parlementary negotiations, the precedent of the Treaty of Rueil, in 1649, perhaps still in his thoughts. Mazarin knew that the parlementary decrees

[49] See Kossman, *La Fronde*, pp. 215-221, for an assessment of Condé's and Mazarin's attitudes toward Paris.

against him stood in the way, and he must have realized that it would not be easy to repeat the tactic of bypassing the noble rebels, but he optimistically urged his Parisian agents to try to bring wavering parlementarians around to dropping charges against him. The administration also tried to ease parlementary opposition by temporarily withdrawing its civilian and military personnel from the Parisian area.[50]

The Mazarinist ministers' guarded approach to the explosive issue of state reform proved how important the support of the Parlement was for Anne's regime. *Surintendant des Finances* La Vieuville needed money desperately, but still found ways to reduce arbitrary fiscal procedures which ran counter to the Declaration of October 1648. He was particularly careful to allocate funds for the payment of officials' salaries and interest on the Parisian rentes rather than diverting that revenue to the royalist armies. Parlementarians in Paris continued to complain that the rate of payment fell below the levels guaranteed by law, but the flow of money to officiers and rentiers did not cease altogether until Condé seized control of the capital in July 1652. Meanwhile, the finance minister was working toward a compromise solution of the royal-official quarrel over intendancies. At the end of 1651, a conciliar *arrêt* specified that special tax-collecting commissaires were to verify their commissions at the parlement of their region before assuming their duties. Despite La Vieuville's care in having his commissioners registered as "maîtres des requêtes *en chevauchées*" (i.e., the pre-intendant maîtres who had worked as circuit riders through the local bureaus of *trésoriers* and *élus*), these royal agents did exceed their authority by collecting taxes on their own. Yet once the principle of restricting the intendancies had been conceded by a royal council, it was difficult to defend their illegal practices in the face of opposition from the Parlement of Paris and other corporations. La Vieuville was quick to understand objections by the parlementarians at Paris and Rouen, as well as a desperate appeal to the Parlement of Bordeaux by *trésoriers* at Limoges. Immediately after the Parlement of Paris forbade all maîtres to act as intendants, the *surintendant* made a major substantive concession. On February 14, 1652, he issued a harsh reprimand to the most controversial of all his commissaires, Jean Balthazar at Limoges. That

---

[50] See Mazarin, *Lettres* v, 69, 89, 101-103, 107, 109, 113, 123-124; Chéruel, *Ministère de Mazarin* I, 177.

maître-intendant was ordered to work through the local financial bureaus instead of usurping their functions. If Balthazar discovered administrative malpractices in the financial bureaus he was not to take the law into his own hands, but merely to forward a report, for consideration, to the royalist regime at Poitiers.[51] La Vieuville's open attack on the intendants was part of a carefully conceived scheme to turn the Parlement of Paris against the lesser financial officials and toward a moderate royalist position. While the *surintendant* was wooing the parlementarians with attacks on intendants, his underling at Paris was inflaming the Parlement's suspicions of embezzlement by individual *trésoriers* and *élus*. After hearing *Intendant des Finances* Morangis cite case after case of maladministration in the financial bureaus, the parlementary judges were more certain than ever of wrongdoing by the intendants' local rivals.[52] The Mazarinists' tactic of yielding on principle, conceding specific points when challenged, and turning the Parlement of Paris against lower corporations succeeded as well as La Vieuville could have expected. When the Parisian high court resumed its investigation of royalist intendants in April, the judges were very uncertain of their position. Speech after speech betrayed the fact that they did not know whether the *surintendant* was an enemy who was secretly backing the intendants or a friend who was trying to carry through on his promises. Under the circumstances, it was impossible for the Parlement to launch a massive attack on the queen mother's financial administration.[53]

From the perspective of the Palace of Justice, these pressures from Mazarinists and Condéans and the closely connected misery of Parisians were two sides of the same coin. The general drift toward neutrality of Parisians and provincials during previous months had been a sign of desperation. Now, during the summer of 1652, panic swept through the capital and its environs. Many persons simply wanted an end to the war and did not care whether this was accomplished by a Condéan dictatorship or the triumph of an authoritarian Mazarinist regime. Others were so desperate that they chose one side, even

---

[51] Charmeil, *Les Trésoriers de France*, pp. 383-384; Mousnier, "Recherches sur les syndicats d'officiers," p. 99.

[52] Courteault, "Journal inédit," p. 109. Ex-Superintendent de Maisons also leveled charges at the lesser financial officials, stating that they padded their salaries so much that the amount was greater than the *gages* of all other officiers. B. U. P. Ms. 69, fols. 177-178.

[53] B. U. P. Ms. 69, fols. 411-420.

though they knew they were supporting the lesser of two great evils. Still others completely lost their senses, looting, rioting, and killing to stave off starvation or to ease their frustrations. Inflammatory pamphlets and bribes of a few *sous* played their part in turning Parisians into wild mobs demonstrating on behalf of Mazarin or Condé. The displacement of peasants by the contending armies added greatly to the turmoil; refugees from places like Montargis and Estampes flocked into Paris, seeking refuge and a chance to clamor for help at the Hôtel de Ville and Palace of Justice.[54]

There was little pattern to the constant round of demonstrations, pleas for help, threats of violence, and offers of support for any public authority caught in the crossfire of conflicting passions. Hostility between social groups over the issue of peace was common, but no more prevalent than disagreements within each. As hard as Mazarin's agents tried to secure bourgeois support, there were still wealthy Parisians who remained violently anti-Mazarinist. For example, bourgeois from the rue de Grenelle and rue Saint Honoré actually broke up pro-Mazarin demonstrations by other bourgeois Parisians. Some *bons bourgeois* concentrated on defending their rural *châteaux* against royal forces. Still others, notably the very wealthy members of the guild of silversmiths, offered their support to Orléans against Mazarin.[55] A well-informed observer summed up the bourgeois attitudes well when he wrote in July:

> As for the *bons bourgeois*, there are few who do not desire the exclusion of C[ardinal] M[azarin], but the [administration] is working hard to win over the six merchant guilds. Those among them who have given in say publicly that it is better to have peace with Maz[arin] than to remain at war, although the most sensible avow that it is extremely difficult to ensure peace as long as Maz[arin] stays in power.[56]

The only difference between the badly divided *bons bourgeois* and the equally confused social elements beneath them was the latter's more pronounced tendency toward violence. Mobs of craftsmen and

<hr />

[54] There are vivid accounts of the situation in many contemporary writings. See, inter alia, B. N. Ms. Fr. 25026, especially fols. 43r, 48, 68v; Talon, *Mémoires*, p. 487; Cubells, "Le Parlement de Paris," pp. 196-197.

[55] B. N. Ms. Fr. 25026, fols. 106-107, 154v; Ms. Fr. 17560, fols. 260-263.

[56] B. N. Ms. Fr. 25026, fol. 104r.

laborers clashed with each other, some crying, "Union of the Parlement with the people and down with Mazarin," others shouting, "Peace at any price."[57]

The public authorities of Paris were almost as confused as those who demonstrated before their chambers. The civic government was too Mazarinist to support either the Parlement or the princes; and when it sent the civic militia to protect the parlementarians from anti-Mazarinist mobs, these guards proved to be ineffective since they were hated as Mazarinists. (Ironically, some guardsmen were actually anti-Mazarinists who worked with Orléans to keep Mazarinist judges from leaving Paris.)[58] The Chambre des Comptes and Cour des Aides were still bitter over the rude treatment accorded them by the Parlement during the ill-fated Chambre Saint Louis of March-April 1652. The Grand Conseil was of no help, since it had always been more royalist than any other sovereign court in the capital and had ceased to play an important part in the Fronde at the beginning of the siege of Paris in 1649. The sole Parisian institution retaining enough prestige to influence Parisians, and independence to find a compromise, was the Parlement.

When Condé made his dramatic entry to Paris in April 1652, the parlementarians thought they saw an opportunity to end the Fronde. Condé had come to them in person with his latest appeal for support, and Anne's administration was close enough to the capital to be contacted at short notice. The Parlement promptly voted to turn down Condé's appeal for union, and at the same time agreed to remonstrate with Anne for Mazarin's dismissal. The parlementarians' plan seemed reasonable: with subjects placated by the cardinal's removal and the queen mother mollified by parlementary resistance to Condé, there would at last be some chance for a negotiated settlement of the civil war. Prospects of peace were momentarily enhanced when other Parisian authorities followed the Parlement's lead. The Chambre des Comptes and Cour des Aides added their remonstrances to the Parle-

[57] On both types of demonstrations, incited partly by Mazarinist and Condéan bribes of a few *sous*, see ibid., fols. 98-99; Aumale, *Histoire des princes de Condé* VI, 529-530.

[58] The divisions within the civic administration among *prévôt*, *échevins*, district representatives (*quarteniers*), militia captains, and guardsmen have never been thoroughly examined. But see B. N. Ms. Fr. 25026, fols. 67, 77-78; B. U. P. Ms. 69, fol. 188; and Broussel's memorandum, B. N. Ms. Baluze 291, fols. 101-102. There is some information in Kossman, *La Fronde*, especially p. 218.

ment's decree when Condé visited their chambers, and a similar resolution was passed at an immense gathering of sovereign court judges and guildsmen, convoked by the Hôtel de Ville on the insistence of the Parlement, Condé, and Orléans.[59]

These peace feelers were premature; Condé was unwilling to give in while he retained a chance to dominate the capital, and Mazarin had no intention of fleeing from France a second time when his troops were on the outskirts of Paris. Nevertheless, the Parlement persisted in its quest for peace: Condé and Orléans were rebuffed every time they renewed their calls for parlementary support, and the Parlement just as grimly held out against constant terrorist attacks by mobs incited by Condé and Beaufort against what they called "Mazarinist" judges.[60] And while the Chambre des Comptes began to request the king's return without conditions, the Parlement continued to remonstrate for the removal of Mazarin as the price of capitulation. This shocked the chief minister, who had convinced himself that the parlementarians were ready to accept the royal family's unconditional return to Paris.[61]

The Parlement even found time to deal with the violence and suffering in Paris. Harsh treatment of rioters was balanced by aid for those who suffered in silence or demonstrated peacefully. Rioters were hanged by orders of the *chambre de la tournelle*, while indigent occupants of rented dwellings saw their rents waived by parlementary decree. The thousands of peasant refugees could not be so easily cared for, but the parlementarians set an example for other public authorities by volunteering some of their wealth for relief, and by preventing financial officials from charging import taxes on the goods of incoming persons.[62]

In the short run, these measures failed, since the war continued and the mob scenes and threats on the judges' lives became uglier with every day. But the parlementarians' refusal to turn to either revolution or abject royalism set the stage for a settlement of the civil war which was to salvage many of the reforms secured in 1648.

[59] Conrart, *Mémoires*, pp. 541-543; *Registres de l'Hôtel de Ville* ii, 236-272; Vallier, *Journal* iii, 198-210.

[60] Conrart, *Mémoires*, pp. 561-564; Vallier, *Journal* iii, 270-285.

[61] Mazarin, *Lettres* v, 123-124.

[62] See especially Actes Royaux, F 23669, nos. 212, 214, 216, 222-224, 227; B. N. Ms. Fr. 25026, fol. 98v; Aumale, *Histoire des princes de Condé* vi, 529.

4

EARLY IN July 1652, Paris was engulfed in a political upheaval which, initially, seemed to spell disaster for the Parlement but turned out to be the first step on the road to internal peace. On July 2, Condé and Turenne fought a pitched battle just outside the city's gates. Condé's army was routed, but the survivors managed to flee to the capital, and their leader found himself virtual master of Paris in spite of that military disaster. Immediately, the prince launched a massive appeal to Parisians to legalize his dictatorship. Condé could not tolerate the parlementarians' refusal to support him, nor would he stand by and let them continue to send the regent new remonstrances which might bring a parlementary-royal settlement mirroring the Treaty of Rueil. On July 4, he appealed directly to a huge assembly of judges, guildsmen, and religious leaders at the Hôtel de Ville. Meanwhile an anti-Mazarinist crowd of inebriated, half-crazed soldiers and civilians gathered outside. After waiting and demonstrating for hours, the crowd became enraged when they were finally told that the Hôtel de Ville's assembly had simply endorsed the Parlement's neutral stand. The city hall was set on fire; and as the delegates tried to escape, some were killed and others beaten.[63] For a short time, this mob action accomplished for Condé what his personal appeals had failed to achieve. The Parlement, half-deserted during the violence of the preceding weeks, was now reduced to a rump assembly of judges who dared remain in the city. On July 20, by a very narrow majority, that pathetic remnant of the proud tribunal legalized Condé's control of the capital. They declared that Mazarin had seized the helpless young king and that the only remaining free representative of the administration was Orléans. The duke was invested with emergency royal powers as *"lieutenant général"* of the realm. The Parlement then authorized him to command the royal armies, and establish a council composed of members of the sovereign courts, rebel nobles, and a few ex-ministers (notably Séguier and Chavigny) who were in Paris.[64] Meanwhile, the Duke of Beaufort

---

[63] The best accounts are Conrart, *Mémoires*, pp. 567-579; Vallier, *Journal* III, 314-327; Dubuisson-Aubenay, *Journal* II, 248-249; Talon, *Mémoires*, pp. 494-496. Kossman, *La Fronde*, pp. 221-223, has a fair assessment of Condé's role.

[64] There are several versions of the vote: 74-69, 74-65, 76-59, 74-66. Of the two motions which were defeated, one called for negotiations between the princes and the administration, while the other asked Orléans to employ his existing authority

became governor of Paris, and Broussel took charge of the civic government as *prévôt des marchands*.

Ironically Condé's *coup d'état* proved fatal to his rebel movement in the long run. Parisians of every background were sickened by the bloodbath of July 4, which had claimed the lives of neutralists and Condé's own supporters, as well as avowed Mazarinists. Some of his long-time supporters in the Parlement of Paris broke from his party in disgust.[65] Both Condé and Mazarin realized that the Parisians' will for peace could not be held back now. While the prince lingered in the capital, not knowing what to do, Mazarin used all his diplomatic skills to bring Paris into the royalist camp. Wavering merchants were brought into line through well-organized demonstrations by Mazarinist judges and bourgeois, led by the parlementarian Le Prévôt.[66] The sovereign courts of Paris were placed on the defensive by the king's personal order for their transfer to Pontoise. Country estates of judges and other Parisians were either threatened with special taxes or razed by royalist forces. Perhaps the best indication of the Mazarinist offensive's seriousness was the decision to use selective withholding of payments on rentes and *gages* as a weapon against wavering Parisians. Conciliar *arrêts* ordered the royal payers of these funds to move from Paris to the royal residence outside, thereby making it possible to pay only those rentiers and sovereign court judges who deserted the Parisian cause and joined the royal entourage.[67]

Despite these awesome pressures and Mazarin's efforts to turn the rest of France against the capital's opposition to an unconditional restoration, the revival of the royalist-Mazarinist fortunes was painfully slow. The way in which many subjects held out despite the universal anarchy goes far in explaining why the collapse of the Parisian Fronde in October gave the monarchy such a limited victory.

---

against Mazarin. The fact that such proposals could be brought to a vote indicates that the Parlement was by no means totally Condéan in composition at this time. See B. U. P. Ms. 69, fols. 150-178.

[65] For the reaction, see ibid., fols. 120, 188-189; Conrart, *Mémoires*, pp. 575, 580; Vallier, *Journal* III, 325-326; Montglat, *Mémoires*, p. 271; *Extrait du livre des choses mémorables de l'Abbaye de Saint Denis* (in *Registres de l'Hôtel de Ville* III), p. 421.

[66] Chéruel, *Ministère de Mazarin* I, 318-322, is an excellent account, but his implication that the Parisian bourgeoisie was enthusiastically royalist is a distortion of the facts. About fifty bourgeois appealed to Orléans against the Mazarinist demonstrators. B. N. Ms. Fr. 25026, fols. 154-156.

[67] See Actes Royaux, F 23631, nos. 571, 574, 578, 580.

The difficulties lying in the path of a complete royalist restoration were most clearly demonstrated by the stands of the provincial parlements, which were generally ambivalent, even though their avowed anti-Mazarinist members had to endure royalist plundering on their country estates, and despite unequivocal royal orders not to side with the Parlement of Paris.[68] For example, the Parlement of Toulouse hedged by making startling concessions and at the same time clinging to its anti-Mazarinist position. The lure of bribes to key members, a barrage of commands from the royal administration, and the use of their region as a major battleground for the rival military forces were powerful incentives for capitulation. Consequently, the Parlement of Toulouse broke sharply with Governor Orléans and the Parlement of Paris, to which it had made so many futile appeals during the Fronde. The Parisian judges' decision to make the duke a provisional lieutenant general was quashed in Toulouse, and all subjects were ordered to obey only the officials and commanders loyal to the king. Yet the Languedocian parlementarians persisted in remonstrating for Mazarin's removal! The bewildered parlementarians at Rouen were also conciliatory toward the administration, but more through evasion than a decisive vote of confidence in the royalist cause. For months, the Norman judges could not bring themselves to a vote on royal orders demanding a repudiation of the Parlement of Paris and the lieutenant general, Orléans. The only concession those northern officials would make was to obey royal orders not to communicate with their sister court in the capital. To the west, the Parlement of Rennes patched up its quarrel with La Meilleraye. Conveniently overlooking the Parisian judges' earlier assistance on that issue, the Breton court commanded subjects to resist Condéan armies and suspended its decrees against Mazarin. However, the suspension of opposition to the cardinal was a provisional one, binding the court only until the Condéans laid down *their* arms. The situation in Guienne cannot be considered typical since the city of Bordeaux was under a reign of terror led by pro-Condéan mobs of poor Bordelais. Nevertheless, the Parlement and inhabitants of Bordeaux did remain unalterably opposed to any concessions.[69]

In Paris, the various public authorities and social groups were lean-

<hr />

[68] B. N. Ms. Fr. 25026, fol. 120 (circular royal letter to the sovereign courts); ibid., and Ms. 17560 (scattered references to royalist devastation of judges' estates).

[69] See B. N. Ms. Fr. 25026, especially fols. 78r, 94v, 120, 124v, 127r, 134r, 136r, 154v.

ing toward unconditional capitulation. However, there was resentment against the massive pressures from the administration, a fact
overlooked by historians eager to anticipate the fervent royalism of
Louis XIV's personal reign after 1661. To be sure, many Parisian
merchants continued to demonstrate for the king's unconditional
return, and the six major guilds were prominent in delegations to
the royal entourage; but they did not voice enthusiasm for the Mazarinist regime. Their royalism was one of desperation, bred of the
need to accept the lesser of evils, and even this did not stop the *petits*
and *bons bourgeois* from resisting royal taxation after the Fronde.
The bourgeoisie had lost all faith in the Parlement of Paris as mediator, and immediately after the royal return to Paris they opposed plenary sessions of that court out of fear of another Fronde.[70] Yet they
could still take advantage of parlementary agitations after 1652.
Actually, the Grand Conseil was far more royalist than merchant
groups. As in 1649, that least obstinate of all French courts tried to
comply with royal orders to leave Paris. Some members slipped out
of the capital despite the watchfulness of anti-Mazarinist guards,
while those who could not escape suspended the functions of their
tribunal to show their loyalty to the king. The Cour des Aides, on
the other hand, made no effort to comply with similar royal orders.
Whether its members were intimidated by Condéan mobs or, more
likely, simply wary of making any agreement with Mazarin, they
delayed making any definite response as long as they could. Then,
after royal decrees solemnly accused them of criminal action against
the state, they suspended their functions—an act similar to that of the
Grand Conseil, but done much later and with the objective of avoiding royal punishment rather than aiding the royalist cause. The
Chambre des Comptes assumed a posture that attempted to avoid the
obsequiousness of the Grand Conseil and the culpability of the Cour
des Aides. On receiving orders to leave Paris, its members notified
the king that they would leave the capital if the administration considered it absolutely necessary, and then when commanded to obey
the orders of transfer, suspended their court's functions.[71] The his-

---

[70] B. U. P. Ms. 70, fol. 209.

[71] See, inter alia, Talon, *Mémoires*, p. 510; B. N. Ms. Fr. 25026, fols. 138-144;
Boislisle, *Chambre des Comptes*, pp. 452-458. Le Tellier's correspondence with Mazarin proves that the Chambre des Comptes' stalling tactics were embarrassing for the
royalist regime. B. N. Ms. 4212, fol. 12r.

torical image of an enthusiastically royalist Paris is further contradicted by the attitude of those maîtres des requêtes who had been left in the capital throughout the civil war and then were commanded to join the royal entourage during the last months of the Fronde. Some complied; some refused.[72] For a group of officials who had been generally royalist and, in some cases, had even acted as new intendants after their brief feud with the administration in 1648, this was astonishing.

The tempered opposition or, at best, reluctant royalism, of Parisians and provincials was one factor working against Mazarin's plan for a triumphant return to Paris. But it was the Parlement of Paris which frustrated the chief minister's plan most of all. For a corporation which had become more and more isolated from other groups in the realm, this was a remarkable demonstration of strength. The rump Parlement of July-October 1652 managed to stave off attacks from Condéan mobs, pressures from Condé and Orléans to shun negotiations with the queen mother, and royalist demands for unconditional surrender. The parlementarians knew that they were negotiating from weakness, but they were equally aware of hidden strengths. Despite the Parlement's precipitous decline in power, it maintained a measure of prestige. Even the judges' illegal election of Orléans as provisional lieutenant general could not overshadow their record of persistent legalism during most of the Fronde.[73] And, finally, the widespread hostility of subjects to both Condé and Mazarin worked to their benefit. Hence the Parlement's mere advocacy of a compromise settlement tipped the balance scales toward that solution.

Although Mazarin had been desperately trying to avoid a second exile, he gradually yielded to pressures from the Palace of Justice. In June, the regent had informed the Parlement of Paris that the chief minister would withdraw from the realm if the Condéan rebels stopped fighting.[74] But since the judges would not alter their demand for an unconditional exile, Mazarin tried to undermine their prestige

---

[72] B. N. Ms. Fr. 25026, especially fols. 12r, 22r.

[73] Barely a week before the formal conclusion of the Parisian Fronde, Anne's ministers were concerned with a threatened appeal to the Parlement by disgruntled Mazarinist governors of border fortresses. B. N. Ms. Fr. 6891, fol. 184.

[74] Talon, *Mémoires*, pp. 486-488.

by establishing an anti-Parlement at Pontoise in August. Although that rival court had only approximately twenty-five members, they represented some of the most prestigious members of the Parlement of Paris who had fled from the capital to the royal residence in previous weeks. Molé acted as first president of the Parlement of Pontoise, while retaining his governmental post as keeper of the seals. He was joined by three *présidents à mortier*, several parlementary councilors, and a few maîtres des requêtes.[75] But not even the brilliance of its membership could make the anti-Parlement a viable alternative to the main Parlement of Paris. Moreover, the tactics Mazarin and his agents had used to lure the small group of parlementarians to Pontoise turned against the chief minister. He had promised to let the Parlement of Pontoise order him out of the realm, on the understanding that he could return as soon as his absence brought internal peace. To his regret, the supposedly Mazarinist judges at Pontoise kept Mazarin to his word, the movement to carry out the banishment being headed by the staunchly Mazarinist judge, President de Novion, and supported by First President Molé who threatened to resign unless the chief minister yielded.[76] With assistance from Anne's ministers, the Parlement of Pontoise drafted a mild remonstrance for Mazarin's banishment, and the cardinal set out for the German border on August 19—after also receiving a royal command which read more like a eulogy than a criminal indictment.[77]

Mazarin's departure from the realm opened the way for serious negotiations to end the civil war. No one could justify continued military resistance, even if many subjects suspected that the second exile of the chief minister was a temporary concession by Anne, designed to undercut the rationale of the rebellion. By indicating their willingness to reach an accord with the administration, the parlementarians and other authorities at the capital ended the nobles' last hope of victory. Condé, Orléans, and Gondi-Retz all tried to make private agreements with Mazarin, but only the king's uncle succeeded in obtaining an honorable settlement—at the urging of Le Tellier, Mazarin agreed to let the duke go into exile at Blois with-

[75] The register of the Parlement of Pontoise is in B. N. Ms. Fr. 21307.
[76] See especially B. N. Ms. Fr. 25026, fols. 112, 120r, 132v. Mazarin, *Lettres* v, 159 (including fn. 4), 169, 171, reveals only the original agreement.
[77] Chéruel, *Ministère de Mazarin* I, 245-249.

out further punishment.[78] Condé fled from Paris and continued his rebellion, first as leader of the parlementary-noble coalition in Guienne until its collapse in 1653, and then as a general in the Spanish armies. Although the *Grand* Condé did not come to terms until a Franco-Spanish peace was arranged in 1659, his opposition after the Fronde did not affect France's internal affairs. From 1654 to 1659, he was viewed by Frenchmen as a traitor, not a rebel. Gondi-Retz's fate was worse. His failure to erect a neutralist third party, followed by Mazarin's refusal to ally with him against Condé during the last days of the Parisian Fronde, led to his imprisonment at the end of the year.

By comparison with *les grands*, the parlementarians and inhabitants at Paris were very successful in their maneuvering with Anne's regime. It is true that the Parlement could not model the peace of 1652 on the Treaty of Rueil, since general war weariness made the situation different from that at the end of the siege of Paris. On the other hand, Anne's ministers wanted the royal restoration to the capital to be peaceful; their aims were to avoid savage repression which would antagonize Parisians for years to come, and to make the reentry of the royal family look like a popular act.[79] Unfortunately, the outward appearance of a peaceful royal restoration has obscured the underlying subtleties of the parlementarians' achievements before the actual return of the royal family. Thus, while scholars have noted the royalists' success in inducing various Parisian groups to beg the king to return without condition, they have overlooked the more important fact that at the same time the Parlement of Paris was laying the foundation of a compromise settlement by refusing to admit that it was a rebel body, punishable for crimes against the state. In its battle to preserve its integrity, that parlement placed enormous pressure on its members at Pontoise to return to the capital before the royal reentry. Although Anne's ministers assisted the judges at Pontoise during the battle of *arrêts* and counter-*arrêts* between Paris and Pontoise in September and October, they failed to

[78] Dethan, *Gaston d'Orléans*, p. 414. The full story of Mazarin's negotiations with Condé and Gondi-Retz has not been told. See the Mazarinist and anti-Mazarinist versions in Chéruel, *Minorité de Louis XIV* I, 166-168, 283ff.; Kossman, *La Fronde*, p. 235; and two collections of letters between Le Tellier and Mazarin, B. N. Mss. Fr. 4212, 6891.

[79] Chéruel, *Ministère de Mazarin* I, reveals the strategy. See especially Servien to Mazarin, Sept. 24, ibid., pp. 313-315.

increase the size of the tribunal at Pontoise;[80] on the contrary, the Parisian judges were so successful in their legalistic attacks on their departed colleagues that at least two judges slipped back into the capital rather than risk the wrath of their colleagues in the future, and royal guards had to be placed around Pontoise to prevent others from defecting.[81]

The queen mother's only major victory over the Parisian judges before returning was her refusal to recognize the existence of the Parlement of Paris as a legal body. Parlementary delegations were turned away when they went to the royal residence to negotiate a settlement, and Anne demanded that the city be represented by the old Mazarinist civic government. Beaufort reluctantly resigned as governor of Paris. Pierre Broussel yielded more graciously in handing over his illegal position as *prévôt des marchands* to the Mazarinist official who had been ousted after the Condéan *coup d'état* of July. The venerable judge knew his duty; if peace could be obtained by his removal, he would not stand in the way.[82] It was a selfless act by a man who had fought consistently during the Fronde against administrative evils. Once the civic government had been restored to legal authorities, it requested the king's return, and a grand entry of the royal family was quickly arranged. On October 21, they arrived in Paris without Mazarin, who remained at a comfortable distance. The following day, the parlements of Paris and Pontoise were united in a *lit de justice* at the Louvre.[83] But even to the end, the Fronde in Paris was preeminently a legalistic maneuvering: while giving the appearance that the royalist restoration was totally devoid of coercion, the final act of the administration was the recognition of the legal existence of the Parlement of Paris.

The *lit de justice* of October 22, 1652, has been described by historians as a crushing defeat for the Parlement of Paris, and a decisive

---

[80] The actions of the Parlement of Pontoise can be followed in B. N. Ms. Fr. 21307, while the *arrêts* by the Parlement of Paris are in Actes Royaux, F 23669. Even agents of Mazarin acknowledged the success of the Parisian judges. See Chéruel, *Ministère de Mazarin* I, 243.

[81] B. N. Ms. Fr. 25026, especially fols. 134v, 138r. See also Ms. Fr. 4212. Many judges had simply fled from Paris to their country estates and refused either to return to the terror-ridden capital or to obey royal commands to go to Pontoise.

[82] B. N. Ms. Fr. 25026, fols. 154-156.

[83] On the ceremony, see *Relation contenant la suite et conclusion du journal de tout ce qui s'est passé au Parlement*, Paris, 1653, pp. 235-251.

factor in the collapse of the Fronde.[84] Compared with the royal declaration concluding the parlementary Fronde four years, to the day, earlier, this was true. But though the Parlement failed to win a clear-cut victory at the end of the Fronde, it did prevent the royal administration from emerging with the sweeping triumph that Anne and Mazarin wanted. The major concession by the judges at the *lit de justice* was their registration of a declaration forbidding all parlementary interference with so-called state affairs. As a royal propagandistic gesture, this was an important act; but in relation to the actual structure of the French government, which retained its confusion of powers and allowed the parlementarians to counter royal absolutism without breaking with it, the declaration had a hollow ring. Far more significant was the psychological defeat of the parlementarians and the other anti-Mazarinist elements of the state. They could, and would continue to, interfere with state affairs, since they were representatives of the king and their tribunal was an important element of the Crown; but they would not dare risk a major confrontation for some time, having learned from the chaos and near-disaster for France and themselves.

The second concession won by the royalists was the agreement that no judge could enter the service of a nobleman or join a noble party. This was a symbolic act rather than a legal change: everyone already knew that the parlementarians had suffered from their association with the noble Frondes and did not intend to court such a disaster again. Actually the true strength of the Fronde had never been the close association of nobles and judges or a broader union with diverse groups of officers and classes. Its strength had derived from the opposition of corporations, social groups, and provinces to royal oppression, all reacting at roughly the same time, though in their own way. The royal enforcement of the separation of judges and nobles was, in a sense, a blessing for the parlementarians. They lost an uncertain ally and they regained their independence. This fact was recognized even by *les grands*. Unable to write the judges' *arrêts*

---

[84] Doolin, *The Fronde*, p. 56, states that the Parlement lost "much of what had been gained in 1648-1649." Shennan, *The Parlement of Paris*, p. 275, is more emphatic, declaring that "the Parlement's antagonism toward Mazarin and its record of opposition to the government condemned it in the king's eyes and caused him to deprive it of all the hard-won gains of 1648 and 1649." It should be noted that those two scholars are more favorable to the parlementary Fronde than any other recent historian.

despite their virtual dictatorship over Paris, the Condéans had left the capital before the end of the Parisian Fronde. The *Grand* Condé was particularly disillusioned by his attempts to control the Palace of Justice. The formation of a rebel administration composed of nobles and judges had been the most humiliating act of Condé's life. His position was stated bluntly by one of his supporters, who wrote to a friend: "See how the civil wars have reduced the position of the princes of the blood, and how miserable they are to be compelled to act deferentially toward men who are infinitely beneath their rank."[85]

The banishment of a few unrepentant parlementarians was probably more significant than this legal separation of judges and nobles. The men whose exile was announced at the time of the *lit de justice* (Broussel, Viole, Coulon, de Thou, Bitaut, and other radicals) were precisely those persons who had led their tribunal against the administration throughout the Fronde, and their departure left a vacuum which could not be filled. Yet the significance of that purge should not be exaggerated. Not only was the number of exiled judges much smaller than Anne's regime had desired, but the very fact that her ministers had originally envisaged a rather extensive change in the composition of the Parlement indicates their awareness that it would take more than a few exilings to subdue the tribunal. Indeed, the radicals had never dominated the Parlement on their own. Parlementary decisions on many ocasions during the Fronde had been the result of compromises between conservatives and radicals. When the radicals had managed to gain a majority for their proposals, it was largely due to external factors which made more moderate members willing to side with them. While it is true that the disappearance of leading radicals shifted the balance within the Parlement toward conservatism, the court as a whole—including some Mazarinist judges who had temporarily defected to Pontoise—did not lose its will to resist the administration. Actually, and perhaps just as significant, was the less-heralded loss of some of the leading conservatives during the last months of the Fronde. Omer Talon and Henri de Mesmes had died, and Molé was soon to relinquish his office of first president to give full service to the administration as keeper of the seals. Other men were taking the place of these eminent conservatives, just as new radicals tried to assume the role of men like Brou-

[85] Marigny to Lenet, Aug. 4, 1652, quoted in Aumale, *Histoire des princes de Condé* VI, 544.

sel—but in both cases, the new men lacked the sheer genius of their fallen colleagues. The Parlement would continue to balance conservative and radical interests after the Fronde, but its new leaders could not play the game on the same grand scale.

Significantly, nothing was done at the *lit de justice* of October 22, 1652, to undo the reforms enacted four years earlier. That omission, more than any pronouncement at the ceremony, indicated the limitations of the royalist victory over the Fronde.[86] The constant legalism of the Parlement throughout the Fronde had prevented Anne, Mazarin, Séguier, and other ministers from destroying the prestige of the court, and it could still fight a defensive campaign to hold on to those reforms which had been preserved from 1648 to 1652. It was also obvious that other corporations and many social groups within Paris and throughout the provinces were neither enthusiastic royalists nor potential traitors of the cause of reform. It is true that Mazarin was able to return from exile and enter Paris without incident in February 1653. The Fronde in Bordeaux was also crushed later that year, leaving the nobles militarily defeated and thoroughly discredited as rebels. Yet, while few Frenchmen wanted another Fronde and no one had the resources to revive it, there would be sullen resistance to arbitrary taxation, executive justice, and the new intendants in the years to come. And, despite widespread disenchantment with the anarchic results of the original parlementary Fronde, the financial courts in Paris, provincial parlements, and various social groups could still take advantage of any new disagreements between the chief Parlement and the administration. This was the strange and ambiguous legacy of a series of revolts which had ended in a royalist revival, without giving the royal administration the sweeping victory so often described by historians.

---

[86] The mild restrictions imposed by the *lit de justice* on the Parlement of Paris contrast sharply with the harsh, comprehensive demands outlined in the letters of Secretary of State Le Tellier and *Intendant des Finances* d'Aligre during preceding weeks. One by one, those crippling limitations were set aside by the realistic ministers, who candidly admitted the impossibility of securing peace on any other terms. See B. N. Mss. Fr. 4212 and 6891.

EPILOGUE

AFTER THE FRONDE

THE AMBIGUOUSNESS of the legacy of the Fronde became readily apparent during the last decade of Mazarin's ministry, and continued to cast its shadow over the personal reign of Louis XIV after 1661. On the one hand, Mazarin had an excellent opportunity to resume the centralizing work of Louis XIII and Richelieu in 1653, and not even the continuation of war with Spain, until 1659, prevented the king's administration from pursuing some of the goals of the earlier governmental revolution. On the other hand, the stubborn resistance of so many corporations of officers and social groups could not be abruptly swept aside after a decade of relatively successful agitations on behalf of state reform. Also, behind the reform movement still lay the entrenched corporative society and confusion of governmental powers which had made the Fronde possible. The royal administration could enhance its authority and power, but only by superimposing centralization on all disparate groups. The ambiguity of this legacy makes the strengths and weaknesses of the Age of Louis XIV far more intelligible than the historical truism that the Sun King capped a pathetic, chaotic, and hopeless Fronde with a royal triumph. For the personal reign of the greatest Bourbon ruler did not eliminate the underlying confusion of powers, despite the fact that intendants, councils, and ministers were placed more firmly over the holders of permanent, purchasable offices. During his reign, an impersonal bureaucracy began, in practice, to give orders to subjects just as if they were coming from the king himself and invoking his so-called "personal will"; yet that reign failed to provide a comprehensive theory capable of destroying the ideological basis of the permanent officials' evading of those same commands of the monarch and his bureaucrats. Arbitrary imprisonment and the tactic of dividing and ruling were all employed to keep the officers in their place; but their place still assured them of the role of legalistic opposition, buttressed as it was by *vénalité*, an *esprit de corps* within each corporation, and deeply rooted social privilege. Their obstructionism was subdued; it was not eradicated. The absolutism of Louis XIV was in many respects a façade.

The restoration of intendancies throughout France after the hap-
hazard and often ill-fated adventures of individual intendants
between 1649 and 1652 illustrates the nature of the continuing royalist revival. Wary of blatantly casting aside the royal declarations of
1648, which had abolished that special type of commission, the central administration proceeded cautiously. In 1653, intendants spread
out to one province after another, but not as the intendant-administrators of the 1630's and 1640's. They were officially described merely
as maîtres des requêtes commissioned to oversee the activities of local
officials (thereby bypassing the laws against intendancies, which
were never revoked under Louis XIV or even during the eighteenth
century). A twenty-five-year period of experimentation, after 1653,
indicated the king's advisers' uncertainty about the role these watchdogs of the state should play within the government. In 1658, the
number of intendant-commissioners was sharply reduced by dou-
bling the territory under each, which made the intendant even less of
an administrator, and more of a general supervisor. By 1665, their
powers were strengthened, combining the characteristics of both the
intendant-administrators of old and the supervising commissioners
of 1653 and 1658. Finally, in 1679, the territory of each intendant
was again substantially decreased, permitting him to function effectively as an administrator. The development of subdélégués under
intendants and the addition of a staff of petty bureaucracy con-
summated the development of the central administration's local
agencies.[1]

The evolution of the intendant-administrator was complemented
by a gradual extension of the authority previously held by royal
councils and auxiliary bodies over sovereign courts. In 1661, a conciliar decree legalized this often asserted superiority. Henceforth,
parlements, chambres des comptes, cours des aides, and the Grand
Conseil were asked to defer to conciliar decisions just as they would
if the king's personal will were in question.[2] Judicial review by the
sovereign courts was restricted by the more formal device of royal
declarations issued in 1667 and 1673. No modification or rejection of

[1] On the restoration and evolution of the intendants after the Fronde, see especially
Esmonin's articles, "Les intendants du Dauphiné," and "Origine des intendants," in
his Etudes.

[2] Isambert, Anciennes lois françaises XVII, 403-406; Colbert, Lettres VI, 487.

legislation was permitted, and remonstrances were to follow rather than precede registration.[3]

The imposition of these broad controls over the law courts and taxing bureaus was by far the most successful aspect of the continuing royalist revival after the Fronde, but even so the general centralizing tendency developed only very gradually. In fact, there were few comprehensive attempts to control the officiers until Mazarin's death a decade after the Fronde. The real architect of royal centralization, Jean-Baptiste Colbert, was constantly hampered between 1653 and 1661 by the cardinal-minister himself, who simply did not possess the will or interest to undertake any basic overhauling of the governmental structure. This kind of post-Fronde inertia of the monarchy was added to by the promotion of parlementary *procureur général* Nicolas Fouquet to finance minister. Fouquet was another d'Emery, living from expedient to expedient until his fall from power after Mazarin's death.[4] So the Mazarinist regime of 1653-1661 made only piecemeal attacks on specific aspects of the reforms of 1648 and occasional Colbertian attempts to strike out against basic reform principles. Even more disconcerting than such inertia from within the central administration was the wave of opposition from outside. Whether Mazarin's fellow ministers were trying to strike down a particularly obnoxious restriction on royal taxation or groping toward more comprehensive solutions, they encountered hostility. The decade of 1652 to 1661 was, in reality, a miniature Fronde, involving strikes or threatened strikes by judges, lawyers, merchants, rentiers, and peasants.[5]

The first indication that reformism had not died with the collapse of the Fronde came at the end of 1652. The king used a *lit de justice* at the Parlement of Paris to reimpose many of d'Emery's outlawed expedients, including tariffs and fees on alienated domains. At the

[3] Cf. Glasson, *Le Parlement de Paris* I, 413-414.

[4] See J. Dent, "An Aspect of the Crisis of the Seventeenth Century: The Collapse of the Financial Administration of the French Monarchy (1653-1661)," *Economic History Review*, 2nd ser., xx (1967), 241-256. For a different interpretation of Fouquet (and Colbert), see L. Rothkrug, *Opposition to Louis XIV. The Political and Social Origins of the French Enlightenment*, Princeton, 1965, especially pp. 193ff.

[5] There is an excellent account of the 1650's in Chéruel, *Histoire de l'administration monarchique* II, pp. 28ff. Chéruel was also convinced that the opposition in that decade constituted a near-Fronde.

Parisian Chambre des Comptes, a similar ceremony was enacted, with the king's brother formally overruling that high court's restrictions on the use of *comptants*.[6] These attacks on the reforms of the Fronde set in motion a series of counterattacks. Parisians, from wealthy rentiers to mere butchers, demonstrated. The sovereign courts not only assailed the forced registration of financial legislation, but coupled their defense of reform with agitation for the return of their colleagues who had been exiled at the end of the Parisian Fronde in October.[7] The six merchant guilds were placated somewhat by major reductions in the new taxes and the preservation of their commercial monopolies. But even when the king's ministers managed to satisfy the *bons bourgeois*, artisans and laborers raised their own objections, arguing vociferously that the reduced taxes on meat and wood were still too much to bear after the economic hardships of the Fronde. The embattled administration was forced to abolish some new taxes altogether.[8] Rentiers who objected to the suspension of interest payments were slightly mollified by a similar compromise. Nevertheless, Chancellor Séguier sensed further trouble and persuaded Mazarin to forbid all intervention on behalf of the rentiers by the Parlement and civic government of Paris. When the parlementarians issued a decree authorizing a meeting of the syndicate of rentiers' representatives, additional royalist controls were imposed. The parlementary first president dutifully avoided a plenary session, and the *bons bourgeois* were ordered not to assemble under any circumstances. Eventually, the rentiers became reconciled with partial satisfaction of their grievances, bringing the immediate dispute to an end.[9]

The sovereign courts were far from subdued, however. Between 1654 and 1656, all four sovereign courts in Paris, including the usually docile Grand Conseil, persisted in blocking royal legislation. In the provinces, the Parlement at Toulouse took a similar stand. By July 13, 1654, Colbert was almost beside himself, and foot-dragging by

[6] *Relation contenant la suitte et conclusion du journal*, pp. 1-2; Boislisle, *Chambre des Comptes*, pp. 465-467.

[7] Boislisle, *Chambre des Comptes*, p. 466, fn. 1, 472-473; A. N. U 30, fol. 210ff.; B. N. Ms. Fr. 25026, fols. 180v, 188.

[8] B. N. Ms. Fr. 25026, fols. 206v, 208r, 210r; Ms. Fr. 17560, fols. 363-366; Ms. Fr. 10276, pp. 7-9; Rothkrug, *Opposition to Louis XIV*, pp. 184-186.

[9] B. N. Ms. Fr. 25026, fols. 184v, 196v, 238; Ms. Fr. 17560, fols. 325-326 (letter from Séguier to Mazarin), 367-370.

the Chambre des Comptes in Paris brought forth his particularly revealing comment to Mazarin: "The sovereign [courts] are acting in an insufferable manner. I think that M. de Plessis will send a [*lettre de*] *jussion* promptly. We will surely have the same refusal at the cour des aides, since these [courts] follow each other's lead."[10] The following month, it was the Parlement's turn to anger Colbert by its employment of judicial review.[11] By March 1655, the situation had become so critical that the king was compelled to register fourteen fiscal edicts at a parlementary *lit de justice* and send his brother to similar ceremonies at the Chambre des Comptes and Cour des Aides. The Parlement was unmoved by this expression of the king's personal will; after the ceremony its members began to reexamine the legislation. The other courts were equally opposed to the edicts, and the first president of the Chambre des Comptes said so in the presence of the king's brother.[12]

The situation was similar to the *lit de justice* of January 15, 1648, which had led to the Fronde. This time, on April 13, 1655, Louis XIV took personal charge, entering the Parlement unannounced and without formal dress. It was one of the few occasions when the Sun King could not hide his emotions. "He showed only too clearly on his face the exasperation which lay in his heart," wrote an eyewitness. And he declared:

Everyone knows how much your assemblies have incited troubles in my State, and how many dangerous effects they have produced. I have learned that you presume to continue them again under the pretext of deliberating on the edicts which not long ago were read and published in my presence. I have come here expressly to forbid (pointing to *messieurs des enquêtes*) the continuation [of debate], and [to forbid] you, M. first president (pointing also to him), to allow or agree to it, whatever requests the *enquêtes* judges may make.[13]

This most famous incident of Louis XIV's life (when he allegedly said "*L'Etat, c'est moi*") was a spectacular display of royal will, but

---

[10] Quoted in Chéruel, *Histoire de l'administration monarchique* II, 28-29.

[11] Ibid. II, 29.

[12] The entire affair is recounted in detail by ibid. II, 30ff., which is based on B. N. Ms. Fr. 10276, pp. 311ff. There is another reliable contemporary account in B. N. Ms. Fr. 5844, fols. 422ff.

[13] B. N. Ms. Fr. 10276, pp. 326-327.

it had a peculiar ending. The parlementarians remained bitter and ordered their first president to protest to the king and Mazarin. The first president's speech left no doubt that the entire parlement was shocked at the king's behavior, "so very far removed from that of his predecessors." Without thinking of the consequences, Mazarin replied by "explaining" that Louis XIV was simply talking like a father and would welcome remonstrances on the edicts after a face-saving delay of time. Mazarin's fellow ministers were upset by this implicit capitulation, and ordered the hapless cardinal to reverse his stand. They knew all too well that the legalistically inclined judges would interpret his disarming words as a promise to back down. So in a conference with the *présidents à mortier*, Mazarin abruptly changed his tone, indicating that the Parlement must postpone any consideration of the contentious edicts. The high court decided not to risk a showdown, and the edicts remained in force.[14]

The bizarre events after the *lit de justice* of 1655 were followed, the following year, by another major confrontation between administrators and parlementarians. Echoing the reforms of 1648, a parlementary *arrêt* recapitulated the sixteenth-century restrictions on conciliar interference with the judiciary. To enforce their decision, the parlementarians decided to interrogate all maîtres des requêtes who were responsible for illegal conciliar actions. Some judges wished to go further, suggesting that the chancellor could be summoned for questioning. The threat was ominous, since it coincided with parlementary opposition to new fiscal measures and negotiations over the renewal of the paulette. Mazarin was shaken by the crisis, the maîtres des requêtes were furious, and the royal entourage was in an uproar. Colbert was less decisive than usual, being hesitant to bargain over the paulette, because he suspected that this would not subdue the judges. The details of the final settlement remain obscure, but its main outlines were clearly a compromise. The first president refused to have the objectionable decree withdrawn, arguing that it conformed to past royal ordinances. When he insisted that he could not resist the entire Parlement on this issue, the king's ministers gave in

[14] Ibid., pp. 327-331. Chéruel, *Histoire de l'administration monarchique* II, 37-38, in characteristic fashion, quoted the manuscript account, complete with the evidence of Mazarin's ineptitude, and then concluded that Mazarin vanquished the opposition of the Parlement. It is an incredible example of that historian's combination of impeccable scholarship and *parti pris*.

graciously. A royal declaration confirmed the restrictions on conciliar actions, although the councils continued to evade the law in succeeding years.[15]

Since the post-Fronde monarchy could not be sure of breaking down a sovereign court's collective resistance by direct methods, the old Mazarinist tactic of bribing and arbitrarily detaining individual judges was continued after 1652, but the results were far from pleasing to Mazarin and his colleagues, especially when they tested their indirect control over the Parlement of Paris. First President Molé's usefulness to the royalist side had been impaired by his appointment as keeper of the seals; his fellow judges suspected that his recommendations were made as a royal minister, not as head of the Parlement, and when that suspicion was confirmed by his obsequiousness to the unwavering royalist Chancellor Séguier in 1653, Molé became so disliked in the Parlement that he resigned his post of first president.[16] His successor, President Pompone de Bellièvre, was even less successful than Molé in bringing the Parlement in line with royal interests, although he certainly tried on several occasions to act on behalf of the administration. Sometimes the hapless first president tried to win the Parlement's confidence by evading royal directives, only to discover that Colbert distrusted him![17] Whenever the administration exiled recalcitrant parlementarians, relations with the high court deteriorated. Immediately after the *lit de jusitce* which marked the end of the Parisian Fronde in 1652, parlementarians protested against the banishment of their radical leaders. In order to prevent a threatened plenary session of the court, the administration decided to yield. One by one, the exiled judges were allowed to take their seats in the Parlement. But their restoration simply gave those inveterate radicals an opportunity to agitate against new administrative

[15] Colbert, *Lettres* I, 239, fn. I, 250-258, 250, fn. I; Chéruel, *Histoire de l'administration monarchique* II, 38-41, 41, fn. I (including correspondence between Colbert and Mazarin). There was also an intriguing "project" in 1653 for a *règlement* restricting the Parlement of Paris' activities and powers, to be found in Séguier's papers, B. N. Ms. Fr. 17560, fols. 321-323.

[16] On Molé's change of character, see Ormesson, *Journal* II, 676.

[17] See especially Colbert to Mazarin, July 19, 1656, quoted in Chéruel, *Histoire de l'administration monarchique* II, 38-39. The inner circle of royal administrators had originally preferred President de Novion's candidacy for the first presidency. B. N. Ms. Fr. 25026, fol. 208v. Perhaps de Bellièvre was chosen because he had not had as strong connections with Condé (who was still resisting the Crown with arms), and because of his experience as a diplomat in the French foreign service.

abuses, and the ministers were compelled to exile the judges a second time. The political atmosphere was highly explosive, since a few judges had resumed contacts with Condé, now fighting against the French monarchy as a general in the Spanish armies. Thinking that the Parlement might be trusted to punish them, the ministers decided to let the high court try them for treason. But the Parlement's deliberate slowness in prosecuting made it necessary to evoke the litigation to special conciliar commissions prepared to hand down sentences, which in turn opened up a chance for the Parlement to object vigorously against what it called arbitrary and illegal proceedings by a type of judicial body suppressed by the reforms of 1648. Eventually, Mazarin found ways to rid himself of certain radicals. He persuaded men like Machault-Fleury and Fouquet de Croissy to sell their parlementary offices and leave France; and the entire parlementary branch of the Potier family he had guarded closely, and constantly moved them from place to place. Even the parlementary presidents objected to such harassment, and the family became a symbol of royal tyranny. The Potiers were finally permitted a gentlemanly exile free of coercion.[18] So it became clear that this kind of solution was almost as unsatisfactory as harsh punishment. Such examples, between 1653 and 1661, show that the monarchy was more powerful than during the Fronde, but they do not exemplify unlimited royal power.

In general, it was the lesser courts and bureaus, rather than the sovereign tribunals, which bore the brunt of royalist attacks immediately after the Fronde. The *trésoriers de France* courted disaster by resisting the intendants' restoration in 1653, and by issuing an *ordonnance* aimed at preventing any wavering officials from being enticed or frightened into collaborating with the rival intendants. This provoked the irate ministers into centering their attention on the *trésoriers'* general syndicate. The chancellor temporarily suspended the syndics' functions, and ordered all officials to comply with royal orders, even if they conflicted with existing royal ordinances. The *trésoriers'* organs of protest were just as brusquely struck down; their syndicate in Paris was forbidden to assemble in the future, and *trésorier* complaints against the central administration were henceforth to be presented in the innocuous form of "very humble prayers and supplications" instead of the traditional remon-

[18] B. N. Ms. Fr. 25026, fols. 167ff.; Ms. Fr. 10276, fols. 9ff.

strances. Not all *trésoriers* were convinced that Séguier would enforce these restrictions, however, and they held secret assemblies in the apartment of *trésorier* Fournival. By 1657, both the *trésoriers de France* and the *élus* were bold enough to hold meetings in the open. The administration responded slowly but firmly. In 1661, a conciliar decree banned all representative assemblies of both groups of financial officials, and though the final version of the decree deleted reference to punishment in case of disobedience, its tone made clear that the ministers intended to be obeyed.[19]

After 1661, relations between the central administration and its officers were less troubled than during the last decade of Mazarin's ministry. The reasons for this outward calm have not been thoroughly examined. Until recently, it was thought that the paucity of remonstrances by the Parlement of Paris between 1661 and 1715 indicated the courts and bureaus of the realm were too weak to cause major trouble, and that Colbertian controls sufficed to stifle the faint opposition that officials dared to raise against councils and intendants.[20] But now a number of scholars are suggesting that the counting of remonstrances is not an accurate way to measure officials' opposition to Louis XIV's personal reign, since it overlooks their highly effective tactic of retreating to secondary and even tertiary defense and their equally successful substitution of the tactic of slowing down implementation of royal decisions in place of openly remonstrating against them.[21] In addition, it is clear from a perusal of even the most commonly consulted collections of published governmental documents that remonstrances and other types of more formal protest did not fall off as much as was formerly believed,

[19] Charmeil, *Les Trésoriers de France*, pp. 397-408; Esmonin, "Un Episode du rétablissement des intendants après la Fronde: Les Maîtres des requêtes envoyés en chevauchées," *Revue d'Histoire Moderne et Contemporaine* XII (1965), pp. 219-228. In 1653, the administration planned to abolish the *élus*' offices; those officials barely escaped total annihilation. Mousnier, "Recherches sur les syndicats d'officiers," p. 116. But the continuing and frequently successful opposition by local officials, nobles, and other persons can also be seen in Colbert, *Lettres* I, 360-363.

[20] Glasson, *Le Parlement de Paris* I, 408-413; Chéruel, *Histoire de l'administration monarchique* II, chaps. IV, V, VI, VII.

[21] See the author's essay, "Law and Justice under Louis XIV," in J. C. Rule, ed., *Louis XIV and the Craft of Kingship*, Columbus, Ohio, 1969, pp. 229-231. There is a well-balanced treatment of one particular corporation, J. J. Hurt, "The Parlement of Brittany and the Crown: 1665-1675," *French Historical Studies* IV (1966), pp. 411-433.

provincial parlements remaining obstinate to the point of modifying important edicts, and subordinate bureaus and courts being sometimes just as stubborn. In 1672, several *présidial* courts angered Chancellor Le Tellier by delaying punishment of known criminals, and as late as 1710, bureaus of *trésoriers* issued ordinances which countermanded royal decisions.[22]

This sullen resistance, unspectacular as it was, by Louis XIV's officiers helps to explain the outward calm of royal-official relations between 1661 and 1715. By permitting minor friction, the Sun King avoided a major confrontation. Had his ministers taken drastic measures to eradicate what remained of the officiers' independence after the Fronde, the repercussions would have been serious. To be sure, Colbert's codification of French legal procedure marked a step toward a radical attack on the law courts; but the judiciary frequently refused to apply the new procedures, and, significantly, the king often ignored this. Moreover, the new law codes left French law, itself, untouched: procedure was changed on paper, but the laws remained a hodgepodge. As Colbert realized, that allowed the judiciary to interpret the law. And, as he admitted with equal candor, the sovereign courts' excellent archives gave them a much better knowledge of legal precedents than the monarchy. Whenever courts and councils clashed, the judicial officials could back up their actions by quoting from past registers, while the king could do nothing more than argue from the principle of royal authority.[23] As long as such basic weaknesses bedeviled the monarchy, it was almost pointless for the king to proclaim that officials were not to interfere with state affairs. Separation of powers remained an ideal, and confusion of powers the practice, despite the pronouncements of the 1660's which placed the councils over the judiciary.

The confusion of powers might have been less of a problem had Louis XIV abolished *vénalité* and the paulette, but this proved as

[22] G. P. Depping, ed., *Correspondance administrative sous le règne de Louis XIV*, 4 vols., Paris, 1850-1855, II, passim, and especially pp. 13-17, 22-24, 25-26, 29-31, 172-173, 187-188, 213-214, 325-326, 343-345; Charmeil, *Les Trésoriers de France*, p. 178, fn. 123.

[23] On these points, see Colbert, *Lettres* I, 252; VI, 5, 20-21. In 1700, Chancellor Pontchartrain sent to the sovereign courts a circular requesting information which could lead to a new compilation of royal ordinances. He included a plea that the first presidents of the courts note what ordinances had been registered without changes, and what ones had been modified. Depping, *Correspondance administrative* II, 303-304.

impossible under Colbert as it had with Richelieu.[24] The reasons are legion, but one stands out above the others. The venal officials were too numerous, and their wealth too closely connected with the economic wellbeing of state and society to permit a ruthless suppression of the practice of selling offices. If threatened with the loss of their investment in offices, many officials would surely have resumed the tactics of the parlementary Fronde—despite their memory of its anarchical results. In any case, no monarch could be driven to such an extreme solution unless unduly provoked by the officers. By liquidating their investment the king would impoverish a large segment of French society and severely damage state credit. Officials were creditors of the state's financiers in many instances, and many outside persons were creditors of venal officials, having advanced the capital with which they purchased their governmental positions.[25] Moreover, royal subjects would surely view an attack on the wealth of the officials as proof of the monarchy's unwillingness to honor its commitments with other creditors. Perhaps the monarchy could have afforded a gradual abolition of *vénalité*, with compensation, but such a project would have taken years to accomplish, and while the transition was in process the financial structure of French society would have been thrown into disorder. Only the extraordinary crises, first in 1771 and then in the 1780's, eventually convinced the monarchy that *vénalité* must go regardless of the risks.

Since the corporate world of officiers remained, protected by *vénal-*

---

[24] For Richelieu's views on *vénalité*, see Mousnier, *Vénalité des offices*, pp. 604-621.

[25] Colbert's views can be found in succinct form in Colbert, *Lettres* VI, 11-12, 15-16, 247-249. Cf. Chancellor Pontchartrain's almost pathetic comment in 1713: "How can we stop the sale of offices since they are patrimonial and the principal wealth of families?" Depping, *Correspondance administrative* II, 366. See also the public defense of *vénalité* in the royal decrees renewing the paulette for both lesser and sovereign court officials in 1648. B. N. Actes Royaux, F 23611, nos. 882, 887. There is a marked difference in the tone of the apologies for *vénalité* made by Richelieu and Colbert. Richelieu lamented the corruption of the time which made *vénalité* a necessary evil. Colbert thought that the reformation of justice and the subordination of the judges would be greatly facilitated through the abolition of *vénalité*. But he was convinced that a strong king (like Louis XIV) could manage without such extreme action. He was also skeptical of the advisability of tampering with the paulette and *vénalité*, considering it a poor form of political blackmail that could stiffen the officers' resistance, at least in the case of the sovereign tribunals of the realm. It is possible that he realized the full implications of d'Emery's mishandling of the paulette crisis in 1648.

ité and confusion of powers, the administration had to find a formula for resolving differences between the strengthened conciliar agencies and the weakened courts and bureaus. Colbert established the guidelines, and they dominated the thinking of royal ministers throughout the remainder of Louis XIV's personal reign. The councils and intendants were to be backed up by all means, including military support, whenever the courts and bureaus openly defied royal policies. However, officiers also were to be authorized to execute royal policies, either on their own or in cooperation with royal agents such as the intendants. Colbert repeatedly urged the intendants to act through and with the normal official bodies. His letter to intendant Morant at Aix, in 1681, was typical in stating that Morant must act very cautiously even when explicitly instructed by the king to mete out justice to a criminal without bringing the sovereign courts into the litigation. While he should not let those tribunals exercise their appellate jurisdiction, he was advised to conduct the trial in a lower court at the *bailliage* or *sénéchaussée* level, if possible. Such a procedure was preferable to the intendant acting with judicial officials drawn from several petty tribunals, for the latter procedure would look too much like the extraordinary commissions abolished during the Fronde. The least desirable action was a judgment by the intendant and assistants holding legal degrees, but no judicial offices.[26] The spirit of Colbert's policy was followed closely by Chancellor Le Tellier, who revealed his moderation in an exchange of views with the *avocat général* of the Parlement of Bordeaux during 1685. Le Tellier wrote that the king would refrain from interfering with the parlements' "jurisprudence," especially when their decisions did not directly contravene royal ordinances or injure the "service of the king's subjects."[27] After the turn of the century, Chancellor Pontchartrain displayed the same restraint, despite trying circumstances. Indeed, that *fin de siècle* minister did little more than bemoan the judiciary's "excessive rights," dilatory prosecution of criminals, inexecution of royal ordinances, and general decadence.[28]

Certainly, local intendants frequently went beyond their instruc-

[26] Colbert, *Lettres* VI, 71-72.

[27] Depping, *Correspondance administrative* II, 252.

[28] Ibid. II, 325-326, 343-345, 357, 359-360. Pontchartrain frequently scolded intendants and other conciliar agents for enforcing new laws without prior registration by the regular courts. See especially ibid. II, 473-474 (Pontchartrain to La Bourdonnaye, intendant of Bordeaux, letter of Aug. 3, 1709).

366

tions, but the avowed royal policy was to work within the framework of existing institutions and practices. Not only was such a policy meant to satisfy and quiet the venal officials; it was clearly designed to avoid the growth of another echelon of independent governmental agents. Colbert wanted the intendants to be the state's watchdogs, not its masters.[29] Strangely enough, some intendants began to act independently of the central administration and sometimes became so attached to their community that they defended its interests against royal directives. For example, as early as the Colbertian period intendants had to be replaced because they sided with local rebellions.[30] According to intendant Foucault, Colbert was equally dissatisfied with the intendants' practice of using *subdélégués* extensively. For those subordinates had "abused the confidence" of the previous intendant, and exercised extremely bad judgment in forcing taxes on reluctant subjects.[31]

Thus the personal reign of Louis XIV continued the old royal-official struggles in an attenuated form, while one more troublesome echelon (the machinery and staff of the intendancies) was added to the French government. The distinct but limited royal advantages stemming from the collapse of the Fronde, combined with prudent and careful royal handling of the venal officials, carried the monarchy through the reign. Given the sociolegal framework of the time, the achievements of Louis XIV and Colbert were as much as could have been expected: a temporarily successful grappling with the ambiguity of the legacy of the Fronde.

The last chapter in the history of royal-official conflict remained to be written. The French Revolution, springing in part from similar bitter feuding in the eighteenth century, cannot be viewed as the end product of Louis XIV's failure to find a final solution to the problems confronting the realm. Indeed, final solutions are rarely determined by the acts of a single generation.

[29] See Pagès, "Essai sur l'évolution des institutions administratives," and that author's recapitulation in *La Monarchie d'ancien régime*.

[30] Colbert, *Lettres* I, 357-358.

[31] Chéruel, *Histoire de l'administration monarchique* II, 342.

CONCLUSION

BOTH GEOGRAPHICALLY and socially, the Fronde was the most widespread of all the rebellions in mid-seventeenth-century Europe. Logically, it should have resulted in some sort of revolution or political transformation far more fundamental than the republican achievements of the Long Parliament in England, the Catalan protest against Spanish centralization, or the peaceful change in Dutch leadership from centralizing Orangists to the republican regents of Holland. For it rallied to its side central provinces as well as outlying districts, in contrast to the Spanish experience; and, in contrast to the Dutch regent movement of officeholders and other well-to-do commoners, and to England's narrowly bourgeois-gentry rebellion, it gathered in all social groups. Also, initially, the sharp division between nobles and other social groups which doomed the protest movements in Denmark, Sweden, Poland, Russia, Brandenburg, and Spain's Italian possessions, did not exist. However, despite these factors, the Fronde was a revolution which misfired—"*une révolution manquée,*" as the title of Louis Madelin's book on that upheaval states. Indeed, the self-centeredness of the institutions and social groups within the corporative society of early seventeenth-century France should have spelled failure for the Fronde from the very beginning, and the degeneration of the parlementary Fronde into an anarchical noble Fronde should have resulted in a massive, postwar movement for unfettered monarchical authoritarianism. Yet the latter, too, failed to emerge from the chaotic events of the 1640's and early 1650's. Instead, as the epilogue of this book has attempted to demonstrate, the legacy bequeathed by the Fronde was an ambiguous one. Noble rebellion was thoroughly discredited, and royal authority increased (far more than in Spain or England, which came closest to experiencing the French anarchy), but the royal administration could not destroy the lingering power of the Parlement of Paris. Moreover, the postwar administrations of Mazarin and then Louis XIV and Colbert proceeded very slowly in attacking the reforms of 1648.

How does one evaluate a so-called revolution which failed and yet prevented the other side from winning a clear-cut victory? In a sense, as Ernst Kossman's admirable study has so convincingly shown, it is misleading even to call the Fronde either a "revolution" or a "revolution which misfired." From the very beginning, the opposition to the administration was too divided to seize power and too narrowly concerned with obstructing royal power to think of seizing and wielding it. Lacking direction, its actions were merely negative, against executive justice, oppressive taxation, the hated *traitants*, and the symbols of all these things—first d'Emery and then Mazarin. It lacked an institution similar to the central Parliament which initially united the English rebels behind a tangible alternative to monarchy. It did not even have the sense of purpose which English puritanism gave to many of the revolutionaries to the north. France had its Jansenism, but that Catholic counterpart of predestinarian Protestantism was pessimistic about changing society and almost otherworldly, as Lucien Goldmann has explained. Moreover, Jansenism never influenced more than a minority of nobles and parlementarians. Philip Knachel has shown that French subjects of varying backgrounds, including the noble Frondeurs, led by Gondi-Retz, and their pamphleteers, were horrified by English republicanism, and Ernst Kossman has stated that the Parlement of Paris was too committed to divine-right absolutism to challenge basic monarchical principles. One could also argue that the Fronde of the sociopolitical elite, who alone had any chance of assuming power, was simply a protest by "outs" versus "ins." Clearly, judges and nobles who are temporarily alienated but know that their destiny lies within the establishment make poor revolutionaries.

This is all true, but it does not account for the duration and tenacity of the opposition. European conditions were, to a degree, responsible for the original intensity of French protest movements. Yet Louis XIII's and Richelieu's questionable subordination of internal grievances to the external Hapsburg problem added to these ingredients of violent protest; and Mazarin's view that politics were to be used for bribing and dividing men, combined with his understandable but misplaced fears, made matters worse and helped turn the rebellions into another more violent phase. Without these decisions and miscalculations by the royal administration, the parlementary Fronde might not even have occurred, and it surely would not have resulted in civil war. The most crucial of all decisions was made at the beginning of 1648 when d'Emery was allowed to combine withholding of the paulette with a *lit de justice*. It was an almost fatal blunder, for it provoked the reluctant, divine-rightist Parlement of Paris into turning from piecemeal attacks on governmental abuses to a much more comprehensive assault on the administration. The parlementarians united temporarily with the other sovereign courts of Paris, and even with the maîtres des requêtes, over their common, selfish interest in officeholding. Thanks to the Parlement's prestige, its carefully constructed legalism, the alliance with other officers in Paris, and the tacit support by Parisians and provincial officials, the administration had to yield. Reforms comparable to those arising from the initial phase of the English Great Rebellion in the early 1640's were the result. In both countries, arbitrary detentions were curbed, taxes reduced, fiscal expedients subjected to institutional approval, and ministers overthrown. In France, there were other reforms. All but six intendants were withdrawn, extraordinary commissions were sharply curtailed, and the legal powers of the councils were restricted. Some of these French reforms were guaranteed on paper only, but so were several English reforms, initially. Moreover, in practice, several reforms in France went far beyond legal provisions, because chaotic conditions throughout the realm and confusion within royal circles enabled courts, bureaus, and social groups to make further changes with impunity.

If the administration of Anne and Mazarin stumbled into a crisis, the parlementarians in Paris played a significant and astute role in controlling events. Bad luck and mismanagement on the administration's part, the fact that a coalition against it came into being and asked for parlementary support, the inability of French troops to leave the Spanish campaign and crush the rebels, and the Parisian *émeute* of the Days of Barricades all helped the Palace of Justice. Nevertheless, as this study has emphasized, the most important factor was the parlementarians' legalistic *via media,* fostered both by compromises between radical and conservative judges and by sheer luck and corporate pride during crucial votes. Proclaiming belief in royal absolutism and yet using every legal power at their command, the parlementarians steered reforms past the administration while avoiding the self-defeating label of rebels. The parlementary Fronde was not entirely legal, but it certainly was legalistic. The judges managed not only to bring about reform, but to avoid a major civil war and blatantly illegal actions of the sort which allowed the English Parliament to be crushed between the extremes of Caroline absolutism and Cromwellian dictatorship. Without that ambivalent position of the Parlement, the reforms of 1648 would have been stillborn. It is true that even those reforms which the cautious judges dared support were negative in that they constituted attacks on royal power and policies. They were also far from being revolutionary, for they failed to make basic changes in government and society. For example, the reformers left basically untouched many built-in evils of contemporary France: the tax exemptions of privileged persons, the confusion of powers within the government, the treatment of public offices as private possessions, and the mutual suspicion between state and wealthy subjects which prevented fiscal cooperation and strong state credit. Sweeping changes in these areas would have destroyed the power of the parlementarians, other officiers, the *bons bourgeois*, and *les grands*; they were inconceivable in seventeenth-century France.

The task of the parlementarians after the siege of Paris was staggering, and their limited success in avoiding the twin evils of royal authoritarianism and noble rebellion goes far in explaining the royalist revival at the end of the Fronde. The judges' revolt gave *les grands* an opportunity to rebel on their own, and Mazarin's inept handling of the noble factions led directly to civil war. From the perspective of the Palace of Justice, noble rebellion and the related war with Spain were twin disasters. At best, these conflicts diverted the regent from her avowed aim of overturning the reforms of 1648. That windfall was of little solace to the parlementarians, however, when set side by side with the other effects of the noble Fronde on the officiers. The judges' antipathy to lawlessness and fear of the loss of their vaunted legalism prevented a united noble-parlementary Fronde. In addition, the realization that their own *gages*, rentes, and country estates were being jeopardized by civil war forced the parlementarians to modify their opposition to the administration. The chaos in the provinces, whose sovereign courts went their own individual ways, determined by local circumstances, also handicapped the Parisian judges. And, finally, the self-centered *esprit de corps* at the Palace of Justice contributed to the breakdown of the officiers' shaky coalition which, in 1648, had helped build up the cause of reform.

In the face of these overwhelming problems, the Parlement of Paris had difficulty preserving anything. To be sure, in 1649 and

1650, its members aided in keeping Paris relatively calm and in bringing an end to the first Condéan rebellion, without sacrificing the reforms of 1648 or parlementary legalism. But in 1651, the judges were swept along by the anti-Mazarinist contagion, unable to resist the pressure to "save" France by ousting Mazarin, and incapable of controlling the anti-Mazarinist coalition which tried to fill the power vacuum. The siege of Paris had set the stage for the first Condéan revolt; the banishment of Mazarin led to the anarchical second Condéan rebellion. Not only had the parlementarians failed to prevent a dreaded and self-defeating civil war; they were compelled to defy the personal will of Louis XIV when, after attaining his majority late in 1651, the king recalled Mazarin. Yet, although unable to preserve order, the judges staved off total defeat by clinging to the position that their opposition was legal. Hence they invoked the king's solemnly registered anti-Mazarinist declarations of the past to defend their own current anti-Mazarinist position against the king's personal wishes. They also continued to combat royal evasions of the reforms of 1648 as they had throughout the Fronde, again through legalistic means, although less enthusiastically and thoroughly than before. And, on the other hand, they refused to authorize the collection of royal taxes and raising of forces by the Condéans against Mazarin, until the massacre of July 4, 1652, gave Condé dictatorial control over Paris.

Even then, they salvaged something from that debacle. While Parisians and provincials inclined reluctantly toward accepting the restoration of royal power in revulsion against the attacks of *les grands*, the Parlement of Paris drew unexpected strength for its own cause from its past adherence to a *via media*. The royal administration, which had cautiously tried to evade the reforms of 1648 after the siege of Paris and then sought to placate the parlementarians on the issues of *gages*, rentes, and intendants during the first months of 1652, could not force an unconditional surrender on the parlementarians when the noble Fronde collapsed later that year. To be sure, the judges at the Palace of Justice could not have accomplished what they did alone. The stubborn, if limited, opposition to Mazarin by the Chambre des Comptes and Cour des Aides of Paris, and by many Parisians and provincial officers, provided help indirectly even though these groups were concerned with their own fate rather than the problems of the Parlement of Paris. Nevertheless, it can be argued that without the constant role of that tribunal as a moderate opponent of the central administration during the course of the Fronde, the other resisters of a royalist revival would never have had the determination to take a stand similar to the Parlement's in 1652. Moreover, during the last frightening months of the Fronde, the Parisian parlementarians helped protect their corporation and the reforms it supported by showing that they were willing to desert the nobles in order to obtain a compromise settlement. Both the Mazarinist judges at Pontoise and the anti-Mazarinist judges still in Paris forced the administration to make the one concession that could bring such a settlement, namely, a second, temporary banishment of the still universally hated Mazarin. Finally, the parlementarians at Paris won the legalistic battle of *arrêts* with their colleagues at Pontoise, thereby preventing the royal administration from treating their institution as an illegal, rebellious body (just as they had succeeded in parrying such royal charges during the siege of Paris in 1649). All these factors, along with the Mazarinist ministers' determination to make the royal return to Paris look popular and peaceful, led to the surprisingly moderate *lit de justice* of October 22, 1652, which ended the Fronde in Paris without abolishing the reforms of 1648.

The fact that the post-Fronde administrations gradually removed most of the reforms of 1648 and went on to strengthen the control of ministers, councils, and intendants over the officiers raises important questions. If the reforms gradually disappeared, was the Fronde a total failure despite the moderation of the settlement in 1652? Would conditions have been any different without the Fronde? To these all-important questions there can be no documented answer. Appearances indicate a steady increase in royal power from Henri IV, through Louis XIII and Richelieu, to Louis XIV, except for an aberration under Mazarin and Anne. And, not unexpectedly, it has been the verdict of historians that appearances were the reality. The only unresolved argument has been whether the resumption of the "inevitable" progression of royal centralization took place during the last decade of Mazarin's ministry or awaited the genius of Louis XIV and Colbert in the 1660's and 1670's. Yet the very fact that almost all historians have debated this last question is a sign of their uncertainty about the Fronde's legacy. Most scholars believe that the Fronde ended in 1652 (or, at the latest, 1653), implying or categorically stating that the reforms of 1648 were immediately overthrown (an obvious factual error). These same scholars then praise Louis XIV and Colbert for achieving those things which were supposedly realized between 1653 and 1661 by Mazarin. But if Louis XIV and Colbert are to be congratulated, they must be congratulated for overcoming the legacy of the Fronde and Mazarin's post-Fronde ineptitude.

Here one begins to see a way out of the historiographical dilemma. While this study is not meant to explain the early years of Louis XIV's personal reign, it can be submitted as an hypothesis that Louis XIV was successful because Colbert recognized the troublesome legacy of the Fronde. On the one hand, the organs of the central administration were placed more firmly over the officers in order to lessen some of the confusion of powers which had made the Fronde possible. Yet, Colbert was able to tame the post-Fronde officers, in large part, because he also compromised with them—though this was not in his nature. One can only assume that he had read the lessons of the Fronde, that he knew that an absolute monarch could not run roughshod over the Parlement of Paris, the French officers' common interest in *vénalité* and the paulette, or their position as representatives of the Crown. Why else would he avoid using the renewal of the paulette as a club, in contrast to Louis XIII's finance ministers, and then Mazarin and d'Emery? Why, indeed, did he tell intendants that they should work with the local officers? Why did he retain judicial review, although admittedly in attenuated form, for the sovereign courts? The only example of thorough, ruthless control over officers after the Fronde was the suppression of the *trésoriers'* and *élus'* syndicates. Those petty officials had been far weaker than the sovereign court judges before the Fronde, and had survived during that upheaval only because of the assistance of the sovereign tribunals. It was relatively easy for Colbert to attack them, and they were attacked. The Fronde had demonstrated the resiliency of the higher officials, especially in the Parlement of Paris, and they were treated far more gently. The flood of new offices to compete with older ones under Louis XIV was, significantly, directed against the lesser officers, not the sovereign courts.

So the personal reign of Louis XIV does bear the imprint of the Fronde, despite Mazarin's apparent triumph in 1652. Indeed, the many-layered administration of eighteenth-century France cannot be imagined without the Fronde. After studying the place of the

Fronde in the evolution of absolute monarchy, this author has been led to the conclusion that if the Fronde had not checked this trend, the progression from Henri IV to Louis XIV would have resulted in a much more powerful monarchy. The mild victory-in-defeat of the parlementary Fronde might have been greater if Colbert had not learned another lesson from the setback to the administrative revolution of Louis XIII. Colbert was a very efficient and relatively uncorrupt financier under Louis XIV. He must have known that the baneful influence of the *traitants* had to be eradicated in order to turn reluctant absolutist subjects and officiers into firm supporters of responsible absolute monarchy. (Certainly his attack on the *traitants* in the 1660's broke with his previous activity as Mazarin's financial agent, during which he had copied the *traitants'* practices by buying depreciated rentes for Mazarin and redeeming them at the treasury for their original high price.) Freed from Mazarin's control, eager to oust his greatest rival, the corrupt *surintendant* Fouquet, in 1661, but also free and eager to end the abuses which had galvanized ubiquitous hatred of the corrupt Mazarinist administration during the Fronde, Colbert acted decisively after 1661. If the Fronde had no other legacy, its ultimate success in reforming the corrupt politics against which it had so fiercely protested would have made it a significant movement.

One additional question remains to be raised and its answer recapitulated here: Might the Parlement of Paris have achieved greater success than its mere victory-in-defeat by altering its tactics? The results of the upheavals throughout mid-seventeenth-century Europe testify sufficiently to the fact that the judges were as successful as was possible. (Only in England did the rebels win, and there, it was the Cromwellian military and gentry, not the institutional arm of the rebellion, which triumphed.) In most countries, the confused social situation, the lack of an ideology, the absence of an institution able to cut across or obliterate the divisions common to any national revolutionary movement fostered violent movements of protest, but these conditions were not conducive to the replacement of absolute monarchy by any alternative. That was as true of France as it was of Spain, Brandenburg, Sweden, and Russia, to give but a few examples. This situation was in sharp contrast to that of the next century in the few states which did achieve change through revolution during the late 1700's. It cannot be said that the Parlement of Paris lost its chance to succeed by preventing an Estates General in 1651, for such an assembly would have further divided the opposition. Nor did it lose an opportunity because of its cool and eventually hostile response to the noble Fronde. *Les grands* had no program of their own, for the Frondeurs merely wanted Mazarin's position, and the Condéans did not know what they wanted beyond control of provincial governorships. In any case, a parlementary-noble alliance would have shattered the judges' treatment of the parlementary Fronde as a legitimate form of protest within the framework of the existing government. Without that political *via media,* the Fronde would have been a total failure. Needless to say, the parlementarians were fortunate and wise in refusing to purge the Mazarinist civic government during the siege of Paris. When they allowed the Condéans to do this in 1652, they almost lost their chance of salvaging some of their gains of earlier years. Their legalism had its weaknesses, as we have said, for it contributed to their refusal to authorize the unrestrained recruitment and use of soldiers time after time when that might have resulted in a decisive defeat of Anne's regime. Their narrow corporative pride antagonized the other Parisian courts and helped to keep the Frondes of the provincial courts parochial and uncoordinated. Yet the lost opportunities have to be set against the disaster which a departure from legalism would have produced. The Parisian judges were fortunate that their curious style of debating and voting, as well as their division into radical and conservative elements, made compromise possible throughout the Fronde. Had conservatives like Molé, de Mesmes, and Talon prevailed exclusively, the central administration would have shattered the parlementarian opposition and ignored the pleas of those men for responsible authoritarianism. And if radicals like Broussel, Deslandes-Payen, and Viole had prevailed, Anne and her ministers would easily have made the parlementary Fronde look rebellious, illegal, and perhaps even treasonous. Without the compromise between radicalism and conservatism, the Parlement could never have achieved the initial reforms of 1648, prevailed against the siege of Paris, forced a settlement of the first Condéan rebellion, or bequeathed the ambiguous legacy of the Fronde to the France of Colbert and Louis XIV.

BIBLIOGRAPHY

I. Manuscript Sources

Archives des Affaires Etrangères (A.A.E.)

Mémoires et Documents, France (France, Ms.)

Scattered governmental papers related to the Parlement of Paris, notably in the following mss.

848 (1643-1645, a check list of the judges' political leanings)

850 (1644, newsletters)

852 (1645, *taxe des aisés*)

860 (1648, Declaration of October 22)

861 (1648, Chambre Saint Louis and tax relief)

Archives Nationales (A.N.)

Series U:

28, 29, 30 (copy of registers of the Parlement of Paris' *conseil secret*, 1646-1655; original destroyed by order of Louis XIV)

336 (anonymous journal of debates in the Parlement of Paris, 1648-1649)

Bibliothèque de l'Institut (B.I.)

Collection Godefroy (Ms. Godefroy):

274: (1649-1659, Anne's return to Paris after the siege of 1649)

Bibliothèque de l'Université de Paris (B.U.P. Ms.)

64, 65, 66, 67, 68, 69, 70 (Pierre Lallement's journal of debates in the Parlement of Paris, 1648-1652, minus two volumes for late 1648 and early 1649 which were destroyed by fire)

Bibliothèque Mazarine (B.M. Ms.)

2239 (introduction, on officials in the financial districts called *élections*)

Bibliothèque Nationale (B.N.)

Collection Baluze (Ms. Baluze):

291 (papers of Pierre Broussel)

Fonds Français (Ms. Fr.):

4212 (copies of Le Tellier's letters to Mazarin, 1652)

5844 (newsletters, 1652-1655)

6891 (correspondence of d'Aligre, Le Tellier, and Mazarin, 1652)

7549 (contains memoir by *Garde des Sceaux* de Marillac on the Parlement of Paris)

10276 (unpublished part of Jean Vallier's *Journal*, 1654-1655)

17560 (papers of Chancellor Séguier)

18367 (papers of Chancellor Séguier)

18431 (Séguier collection on crimes of *lèse-majesté, rébellions, abolitions*, etc.)

21307 (registers of the Parlement of Pontoise, 1652)

23319 (debates of Parlement of Paris, etc.)

25025, 25026 (newsletters, Dec. 25, 1648-Aug. 26, 1653)

II. Printed Sources

A. *Collections of Laws, Decrees, Règlements*

Bibliothèque Nationale, Actes Royaux

F 23611 (1645-1649, nos. 681-1015, royal letters, declarations, etc.)

F 23612 (1650-1652, nos. 1-161, same)

F 23631 (1648-1652, nos. 494-597, *arrêts* of *conseil d'état*)

F 23668 (1642-1649, nos. 584-889, *arrêts* of Parlement of Paris)

F 23669 (1650-1654, nos. 1-372, same)

Isambert, F. A. et al., eds. *Recueil général des anciennes lois françaises depuis l'an 420 jusqu'à la révolution de 1789.* 29 vols. Paris, 1822-1833.

Isnard, A.L.P. *Catalogue générale des livres imprimés de la Bibliothèque Nationale: Actes Royaux.* 7 vols. Paris, 1910-1960.

Mousnier, R., ed. "Les Règlements du conseil du roi sous Louis XIII," *Annuaire-Bulletin de la Société de l'Histoire de France.* Paris, 1948.

Néron, P., and Girard, E., eds. *Recueil d'édits et d'ordonnances royaux.* 2 vols. Paris, 1750.

B. *Administrative Correspondence and Memoranda*

Chéruel, P. A., ed. "Les Carnets de Mazarin pendant la Fronde." *Revue Historique* IV (1877): 103-138.

Colbert, J.-B. *Lettres, instructions, et mémoires*, ed. P. Clément. 7 vols. Paris, 1861-1882.

Depping, G. P., ed. *Correspondance administrative sous le règne de Louis XIV.* 4 vols. Paris, 1850-1855.

Mazarin, J. *Lettres*, ed. P. A. Chéruel. 9 vols. Paris, 1872-1906.

———. *Lettres à la reine, à la Princesse Palatine ...* ed. J. Ravenel. Paris, 1836.

Mousnier, R., ed. *Lettres et mémoires adressés au Chancelier Séguier (1633-1649)*. 2 vols. Paris, 1965.

Richelieu, Cardinal de. *Lettres, instructions diplomatiques, et papiers d'état*, ed. M. Avenel. 8 vols. Paris, 1835-1877.

C. *Parlement of Paris*

Courteault, H., ed. "Complément au *Journal du procès du Marquis de la Boulaye*," *Annuaire-Bulletin de la Société de l'Histoire de France*. Paris, 1911.

———, ed. "Journal inédit du Parlement de Paris pendant la Fronde" (Dec. 1, 1651-Apr. 12, 1652), *Annuaire-Bulletin de la Société de l'Histoire de France*. Paris, 1916.

Histoire du temps, ou le véritable récit de ce qui s'est passé dans le Parlement de Paris (Aug. 1647-Apr. 1649). 2 vols. Paris, 1649.

Journal du Parlement de Paris (1648-1652) (individual, titled volumes cited chronologically):

> *Journal contenant tout ce qui s'est fait et passé en la cour de Parlement de Paris* (May 13-Sept. 23, 1648). Paris, 1649.

> *Suite du journal contenant tout ce qui s'est fait et passé en la cour de Parlement de Paris* (Sept. 24-Dec. 31, 1648). Paris, 1649.

> *Journal de ce qui s'est fait ès assemblées du Parlement* (Jan. 1-Feb. 28, 1649). Paris, 1649.

> *Suitte du journal de ce qui s'est passé au Parlement* (Mar. 1-Apr. 1, 1649). Paris, 1652.

> *Journal ou histoire du temps présent, contenant toutes les déclarations du roy verifiées en Parlement* (May 12, 1651-May 29, 1652). Paris, 1652.

> *Relation contenant la suitte et conclusion du journal de tout ce qui s'est passé au Parlement* (May 31-Oct. 22, 1652). Paris, 1653.

Journal du Procès du Marquis de la Boulaye (in volume entitled *Mémoires du Marquis de Beauvais-Nangis*, eds. M. Monmerqué and A. H. Taillandier. Paris, 1862).

Molé, M. *Mémoires*, ed. A. Champollion-Figeac. 4 vols. Paris, 1855-1857.

Procès-Verbal de la conférence à Ruel (1649), in M. Petitot, ed., *Collection des mémoires relatives à l'histoire de France* XLVI. Paris, 1825.

Talon, O. *Mémoires.* Michaud and Poujoulat collection (ser. III, vol. VI). Paris, 1839.

D. *Other Primary Sources*

Berthod, P. F. *Mémoires.* Michaud and Poujoulat collection (ser. II, vol. X). Paris, 1838.

Boislisle, A. de, ed. *Chambre des Comptes de Paris: Pièces justicatives pour servir à l'histoire des premiers présidents, 1506-1791.* Nogent le Rotrou, 1873.

Brienne, H. A. de Loménie de. *Mémoires.* Michaud and Poujoulat collection (ser. III, vol. III). Paris, 1838.

Commission envoyé par Monseigneur le Duc d'Orléans aux trésoriers de France à Caen, pour l'établissement de la subsistance des gens de guerre pour le service du roy. Paris, 1652.

Conrart, V. *Mémoires.* Michaud and Poujoulat collection (ser. III, vol. IV). Paris, 1838.

Courier françois, apportant toutes les nouvelles véritables de ce qui s'est passé depuis l'enlèvement du roy, tant à Paris qu'à S. Germain-en-Laye. 12 pts., or *arrivées.* Paris, 1649.

Dubois, M. *Relation véritable de ce qui s'est passé de plus remarquable en la sédition arrivée à Paris le 26 août 1648,* ed. A. Feillet (in *Revue des Sociétés Savantes des Départements,* ser. IV, vol. II. 1864).

Dubuisson-Aubenay, F.N.B. *Journal des guerres civiles,* ed. G. Saige. 2 vols. Paris, 1883-1885.

Estrées, F. Annibal, Maréchal d'. *Mémoires,* ed. P. Bonnefon. Paris, 1910.

Extrait du livre des choses mémorables de l'Abbaye de Saint Denis en France, pour l'année 1649 et suivantes, eds. Le Roux de Lincy and Douët-d'Arcq (in edition cited of *Registres de l'Hôtel de Ville de Paris pendant la Fronde* III).

Goulas, N. *Mémoires,* ed. C. Constant. 3 vols. Paris, 1879-1882.

Joly, C. *Mémoires.* Michaud and Poujoulat collection (ser. III, vol. II). Paris, 1838.

Joly, G. *Mémoires.* Michaud and Poujoulat collection (ser. III, vol. II). Paris, 1838.

Journal de l'assemblée de la noblesse tenue à Paris en l'année mil six cens cinquante-un. Paris, 1651.

La Rochefoucauld, F. de. *Oeuvres*, ed. D. L. Gilbert and J. Gourdault. 4 vols. Paris, 1868-1912.

Lenet, P. *Mémoires*. Michaud and Poujoulat collection (ser. III, vol. II). Paris, 1838.

Marigny, *Lettres à Lenet pendant la Fronde* (in *Cabinet Historique* I-IX, 1855-1863).

Mayer, C. J., ed. *Des Etats Généraux et autres assemblées nationales*. 18 vols. The Hague, 1789.

Mercure François. 25 vols. Paris, 1605-1644.

Montglat, F. de P. de Clermont, Marquis de. *Mémoires*. Michaud and Poujoulat collection (ser. III, vol. IV). Paris, 1838.

Montpensier, A.M.L. d'Orléans, Duchesse de. *Mémoires*. Michaud and Poujoulat collection (ser. III, vol. IV). Paris, 1838.

Moreau, C. *Bibliographie de Mazarinades*. 3 vols. Paris, 1850-1851.
———. *Choix de Mazarinades*. 2 vols. Paris, 1853.

Motteville, F. B. de. *Mémoires*. Michaud and Poujoulat collection (ser. II, vol. x). Paris, 1838.

Nemours, Duchesse de. *Mémoires*. Michaud and Poujoulat collection (ser. II, vol. IX). Paris, 1838.

Ordres du Prévôt de Paris adressés à M. de Lamoignon, colonel du quartier de St. Denis, 1649-1652 (in *Cabinet Historique* XX, 1874).

Ormesson, O. L. d'. *Journal*, ed. P. A. Chéruel. 2 vols. Paris, 1860-1861.

Patin, G. *Lettres*, ed. J. H. Reveillé-Parise. 3 vols. Paris, 1846.

Peiresc, N.C.F. de. *Lettres aux frères Dupuy*, ed. P. T. de Larroque. 7 vols. Paris, 1888-1898.

Pontchartrain, P. de. *Mémoires*. Michaud and Poujoulat collection (ser. II, vol. v). Paris, 1837.

Priolo, B. *History of France under the Ministry of Cardinal Mazarine*, trans. C. Wase. London, 1671.

Rapin, P. R. *Mémoires sur l'église et la société*, ed. L. Aubeneau. 2 vols. Paris, 1865.

Recueil de divers pièces qui ont paru durant les mouvemens derniers de l'année 1649. Paris, 1650.

Registres de l'Hôtel de Ville de Paris pendant la Fronde, eds. Le Roux de Lincy and Douët-d'Arcq. 3 vols. Paris, 1846-1848.

Retz, P. de Gondi, Cardinal de. *Oeuvres*, eds. A. Feillet et al. 10 vols. Paris, 1870-1896.

Richelieu, Cardinal de. *Mémoires,* ed. Société de l'Histoire de France. Paris, 1907-1931. Also eds. Michaud and Poujoulat. Paris, 1837.

Rohan, Duc de. *Mémoires.* Michaud and Poujoulat collection (ser. II, vol. v). Paris, 1837.

Sévigné, Chevalier de. *Correspondance avec Christine de France, Duchesse de Savoie,* eds. J. Lemoine and F. Saulnier. Paris, 1911.

Sirot, Baron de. *Mémoires.* Paris, 1683.

Tallemant des Réaux, G. *Historiettes,* eds. M. Monmerqué and P. Paris. 6 vols. Paris, 1862.

Vallier, J. *Journal,* eds. H. Courteault et al. 4 vols. Paris, 1902-1918.

Vineuil, L. A. de. *Mémoires* (in edition cited of La Rochefoucauld. *Oeuvres* II).

III. Secondary Works

A. *French Law and Institutions*

Aubert, F. *Histoire du Parlement de Paris de l'origine à François Ier, 1250-1515.* 2 vols. Paris, 1894.

Avenel, Vicomte G. d'. *Richelieu et la monarchie absolue.* 4 vols. Paris, 1895.

Bluche, F. *Les Magistrats du Parlement de Paris au XVIII siècle.* Paris, 1960.

Brissaud, J. B. *A History of French Public Law.* Boston, 1915.

Caillet, J. *De l'administration en France sous le ministère du Cardinal de Richelieu.* Paris, 1863.

Camoin de Vence, C. E. *Magistrature française, son action et son influence sur l'état et la société aux diverses époques.* Paris, 1862.

Charmeil, J. P. *Les Trésoriers de France à l'époque de la Fronde.* Paris, 1964.

Chénon, E. *Histoire générale du droit français public et privé des origines à 1815.* 2 vols. Paris, 1926-1929.

Chéruel, P. A. *Dictionnaire historique des institutions, moeurs et coutumes de la France.* 2 vols. Paris, 1910.

———. *Histoire de l'administration monarchique en France depuis l'avènement de Philippe-Auguste jusqu'à la mort de Louis XIV.* 2 vols. Paris, 1855.

Dareste, R. *La Justice administrative en France.* Paris, 1898.

Déclareuil, J. *Histoire générale du droit français des origines à 1789.* Paris, 1925.

Doucet, R. *Les Institutions de la France au XVIe siècle*. 2 vols. Paris, 1948.

Ellul, J. *Histoire des institutions*. Paris, 1956.

Esmein, A. *Cours élémentaire d'histoire du droit français*. Paris, 1925.

Esmonin, E. *Etudes sur la France des XVIIe et XVIIIe siècles*. Paris, 1964.

———. *La Taille en Normandie au temps de Colbert (1661-1683)*. Paris, 1913.

Forbonnais, F.V.D. de. *Recherches et considérations sur les finances de France depuis 1596 jusqu'en 1721*. 6 vols. Liège, 1758.

Fréville, H. *L'Intendance de Bretagne (1689-1790)*. 3 vols. Rennes, 1953.

Glasson, E. D. *Histoire du droit et des institutions de la France*. 8 vols. Paris, 1887-1903.

———. *Le Parlement de Paris, son rôle politique depuis le règne de Charles VII jusqu'à la Révolution*. 2 vols. Paris, 1901.

Göhring, M. *Die Amterkauflichkeit im ancien regime*. Berlin, 1938.

Hanotaux, G. *Origine des intendants de province*. Paris, 1884.

Livet, G. *L'Intendance d'Alsace sous Louis XIV*. Paris, 1956.

Marion, M. *Dictionnaire des institutions de la France aux XVIIe et XVIIIe siècles*. Paris, 1923.

Maugis, E. *Histoire du Parlement de Paris de l'avènement des rois Valois à la mort d'Henri IV*. 3 vols. Paris, 1913-1916.

Michaud, H. *La Grande Chancellerie et les écritures royales au XVIe siècle*. Paris, 1967.

Mousnier, R. *La Vénalité des offices sous Henri IV et Louis XIII*. Rouen, 1945.

Olivier-Martin, F. *Histoire du droit français des origines à la Révolution*. Paris, 1951.

Pagès, G. *Les Institutions monarchiques sous Louis XIII et Louis XIV*. Paris, 1933.

———. *La Monarchie d'ancien régime en France (de Henri IV à Louis XIV)*. Paris, 1946.

Shennan, J. H. *The Parlement of Paris*. Ithaca, 1968.

Viollet, P. M. *Histoire des institutions politiques et administratives de la France*. 4 vols. Paris, 1890-1912.

Zeller, G. *Les Institutions de la France au XVIe siècle*. Paris, 1948.

B. *Studies Relating to the Fronde*

Aumale, Duc d'. *Histoire des princes de Condé.* 8 vols. Paris, 1885-1896.

Barante, A. de. *Le Parlement et la Fronde: La Vie de Mathieu Molé.* Paris, 1859.

Batiffol, L. *Biographie du Cardinal de Retz.* Paris, 1929.

Bazin, A. de R. *Histoire de France sous Louis XIII et sous le ministère du Cardinal Mazarin, 1610-1660.* 4 vols. Paris, 1846.

Bitton, Davis. *The French Nobility in Crisis, 1560-1640.* Stanford, 1969.

Blet, P. *Le Clergé de France et la monarchie, 1615-1666.* 2 vols. Rome, 1959.

Boulenger, M. *Mazarin, soutien de l'état.* Paris, 1929.

Capefigue, J. B. *Richelieu, Mazarin et la Fronde.* 2 vols. Paris, 1844.

Chéruel, P. A. *Histoire de France pendant la minorité de Louis XIV.* 4 vols. Paris, 1879-1880.

————. *Mémoires sur la vie publique et privée de Fouquet.* 2 vols. Paris, 1862.

————. *Histoire de France sous le ministère de Mazarin.* 3 vols. Paris, 1882.

Church, W. F. *Constitutional Thought in Sixteenth-Century France.* Cambridge, 1941.

Cosnac, G. J. de. *Souvenirs du règne de Louis XIV.* 8 vols. Paris, 1866-1882.

Coste, P. *Histoire de Louis de Bourbon, second de nom (1646-1686).* The Hague, 1748.

Courteault, H. *La Fronde à Paris, premières et dernières journées.* Paris, 1930.

Cousin, V. *Madame de Chevreuse.* Paris, 1886.

————. *Madame de Longueville pendant la Fronde, 1651-1653.* Paris, 1859.

Debû-Bridel, J. *Anne-Geneviève de Bourbon, Duchesse de Longueville.* Paris, 1938.

Dethan, G. *Gaston d'Orléans: Conspirateur et prince charmant.* Paris, 1959.

Doolin, P. R. *The Fronde.* Cambridge, 1935.

Feillet, A. *La Misère au temps de la Fronde et Saint Vincent de Paul.* Paris, 1862.

Ford, F. L. *Robe and Sword: The Regrouping of the French Aris-tocracy after Louis XIV*. Cambridge, 1953.

Goldmann, L. *Le Dieu caché. Etude sur la vision tragique dans les Pensées de Pascal et dans le théatre de Racine*. Paris, 1955.

Grand-Mesnil, M.-N. *Mazarin, la Fronde et la presse, 1647-1649*. Paris, 1967.

Hanotaux, G., and La Force, Duc de. *Histoire du Cardinal de Riche-lieu*. 6 vols. Paris, 1933-1947.

Knachel, P. A. *England and the Fronde: The Impact of the English Civil War and Revolution on France*. Ithaca, 1967.

Kossman, E. H. *La Fronde*. Leiden, 1954.

Lacour-Gayet, G. *L'Education politique de Louis XIV*. Paris, 1923.

Lavisse, E., ed. *Histoire de France depuis les origines jusqu'à la Révolution* VI-ii, VII-i. 9 vols. Paris, 1900-1911.

Lecestre, L. *La Bourgeoisie parisienne au temps de la Fronde*. Paris, 1913.

Lemaire, A. *Les Lois fondamentales de la monarchie d'après les théoreticiens de l'ancien régime*. Paris, 1907.

Logié, P. *La Fronde en Normandie*. 3 vols. Paris, 1952.

Lorris, P. G. *Un Agitateur au XVIIe siècle: Le Cardinal de Retz*. Paris, 1956.

———. *La Fronde*. Paris, 1961.

Lublinskaya, A. D. *French Absolutism: The Crucial Phase, 1620-1629*, trans. B. Pearce. Cambridge, 1968.

Madelin, L. *Une Révolution manquée: La Fronde*. Paris, 1931.

Mailfait, H. *Un Magistrat de l'ancien régime: Omer Talon, sa vie et ses oeuvres*. Paris, 1902.

Mandrou, R. *Classes et luttes de classes en France au début du XVIIe siècle*. Florence, 1965.

Martin, H. *Histoire de France depuis les temps les plus reculés jusqu'en 1789* XII. 17 vols. Paris, 1855-1860.

Merriman, R. B. *Six Contemporaneous Revolutions*. Oxford, 1938.

Méthivier, H. *L'Ancien Régime*. Paris, 1964.

Mousnier, R. *Les XVIe et XVIIe siècles*. Paris, 1954.

———. *Paris au XVIIe siècle*. 3 vols. Paris, 1961.

———. *Fureurs paysannes: Les Paysans dans les révoltes du XVIIe siècle*. Paris, 1967.

Normand, C. *La Bourgeoisie française au XVIIe siècle: La Vie publique, les idées et les actions politiques, 1604-1661*. Paris, 1908.

Perkins, J. B. *France under Mazarin, with a Review of the Administration of Richelieu.* 2 vols. New York, 1886.

Porchnev, B. *Les Soulèvements populaires en France de 1623 à 1648.* Paris, 1963.

Préclin, E., and Tapié, V.-L. *Le XVIIe siècle.* Paris, 1955.

Ranum, O. A. *Paris in the Age of Absolutism.* New York, 1968.

——. *Richelieu and the Councillors of Louis XIII.* Oxford, 1963.

Rothkrug, L. *Opposition to Louis XIV: The Political and Social Origins of the French Enlightenment.* Princeton, 1965.

Saint-Aulaire, A.F.C. de B. de. *Mazarin.* Paris, 1946.

Sainte-Aulaire, L. C. de Beaupoil, Comte de. *Histoire de la Fronde.* 2 vols. Paris, 1841.

Sée, H. *Les Idées politiques en France au XVIIe siècle.* Paris, 1923.

Tapié, V.-L. *La France de Louis XIII et de Richelieu.* Paris, 1952.

Venard, M. *Bourgeois et paysans au XVIIe siècle: Recherches sur le rôle des bourgeois parisiens dans la vie agricole au sud de Paris au XVIIe siècle.* Paris, 1957.

Wolf, J. B. *Louis XIV.* New York, 1968.

C. *Articles*

Bernard, L. "French Society and Popular Uprisings Under Louis XIV," *French Historical Studies* III (1964): 454-474.

Bluche, F. "L'Origine des magistrats du Parlement de Paris au XVIIIe siècle," *Paris et Ile de France, Mémoires* V (1953-1954).

Bourgeon, J. L. "L'Ile de la Cité pendant la Fronde: Structure sociale," *Paris et Ile de France, Mémoires* XIII (1962): 23-144.

Boutarel, P. de. "Les Mobiles d'un faction au XVIIe siècle," *Séances et Travaux de l'Académie des Sciences Morales et Politiques* CLII (1899): 51-92.

Cans, A. "Le Rôle politique de l'assemblée du clergé pendant la Fronde, 1650-1651," *Revue Historique* CXIV (1913): 1-60.

Chauleur, A. "Le Rôle des traitants dans l'administration financière de la France de 1643 à 1653," *XVIIe Siècle*, no. 65 (1964) pp. 16-49.

Church, W. F. "Publications on Cardinal Richelieu since 1945. A Bibliographical Study," *Journal of Modern History* XXXVII (1965): 421-444.

Cubells, Mme. "Le Parlement de Paris pendant la Fronde," *XVIIe Siècle*, no. 35 (1957), pp. 171-199.

Degarne, M. "Etudes sur les soulèvements provinciaux en France avant la Fronde: La Révolte du Rouergue en 1643," *XVIIe Siècle*, no. 56 (1962), pp. 3-18.

Dent, J. "An Aspect of the Crisis of the Seventeenth Century: The Collapse of the Financial Administration of the French Monarchy (1653-1661)," *Economic History Review*, 2nd ser., xx (1967), pp. 241-256.

Dethan, G. "Mazarin avant le ministère," *Revue Historique* ccxxvii (1962): 33-66.

Deyon, P. "A Propos des rapports entre la noblesse française et la monarchie absolue," *Revue Historique* ccxxxi (1964): 341-356.

Dillay, M. "Les Registres secrets des Chambres des Enquêtes et des Requêtes du Parlement de Paris," *Bibliothèque de l'Ecole des Chartes* cviii (1950): 75-123.

Dumont, F. "Royauté française et monarchie absolue au XVIIe siècle," *XVIIe Siècle*, nos. 58-59 (1963), pp. 3-18.

Esmonin, E. "Les Arrêts du conseil dans l'ancien régime," *Bulletin de la Société d'Histoire Moderne* (1938): 6-10.

———. "Un Episode du rétablissement des intendants après la Fronde: Les Maîtres des requêtes envoyés en chevauchées," *Revue d'Histoire Moderne et Contemporaine* xii (1965): 217-228.

———. "Un Episode du rétablissement des intendants: La Mission de Morant en Guienne (1650)," *Revue d'Histoire Moderne et Contemporaine* i (1954): 86-101.

———. "Observations critiques sur le livre de M. Hanotaux: 'Origines de l'institution des intendants de province,'" *Bulletin de la Société d'Histoire Moderne* (1932-1933): 6-9.

———. "La Suppression des intendants pendant la Fronde et leur rétablissement," *Bulletin de la Société d'Histoire Moderne* (1935): 114-119.

Feugère, A. "La Fronde et les mémoires du temps," *Revue Bleue*, ser. ii, vol. x (January 1, 1876).

Goubert, P. "Les Officiers royaux des présidiaux, bailliages et élections dans la société française au XVIIe siècle," *XVIIe Siècle*, nos. 42-43 (1959), pp. 54-75.

Hartung, F., and Mousnier, R. "Quelques Problèmes concernant la monarchie absolue," *Relazioni X Congresso Internazionale de Scienze Storiche*, Rome and Florence 1955, iv, 3-55.

Hurt, J. J. "The Parlement of Brittany and the Crown: 1665-1675," *French Historical Studies* iv (1966): 411-433.

Jacquart, J. "La Fronde des princes dans la région parisienne et ses conséquences matérielles," *Revue d'Histoire Moderne et Contemporaine* VII (1960): 257-290.

Kossman, E. H. "Een Blik op het Franse absolutisme," *Tydschrift voor Geschiedenis* LXXVIII (1966): 52-58.

Labatut, J.-P. "Situation sociale du quartier du Marais pendant la Fronde parlementaire (1648-1649)," *XVIIe Siècle*, no. 38 (1958), pp. 55-81.

Mandrou, R. "Les Soulèvements populaires et la société française du XVIIe siècle," *Annales: Economies, Sociétés, Civilisations* XIV (1959): 756-765.

Meuvret, J. "Comment les Français du XVIIe siècle voyaient l'impôt," *XVIIe Siècle*, nos. 25-26 (1955), pp. 59-82.

Moote, A. L. "The French Crown versus its Judicial and Financial Officials, 1615-1683," *Journal of Modern History* XXXIV (1962): 146-160.

———. "The Parlementary Fronde and Seventeenth-Century Robe Solidarity," *French Historical Studies* II (1962): 330-355.

Mousnier, R. "Comment les français du XVIIe siècle voyaient la constitution," *XVIIe Siècle*, nos. 25-26 (1955), pp. 9-36.

———. "Le Conseil du roi de la mort de Henri IV au gouvernement personnel de Louis XIV," *Etudes d'Histoire Moderne et Contemporaine* I (1947): 29-67.

———. "Etat et commissaire. Recherches sur la création des intendants des provinces (1634-1648)," in *Forschungen zu Staat und Verfassung. Festgabe für Fritz Hartung.* Berlin, 1958.

———. "L'Evolution des institutions monarchiques en France et ses relations avec l'état social," *XVIIe Siècle*, nos. 58-59 (1963), pp. 57-72.

———. "Notes sur les rapports entre les gouverneurs de province et les intendants dans la première moitié du XVIIe siècle," *Revue Historique* CCXXVIII (1962): 339-350.

———. "Quelques raisons de la Fronde: Les Causes des journées révolutionnaires parisiennes de 1648," *XVIIe Siècle*, nos. 2-3 (1949), pp. 33-78.

———. "Recherches sur les soulèvements populaires en France avant la Fronde," *Revue d'Histoire Moderne et Contemporaine* V (1958): 81-113.

———. "Recherches sur les syndicats d'officiers pendant la Fronde.

Trésoriers généraux de France et élus dans la révolution," *XVIIe Siècle*, nos. 42-43 (1959), pp. 76-117.

Pagès, G. "Autour du grand orage: Richelieu et Marillac, deux politiques," *Revue Historique* CLXXIX (1937): 63-97.

———. "Le Conseil du roi sous Louis XIII," *Revue d'Histoire Moderne* XII (1937).

———. "Essai sur l'évolution des institutions administratives en France du commencement du XVIe siècle à la fin du XVIIe," *Revue d'Histoire Moderne* VII (1932): 8-57.

———. "Quelques Reflections sur la centralisation administrative dans l'ancienne France," *Bulletin de la Société d'Histoire Moderne* (1935): 105-109.

———. "Sur le Développement de l'administration monarchique en France du début du XVIe siècle à la fin du XVIIIe," *Bulletin de la Société d'Histoire Moderne* (1931), pp. 18-20 (Esmonin's comments, pp. 29-42, 54-57).

———. "La Vénalité des offices dans l'ancienne France," *Revue Historique* CLXIX (1932): 477-495.

Ricommard, M. "Les Arrêts du conseil sous l'ancien régime," *Bulletin de la Société d'Histoire Moderne* (1936): 6-9.

Salmon, J. H. "Venal Office and Popular Sedition in Seventeenth-Century France," *Past and Present*, no. 37 (1967), pp. 21-43.

Tapié, V.-L. "Comment les Français du XVIIe siècle voyaient la patrie," *XVIIe Siècle*, nos. 25-26 (1955), pp. 37-58.

Timbal, P. J. "L'Esprit du droit privé au XVIIe siècle," *XVIIe Siècle*, nos. 58-59 (1963), pp. 30-39.

Trevor-Roper, H. R. "The General Crisis of the Seventeenth Century," *Past and Present*, no. 16 (1959), pp. 31-64 (comments by Kossman, Mousnier et al., in no. 18, 1960, pp. 8-42).

Vernes, S. "Un Frondeur: Le Président Viole," *Revue d'Histoire Diplomatique* (1951), pp. 16-38.

Wolf, J. B. "The Formation of a King," *French Historical Studies* I (1958): 40-72.

———. "The Reign of Louis XIV: A Selected Bibliography of Writings Since the War of 1914-1918," *Journal of Modern History* XXXVI (1964): 127-144.

Zeller, G. "L'Administration monarchique avant les intendants: Parlements et gouverneurs," *Revue Historique* CXCVII (1947): 180-215.

INDEX

absolutism, royal: principle of, 4;
royal officers hide behind, 11-12;
royal officers defend, 23-24, 30; Louis
XIII's approach toward, 41-43;
Parlement of Paris' *via media* on
during the Fronde, 109; councilor
Pierre Broussel's complex position
on, 110, 134; First President Mathieu
Molé virtually repudiates principle of,
139, 211; *Président à mortier* Nicolas
Potier de Novion virtually denies
principle of, 182; Anne of Austria's
inflexibility on, 184; Louis XIV and,
355, 359-60. *See also* divine right of
kings; king's personal will; Parlement
of Paris; *raison d'état*

administration, royal: defined, 3n, 48;
changes in personnel of: under Louis
XIII and Richelieu, 36, 47-48;
according to Louis XIII's political
testament, 64-65; as altered by Anne
of Austria and Mazarin, 66-70; in
1648, 154-56; during the noble
Fronde (1649-52), 228-30; Condéan
domination of late in 1649, 243;
Frondeur-Mazarinist coalition of
1650, 256-57, 265-67; post-Mazarinist
coalition of 1651, 290-99; dismissal
of Mazarin's and Condé's supporters
in 1651, 304-5; post-regency coalition
of anti-Condéans, 318-20; Mazarin's
restoration 1651-52, 325-28; royal
administration during Mazarin's 1652
exile, 349-51; rebel administration in
1652, 344-45; Mazarin's post-Fronde
administration, 357, 361. *See also*
councils, royal

aides, 37, 62, 77. *See also* tariff, Paris

Aix, Parlement of, *see* Parlement of Aix

Alais, Louis-Emmanuel de Valois,
Count of, governor of Provence, 177,
191-92, 225, 240, 242-43, 262-63,
283-84, 312, 319, 325

Aligre, Etienne d', *intendant des
finances,* 326-27, 353n

Anjou, Fronde in, 191, 191n, 284

Anne of Austria, queen mother and
regent, 64, 84, 86, 101, 153, 184,
202; and the Parlement of Paris,
65-66, 100-101, 105, 108, 113-16,
115n, 132-33, 146, 184, 186-88, 209,
237-39, 275, 289-90, 301-6, 326-27;
relations with Cardinal Mazarin, 66,
75, 107, 214, 229-30, 236, 292-94,
299-301, 325; character of, 68, 87,
184, 211, 304; unpopularity of, 68,
156, 194, 236; position as regent,
71-73, 184, 316; and the Duke of
Orléans, 76, 105, 178, 190, 228, 292-
93, 301, 322, 327; and state reform,
132, 134-37, 139, 141-42, 167-68, 180;
views on the English civil war, 184,
186; and the siege of Paris in 1649,
186-88; and Condé, 190, 298-306,
316-18; welcomed by Parisians in
1649, 241

arrêts: *de règlement*, 8; of union, 16,
126-27; conciliar (as substitutes for
legislation), 33, 44, 48, 170; conciliar
(*de cassation*), 57, 127, 329-30; battle
of conciliar versus parlementary *arrêts*
in 1649, 205-6; use of *arrêts* by the
Parlement of Paris to implement
reforms conforming to existing law,
145; refusal by the Parlement of
Paris to issue *arrêts* in areas outside
its jurisdiction or within the royal
prerogative, 145-46, 206-7; battle of
conciliar versus parlementary *arrêts*
in 1649, 205-6; battle of *arrêts*
between the Parlement of Paris and
Parlement at Pontoise in 1652, 351-52

artisans, 23, 25, 78, 95-97, 204, 336-37,
341-42, 358; and the Parlement of
Paris, 29, 97-98, 151, 204; and Condé,
Mazarin, and the Parlement of Paris,
341-42. *See also* society, Parisian

Avaux, Claude de Mesmes, Count
of, 137

avocats généraux (Parlement of Paris),
21, 49; *see also gens du roi*; Talon;
Bignon

Nesmond, François Théodore de, *président à mortier* in the Parlement of Paris, 63, 189, 226

noblemen, 24-26, 37, 39, 77, 306, 314, 336-37; officiers as nobles, 26-27, 83; officiers and nobles, 28, 50, 268, 294-96, 306, 308; revolts by, 37, 39, 235, 239-40, 262, 308; assembly of nobles in 1651, 268, 285, 294-96; *see also grands*

Normandy, revolt of 1639-40, 39, 45, 61; Fronde in, 137, 157, 191, 208-9, 215, 260-61. *See also* for the Norman Fronde, Longueville, Anne-Geneviève de and Henri de; Parlement of Rouen

notables, assembly of: question of convoking, 57-60, 155

Novion, Nicolas Potier de, *président à mortier* in the Parlement of Paris, 63, 154, 154n, 179, 182, 202, 204, 231-32, 245-46, 349, 361n

officials, royal, *see* officiers

officiers, royal: described, 5-9; compared with officials in other 17th c. states, 7; security of tenure, 7, 42, 162-63; corrupt practices among, 18, 18n, 81, 120; and French society, 23-24, 26-29. *See also gages*; paulette; *vénalité*; and specific categories or institutions of officiers

ordinances: by officiers, 8; of Orléans, 33; of Blois, 33, 42n, 161; of Moulins, 33, 42n; royal, 121, 145, 160-61

Orléans, Fronde in, 206, 336-37

Orléans, Gaston, Duke of: under Louis XIII, 39, 45, 61, 227; and the Parlement of Paris, 61, 76, 105, 113, 135, 149-50, 155, 178, 182-83, 216, 227-28, 270-75, 290-93, 204-5, 310, 324, 330-32, 343, 348; as *lieutenant général* of the kingdom under Anne of Austria, 65-66, 319; career, 76-77, 227-28; and Mazarin, 76, 137, 153, 155, 178-79, 220, 227-28, 256-58, 266, 270, 274-75, 281-82, 290-93, 319, 326-28, 349-50; and Anne of Austria, 76, 105, 178, 190, 228, 292-93, 301, 322, 327; as governor of Languedoc, 129, 137, 208, 283, 312-13, 320, 322,

335-36, 346; mediator of reform issue in 1648, 135, 146, 153, 178; and Condé, 153, 256, 296, 299, 319, 327-28; and arbitrary detention, 162, 256, 270-71; and the siege of Paris in 1649, 179, 190; heads Paris branch of the administration in 1650, 229, 237, 266, 268-75; mediator of Paris and provincial trouble after Rueil, 231, 237, 242, 251-52; futile position in late 1650, 281-83; as catalyst of anti-Mazarinist coalition of 1651, 290-99; mediator between Anne of Austria and Condé, 301, 303-5, 311, 319, 323-24; and Gondi, 319, 323, 328, 337; as a Condéan in 1652, 327-28, 331, 343, 348-50; as rebel "lieutenant general" in 1652, 344, 346, 348

Paris, *see* society, Parisian; and specific institutions and other items connected with Paris, e.g., Hôtel de Ville, *bourgeois*, guilds, merchants, rentes, tariff, *toisé*, Chambre des Comptes, Cour des Aides, Grand Conseil, Parlement

Parlement of Aix (Provence), 78-79, 92, 112, 144, 160, 177, 191-93, 210, 240-46, 261-63, 284, 312-13, 328, 335; and reforms of 1648, 144, 160; and the Parlement of Paris, 191-92, 207-8, 212, 241-42, 244-46, 284, 312, 314, 322, 335; and the Parlement of Dijon, 208n; and the Parlement of Toulouse, 240

Parlement of Bordeaux (Guienne), 128-29, 158, 240, 243-46, 252, 261-62, 264-65, 269-76, 284, 311-12, 321-22, 335, 339, 346; and reforms of 1648, 128-29, 144, 158; and the Parlement of Toulouse, 240; and the Parlement of Paris, 241-42, 244-46, 265, 269-76, 284-85, 311-12, 314, 323; and the peace of Bordeaux, 252

Parlement of Dijon (Burgundy), 129, 208, 260-62, 311, 313, 322, 335; and reforms of 1648, 129; and the Parlement of Aix, 208n; and the Parlement of Paris, 311, 335

401